palgrave macmillan law masters

landlord and tenant law

margaret wilkie
Visiting Lecturer in Law, University of Sheffield

peter luxton
Professor of Property Law, University of Sheffield

jill morgan
Reader in Law, University of East Anglia;
Affiliated Lecturer, Department of Land Economy,
University of Cambridge

and

godfrey cole
Barrister, District Chairman, the Appeals Service

Fifth edition

Series editor: Marise Cremona
Professor of European Law
European University Institute
Florence
Italy

palgrave
macmillan

First edition 1989
Reprinted once
Second edition 1993
Reprinted twice
Third edition 1997
Reprinted twice
Fourth edition 2000
Fifth edition 2006

Published by
PALGRAVE MACMILLAN

Palgrave Macmillan in the UK is an imprint of Macmillan Publishers Limited,
registered in England, company number 785998, of Houndmills, Basingstoke,
Hampshire RG21 6XS.

Palgrave Macmillan in the US is a division of St Martin's Press LLC,
175 Fifth Avenue, New York, NY 10010.

Palgrave Macmillan is the global academic imprint of the above companies
and has companies and representatives throughout the world.

Palgrave® and Macmillan® are registered trademarks in the United States,
the United Kingdom, Europe and other countries.

ISBN-13: 978-1-4039-1754-6
ISBN-10: 1-4039-1754-X

This book is printed on paper suitable for recycling and made from fully
managed and sustained forest sources. Logging, pulping and manufacturing
processes are expected to conform to the environmental regulations of the
country of origin.

A catalogue record for this book is available from the British Library.

10   9   8
15   14   13   12   11

Printed and bound in Great Britain by
CPI Antony Rowe, Chippenham and Eastbourne

PALC

Serie:

Trusts Law Charlie Webb and Tim Akkouh (spring 2008)

Titles in this series

Available from good
booksellers

Contents

Preface

The aim of this book is to provide a sound basic text on the law of landlord and tenant, a subject which is included in many professional courses, and which is essential to practitioners in property management. It is also sufficiently detailed to be used as a primary text for those studying the subject in more depth such as undergraduate or postgraduate law students and as a first point of reference for solicitors, barristers and legal executives dealing with problems in this area.

It is some years since the previous edition was published, but it is fair to say that there is never a 'quiet' time in the area of landlord and tenant law. Inevitably, there has been a number of important new decisions and some new legislation.

In the general law of landlord and tenant, the Landlord and Tenant (Covenants) Act 1995 has been judicially considered on several occasions, and the House of Lords in *Avonridge Property Co. Ltd.* v. *Mashru* has resolved one specific area of uncertainty as to the scope of that Act. There have been cases on covenants against assignment or under-letting, including cases applying the Landlord and Tenant Act 1988, and cases on under-letting in an economic environment where tenants have found it difficult to dispose of premises at the rent which they are paying. The Town and Country Planning (Use Classes) Order 2005 amends the use classes, and *Williams* v. *Kiley* (2003) applies a scheme of development, which can create what one judge referred to as a kind of 'local law' in freehold property, to a leasehold development. There are new lease/licence cases, and cases on repairs and rent review. The Land Registration Act 2002, which came into force on 13 October 2003, makes substantial changes to the registration of leases and abolishes the rules, which could apply in certain circumstances, limiting the title available to a lessee or sublessee.

Importantly for public housing authorities, the impact of the European Convention on Human Rights on the domestic law of eviction was recently considered by the House of Lords in *Kay* v. *Lambeth LBC* (2006).

Although the principal statutory codes – the Rent Act 1977 and the Housing Acts of 1985, 1988 and 1996 – remain in place, important developments have taken place within the context of both private and public residential accommodation, not least the extension of succession rights to same-sex partners. The chapter on private residential accommodation has been extended to cover the Mobile Homes Act 1983 and the chapter on public residential accommodation now includes a section on the new 'demoted tenancies'. The Commonhold and Leasehold Reform Act has significantly altered many of the existing measures to which tenants with long leases are subject, as well as introducing a new Right to Manage. These are all dealt with in Chapter 17.

For those familiar with previous editions of this book there are a few important changes which we have made in order to make the book more accessible and to provide greater coverage:

- The long Chapter 8 (dealing with certain covenants in leases) in previous editions has been divided up into six new chapters, each dealing with a particular type of covenant.
- The new Chapter 12 dealing with insurance now also covers service charges under leases where parts of a building are let.
- Chapter 19 on business leases has been considerably expanded, and deals fully with the impact of the Regulatory Reform (Business Tenancies) (England and Wales) Order 2003. This Order, which came into force on 1 June 2004, has made the most important changes to the security of tenure provisions in Part II of the Landlord and Tenant Act 1954 since its enactment over fifty years ago.
- Chapter 20 on agricultural tenancies has been revised and updated.

This book is dedicated to Margaret's grandson Freddie, who came into the world at roughly the same time as this fifth edition, but whose period of gestation was considerably shorter than that of this book!

MARGARET WILKIE
PETER LUXTON
JILL MORGAN

Table of cases

Table of Statutes

Part I

Leases: the general law

Chapter 1

Essential characteristics of a lease

1.1 An Estate in Land

Most people who see particulars in an estate agent's window offering for sale a desirable leasehold residence (often a flat) are aware that what is offered is something for a certain period, such as 'the remainder of a ninety-nine-year lease', and that this is less than a freehold, which connotes an unlimited and indefinite ownership. Few people would realise, however, that the basic distinction between the two derives from the historical development of land law.

Both leaseholds and freeholds are 'estates' in land. In the feudal society of medieval England, it was not possible to own land as all land belonged to the King. The King would graciously grant tenure of the land to his lords In return for certain services (often the provision of men and horses for battles, a form of tenure known as Knight Service), and the lords would in turn grant tenure of plots of land to the villeins in the manor in return for their services. Neither the lord nor his villeins owned the land itself, however. The extent of their interest in the land was therefore determined by the duration of the tenure granted to them, and this was known as their 'estate' in the land.

From early times, there was always a distinction between estates of an uncertain duration (such as life estates, or estates which were inheritable by certain heirs and so would continue until there were no such heirs capable of taking) known as *freehold* estates, and estates of a limited and definite duration which were estates of less than freehold, later known as 'term of years' or *leasehold* estates.

The 1925 property legislation radically changed English land law with the ultimate aim of simplifying the conveyancing process for a purchaser. Since 1 January 1926, when the legislation came into force, only two estates in land may subsist at law, those being (a) the fee simple absolute in possession (or what is now commonly known as freehold) and (b) the term of years absolute (leasehold). Because s.205 (xix) of the Law of Property Act 1925 (LPA 1925) defines 'possession' as including receipt of the rents and profits of the land, it is possible for a person who has a freehold estate, who creates a lease on which he receives rent, to still have a legal freehold estate. The lease which he creates may also be a legal estate, and the two legal estates may subsist in the land concurrently.

The definition of land in English land law is to be found in a Latin phrase *'cujus est solum, ejus est usque ad caelum et ad inferos'* adopted by English law, meaning that with ownership of land goes ownership of the subsoil and air space above and any premises and fixtures on the land. This maxim is subject to many restrictions nowadays, and must necessarily be revised. For example, British Coal may have mining rights under a person's land and civil aviation authorities a right to fly aeroplanes through air space over land, and clearly a block of flats creates horizontal rights of ownership and not vertical ones.

Notwithstanding that a lease creates an estate in land, it is also a contract between two parties – a landlord and a tenant. It will often contain a number of covenants by both of them, and there is an increasing tendency for the courts to recognise this contractual nature of a lease as well.[1]

1.2   Fixed Duration

A lease, then, is an estate in land of a fixed and definite duration. Although the technical name for it is 'a term of years', it may in fact be for any term less than a year – a week, a month or even a day – as well as for any number of years. It must, however, be for a *definite* or *determinable* duration, and the grant of an interest in land which does not comply with this requirement will not create a lease. Thus in the case of *Lace* v. *Chantler* (1944) a lease 'for the duration of the war' was held to be void.[2]

A very usual provision included in a lease for a fixed term is a proviso for re-entry by the landlord and forfeiture of the term if the tenant does not pay the rent or is in breach of any of the covenants contained in the lease. It is specifically provided by s.205(1)(xxvii) LPA 1925 that such a clause for premature defeasance of the term on certain events will not invalidate a lease.

A periodic tenancy, running automatically from one period to another unless terminated by either party, also falls within the definition as it is regarded as being a tenancy for that period. Examples of periodic tenancies are weekly, monthly, quarterly or yearly tenancies. Leases for life or until marriage are clearly outside the scope of the definition, but special provision is made for such leases in s.149(6) LPA. The particular characteristics of these and periodic tenancies will be dealt with in Chapter 2.

1.3   Exclusive Possession of Land

Because a tenant is given an estate in the land, he is entitled to exclusive possession of it and may exclude from it the landlord or anyone else. For this reason, it is usually necessary for a landlord who requires entry onto premises during the term of the lease (e.g. to inspect the state of repair) to reserve a right of entry in the lease itself.

A grant of anything less than exclusive possession will not create a leasehold estate. Thus in *Clore* v. *Theatrical Properties Ltd.* (1936) a right to sell refreshments in a cinema which did not give the grantee exclusive possession was held not to be a lease but merely a licence.

The House of Lords in *Street* v. *Mountford* (1985) has reasserted this basic difference between a lease and a licence. A lease is a proprietary interest in land whereas a licence is merely permission for user of, or entry on to, the land. There are, however, some circumstances where an occupier may have only a licence notwithstanding that he has exclusive possession, and these circumstances will be examined in more detail at the end of this chapter.

1.4   Rent

Rent is the consideration for the possession of the land enjoyed by the tenant, and as such is usually one of the basic characteristics of a lease. This commercial nature of a lease often distinguishes it from interests which are gratuitous and which may then take effect under a trust. Nevertheless, it is possible to have a gratuitous lease. This is specifically envisaged by the definition of a term of years in s.205(1) (xxvii) LPA, which states 'whether or not at a rent', and it was recognised by the Court of Appeal in *Ashburn Anstalt* v. *W.J. Arnold & Co.* (1987) that rent-free occupation could nevertheless be a lease.

Rent is usually a money payment, of course, but it does not have to be. The most common alternative to a money payment is services, where the property is leased in return for the tenant's services.

Rent is an acknowledgement of the landlord's reversionary title, and failure to pay rent for twelve years may result in his reversionary title being extinguished under the Limitation Act 1980. Alternatively, lack of rent may be a factor which indicates that the agreement between the parties is not a lease at all, but is merely a licence, as in the case of *Heslop* v. *Burns* (1974).[3]

1.5   Reversion Expectant upon the Term

Because a lease is for a definite and limited duration, there must always be a reversionary interest expectant upon its determination. This will usually be a freehold estate, but need not necessarily be so. For example, a person who has himself a lease for ninety-nine years may grant out of it a lease for any lesser term, called a sublease or underlease.

If the sublease is for, say, fifty years, it is then possible to grant a further sublease for any term less than fifty years. The reversion on this last lease would be the sublease of fifty, years, the reversion on the sublease of fifty years would be the lease of ninety-nine years, and the reversion on the ninety-nine-year lease would be the freehold.

The lease and the immediate reversion must be vested in different persons, however, and should they become vested in the same person, then the lease will cease to exist. This principle was illustrated by the House of Lords case of *Rye* v. *Rye* (1962), where it was held that co-owners could not grant a valid lease to a partnership of which they themselves were the partners, as a partnership (unlike a limited company) does not have any distinct identity separate from the partners in it.

1.6   Distinction between a Lease and a Licence

It was at one time believed that the essential difference between a lease and a licence was that a lease gave the tenant exclusive possession of the property, whereas a licence did not.

Under the Rent Acts, extensive protection was given to tenants both as regards security of tenure and rent control. In the majority of leases, when the contractual term of the lease expired, the tenant would have a statutory tenancy which the landlord would be able to terminate only on certain grounds, and which could pass on the tenant's death to certain members of his family living with him in the leased premises.

Not surprisingly, many landlords were anxious to avoid creating a lease which might not be terminable for many years to come, and attempted (with varying degrees of success) to avoid the effect of the Rent Acts by creating a licence instead. Moreover, there have been circumstances where, although the logical interpretation of an agreement would suggest that a lease has been created, the judges have concluded that it was merely a licence in order to avoid undue hardship to the landlord. The distinction between leases and licences is therefore blurred. It is certainly no longer defined by the simple criterion of exclusive possession, and it requires an examination of the principles applied by the courts to determine which side of a rather wavering line any particular agreement may fall.

First, it is clear that if there is no exclusive possession, then the occupier of premises cannot have a lease but only a licence. 'Exclusive possession' means the right to exclude everyone else, including the landlord, from the premises, and in *Luganda* v. *Service Hotels Ltd.* (1969) this was distinguished from 'exclusive occupation', which gave the occupier the right to exclude everyone except the landlord – a circumstance usually typical of a lodger's rights.[4] In the decision of *Brooker Settled Estates Ltd.* v. *Ayers* (1987) the Court of Appeal ruled that whether exclusive possession exists or not is a matter of fact for the trial judge to determine in every case, and it is not a proper inference to draw that a person in possession of premises who is not a lodger necessarily has exclusive possession and is a tenant.

Secondly, it is abundantly clear from *Addiscombe Garden Estates Ltd.* v.

Crabbe and Others (1958),[5] and from the House of Lords' decision in *Street* v. *Mountford* (1985), that what the parties call their 'agreement' is by no means conclusive and it is primarily the intention of the parties which the court will look at in deciding whether the agreement creates a lease or a licence. Moreover, this intention is to be deduced from the realities of the arrangement in practice, and not as may be expressed in the agreement.

Since the decision in *Street* v. *Mountford*, the presumption is in favour of a lease wherever exclusive possession of premises is granted for a term at a rent. However, the speech of Lord Templeman in *Street* v. *Mountford* clearly recognises that there will be some instances where this will still not apply. These are where the occupation of premises by someone is referable to legal relations other than a tenancy – e.g. a service occupancy, or occupation under a contract for the sale of property.

Alternatively, the arrangement between the parties may not have been intended to create legal relations at all. In the case of *Facchini* v. *Bryson* (1952) Denning L.J. referred to the possible existence of 'circumstances such as family arrangement, an act of friendship or generosity, or such like, to negative any intention to create a tenancy'. Lord Templeman cites these situations as ones which may not give rise to a tenancy, in spite of exclusive possession, as they may not create legal relations at all between the parties.

There have been cases of family arrangement (*Cobb* v. *Lane* (1952),[6] friendship (*Heslop* v. *Burns*)[3] and generosity (*Marcroft Wagons Ltd.* v. *Smith* (1951))[7] where the courts have decided that a licence and not a lease had been created. In *Ward* v. *Warnke* (1990), however, it was said that a family relationship is not conclusive of a licence and there may still be a tenancy if the circumstances support this.[8] Whilst the decision in *Street* v. *Mountford* clearly gives the courts the power to expose any 'sham' licences, which are in reality leases, certain well-established types of occupancy will still not be within the definition of leases as they are not agreements which were intended to create legal relations.

In *Bruton* v. *London & Quadrant Housing Trust* (1999), the House of Lords applied the principle of *Street* v. *Mountford* to a licence granted by a Housing Trust which was a charity. The Trust itself was a licensee of a block of flats from Lambeth LBC for the purpose of providing temporary accommodation for homeless persons. The House of Lords held that the licence granted to Mr. Bruton had all the hallmarks of a lease, giving him exclusive possession of premises for a period in return for a payment. It was irrelevant that the Housing Association itself only had a licence from the council, and they were estopped from denying the tenancy which they had created. This decision has recently been reviewed by Lord Scott in *Kay* v. *Lambeth LBC* (2006), where he said that the 'non-estate' Bruton tenancies granted by the Trust, although binding on them, could not be binding on the Lambeth Borough Council.[9]

Another way in which landlords have sought to ensure that they grant an occupier of premises a licence rather than a lease is to grant rights of shared occupation only to two or more persons, reserving to the landlord the right to select another occupier if one should vacate the premises. It may then be argued that no one occupier has exclusive possession of the premises.

The decision of the House of Lords in *A.G. Securities* v. *Vaughan and Others* (1988) accepted that four occupiers, who each signed different licence agreements on different dates at varying rents, which expressly negatived exclusive possession of any part of the premises, could not have a joint tenancy of a four-bedroom flat which gave them *'in toto'* exclusive possession.

The essential ingredients of a joint tenancy – which would have to commence at the same time and give each of the joint tenants identical rights in the whole of the property – were missing. In *Mikeover* v. *Brady* (1989) two licensees paid identical monthly sums under two licence agreements. When one vacated the premises the landlord refused to accept any payment from the remaining licensee other than that under his agreement. It was held that as they were clearly liable individually for their own payments there was no unity of interest essential for a joint tenancy and they were necessarily licensees.

In the case of *Antoniades* v. *Villiers and Another*, however (1988, heard on appeal along with *Vaughan*) the House of Lords decided that occupation of a one-bedroom flat given to two people at the same time, where they both paid equal contributions to periodic payments of rent, was in fact a lease and not a licence as it described itself. The landlord's right of entry and occupation, expressly reserved for the purpose of avoiding exclusive occupation by the two occupiers, was unrealistic in a one-bedroom flat and amounted to a sham. The two occupiers together had exclusive possession for a term at a rent, and therefore had a tenancy.

Two further cases in which the landlord purported to reserve a right of entry which the court decided was not real are *Aslan* v. *Murphy* (1990)[10] and *Family Housing Association* v. *Jones* (1990).[11] In each case the court found that a lease had been created, and in the latter case, the court was not prepared to find that the retention of a key by the landlord was in itself sufficient to indicate shared possession.

Although the virtual abolition of security of tenure now means that the creation of a lease will not have the same far-reaching effects for a landlord, and the deluge of litigation in this area has abated, the distinction is still important as a lease creates an estate in land, with all that this entails, whereas a licence is still only an agreement.

A lease will often give a tenant certain important statutory rights which may not attach to a licence. A licence is usually more easily revoked and will not give rise to the same rights which a tenant would have against a landlord. In *Monmouth Borough Council* v. *Marlog* (1994), the tenant of a three-bedroom house, under a written tenancy agreement, allowed a woman and her two children to share the house with him. He later left the house and the Council sought to recover possession of it. It was held that the woman was merely a licensee under an informal house-sharing arrangement, and not a subtenant, so that the Council could recover possession against her. Also, the rights of a tenant are much more likely to be binding on a third party than the rights of a licensee. In *Skipton Building Society* v. *Clayton* (1993), a 'Licence' whereby vendors of property occupied it for their lives was held to be a lease within S.149(6), LPA (see section 2.4) and so binding on the Building Society, to which the purchaser had mortgaged the property.[12]

The distinction between a lease and a licence may also be important in relation to business premises where a lease (even a periodic one) will be within the provisions of the Landlord & Tenant Act 1954, Part II, whereas a licence will not be. In *Esso Petroleum Co. Ltd.* v. *Fumegrange Ltd.* (1994), a filling station, shop and car wash was managed by the occupiers on behalf of Esso under three separate licence agreements. The occupiers tried to claim that they had exclusive possession and were lessees. Esso exercised considerable control over the management of the businesses, however, and issued a manual of operating standards. It was held that this degree of control negatived any intention to create a lease, and although the licensees had exclusive occupation, they did not have exclusive possession as regards the landlord. A decision to the contrary, where a management agreement on restaurant premises gave the sole and exclusive right to operate the restaurant business to the restaurant proprietor, was held to create a lease and not merely a licence.[13]

In *Clear Channel Ltd.* v. *Manchester City Council* (2006), the Council entered into two agreements with the claimants for the erection and use of advertising hoardings on sites. The first agreement, which described itself as a licence and stated that no tenancy was to be conferred, concerned thirteen sites which were identified only by general addresses and not specifically described. The judge (whose decision was confirmed by the Court of Appeal) concluded that the agreements conferred merely a right to use the sites rather than any exclusive possession of them and that they were not sufficiently described to be an area of land contained in a lease. Jonathan Parker L.J. said that he would have had great difficulty in construing an agreement as a lease when the parties, who had received legal advice and were of equal bargaining power, had expressly stated in the agreement that it was not. The 1954 Act did not therefore apply. The second agreement, contained in a letter, set out terms entirely consistent with a tenancy granting rights and obligations with regard to clearly identified land which could be the subject matter of a lease, and the user of the site for advertising was sufficient business user for the 1954 Act to apply.

In *Hunts Refuse Disposals Ltd.* v. *Norfolk-Environmental Waste Services Ltd.* (1997) the Court of Appeal accepted that while the principles of *Street* v. *Mountford* apply to both residential and business premises, their application in practice may be very different to business premises. In that case, it was held that the exclusive right to deposit waste on a thirty-one-acre site, for twenty-one years, part of which was used for quarrying, created a licence and not a lease. Similarly, the judgment of Jonathan Parker L.J. in *Clear Channel* above demonstrates the possibility that the courts may not apply the principles of *Street* v. *Mountford* so rigorously in commercial transactions.

Notes

▶ 1 Luxton, 'Termination of Leases: from Property to Contract?', in Birds, Bradgate and Villiers (eds.), *Termination of Contracts*, 1995, Wiley Chancery, Chapter 7.

▶ 2 Because a number of leases had been made in this form during the war, the Validation of War-time Leases Act 1944 was passed specifically to validate them.

▶ 3 *Heslop* v. *Burns* [1974] 3 All ER 406

An elderly man who had befriended a young couple allowed them to live in a property of his. No rent was paid and he paid the rates. After his death, his executors brought an action for possession of the property. They were successful as the court decided that the couple had only a licence and not any kind of tenancy.

▶ 4 *Luganda* v. *Service Hotels Ltd.* [1969] 2 Ch 209

Rooms were let to occupiers and the landlords provided some porterage and room services. It was held that, although the occupant had exclusive occupation in

that he was able to exclude everyone but the landlord (and had limited protection under Part VI, Landlord & Tenant Act 1968), he did not have exclusive possession which enabled him to exclude the landlord and was not therefore a lessee.

▶ 5 *Addiscombe Garden Estates* v. *Crabbe & Others* [1958] 1 QB

A document, which described itself as a licence, gave the trustees of a tennis club the right to use tennis courts for a fee. There was a right of re-entry on non-payment of the fee and an agreement for quiet enjoyment, and the trustees were to repair and maintain the premises and to permit the grantors to enter and inspect. It was held that the terms were indicative of a lease rather than a licence.

▶ 6 *Cobb* v. *Lane* [1952] 1 All ER 1199

A sister allowed her brother to occupy a house belonging to her, she paying the rates. It was held that this was a family arrangement, creating a licence rather than a tenancy.

▶ 7 *Marcroft Wagons Ltd.* v. *Smith* [1951] 2 All ER 271

A landlord permitted the daughter of a protected tenant, who had lived in the cottage for many years, to remain there after her widowed mother's death. He refused to put her name in the rent book but accepted rent for six months. It was held nevertheless that she was not a tenant but only a licensee, as she had only permissive occupation.

▶ 8 *Ward* v. *Warnke* [1990] 22 HLR 496

The plaintiff's daughter and her husband occupied a holiday cottage belonging to the plaintiff. They paid all outgoings and a small sum of £3 per week which later rose to £6 per week. The daughter left but her husband and child remained there. It was held that the husband was a tenant as the premises were let for a term at a rent and the family relationship did not prevent this.

▶ 9 In *Bruton*, the London Quadrant Housing Trust had surrendered its licence and been granted a tenancy by the Lambeth Borough Council in 1995, which the Council terminated after the decision in the Court of Appeal. Lord Scott said that the tenancies created by the Trust thereupon became 'estate' tenancies, but still fell when the lease to the Trust was terminated. In *Kay* v. *Lambeth LBC* (2006), the tenant also pleaded Article 8(2) of the Human Rights Act 1998 as a defence to his eviction, but the House of Lords applied their previous decision on this in *Harrow LBC* v. *Qazi*. For a discussion of this, see section 15.2.

▶ 10 *Asian* v. *Murphy (Nos. 1 & 2)* [1990] 1 WLR 766

The licensee's agreement allowed him to occupy the premises from midnight until 10.30a.m. and from midday to midnight. It was held that the break of one and a half hours each day was a pretence and to be ignored, and he therefore had a lease.

▶ 11 *Family Housing Association* v. *Jones* [1990] 1 All ER 385

The Housing Association, which had granted a licence of temporary accommodation to a homeless person, retained keys to the premises. The purpose of this was to discuss rehousing with the occupier and inspect the state of repair and not to introduce another occupier. The Court of Appeal held that retention of keys alone was not sufficient to indicate a licence where the purpose of retention did not relate to shared occupation.

▶ 12 *Skipton Building Society* v. *Clayton* (1993) 66 P&CR 223

The vendor of a flat sold it to the purchasers at one-third of the market value in return for the purchasers granting a 'licence' to him and his wife to live there for the rest of their lives. The licence purported to give the purchasers' 'possession, management and control' of the property. They did not have any key to the property however and the judge found that this clause, along with the description of the agreement as a 'licence', was a sham. The reality was that the vendor and his wife had sole possession. It was held that the agreement created a lease and not a licence, to which s.149(6) LPA applied as the sale at one-third of the market price amounted to a 'fine' within the section (see section 2.4). It therefore became a lease for ninety years and was binding on the Building Society to which the purchasers mortgaged the property.

▶ **13** *Bon Appetito* v. *Michael Poon* **(2005) Unreported Newcastle CC 18.1.05.**

Summary

▷ A lease is a contract between a landlord and a tenant which creates an estate in land. It may be a legal estate (term of years absolute).

▷ A lease must be for a fixed and definite duration and must give the tenant exclusive possession of the property.

▷ Rent will usually be payable although it is not essential.

▷ The landlord (who owns the reversion) and the tenant (who owns the term) must be different persons.

▷ It is not always clear whether an agreement is a lease or a licence. After the case of *Street* v. *Mountford,* there is a presumption of a lease, but circumstances such as lack of legal relations or no exclusive possession, may mean that the agreement is merely a licence.

▷ The distinction is still important as regards certain statutory rights and as regards the enforceability of a lease against third parties.

▷ In commercial transactions, there may be reasons for not applying the principles of *Street* v. *Mountford* too rigidly.

Exercises

1.1 What is an estate in land?

1.2 What is the essential difference between a freehold and a leasehold estate?

1.3 Does a right of re-entry reserved to the landlord in certain circumstances make a lease invalid?

1.4 What are the essential requirements of a lease?

1.5 How would you define a licence?

1.6 What is rent? Does it have to be a money payment?

1.7 Why have the courts been reluctant in some cases to find that an agreement creates a lease?

1.8 Give examples of circumstances where the courts have decided that a licence rather than a lease has been created.

Workshop

1 Lawrence allowed three students to occupy a three-bedroom flat of his. The students were each given a licence agreement to sign which stated that they did not have exclusive possession and must each contribute a one- third part of the fee for occupation. Recently, one of the students left and the other two advertised his room and have allowed someone else to occupy it.

Discuss whether the agreements between Lawrence and the students create a lease or a licence of the flat.

2 Five years ago, the Ambridge Borough Council entered into a written agreement with Teasmade Ltd. whereby Teasmade Ltd. were to have exclusive possession of a hut on a recreation ground to provide refreshments until such time as the Council demolished the hut in order to build a pavilion. The Council is now ready to proceed with the building and have asked Teasmade Ltd. to vacate the hut. Advise Teasmade Ltd.

Chapter 2
Different types of leases

2.1 Tenancy for a Fixed Term

As we have already seen, one of the essential characteristics of a lease is that it is for a fixed and definite duration (*Lace* v. *Chantler* (1944)). This was more recently confirmed by the House of Lords in *Prudential Assurance Company* v. *London Residuary Body* (1992). Also, although its technical legal name is a term of years, it may in fact be for any period of less than a year, or even for one day.

A lease for a fixed number of years will terminate automatically by effluxion of time, but it may also include a proviso for re-entry by the landlord on non-payment of rent or breach of any other covenant thereby terminating it prematurely. Such a lease still satisfies the definition of certainty of term, as s.205(1)(xxvii) LPA 1925 specifically includes a term which may be liable to premature defeasance. The Leasehold Reform Act 1967 provides for long leases of over twenty-one years to be enfranchised and thereby converted into freeholds in certain circumstances, and s.153(1) LPA also provides for the enfranchisement of certain long leases at very low rents. Otherwise, however, a lease for a fixed term will terminate at the end of the term by effluxion of time.

2.2 Periodic Tenancies

A periodic tenancy is one which runs on automatically from one period to the next until it is terminated. The term of the tenancy may be a week, a month, a year, or a quarter, and it is regarded as being a definite term for whatever period it is. This means that most periodic tenancies will fall within s.54(2) LPA, which provides that parol leases taking effect in possession for a term not exceeding three years, at the best rent obtainable without a fine, may be legal leases. Periodic tenancies will therefore in most cases be legal leases.[1] If rent is paid at different periods than the period by which it is reserved – for example, a yearly rent where the rent is paid monthly – then the tenancy will be a periodic tenancy determined by the period for which the rent is expressed to be reserved and not by the instalments by which it is paid (*Adler* v. *Blackman* (1952)).[2]

Periodic tenancies are usually expressly created by the parties, but they may also arise by implication where a person occupies premises and pays rent by reference to a period.

A periodic tenancy continues until it is terminated by notice. The period of notice required to terminate it may be specified by the parties, but, in the absence of this, the notice required will be a full period's notice to terminate at the end of the period. The exceptions to this are a yearly tenancy where only six months' notice to terminate at the end of the year is required, and notice to terminate a periodic tenancy of a dwellinghouse, for which at least twenty-eight days' notice is required by s.5 Protection from Eviction Act 1977. Notice given by only one joint tenant will be sufficient to terminate the tenancy (see Chapter 15.2).

One of the essential characteristics of a periodic tenancy is that it must be terminable by either party. A restriction on the right of one party to terminate which is not a total abrogation of the right will not make it void, however (*Breams Property Investment Co. Ltd.* v. *Stroulger* (1948)),[3] provided that it is not limited to an uncertain event. Periodic tenancies must also comply with the general requirement for certainty of term, and a provision making it uncertain as to when a party can give notice to terminate the tenancy will make it void. In *Prudential Assurance Company* v. *London Residuary Body* (1992), the Greater London Council had granted the Prudential a quarterly lease of a strip of land and agreed not to give notice terminating the tenancy until such time as the land was required for road widening purposes. The House of Lords (overruling *Re Midland Railway Company's Agreement* (1971)) held that this made the whole agreement void for uncertainty as to its term.

Under Schedule I, Part I of the Limitation Act 1980, a tenancy from year to year or other period without a lease in writing is to be treated as determined at the end of the first year or other period, or when the last payment of rent was made, whichever is later. From that time, the statutory period under the Act runs against the landlord, and after twelve years he will lose his right to recover possession of the premises.

2.3 Statutory Tenancies

Where a residential tenant had a fixed-term tenancy or a periodic tenancy which was protected under the Rent Acts or the Landlord & Tenant Act 1954, Part I, and that tenancy came to an end, a statutory tenancy under the legislation would come into effect. The terms of the statutory tenancy would be those of the previous contractual tenancy in so far as they were not inconsistent with the statutory tenancy. Although statutory tenancies cannot now be created, some which arose under the old legislation still remain.

A business tenant may acquire a new lease in certain circumstances by serving a notice under the Landlord & Tenant Act 1954, Part II, and the Agricultural Holdings Act 1986 gives security to agricultural tenants whose tenancies were created prior to 1 September 1995: no such security is provided by successor legislation, the Agricultural Tenancies Act 1995. All of these statutory regimes are dealt with in Part II of this book.

2.4 Tenancies Terminable on Death or Marriage

Because of the requirement of certainty of the term granted, a lease granted for life or until marriage, or one terminable on a death, would normally be void as an infringement of this principle. Section 149(6) LPA provides that a lease at a rent or in consideration of a fine (that is, a lump sum payment) for life or lives, or for any term determinable with life or lives or on the lessee's marriage, shall take effect as a lease for a term of ninety years terminable by one month's written notice on the death or marriage. It should be noted that, although the life upon which the term of the lease is made dependent may be anyone's, the marriage must be that of the lessee only. The fact that the premium is less than the full market value does not preclude the section from applying (see *Skipton Building Society* v. *Clayton* in Note 12 to Chapter 1).

2.5 Perpetually Renewable Leases

A lease for a term which contains an option for the tenant to renew it for a further term in exactly the same form, including the option to renew, contains the seeds of its own indefinite reproduction and could, if the tenant so wished, continue for ever. Schedule 2, para. 15 LPA 1922 provides that such a lease is converted into a term for 2,000 years, terminable by the tenant only by ten days' written notice to terminate on a day on which it would have expired but for its conversion into a term of 2,000 years.

Because of the drastic consequences of such a lease for the landlord, the courts have construed against finding that an option to renew a lease on the same terms creates a perpetually renewable lease, and have said that it should do so only if that was what the landlord intended. In the case of *Marjorie Burnett Ltd.* v. *Barclay* (1980) the lease provided that the tenant could give notice to the landlord if he wanted a new lease and the landlord would grant him a new lease for a further term of seven years. This was to contain a provision to renew again for a further seven years, and on each renewal the rent was to be agreed. The court construed the agreement as one for renewal twice only and not a perpetually renewable lease. It was said that the provision for rent review every seven years was inimical to a 2,000-year term.

The lease for 2,000 years created by the LPA 1922 differs from other leases in certain respects. The tenant must give notice to the landlord of any devolution or assignment of the term within six months, and the original tenant has never been liable to the original landlord under privity of contract once the lease has been assigned.

2.6 Reversionary Leases

By s.149(3) LPA 1925, a lease, or a contract for a lease, at a rent or for a premium which is to take effect in possession more than twenty-one years after the creation of the lease is void. This will not invalidate an option to renew contained in a lease, however (*Re Strand & Savoy Properties Ltd.* (1960)).[4] Section 27, Land Registration Act 2002, makes reversionary leases which will not take effect in possession for more than three months after the date of their grant registrable dispositions. This means that they will be equitable only until registered substantively and require registration to bind a purchaser of the freehold reversion.

2.7 Concurrent Leases

A concurrent lease arises where a lessor grants a subsequent lease, longer in duration than a previous lease which he has already granted, and which commences during the term of the previous lease. He is, in effect, leasing part of his reversion, and the second or subsequent lessee will have no right to possession until the prior lease terminates. He will, however, be the immediate landlord of the prior lessee and entitled to receive rent from him payable under the prior lease. The device of concurrent leases could be used to create second and subsequent mortgage terms where each mortgagee receives as security a lease for a term one day longer than the prior mortgagee. However, as the grant of a mortgage triggers registration of title, any second mortgage would now be a mortgage of registered title and would be effected by a legal charge.

2.8 Tenancies by Estoppel

Where a person who has no title to land grants a lease of it and subsequently acquires a title, then his subsequent title will 'feed the estoppel' to make good the lessee's title. The most frequent example of this is where an intending purchaser of property leases it before completion of the purchase, and therefore before he acquires a legal title to it. Once the purchase is completed and his title becomes good, the title of the lessee also becomes good and his lease becomes a legal lease. The rule of *scintilla temporis* whereby a mortgagee granting a mortgage to finance the purchase was bound by a lease created by the purchaser was overruled, however, by the House of Lords.[5]

2.9 Tenancies at Will

A tenancy at will usually arises by implication where a person occupies 'at will' property belonging to another – for example, where a tenant holds over at the end of a lease, or where a purchaser of property is allowed into possession before completion. It is terminable by either party without notice. It is not strictly speaking a term of years at all within s.205(1)(xxvii) LPA 1925.

In *Manfield & Sons Ltd.* v. *Botchin* (1970) it was decided that, although it usually arises by implication, a tenancy at will may also be expressly created. In that case, the landlord had made unsuccessful applications to develop a shop property which he owned. Anticipating that he would eventually obtain planning permission, he allowed a tenant to occupy the shop as a tenant at will, reserving an annual rent. It was held that the intention of the parties to create a tenancy at will prevailed, and the tenancy did not become a yearly periodic tenancy merely by the reservation of an annual rent.

The effect of para. 5 of Schedule 1, Part I of the Limitation Act 1980 is to extinguish a landlord's right of recovery of his land after twelve years' adverse possession by a tenant at will once the tenancy at will has ceased.[6] There is now no rule that the tenancy at will ceases automatically after twelve months, and it is therefore a matter of evidence as to when it ends.

Time begins to run against the landlord under the Limitation Act 1980 as soon as the tenancy at will is determined (for example, by the landlord demanding possession) and after twelve years, the landlord's right to recover possession will be extinguished. Any acknowledgement of the landlord's title – by payment of rent, for instance – will start the twelve-year period running again.

Where a tenant at will pays rent by reference to a period, an implied periodic tenancy arises, unless, as in *Manfield & Sons Ltd.* v. *Botchin*, it has been expressly stipulated that the tenancy is a tenancy at will.

A tenant at will, whether of residential or business premises, will not be able to claim any statutory rights which may be available to other tenants.

2.10   Tenancies at Sufferance

A tenancy at sufferance arises where a tenant wrongfully remains in possession after his lease has terminated without the consent of the landlord. It is not a tenancy at all as such and he is in effect a trespasser whom the landlord may evict. If the landlord accepts rent from him, however, then a periodic tenancy may arise by implication. As he is wrongfully holding over, time under the Limitation Act 1980 starts to run against the landlord from the commencement of the tenancy, and after twelve years the landlord's right to recover the premises will be barred.

Notes

▶ **1** A decision at first instance suggests that such a tenancy which does not take effect immediately in possession cannot fall within the section and so must be equitable and not legal (*Long* v. *Tower Hamlets LBC* [1996] 2 All ER 683, the subject of a Case Note by Susan Bright [1998] Conv.229). The point is only likely to be of importance retrospectively, for example in determining when a period of adverse possession might start to run.

▶ **2** *Adler* v. *Blackman* [1952] 2 All ER 945

Premises were let for a year at a weekly rent and the tenant held over at the end of the term. It was held that a weekly tenancy and not a yearly tenancy should be presumed. A yearly tenancy would be presumed only if the rent was reserved as an annual rent.

▶ **3** *Breams Property Investment Co. Ltd.* v. *Stroulger* [1948] 2 KB 1

Premises were let on quarterly tenancies which provided that the landlords should not serve notice to terminate the tenancies within three years of the commencement of the tenancies unless the landlords required the premises for their own use. It was held that the clause was valid and not repugnant to the nature of a periodic tenancy.

▶ **4** *Re Strand & Savoy Properties Ltd.* [1960] Ch 582

A lease dated 1 November 1928 for thirty-eight years to commence in June 1926 contained an option for the tenant to renew it for a further thirty-five years. The option was to be exercised within twelve months before the expiration of the lease. It was held that the option was not a contract caught by s.149(3) (invalidating a contract to grant a lease to commence more than twenty-one years later) as this term was to take effect within twenty-one years from the end of the term of the lease.

▶ **5** *Abbey National Building Society* v. *Cann* [1990] 1 All ER 1085, over-ruling *Church of England Building Society* v. *Piskor* [1954] Ch.553.

▶ **6** If the landlord's freehold reversion is a registered title, then a procedure for serving notices before a landlord's title is barred was introduced by the Land Registration Act 2002 and applies from 13 October 2003. See Chapter 11.1.

Summary

▶ A tenancy for a fixed term which will expire at the end of that term also includes tenancies liable to premature defeasance by forfeiture or notice.

▶ A periodic tenancy runs automatically from one period to another. It is terminable by notice by either party.

Summary cont'd

▶ Statutory tenancies arise where a periodic or fixed-term tenancy is terminated and the tenant becomes protected from eviction under the Landlord and Tenant legislation.

▶ Special provision is made by s.149(6) LPA for certain tenancies terminable by death or marriage, which are converted into tenancies for ninety years terminable by notice on the event.

▶ Perpetually renewable leases are leases providing for their renewal on exactly the same terms, including the same provision for renewal, and are converted into leases for 2,000 years.

▶ By s.149(3) LPA, a lease must take effect in possession within twenty-one years from its creation.

▶ A concurrent lease arises where a landlord grants a subsequent lease to take effect in possession for a term longer than a prior lease he has already granted.

▶ A tenancy by estoppel arises where a person without a title to property grants a lease of it. His subsequent acquisition of a title feeds the estoppel and makes good the lessee's title.

▶ A tenancy at will arises where a person occupies premises at the will of the landlord.

▶ A tenancy at sufferance arises where a person holds over at the end of a tenancy without the consent of the landlord.

Exercises

2.1 How may a fixed-term lease expire?

2.2 Give examples of periodic tenancies. How may they be terminated?

2.3 How does a statutory tenancy arise?

2.4 Why is provision made by s.149(6) for leases terminable on death or marriage to be converted into leases for ninety years? Are all such leases within the section?

2.5 How does a perpetually renewable lease which has been converted into a term for 2,000 years differ from other leases?

2.6 Within what period from its creation must a lease take effect in possession?

2.7 How does a concurrent lease arise?

2.8 Distinguish a tenancy at will from a tenancy at sufferance.

Workshop

1 Joe allowed Leeroy to occupy exclusively a cottage of his which he proposed to demolish as soon as he received planning permission for a new house on the site. Leeroy paid him a weekly sum for the cottage. Joe has now received planning permission. What notice to leave the cottage, if any, does he need to give to Leeroy?

2 Jake and Jane granted a lease of the top floor of their house to Jane's mother, who is eighty, 'for thirty years if she should live so long'. What is the effect of this grant?

3 Peter leased a flat from Laura for three months, paying the rent monthly. The lease expired five months ago and he has remained in possession, continuing to pay rent monthly to Laura. What is Peter's position?

4 Lucy granted a three-year lease to Tom which included an agreement by Lucy to renew the lease on exactly the same terms, including the covenant to renew, at the end of the three-year term. What is the effect of this? Would your answer differ if the agreement provided that the new lease was to be at a new rent to be agreed between the parties?

Chapter 3

Formalities for creating a lease

3.1 Contractual Nature of a Lease Creating an Estate in Land

A lease is essentially a contract between *two parties*, the landlord (or lessor) and the tenant (or lessee). It was held in the House of Lords case of *Rye* v. *Rye* (1962) that the landlord and the tenant must be different persons, and that a lease granted by two persons in their private capacity to a partnership of which they were both partners was void. Viscount Simonds said in the case: 'It is meaningless to say that a man accepts from himself something which is already his own.'

It is also a contract which creates an estate in land. The technical name for the estate which it creates is a term of years, although it does not in fact have to be for a term of years and may be for any lesser period such as a year, a month, or even a day. Section 205 (xxvii) LPA 1925 provides that it will still satisfy the requirement of being for a fixed and definite duration not withstanding that it is a term of years liable to premature defeasance by forfeiture or notice.

It is the only estate in English land law of less than freehold. The essential characteristic of a freehold estate is that it is for an uncertain duration (and a legal freehold nowadays lasts virtually for ever) but a term of years must be for a *fixed and definite duration*. A term of years absolute is one of the two estates which may subsist at law (s.1(1) LPA 1925), although it may also subsist in equity. The word 'absolute' is thought to add little to the definition, other than to emphasise that it must be for a definite duration.

A legal term of years ('legal lease' in layman's language) is a legal estate which is a right *in rem* (that is, in the land itself) binding against everyone. This can be very important if the freehold reversion is sold, and will be dealt with in more detail in Chapter 14. In order to be legal, however, it must comply with certain formalities as to its creation.

3.2 Requirements for a Legal Lease

Section 52 LPA 1925 provides that a deed (that is, a document which is signed as a deed and attested) must be used to create or to transfer a legal estate or interest in land. The document is a formal demise (or lease) of the term to the tenant. It will set out the names of the parties, recite the seisin of the lessor and formally demise the term granted in the premises to the tenant, reserving a rent therefor. There will usually be a number of covenants by both the landlord and the tenant, and most formal leases include a proviso for re-entry by the landlord for non-payment of rent or breach of some other covenant in the lease by the tenant. The lease is the tenant's document of title and the landlord will usually keep a counterpart lease signed by the tenant. A short model of a very simple lease is to be found in Chapter 14.4. (For registration requirements, see Chapter 14.1.)

There is an exception under s.54(2) LPA 1925 for leases which do not exceed three years, at the best rent obtainable without a fine, and which take effect in possession. Such leases may be legal even if created only by parol.[1] The section includes all periodic tenancies (which are regarded as being leases for a week, year, month, and so on) and periodic tenancies arising by implication from occupation and payment of rent. Those leases which comply with the section will therefore be legal.

3.3   Leases Enforceable in Equity: Enforceable Contracts

A lease which is not legal because it does not comply with either s.52 or s.54 may nevertheless be enforceable in equity. The reason for this is that equity will enforce a contract for the creation or disposition of an interest in land if it is in writing and complies with s.2 Law of Property (Miscellaneous Provisions) Act 1989. Section 2 requires that a contract for the sale or other disposition (including a lease) of land must be in writing and signed by both parties, or if the customary way of exchanging contracts on the sale of land is followed, the agreement must be contained in two identical parts, one signed by each party, to be exchanged. If exchange is contemplated but has not actually taken place, then specific performance of the contract will not be available (*Longman* v. *Viscount Chelsea* (1989)).

Section 2(5)(*a*) exempts contracts for a lease within s.54(2) LPA from this provision, so a contract for such a lease may also be oral.

If these conditions are complied with as regards contracts made after 26 September 1989, the contract for a lease is specifically enforceable in equity and there is therefore a valid equitable lease. The enforceability of such a lease against a purchaser of the freehold reversion is dealt with in Chapter 14.3.

3.4   Leases Enforceable in Equity: Part Performance and Other Equitable Principles

Section 40 LPA 1925, the predecessor of s.2, Law of Property (Miscellaneous Provisions) Act 1989, required a contract for the sale or other disposition of land to be evidenced in writing. The courts were always anxious to prevent an unscrupulous defendant from using s.40 to evade his obligations under a purely oral contract if it would be grossly unfair to the plaintiff to do so. Equity therefore developed the doctrine of part performance. This meant that, where a plaintiff who was seeking to enforce an oral contract which did not comply with s.40 had done some act of *part performance*, equity would grant a decree of specific performance of the contract notwithstanding that it did not comply with the section.

In the case of leases, taking possession was a sufficient act of part performance, although remaining in possession at the end of a lease was not sufficient for a contract to renew a lease.

Section 2(8) of the 1989 Act repeals s.40 LPA 1925 as regards contracts created on or after 27 September 1989. Although there was a saving for the equitable doctrine of part performance in s.40(2) LPA, the actual doctrine itself, being a creature of equity, was not enshrined in the statute. It is therefore arguable to what extent the doctrine may have survived the repeal of s.40.[2] In any event, there is nothing in the 1989 Act which would affect the equitable doctrine of estoppel if applicable, or constructive trusts (which are expressly exempted from s.2) or the application of the general equitable principle that equity will not allow a statute to be used as an engine of fraud. In *Yaxley* v. *Gotts* (2000), a builder carried out work for a friend, at his own expense, on the conversion of a building into flats on the understanding that he was to have the two ground floor flats himself. The Court of Appeal held that this created a proprietary estoppel which was not affected by s.2(1) Law of Property (Miscellaneous Provisions) Act 1989, but was protected by a constructive trust, which is expressly exempted from s.2(1) by s.2(5).

There has been some litigation on the section, including a case on what amounts to a necessary signature,[3] and as to what formality is required to vary a s.2 contract.[4] Perhaps more importantly, there have been cases where the courts have been prepared to find that an agreement relating to a land transaction caught by the section was a collateral agreement, not itself within the section and therefore enforceable even though not complying with the section.[5]

3.5 The Nature and Effect of an Equitable Lease

An equitable lease arises where there is an enforceable contract to grant a lease. How does such a lease differ from a legal lease?

First, it depends upon the willingness of a court to grant the equitable remedy of specific performance. The essential nature of all equitable remedies is that they are discretionary, and the equitable maxims apply to them. One of the best remembered of these is that 'He who comes to equity must come with clean hands.' If a claimant seeking to enforce an equitable lease is himself at fault in any way therefore (in breach of a covenant or in arrears with the rent), equity will not exercise its discretion to grant him a decree of specific performance. In *Coatsworth* v. *Johnson* (1886), equity declined to assist a plaintiff lessee of an equitable lease who had failed to cultivate the farm leased to him properly in accordance with a covenant to do so in his lease. Nor will equity grant a decree of specific performance if it necessarily involves a breach of contract with a third person. In *Warmington* v. *Miller* (1973), a tenant granted an oral sublease of part of premises leased to him in breach of a covenant in the lease. The court refused to grant a decree of specific performance of the sublease which would have been in breach of the covenant in the headlease.

Secondly, an equitable lease is not a 'conveyance' within the definition in s.205(1)(ii) LPA 1925. Section 62 LPA 1925 provides (*inter alia*) that 'A conveyance of land shall be deemed to include and shall . . . operate to convey, with the land, all buildings, erections, fixtures . . . liberties, privileges, easements, rights and advantages whatsoever, appertaining . . . to the land or any part thereof'. The section will not therefore apply to an equitable lease of part of a property, although it applies to a legal lease. It has been held to apply however to a lease for one year in writing which was a legal lease under s.54(2) LPA 1925 and therefore within the definition of a conveyance in s.205(1)(ii) (*Wright* v. *Macadam* (1949)).[6] A parol lease, although legal if it complies with the section, would probably not be a conveyance for the purposes of s.62 however.[7]

Thirdly, the assignment of an estate created by a legal lease, or of the reversion on it, has the effect of passing the benefit and the burden of certain covenants contained in the lease to the successors in title of the lessor and the lessee. In the case of a pre-1996 equitable lease, this will not apply. Consequently, the normal rule of benefits and burdens applies, that the benefit of covenants may pass but not the burden (*Purchase* v. *Lichfield Brewery Co.* (1915)). In that case a lease in writing only of a public house was mortgaged by way of assignment of the term. The mortgagees never took possession or attorned tenant of the landlords, so that there were no relationships of privity of contract or estate between them. It was held that they were not therefore liable to pay the rent. As regards a post-1995 lease, the Landlord & Tenant (Covenants) Act 1995 makes all covenants other than purely personal ones pass even where the lease is only an equitable one.

The final important difference between a legal lease and an equitable one is the basic difference in land law between legal estates and interests in land and equitable ones as regards their binding effect upon third parties. A legal estate or interest is a right *in rem* binding against everyone. An equitable estate or interest created before 1 January 1926 (when the 1925 property legislation came into force) would bind everyone except 'equity's darling', the *bona fide* purchaser for value of the land without notice of the equitable interest. Since 1926, the doctrine of notice has been replaced by registration as regards equitable leases, and the binding effect of an equitable lease against a third party who purchases the land has to be considered in both unregistered and registered title. This will be dealt with more fully in Chapter 14.3.

Notes

▶ **1** But see Chapter 2, Note 1, *Long* v. *Tower Hamlets LBC* [1996] 2 All ER 683 as to possible requirements for such leases.

▶ **2** It was doubted (obiter) by Neill L.J. in *Singh* v. *Beggs* (1995) 71 P&CR 120 whether s.2 (8) had abolished the doctrine of part performance.

▶ **3** *Firstpost Homes Ltd.* v. *Johnson* [1995] 4 All ER 355

A signature on a plan, but not on a letter setting out the terms of a proposed contract and referring to the plan, was not sufficient for the section. In this respect, the requirements of s.2 appear to be more stringent than those of s.40 LPA 1925, which did allow for incorporation of an unsigned document by reference.

▶ **4** *McCausland* v. *Duncan Lawrie Ltd.* [1996] 4 All ER 995

Correspondence between solicitors was held not to be sufficient to vary a completion date written into a formal agreement complying with the section.

▶ **5** *Robert Leonard (Developments) Ltd.* v. *Wright* [1994] NPC 49

Contracts were exchanged for the purchase of a leasehold flat which had been a show flat on a development. An oral agreement was made that the price was to include furnishings and appliances in the flat. The vendor subsequently removed these. It was held

that the agreement for the sale of the items was enforceable, not being itself a contract within s.2 but a collateral contract. Similarly, in *Tootal Clothing Ltd.* v. *Guinea Properties Ltd.* (1992) 64 P&CR 452, a contract whereby the landlord agreed to give a tenant of commercial premises £30,000 towards the cost of fitting out was signed by the parties on the same day as the contract for a lease. It was not referred to in the lease contract, which purported to be the entire agreement between the parties, but was held to be enforceable as a collateral agreement.

▶ **6** *Wright* v. *Macadam* [1949] 2 KB 744

Premises were let to a tenant on a weekly basis and she used a shed for storing coal. The landlord gave her a new lease for one year in writing only, which made no reference to the coal shed. It was held that the lease created a legal estate being within s.54(2) LPA and was therefore a 'conveyance' within s.205 LPA. It was therefore effective to pass the right of storage as an easement under s.62 LPA 1925, as the section applies to a 'conveyance'.

▶ **7** *Rye* v. *Rye* [1962] 1 All ER 146, indicating that a conveyance should be a written instrument.

Summary

▷ A lease is essentially a contract between a landlord and a tenant which creates an estate in land.

▷ For that estate to be legal, the contract must be made by deed (s.52 LPA) or comply with s.54(2) LPA 1925.

▷ By s.54(2) LPA 1925, a purely parol lease may be legal if it takes effect in possession, is at the best rent obtainable and does not exceed three years. For this reason, all periodic tenancies will be legal.

▷ If the lease is not a legal lease, it may be enforceable in equity if it complies with s.2 Law of Property (Miscellaneous Provisions) Act 1989.

▷ There are certain important differences between a legal lease and an equitable lease which should be noted.

Exercise

3.1 What kinds of leases do the following contracts create:

(a) a lease by deed for two years;
(b) a lease in writing only for two years;
(c) a lease by word of mouth for three years where the tenant has taken possession;
(d) a lease in writing for five years?

Workshop

1 Sanjay granted a lease of a cottage to Tina for four years to commence in two years' time. The lease was by deed. What kind of lease has Tina?

2 Lucy agreed in writing with Amy to grant her a lease of a lock-up boutique. Both Amy and Lucy signed the agreement. Amy took possession three weeks ago but has not paid any rent yet. Is there an enforceable lease?

Chapter 4

Covenants and conditions in leases

4.1 Difference between Conditions and Covenants

A lease is essentially a contract which creates an interest in land. Any contract may be made subject to certain conditions, and leases are no exception to this rule. The condition may be a *condition precedent*, such as the grant of planning consent to a change of user, so that the lease does not take effect at all unless the condition is fulfilled, or a *condition subsequent*, whereby the lease terminates should the condition on which it is granted cease to apply and the landlord therefore has a right to re-enter.

A covenant contained in a lease, on the other hand, will simply be an agreement between the parties. As with any other agreement, its breach will give rise to a cause of action for which the usual remedies of damages, injunction or specific performance are available. Additionally, most leases will reserve a right of re-entry to the landlord in the event of the tenant being in breach of any of his covenants contained in the lease, including the covenant to pay rent. Such right of re-entry must be expressly reserved, however, if the landlord is to be able to re-enter for a breach of covenant. It is not necessary for re-entry on breach of a condition, although it is still necessary to serve a notice under s.146 LPA 1925 in circumstances where such a notice is required for breach of a covenant (see Chapter 15.5).

4.2 Covenants in Leases

A formal lease for a fixed term will almost certainly contain a number of covenants by the tenant and some covenants also by the landlord. Typical covenants by the tenant, in addition to a covenant to pay the rent, are covenants as to user of the premises, covenants as to repairing and redecorating and covenants as to assignment of the term. Typical covenants by the landlord are covenants to allow the tenant quiet enjoyment of the premises and to keep the premises insured.

A lease granted more informally – for example, orally – may not contain any covenants at all, however. In this situation, the law will imply certain covenants on the part of the landlord and the tenant. There will be covenants for quiet enjoyment and non-derogation from his grant implied on behalf of the landlord. On behalf of the tenant, there are covenants implied to pay the rent agreed, to pay rates, not to deny his landlord's title and, if the landlord is responsible for repairs to the premises, to allow the landlord to enter to view the state of repair. Implied covenants may be varied or negatived by express covenants in the lease, unless the covenants are implied by statute and the statute expressly prohibits 'contracting out' of them. This is the case with certain covenants for repairs (Chapter 5.3).

What will be the position if the parties enter into an enforceable agreement for the grant of a lease, but the terms are not discussed'? To be enforceable, the agreement would have to comply with s.2 Law of Property (Miscellaneous Provisions) Act 1989. Under these circumstances, the law will imply certain covenants known as 'the usual covenants'. The 'usual' covenants have to be determined according to custom and the conveyancing practice of the time, and Jessel M.R. in the case of *Hampshire* v. *Wickens* (1878) decided that these were covenants by the tenant to pay rent, to pay any tenant's rates and taxes, to keep the premises in repair and deliver them up to the landlord at the end of the term. If the landlord has agreed to repair, however, there is a 'usual' covenant by the tenant to allow the landlord to enter to view the state of repair. The only covenant by the landlord is one for quiet enjoyment and a proviso for re-entry by the landlord on non-payment of the rent, but not for breach of any other covenant. Jessel M.R. conceded, however, that these covenants could change over a period of time, and in *Chester* v. *Buckingham Travel Ltd.* (1981) Foster J. was prepared to recognise other covenants as usual.[1] He expressed the opinion that what was a usual covenant was a question of fact in each case having regard to the nature of the premises and their situation, the purpose of the letting, the length of the term and conveyancers' precedents commonly used at the time.

The common law and legislation implies certain covenants as to the maintenance and repair of the demised premises on the part of either the landlord or the tenant according to the nature of the tenancy, and these will be dealt with more fully in Chapters 5 and 6.

There are many important covenants which may not be regarded as 'usual' covenants, however, such as covenants as to user or not to cause a nuisance.

Any covenants by the tenant over and above those which would be implied by the law are regarded as 'onerous' covenants: for example, a covenant not to assign or sublet the premises without the landlord's consent, or a proviso for re-entry for breach of a covenant other than the covenant to pay rent.

▶ **1** *Chester* v. *Buckingham Travel Ltd.* **[1981] 1 All ER 386**

An agreement was made in 1971 to grant a lease of a garage and workshop. Some years after the tenant had taken occupation, it was necessary to determine what covenants should be implied into the lease, Foster J. heard evidence from conveyancing experts as to what covenants might be usual in a lease of such premises, and decided that he could accept the following covenants as usual:

(a) A covenant not to alter the building (because the term of the lease was short and the premises demised were part of other premises).

(b) A covenant not to interfere with easements (for the same reasons).

(c) A covenant not to use the premises for any purpose other than that of a garage and workshop, with the addition of the words 'without the landlord's consent'.

(d) A covenant not to commit a nuisance or cause any annoyance.

(e) A right of re-entry for non-payment of rent or breach of covenant.

He decided that a covenant against assignment without the landlord's consent was not a usual one.

Summary

▷ A lease is a contract which creates an estate in land.

▷ It is necessary to distinguish between a condition upon which the whole contract depends, and a covenant which is one particular head of the agreement.

▷ The landlord's right to re-enter will vary according to whether a condition or a covenant has been broken.

▷ Where there are no express covenants in a lease on a particular matter, the law may imply covenants.

▷ A contract for a lease will be deemed to be for a lease which includes the 'usual' covenants if it does not specifically set out covenants to be included.

▷ Apart from certain basic covenants laid down by Jessel M.R. in *Hampshire* v. *Wickens* (1878), the usual covenants may vary according to current practice and the circumstances of the letting.

Exercises

4.1 Why is it important to distinguish between a covenant and a condition in a lease?

4.2 What are the 'usual' covenants which will be implied into a lease? Can these be varied?

Workshop

Two years ago Leeroy agreed with Tobias that Tobias should have a lease of a yard which Tobias had been using for some time to park cars upon which both he and Leeroy would carry out repairs. The yard is at the back of a large shed which Leeroy uses as a garage for repairing cars. The lease was written on one side of paper only, signed by both of them, and merely states that the yard was demised to Tobias for seven years at a rent of £5,000 per annum.

Consider whether Tobias can claim:

(i) a right to park his breakdown truck on adjoining land belonging to Leeroy.
(ii) a right to carry out repairs on the cars stored involving welding and spraying.

Consider whether Leeroy has a right of forfeiture if:

(i) Tobias is in arrears with the rent
(ii) Tobias uses the yard for storing building materials instead of cars.

Chapter 5

Obligations implied on behalf of the landlord

Landlord's Covenant for Quiet Enjoyment

If a covenant for quiet enjoyment of the property is not expressly given in the lease, then one will be implied. The express covenant is usually qualified to extend to the unlawful acts of the landlord, or the lawful acts of anyone claiming through him. The implied covenant is similarly qualified. It will not therefore apply to an interruption in enjoyment by anyone with a superior title to the landlord, such as a head lessor as regards the lease of a subtenant as in *Celsteel Ltd.* v. *Alton House Holdings Ltd.* (No. 2) (1986),[1] unless the wording of an express covenant is made to cover a head lessor specifically, as it was held to do in *Queensway Marketing Ltd.* v. *Associated Restaurants Ltd.* (1984).[2] The covenant applies to the physical enjoyment of the premises, but not to a mere inconvenience. Thus in *Owen* v. *Gadd* (1956) a tenant was able to recover damages for breach of the covenant where a landlord erected scaffolding outside the door and window of his shop, thereby interrupting his business. In view of the Court of Appeal case of *Goldmile Properties Ltd.* v. *Lechouritis* (2003), the breach of the covenant in this case must be considered in the context of any covenant by the landlord to repair, and provided that the landlord is reasonable in carrying out repairs with the minimum of disturbance to the tenant, scaffolding for six months may not amount to a breach (see Chapter 9.1). In the earlier case of *Yeoman's Row Management Ltd.* v. *Bodentien-Meyrick* (2002), the tenant had covenanted to allow the landlord to enter and carry out 'any repairs or work', which it was agreed was wider than a normal repairing covenant. The landlord wanted temporary possession of the premises to carry out improvements. It was held that this was unreasonable and would have amounted to a breach of the landlord's covenant for quiet enjoyment. In *Browne* v. *Flower* (1911), however, the erection by the landlord of an external staircase passing the tenant's bedroom window, which interrupted his privacy, was held not to amount to a breach of the covenant. The covenant extends to acts which may also amount to the criminal offence of harassment as defined by s.1(3) Protection from Eviction Act 1977. An example of such a case before the Act might have been *Kenny* v. *Preen* (1963), where the landlord wrote threatening letters to the tenant, banged on her door and shouted threats at her. His behaviour was held to constitute a breach of the covenant for quiet enjoyment, and would almost certainly also have been an offence under the Act. The covenant does not cover the unlawful acts of third parties.

The distinction between lawful and unlawful acts of third parties is neatly illustrated by the case of *Sanderson* v. *Berwick on Tweed Corporation* (1884). The Corporation were landlords of two farms. The tenant of one of the farms suffered flooding with water from the other farm. The flooding was due partly to the tenant's lawful use of some of the drains which were badly constructed, and the landlord was therefore held to be liable to this extent. It was also found to be due to the unlawful and excessive use of some of the drains by the tenant, and the landlord was not liable for this.

A tenant's remedies for breach of the covenant are damages and an injunction. Noise which causes interference with the tenant's enjoyment of the property may amount to a breach of the covenant. In *Sampson* v. *Hodson-Pressinger* (1981) footsteps on the tiled roof terrace of the flat above was a nuisance and a breach of the covenant for quiet enjoyment in the lease of the flat below. The landlord was the reversioner of both leases and his predecessor in title had agreed to the construction of the roof terrace. In *Southwark LBC* v. *Mills* (1998) however, the Court of Appeal refused to find a breach of the covenant where the tenant was complaining of the normal living noises of adjoining tenants. These were noises which a tenant leasing such a flat might expect to hear, and did not constitute an 'interruption' by the landlord. In *Mira* v. *Aylmer Square Investments* (1990) damages were awarded for interference from work carried out by the landlord which covered loss of rental income while the tenants were abroad. The tenant may also have an action for damages in tort if the interference amounts to nuisance or trespass, and unlike the damages for breach of the covenant which are contractual, damages in tort may be exemplary, as in *Drane* v. *Evangelou* (1978).[3] In *Baxter* v. *Camden LBC* (1999), the Court of Appeal followed the decision in *Mills* however and held that the normal living noises of adjoining tenants could not constitute a nuisance by the landlord.

In the case of residential tenancies, if the offence of harassment is proved, then the tenant may have a claim for criminal compensation under s.1 of the Protection from Eviction Act 1977 or damages under s.27 and s.28 Housing Act 1988 (see Chapter 16.7). Damages under this section may be assessed on the difference in value of the property tenanted and untenanted if the tenant is not reinstated before civil proceedings are completed. The damages may also be mitigated if the landlord has offered to reinstate the tenant before proceedings commenced and the tenant has unreasonably refused, or the conduct of the tenant or anyone living with him make it reasonable to mitigate them.[4]

Section 27(4) Housing Act 1988 provides that damages under the Act shall be additional to any other damages 'whether in tort, contract or otherwise'. This is to be read subject to s.27(5), however, which provides that there should not be any additional damages under the Act for the tenant's loss of the right to occupy the property. In *Nwokorie* v. *Mason* (1993) the Court of Appeal varied an award of damages by the county court judge by holding that exemplary damages (£1,000) and general damages (£500) should not have been awarded in addition to damages of £4,500 under the Act, as they were damages in respect of the loss of the right to occupy the property and therefore excluded by s.27(5).[5] In *Kaur* v. *Gill* (1995), however, the Court of Appeal distinguished *Nwokorie* v. *Mason* and would not allow damages for breach of the covenant for quiet enjoyment, as distinct from damages for loss of the right of occupation, to be set off against damages under the Act. If the landlord's conduct amounts to harassment as defined by the Protection from Harassment Act 1997, then he will have committed an offence under s.1 of the Act for which the tenant will have a civil remedy in damages for anxiety and any financial loss resulting from the harassment.

Where the wrongful eviction makes no difference to the value of the landlord's interest, no damages can be awarded under the Act.[6]

5.2 Landlord's Covenant not to Derogate from his Grant

This is an application to leases of one of the basic principles of property law. The law will prevent a grantor from acting in such a way as to detract from the value of what he has granted. It usually applies therefore where the landlord has retained ownership or control over adjoining land for which he is seeking to claim a benefit which detracts in some way from the land leased.

It applies to casements, where generally a grantor may not claim an implied reservation of an casement for adjoining land he retains after he has sold off or leased part of a plot of land, e.g. a landlord who leases part of his premises will not usually be able to claim afterwards a right of way across the premises which he has leased.[7]

The principle also applies to prevent a landlord from using retained land so as to render adjoining land which he has leased useless for the tenant's purposes, provided that the landlord was aware of the purpose for which the tenant intended to use the demised premises. Thus in *Aldin* v. *Latimer Clark Muirhead & Co.* (1894), where a landlord let premises to be used only as a timberyard and an assignee of the landlord's subsequently sought to build on adjoining land which the landlord had retained, thereby obstructing the free flow of air essential to the timber yard, this was held to be a breach of the implied obligation of a grantor not to derogate from his grant.

Like the covenant for quiet enjoyment, the covenant has in the past been quite narrowly construeed so as not to extend to the acts of third parties.[8] In *Chartered Trust plc* v. *Davies* (1997) however the Court of Appeal took the view that a landlord letting units in a shopping arcade was liable for derogation from his grant when he let a shop next door to the plaintiff's gift shop to a pawnbroker. The shops were situated in a narrow passageway, and because only one customer at a time was allowed into the pawnbroker's, there was a constant queue of six to eight people outside obstructing the window and entrance to the plaintiff's shop. They would often enter the plaintiff's shop to wait (although they were unlikely customers) and the plaintiff had to employ part-time staff as the shop could never be left unattended. The landlord retained cotrol over the arcade and the tenants paid him a service charge. The Court of Appeal took the view that the landlord was under a duty to ensure that a nuisance caused by other tenants did not render a shop unfit for the purpose for which it had been let. It was unrealistic to expect the tenant herself to bring an action for nuisance given the expense and uncertainty of litigation.

5.3 Implied Obligations as to the State of Fitness of the Premises

Varying obligations as to the state of fitness and as to repair of premises are implied on the landlord's behalf by case law and statute.

A formal lease will usually deal specifically by express covenants with the responsibility for repair of the premises, and in general, an express covenant will override or displace an implied one. This is particularly so with implied covenants deriving from the case law. Some of the statutory obligations imposed upon landlords cannot be contracted out of, however, and will apply despite any provision to the contrary.

5.3.1 Implied condition at common law as to fitness for habitation at the commencement of the tenancy

This applies to the letting of furnished premises only. It is an implied condition, where the tenant is going into immediate possession of the premises, that they are fit for habitation at the commencement of the tenancy only. The condition was held to apply in the case of *Smith* v. *Marrable* (1843) where premises infested by bugs were held not to be fit for human habitation. Similarly, in *Collins* v. *Hopkins* (1923) a house where a person had recently been suffering from pulmonary tuberculosis was held not to be reasonably fit for human habitation.

5.3.2   Implied condition as to fitness for habitation under s.8 Landlord & Tenant Act 1985

This section replaces s.6 Housing Act 1957 and applies only to houses let at very low rents after 6 July 1957. The rent must not exceed £80 in London and £52 elsewhere.

The section implies a covenant that the house is fit for habitation at the commencement of the tenancy and an undertaking that it will remain so during the term of the tenancy. It negatives any express covenant to the contrary. The Court of Appeal held in *Buswell* v. *Goodwin* (1971),[9] however, that the obligation will not apply if the house is in such a dilapidated state that it cannot be made fit for human habitation at reasonable cost.

5.3.3   Section 11(1) Landlord & Tenant Act 1985[10]

This section, which applies to leases for less than seven years (including a term which if renewed by the tenant would not exceed seven years, or a longer term terminable by the tenant within seven years) replaces an earlier statutory provision (s.32 Housing Act 1961). It imposes on the landlord an obligation to keep in repair the structure and exterior of the dwellinghouse, including gutters and drains and external pipes, and to keep in repair and in working order existing installations for water, gas, electricity and sanitation and installations for space and water heating.

In *Brown* v. *Liverpool Corporation* (1969), the 'exterior' of the premises was held to include a flight of stone steps from the street to the front door which were demised with the house. In *Hopwood* v. *Cannock Chase D.C.* (1975), however, it was held not to include a paving slab in the rear yard of the premises, the rear yard not affording an essential means of access to the premises, normal access being from the front. A landlord may be held liable for *injury* caused by disrepair of part of the premises not included in the 'structure' however under s.4(4) Defective Premises Act 1972 (see 5.3.4 below), and in *McAuley* v. *Bristol City Council* (1992) the Council was held liable to a tenant who broke her ankle on a loose step in the garden.

In *Quick* v. *Taff-Ely B.C.* (1986) it was held that the repair of metal windows causing bad condensation was not within the statutory obligation as the problem was a design fault rather than disrepair. In *Minja Properties Ltd.* v. *Cussins Property Group plc* (1998) however, where the metal window frames had actually corroded, replacement was held to be within the scope of a repairing covenant even though it also effected an improvement. The principle in *Quick* v. *Taff-Ely BC* has been applied to damp, which again will only fall within the scope of a repairing covenant if caused by a physical defect.[11]

In *Campden Hill Towers Ltd.* v. *Gardner and Another* (1977) (a case on s.32

Housing Act 1961) a flat was demised for seven years. The demise expressly excluded the walls of the flat and provided that the tenant was to pay a service charge to the landlord for the repair of the gas and water pipes, gutters, sewers and drains in, under and on the block of flats. The tenant claimed that the service charge was not payable as these were included in the 'structure and exterior' and 'installations' of the 'dwellinghouse' within s.32. It was held that the walls of the flat were within the 'dwellinghouse' for the purposes of the section, even though expressly excluded from the lease of the flat, and the service charge was not payable for these or for installations within the curtilage of the flat. The landlord's obligations under the section did not extend, however, to installations outside the curtilage of the flat, such as the central heating boiler for the block, and the service charge was therefore applicable for this. In *Douglas-Scott* v. *Scorgie* (1984) the Court of Appeal indicated that whether or not the roof of a block of flats was included in the demise of a top floor flat must depend upon the circumstances in every case.

Section 11(1) has now been amended by s.116 Housing Act 1988[12] as regards leases made after the Act came into force on 15 January 1989, even though made pursuant to a contract before that date. This section adds two new subsections (1A and 1B) to s.11(1). Where there is a lease of a dwellinghouse which is part only of a building to which the section applies, the landlord will be liable to maintain the common parts of the building, and any installations used in common, which affect the tenant's enjoyment of the dwellinghouse. A definition of the common parts Is to be found in s.60 Landlord & Tenant Act 1987.[13] In leases made after 14 January 1989, therefore, the decision as regards the central heating boiler in *Campden Hill Towers Ltd.* v. *Gardner and Another* will be reversed and any common parts such as the roof area will be clearly within the section. Some disused common part of a building might presumably still not be within the section if it could be said that it did not affect the tenant's enjoyment. A new subsection (3A) to s.11(3) provides that it is a defence to the landlord if he is unable to gain access to the part in disrepair.

Another gap in s.11(1) was exposed by the case of *Niazi Services Ltd.* v. *Van der Loo* (2004). In this case, the yearly tenant of a top floor flat suffered a much diminished water supply because of the conversion of the ground floor and basement into a restaurant which was running off large quantities of water. S.11(1A)(a) states (see Note 12) that in a lease of only part of a building, the section applies only to a part in which the lessor has an 'estate or interest'. His landlord had only a long lease of the top floor flat however, and so was not liable within the wording of the section as he did not have an 'estate or interest' in the basement and ground floor areas.

It was held in the case of *O'Brien* v. *Robinson* (1973) that a landlord would be liable under the section only for patent defects, or latent defects of which he had notice. In this case, a ceiling fell in, but the tenant had mentioned that the ceiling vibrated when the tenants above were dancing only in the course of court proceedings some three years previously. The tenants had stopped dancing and no further complaints were made. This was held to be insufficient notice to make the landlord liable.

It is not necessary for the tenant himself to give notice to the landlord of the disrepair, however. In *Sheldon* v. *West Bromwich Corporation* (1973) the landlord Corporation had been told by its workmen who were sent to investigate noises in the pipes of the premises, of rust in the water tank. They were therefore held liable for its subsequent collapse. This was followed in *Dinefwr B.C.* v. *Jones* (1987), where the local authority learned of disrepair from its Environmental Health Officer.

The requirement that the landlord must know of the disrepair before he can be liable has been limited to disrepair within the demised premises. In *British Telecommunications plc.* v. *Sun Life Assurance Society plc.* (1994) Nourse L.J. regarded *O'Brien* v. *Robinson* as an exception rather than the rule, and the landlord's lack of knowledge of want of repair to retained parts of a building was held to be no defence to a covenant to keep the retained parts in repair. Both this case and the case of *Loria* v. *Hammer* (see Chapter 9.1) concerned express repairing covenants, but the principle would seem to be equally applicable to the implied covenants under s.11(1) and 1A) Landlord & Tenant Act 1985.

The repairing obligation under the section does not require the landlord to rebuild or reinstate premises destroyed or damaged by fire, tempest, flood or other inevitable accident, or to repair tenant's fixtures, or to carry out repairs attributable to the tenant's failure to use the premises in a tenant-like manner (s.11(2)). In *Wycombe Health Authority* v. *Barnett* (1982) a tenant left the premises in very cold weather to visit a friend on Friday evening, intending, to return' the following day. She did not return until Sunday, and during her absence, the pipes froze and the subsequent burst caused damage. The tenant alleged that the landlord was in breach of his obligation under s.32 as he had failed to lag the pipes, and the landlord alleged that the tenant had failed to use the premises in a tenant-like manner by leaving them unattended during a cold spell. It was held that the landlord was not in breach of his duty under the section, which was to keep the pipes in proper working order', referring to the mechanical condition of the water pipes. It was also held, however, that the tenant had not used the premises in an un-tenant-like manner in failing to lag the water pipes and in leaving them for a very short period during cold weather.

The obligations under s.11(1), like those under s.32, of the Housing Act cannot be abrogated by agreement, but s.12(2) Landlord & Tenant Act

1985 provides that the Country Court may make an order excluding or modifying the landlord's obligations if in all the circumstances of the case it is reasonable to do so. The circumstances include the other terms and conditions of the lease.

5.3.4 Section 1 Defective Premises Act 1972

This section provides that a person who takes on work in connection with the provision of a dwelling must ensure that the work is done in a workmanlike manner and with proper materials, and so that the dwelling will be fit for habitation on completion. In *Andrews* v. *Schooling* (1991) it was held that non-feasance, being an omission to carry out necessary work, was also a breach of the section.[14]

Most new buildings are within the National House Builders' Council Scheme, in which case the Act does not apply, but s.1 specifically includes a dwelling provided by 'the conversion or enlargement of a building', and it would therefore apply to flats created by the conversion of a large Victorian-style house.

Section 4 Defective Premises Act 1972[15] imposes upon landlords who are responsible for repairs to premises under the terms of a lease liability for personal injury or damage to property due to a defect in repair. The Court of Appeal said in *McAuley* v. *Bristol City Council* (1992) that the obligation to repair was limited to such repairs as were necessary to remove a risk of injury or damage. Moreover, the principle of *Quick* v. *Taff-Ely B.C.* (*supra*) applies and the obligation does not extend to defects which do not arise from a breach of the landlord's obligation to repair (*McNerny* v. *Lambeth B.C.* (1989).[16]

The liability is a statutory one which extends to all persons who 'might reasonably be expected to be affected by defects', which includes not only the tenant and family, friends and invitees, but also passers-by. The liability would cover an individual flat if the landlord is responsible for repairs, or the common parts of a block of flats for which the landlord is responsible.

The landlord is liable under the section if he knows, or ought to have known, of the defect, and s.4(4) goes even further in imputing knowledge to the landlord where he is given an express or implied right to enter premises and carry out repairs. (*Smith* v. *Bradford Metropolitan Council* – see Case Note 4, Chapter 9.)

5.3.5 Liability in negligence for bad design or construction

Quite apart from liability under the Defective Premises Act 1972, a landlord who designs or builds premises which are dangerous may be liable in negligence for any resulting injury.

In *Cavalier* v. *Pope* (1906) the House of Lords had held that a landlord was not liable for damages in negligence for injury to the tenant's wife in the absence of any contractual obligation to repair. *Rimmer* v. *Liverpool City Council* (1985) imposes a liability in negligence, however, where the landlord designs and builds the property, and the local authority were liable in damages to a tenant who was injured when he fell against a pane of glass which was too thin for its purpose in a house designed and built by them. This was applied in *Targett* v. *Torfaen B.C.* (1992) to a house designed and built by the Council where the tenant fell and was injured on an unlit flight of steps without a handrail. In this case, the court found that the tenant was also negligent, and damages were reduced by 25 per cent for his own contributory negligence. Presumably either the landlord's negligent design or negligent construction which caused injury or damage would suffice.

5.3.6 Obligation to take reasonable care to maintain the common parts and the structure of a building let in units

In *Liverpool City Council* v. *Irwin* (1977) the House of Lords held that a landlord (in this case Liverpool Council) who lets flats in a building has a duty to take reasonable care to ensure that the structure of the building and its common parts, used by all the tenants, are properly maintained and usable in the absence of any express obligation for this being placed collectively upon the tenants.

The case concerned a block of high rise flats in Liverpool let to Council tenants. The tenants complained that the lifts were constantly out of order, the stairs were unlit and dangerous with accesses to the rubbish chutes exposed, and the rubbish chutes themselves were blocked. The tenants had signed Conditions of Tenancy but these made no mention of maintenance and repair of the common parts of the building and the landlords had not undertaken any responsibility for this. The Law Lords expressed the views that the stairs and lifts were essential for the use of the flats, as were the rubbish chutes, and that the tenants must therefore have rights in the nature of easements of necessity over them. It was therefore a necessary implication that the landlords would be liable for their maintenance and upkeep, as the flats were unusable without them.[17] The landlords were held to have fulfilled their obligation as the blocked rubbish chutes, inoperative lifts and unlit staircases were caused by repeated acts of vandalism by the tenants' children and the landlords were not therefore responsible.

The case was applied, and the principle possibly slightly extended, in *King* v. *South Northamptonshire D.C.* (1991) where it was held that the landlord was liable to maintain a rear access to premises. The houses had been designed with rear access for services, and it was therefore implied that the landlord would maintain and repair this.

The duty is not an absolute one to ensure repair, however, but only one to take reasonable care to ensure upkeep of the common parts.

The obligation may be negatived by any express provision in the leases to the contrary. It will be otiose for leases made after 14 January 1989 for repairs falling within the ambit of s.11(1) Landlord & Tenant Act 1985 as enlarged by s.116 Housing Act 1988. Its relevance will remain for leases outside the section by reason of the length of their term, or for repairs still outside the scope of the section as in *King* v. *South Northamptonshire D.C.* (*supra*).

5.3.7   Obligation implied to give business efficacy to an agreement

In *Barrett* v. *Lounova (1982) Ltd.* (1989) a tenant had covenanted to repair the interior of a terraced house but the agreement was silent as to exterior repairs. The tenancy was for one year and then monthly. It was held that a covenant by the landlord to repair the exterior was to be implied to give business efficacy to the agreement. The case of *Liverpool City Council* v. *Irwin* above may also be regarded as an application of this principle.

5.3.8   Obligation to remedy a continuing nuisance

In *Gordon* v. *Selico Ltd.* (1980), but for an exclusion clause, a landlord would have been liable in nuisance for failing to prevent the spread of water or dry rot from the common parts of the building retained by him to the lessees' flats.

As nuisance is a tort, an action may also lie against a third person who is not a party to the lease. In *Abbahall* v. *Smee* (2003), the owner of the second and third floors and roof space of a mews property refused to carry out, or to contribute to the cost of, repairs to the roof. The roof was leaking badly and causing damage to the ground floor, of which the claimant was the landlord, having let it to a business tenant. The Court of Appeal applied the dictum of the House of Lords in *Delaware Mansions Ltd.* v. *Westminster CC* (2001) that a person causing a continuing nuisance is under a duty to abate it. The ground floor freeholder, who had obtained an injunction to allow him to carry out the repairs, was held able to recover one-half of the cost, this being a reasonable amount for the defendant to contribute as the repair benefited both of them.

Notes

▶ **1** *Celsteel Ltd.* v. *Altan House Holdings Ltd.* (No. 2) [1986] All ER 598

C Ltd., erected some flats and garages which were let on long leases. The leases included rights of way for the tenants to use a driveway for access which went along the rear of a site for which C Ltd. had obtained planning permission for a petrol filling station and car wash. C Ltd. transferred the site to L who then gave a lease of the petrol station and car wash site to an oil company. The tenants brought an action and obtained an injunction to stop the car wash from being built as it would have interfered with the rights of access over the driveway. The oil company then sued their landlord for a breach of the covenant for quiet enjoyment. It was held that the covenant did not cover the acts of a predecessor in title to the landlord or rights granted by such a person. For the purposes of the covenant for quiet enjoyment, the tenants of the flats and garages were not persons 'claiming under' the landlord.

▶ **2** *Queensway Marketing Ltd.* v. *Associated Restaurants Ltd.* (1984) 271 EG 1106

The Norwich Union sublet a shop and restaurant and basement premises to Associated Restaurants, being part of larger premises of which they were the lessees. They in turn sublet the shop and basement to clothing retailers, Queensway Marketing Ltd. This sublease included a covenant for quiet enjoyment free from interruption 'by the landlord or any person or persons lawfully claiming through, under or in trust for the landlord'. The term 'landlord' was expressed to include any superior lessor. The Norwich Union then erected scaffolding outside the building to repair crumbling masonry and protect passers by, which was there for two

years. The subtenants Queensway Marketing Ltd., brought an action against Associated Restaurants for breach of the covenant for quiet enjoyment in their lease. It was held that the scaffolding erected by the Norwich Union was a breach of the covenant for quiet enjoyment given by the immediate landlords, and that they had in effect covenanted specifically for the acts of a named person (the superior lessor which was the Norwich Union) and were therefore liable. As to scaffolding erected for a lesser period of six months, see the Court of Appeal case of *Goldmile Properties Ltd.* v. *Lechouritis*, at section 9.1.

▶ **3** *Drane* v. *Evangelou* [1978] 2 All ER 437

In October 1975 the landlord put the tenant's belongings out into the back yard of the premises and installed other people in the premises. The tenant obtained an injunction requiring the landlord to restore him to the premises, but the landlord did nothing until threatened with imprisonment for breach. The tenant was finally reinstated in January 1976 and claimed damages for breach of the covenant for quiet enjoyment. It was held that even though exemplary damages would not have been available for the contractual claim for breach of the covenant, exemplary damages would be awarded for the tort of trespass.

▶ **4** *Tagro* v. *Cafane and Another* [1991] 2 All ER 235

A landlord who evicted a tenant and changed the lock gave her a key a few days later but she found the front door broken and many of her possessions stolen. This was held not to amount to reinstatement and the order for damages of £31,000 stood. In *Murray v. Aslam* [1994] EGCS 163, however, a tenant who was reinstated by the police two hours after the landlord had put him and his possessions out on the street failed to obtain damages under s.27 as he had been reinstated. He did, however, obtain damages of £5,703 for trespass to his property.

▶ 5 For a criticism of this decision and a discussion of what damages would be 'additional', see a case note by Stuart Bridge: [1994] *Conv.* 162.

▶ 6 *Melville* v. *Bruton* [1996] EGCS 57

The Court of Appeal held that no damages could be awarded under the Act where there were two other occupants of the property so that the wrongful eviction did not give the landlord vacant possession.

▶ 7 The law of easements does allow, exceptionally, an easement not expressly reserved to be subsequently claimed if there is no other right of access to the land retained, or if the agreement between the parties necessarily included an easement to give effect to it.

▶ 8 *Port* v. *Griffith* [1938] 1 All ER 295

A landlord who had let shop premises with a specified use as a shop for the sale of wool and trimmings only was held not to have derogated from his grant by letting adjoining shop premises with a specified use of tailor and dressmaking and the sale of trimmings and cloth. This did not interfere with the tenant's use and enjoyment of the demised premises.

▶ 9 *Buswell* v. *Goodwin* [1971] 1 All ER 418

In 1962 the landlord purchased the leasehold premises in question for £2,000.

In 1968 the local authority made a closing order on the premises as they were not fit for human habitation. The landlord therefore claimed possession, but the tenant disputed the claim, arguing that the premises were in such a poor state because the landlord had neglected them. It was held that there had never been any agreement between the landlord and the tenant that the landlord would carry out repairs and there was no obligation on the landlord to do so under s.6(2) Housing Act 1957, as this applied only to premises capable of being made fit for habitation at reasonable expense. Possession was therefore given to the landlord.

▶ 10 S.11 Landlord & Tenant Act 1985

'(1) In a lease to which this section applies ... there is an implied covenant by the lessor

(a) to keep in repair the structure and exterior of the dwellinghouse (including drains, gutters and external pipes),

(b) to keep in repair and proper working order the installations in the dwellinghouse for the supply of water, gas and electricity and for sanitation (including basins, sinks, baths and sanitary conveniences, but not other fixtures, fittings and appliances for making use of the supply of water, gas or electricity), and

(c) to keep in repair and proper working order the installations in the dwelling-house for space heating and heating water,

(2) The covenant implied by subsection (1) ('the lessor's repairing covenant') shall not be construed as requiring the lessor

  (a) to carry out works for which the lessee is liable by virtue of his duty to use the premises in a tenant-like manner, or would be so liable but for an express covenant on his part

  (b) to rebuild or reinstate the premises in the case of destruction or damage by fire, or by tempest, flood or other inevitable accident, or

  (c) to keep in repair or maintain anything which the lessee is entitled to remove from the dwellinghouse.

(3) In determining the standard of repair required by the lessor's repairing covenant, regard shall be had to the age, character and prospective life of the dwellinghouse and the locality in which it is situated.

(4) A covenant by the lessee for the repair of the premises is of no effect so far as it relates to the matters mentioned in subsection (1) (a) to (c), except so far as it imposes on the lessee any of the requirements mentioned in subjection (2) (a) to (c).

(5) In a lease in which the lessor's repairing covenant is implied there is also implied a covenant by the lessee that the lessor, or any person authorised by him in writing, may at reasonable times of the day and on giving 24 hours' notice in writing to the occupier, enter the premises comprised in the lease for the purpose of viewing their condition and state of repair,'

Irvine v. *Moran* [1991] 1 EGLR 261 was a decision at first instance on a lease made in 1978 which considered what parts of a dwelling were within s.32 Housing Act

1961, which was replaced by s.11 (1). Both sections have much the same working and effect.

▶ **11** *Southwark LBC* v. *McIntosh* **[2002] 1 EGLR 25,** *Ball* v. *Plymouth City Council* **[2004] EWHC 134 (QB)**

▶ **12 S.116 Housing Act 1988**

'(1) In Section 11 of the Landlord & Tenant Act 1985 (repairing obligations in short leases) after subsection (1) there shall be inserted the following subsections –

(1A) If a lease to which this section applies is a lease of a dwellinghouse which forms part only of a building, then, subject to subsection (1B), the covenant implied by subsection (1) shall have effect as if –

  (a) the reference in paragraph (a) of that subsection to the dwellinghouse included a reference to any part of the building in which the lessor has an estate or interest; and

  (b) any reference in paragraphs (b) and (c) of that subsection to an installation in the dwelling-house included a reference to an installation which, directly or indirectly, serves the dwellinghouse and which either –

    (i) forms part of any part of a building in which the lessor has an estate or interest; or

    (ii) is owned by the lessor or under his control

(1B) Nothing in subsection (1 A) shall be construed as requiring the lessor to carry out any works or repairs unless the disrepair (or failure to maintain in working order) is such as to affect the lessee's enjoyment of the dwelling-house or of any common parts, as defined in section 60(1) of the Landlord & Tenant Act 1987, which the lessee, as such, is entitled to use.

(2) After subsection (3) of that section there shall be inserted the following subsection –

(3A) In any case where –

(a) the lessor's repairing covenant has effect as mentioned in subsection (1A), and

(b) in order to comply with the covenant the lessor needs to carry out works or repairs otherwise than in, or to an installation in, the dwellinghouse, and

(c) the lessor does not have a sufficient right in the part of the building or the installation concerned to enable him to carry out the required works or repairs

then, in any proceedings relating to a failure to comply with the lessor's repairing covenant, so far as it requires the lessor to carry out the works or repairs in question, it shall be a defence for the lessor to prove that he used all reasonable endeavours to obtain, but was unable to obtain, such rights as would be adequate to enable him to carry out the works or repairs.'

▶ **13 S.60 Landlord & Tenant Act 1987**

' "Common parts" in reference to any building or part of a building includes the structure and exterior of that building or part and any common facilities within it.'

▶ **14** *Andrews v. Schooling* **(1991) 23 HLR 316**

The omission to put in a damp-proof course in a basement flat which consequently suffered from condensation, although non-feasance, was still within s.1 of the Act.

▶ **15 S.4 Defective Premises Act 1972**

'(1) Where premises are let under a tenancy which puts on the landlord an obligation to the tenant for the maintenance or repair of the premises, the landlord owes to all persons who might reasonably be expected to be affected by defects in the state of the premises a duty to take such care as is reasonable in all the circumstances to see that they are reasonably safe from personal injury or from damage to their property caused by a relevant defect.

(2) The said duty is owed if the landlord knows (whether as the result of being notified by the tenant or otherwise) or if he ought in all the circumstances to have known of the relevant defect.

(3) In this section 'relevant defect' means a defect in the state of the premises existing at or after the material time and arising from, or continuing because of, an act or omission by the landlord which constitutes or would if he had had notice of the defect, have constituted a failure by him to carry out his obligation to the tenant for the maintenance or repair of the premises; and for the purpose

of the foregoing provision 'the material time' means –

(a) where the tenancy commenced before this Act, the commencement of this Act, and
(b) in all other cases, the earliest of the following times, that is to say –
    (i) the time when the tenancy commences;
    (ii) the time when the tenancy agreement is entered into;
    (iii) the time when possession is taken of the premises in contemplation of the letting.

(4) Where premises are let under a tenancy which expressly or impliedly gives the landlord the right to enter the premises to carry out any description of maintenance or repair of the premises, then, as from the time when he first is, or by notice or otherwise can put himself, in a position to exercise the right and so long as he is or can put himself in that position, he shall be treated for the purposes of subsections (1) to (3) above (but for no other purpose) as if he were under an obligation to the tenant for that description of maintenance or repair of the premises;

(5) For the purpose of this section obligations imposed or rights given by any enactment in virtue of a tenancy shall be treated as imposed or given by the tenancy.'

▶ 16 *McNerny* v. *Lambeth B.C.* [1989] 1 EG 81

A flat built in the 1940s with solid walls and steel window frames which suffered from condensation was not in disrepair, and there was therefore no liability under the Act.

▶ 17 This obligation may also be regarded as an application of the obligation in 5.3.7 as repairing obligations required to give efficacy to the tenancy agreement.

Summary

- An implied covenant for quiet enjoyment will only cover the acts of the landlord or anyone claiming under him. The covenant will not cover the acts of a superior landlord unless an express covenant is specifically made to do so.

- The covenant may be limited to cover interference with physical enjoyment of the premises, but intimidating acts may also constitute the criminal offence of harassment under the Protection from Eviction Act 1977.

- The tenant may claim damages and an injunction for breach of the covenant, or damages in tort if the landlord's acts amount to nuisance or trespass, or criminal compensation for the offence of harassment.

- The implied covenant not to derogate from his grant will apply only where a landlord retains control over premises adjoining the demised premises. It covers user of the demised premises and any easements which they enjoy.

Summary cont'd

▶ There is a covenant implied by common law that furnished premises are fit for habitation at the commencement of the tenancy.

▶ There is a covenant implied by s.8 Landlord & Tenant Act 1985 that certain premises let at a very low rent are fit for habitation at the commencement of the tenancy and will remain so.

▶ There is a covenant implied into leases for less than seven years by s.11(1) Landlord & Tenant Act 1985 that the landlord will maintain the structure and exterior of the premises and installations for services. A landlord will be liable only for defects which he has been made aware of and will not be liable for damage caused by un-tenant-like user of the premises.

▶ The landlord may be liable in tort under the Defective Premises Act 1972 for injury or damage to the tenant or his lawful visitors due to defective premises where the landlord is liable to repair, or where he has carried out defective work.

▶ In the absence of any express covenant dealing with the repair of hallways, stairs and common parts of a building necessary for tenants' access to and user of the flats therein, there will be an implied obligation on the landlord's part to take reasonable care to maintain these. This is not an absolute covenant (*Liverpool City Council* v. *Irwin*, 1977). This case was applied more recently in *King* v. *South Northamptonshire District Council* (1991).

▶ This obligation may be regarded as part of the more general implied obligation to give business efficacy to an agreement.

▶ A landlord or other person may be liable for damage to premises from a continuing nuisance caused by them.

Exercises

5.1 In what ways may an express covenant for quiet enjoyment differ from an implied one?

5.2 What remedies are available to a tenant for breach of a covenant for quiet enjoyment?

5.3 When will a covenant not to derogate from a grant apply to leased premises?

5.4 In what tenancies are obligations as to fitness for human habitation implied?

5.5 What obligations as to repair are imposed upon a landlord by s.11(1) Landlord & Tenant Act 1985?

5.6 In the absence of any express agreement as to the repair of common parts of a building let off in flats, who will be responsible for this and why?

Workshop

1   Kyle is the freehold owner of No. 7, High Street, which is a shop with a flat above. Two years ago, he granted a lease of the flat to Tom, who is living there. Earlier this year, he granted a five-year lease of the shop (which had been a shoe shop) to John who has opened a fish and chip shop. The shop remains open until 1 a.m. and Tom is disturbed by the noise. There is a constant smell from the frying in his shop. Advise Tom.

2   The Ambridge District Council owns a large block of flats which it has let to tenants on yearly leases. Peter, the tenant of one of the top floor flats, is complaining of dampness to his ceiling due to a leaking roof, graffiti on the walls of the staircase scribbled by the children of some of the tenants, and dripping taps on which the washers need renewing. Advise him.

3   George owned a house with a garage workshop at the end of his garden. He leased the garage to Joe for ten years and agreed that Joe should have access to it along a driveway over his garden. Earlier this year, George sold his house and the reversion on the lease to Tim, who has now withdrawn permission to use the driveway. Advise Joe.

Chapter 6

Obligations implied on behalf of the tenant

6.1 To Pay Rent

Rent is the consideration given by the tenant for occupation of the land or premises. Although almost invariably a money payment, it does not have to be, and in the old case of *Pitcher* v. *Tovey* (1692), bottles of wine were held to be recoverable as part of the consideration under a lease. The most usual alternative to a money payment will be services to be rendered on a service tenancy.

Any formal lease will usually contain an express covenant to pay rent, and such covenants will be dealt with in Chapter 11. Rent will also be an important part of any informal lease: for example, one created by parol under s.54(2) LPA 1925. Although it is possible to have a gratuitous lease, this would have to be expressly stated.[1]

A covenant to pay rent will be implied from words of reservation, such as 'paying therefor' following the demise of the property in the lease. If no fixed sum is agreed for rent, the landlord will be able to recover damages for use and occupation of the premises. A tenant is not liable on an implied covenant to pay rent until he actually takes possession of the premises, and (unlike the position in the case of an express covenant) he will not be liable after he has assigned the term of the lease. An express covenant to pay rent may make the tenant liable to the landlord under privity of contract throughout the term of the tenancy if the lease was made before 1 January 1996 (see Chapter 7.3.1). As regards leases made on or after that date, the tenant's liability will be more limited (see Chapter 7.4.2).

Section 4 Landlord & Tenant Act 1985 imposes an obligation on a landlord to provide a tenant of residential premises with a rent book.

6.2 To Pay Rates and Charges Payable by the Occupier of the Premises

The tenant is the occupier of the premises and, in the absence of any express provision in the lease to the contrary, he will be liable as occupier to pay all outgoings and charges levied against the occupier, such as water rates. It is of course possible for the parties to expressly agree otherwise, and in short leases or furnished lettings a landlord will usually expressly undertake liability for rates.

6.3 Tenant's Implied Obligations as to Maintenance and Repair

The law is reluctant to imply obligations for the repair and maintenance of premises on the part of a tenant, but there are nevertheless some minimal obligations which the courts have been prepared to impose.

6.3.1 Not to commit waste

The underlying principle of the doctrine of waste is that a person who occupies land for the time being shall not destroy its value to the detriment of future owners and occupiers with a reversion or a remainder in the land. It applies to a tenant for life under a settlement and to a tenant for a term of years. An action for waste lies in tort for damages and an injunction if applicable.

The law recognises different categories of waste.

(a) Voluntary waste is a *positive act of commission*. It includes not only damaging acts, such as cutting timber or demolishing buildings, but also ameliorating waste – namely, acts which improve but nevertheless alter the character of the premises. In the latter case, the landlord is unlikely to recover any substantial damages, because a landlord's damages for breach of covenant are limited to the diminution in the value of his reversion. Moreover, in *Doherty* v. *Allman* (1878), where the tenant under a lease for 999 years converted some dilapidated barracks into cottages by the erection of partitions, the court refused to grant an injunction as the structural alterations were only slight and the lease was a long one.

An ameliorating alteration such as this would, however, have been a breach of an express covenant not to make structural alterations to the premises (see Chapter 10.4), so that, if a landlord wishes to preserve the original character of the premises let, it would be preferable to include such an express covenant in the lease.

(b) *Permissive waste* is damage resulting from *neglect* or *inactivity* by the tenant.

All tenants are liable for voluntary waste, but a tenant's liability for permissive waste depends upon his term. A tenant for a fixed term and most periodic tenants will be liable, but it was held in *Warren* v. *Keen* (1954) that a weekly tenant is not liable for permissive waste. Clearly a weekly tenant has a minimal interest in the property, and it would be unfair to impose upon him any substantial liability for repairs.

Damages for waste which is a tort may be recoverable from someone other than the tenant. In *Mancetter Developments Ltd.* v. *Garmanson Ltd.* (1986), holes had been made in the walls of a factory building in order to install pipes and extractor fans. These were later removed by the liquidator of the tenant company, but the holes were not made good. It was held that the removal of fixtures without making good the damage occasioned thereby amounted to waste (although the court were divided as to whether the actual act of waste was committed when the original holes were made or when the fixtures were removed). Although the liquidator was not liable to the landlord under any contractual obligation in the lease, to which he was not a party, he was liable in tort for waste.

6.3.2   Obligation to use the premises in a tenant-like manner

The detailed application of this obligation, which is the only obligation on a weekly tenant, was explained by Lord Denning M. R. in *Warren* v. *Keen* (1953) by a number of illustrations as follows:

> 'The tenant must take proper care of the place. He must, if he is going away for the winter, turn off the water and empty the boiler. He must clean the chimneys when necessary, and also the windows. He must mend the electric light when it fuses. He must unstop the sink when it is blocked by his waste. In short, he must do the little jobs about the place which a reasonable tenant would do. In addition, he must not damage the house, wilfully or negligently; and he must see that his family and guests do not damage it: and if they do, he must repair it.'

In *Wycombe Health Authority* v. *Barnett* (1982) it was held not to be un-tenant-like behaviour for a tenant to go away for a short while (two days) during a very cold spell in winter without turning off the water.

It was said in *Regis Property Co.* v. *Dudley* (1958) that the obligation to use premises in a tenant-like manner entitles a landlord to assume that his tenant is a person of reasonable diligence. He will be liable therefore not only for damage caused by his own negligent acts, but also those of his family and visitors.

6.4   Obligation to Allow the Landlord to Enter and View State of Repair of the Premises

Where there is an obligation on a landlord to carry out repairs, there is an implied right to enter and view the state of repair.

In the case of a weekly tenancy where a landlord is liable for repairs, a right of entry is implied (*Mint* v. *Good* (1950)). In this case Somervell L.J. said that business efficacy requires that the landlord of a weekly tenant should have a right of entry to view the state of repair for which he is responsible. In *Saner* v. *Bilton* (1878) the lease of a warehouse included a covenant by the landlord to keep in repair the structure. It was held that the covenant implied a licence by the tenant to the landlord to enter on the premises for a reasonable time for the purpose of executing the necessary repairs.

Where a landlord is under a statutory obligation under s.11(1) Landlord & Tenant Act 1985 to repair the structure and certain installations of premises let on a lease of less than seven years (see Chapter 5.3.3), then s.11(5) implies an obligation on the tenant's part to allow a landlord or his authorised agent to enter and view the state of repair of the premises at reasonable times during the day upon giving to the tenant twenty-four hours' written notice.[2]

Notes

▶ 1 See Chapter 1.4.

▶ 2 See Chapter 5, Note 10, s.11(5), Landlord & Tenant Act 1985.

Summary

▷ Rent is usually payable for a lease and will be readily implied. It is usually a money payment, but may be payment in kind or services.

▷ A tenant is liable for any charges made against an occupier of premises.

▷ All tenants are liable for voluntary waste. Tenants for a fixed term and most periodic tenants are liable also for permissive waste, but a weekly tenant is liable only to use the premises in a tenant-like manner.

▷ Where a landlord is under a liability to repair premises, there is an implied obligation on the tenant's part to allow him to enter to view the state of repair and an implied licence for the purpose of carrying out any necessary repairs.

Exercises

6.1 When does a tenant become liable to pay rent on an implied reservation?

6.2 Describe, with examples, voluntary, ameliorating and permissive waste.

6.3 What implied responsibilities as regards the state of premises has (a) a fixed-term tenant, (b) a yearly tenant, and (c) a weekly tenant?

6.4 Under what circumstances has a landlord an implied right of access to leased premises?

Workshop

1　Michael gave Tom a ten-year lease of a house and adjoining garage. Tom has erected a partition wall across part of the garage and is using it as a utility room. He has installed a sink and washing machine, making holes in the walls to put in pipes. Advise Michael.

2　Would your answer differ if there had been a covenant in the lease not to make any structural alterations to the premises?

3　Toby granted Doreen, an elderly lady, a six-year lease of a cottage. Part of the chimney stack fell in a recent gale, damaging the roof. Toby has called to see if there is any interior damage, but Doreen, who uses only the downstairs rooms, refuses to have him in. She is very nervous and refuses to have the workmen instructed by Toby to repair the roof. Advise Toby.

Chapter 7

Enforceability of leasehold covenants

7.1   Introduction

The law relating to the passing of the benefit and burden of covenants in a lease has been drastically changed by the Landlord and Tenant (Covenants) Act 1995 (the 1995 Act), which came into force on 1 January 1996. All sections of the Act apply to new leases, *i.e.* to leases granted on or after that date, otherwise than in pursuance of an agreement entered into, or a court order made, before that date. A lease granted pursuant to the exercise of an option is an old lease if the option was granted before 1996. If an old lease is so substantially varied as to effect a surrender and re-grant by operation of law after 1995, the lease that arises in its place is a new lease for the purposes of the Act. An overriding lease granted after 1995 is a new lease only if the lease in respect of which the tenant made payment in accordance with section 17 of the 1995 Act was itself a post-1995 lease (see 7.5.3 below).

It is therefore necessary to consider both the law applicable to pre-1996 leases (which will continue to be important for many years), and the new regime under the 1995 Act applicable only to post-1995 leases. Sections 17–20, which apply to all leases whenever granted, are dealt with at 7.5 below.

7.2   Distinguishing an Assignment from a Sublease

In determining the enforceability of leasehold covenants, it is important to distinguish an assignment of a lease from the creation of a sublease.

An assignment occurs where the tenant (T1) disposes of the whole of the remainder of the term vested in him, retaining no interest. The assignee (T2) then stands in the shoes of T1, as it were; and, although the assignment does not create privity of contract between T2 and the landlord (L), it does create privity of estate.

A sublease arises where the tenant (T) creates a lesser term out of the remainder of the term vested in him, so keeping a reversion for himself. It does not matter if the term created is only one day less than the remainder of T's term, leaving T a reversion of merely one day at the end of the sublease. If T retains any reversion, the disposition is a sublease. The lease which T holds of L is then called a headlease, and the lease which T has granted to the sub tenant (S) is called a sublease. T then occupies two positions - viz. tenant of L under the headlease, and landlord of S under the sublease. The sublease creates the relationship of privity of contract and privity of estate between T and S, by virtue of which all the covenants in the sublease are enforceable between T and S. As between L and S, however, there is neither privity of contract nor privity of estate.

It is the substance of the transaction, not what the parties may label it, which determines whether it is an assignment or a sublease. If a purported sublease is for a term longer than, or equal to, that of the lease out of which it is granted, it takes effect instead by way of an assignment: *Milmo* v. *Carreras* (1946).

An express assignment must be made by deed, even if the lease which is assigned could be created orally (because it falls within the exception within s.54(2)). Thus, it has been held that the express assignment of a weekly tenancy must be by deed: *Crago* v. *Julian* (1992). If, however, a tenant purports to create an oral sublease (which as a sublease would be a legal lease within s.54(2)) for a term that leaves no remainder, the effect is an assignment of the lease by operation of law, which falls outside the formality requirements. This was so held in *Parc Battersea Ltd.* v. *Hutchinson* (1999), where the tenant purported to create an oral subtenancy for a term that exceeded his own. If it had taken effect as a subtenancy, it would, by virtue of s.54(2), have been a valid legal lease without a deed. However, as the grantor had been left with no reversion, the problem was to determine whether, given the absence of formalities, it could take effect as an assignment. The court was tempted to treated the assignment as a conveyance by operation of law, which is exempt the requirements of a deed by section 52(2)(g).[1] It nevertheless rejected this line of reasoning, as it considered, following *Rye* v. *Rye* (1962), that the word 'conveyance' in this context referred narrowly to a document, rather than to the act by which a legal estate is created or transferred. This left s.53(1)(a), under which a disposition of an interest in land must be by signed writing; but it was held that the assignment in this case was within the exception in that paragraph for a disposition by operation of law.

If the title to a lease is registered, it can be assigned at law only by registration at HM Land Registry: LRA 2002, s.27(1),(2)(a). Until it is registered, the assignment takes effect only in equity, i.e. as an equitable assignment. In *Brown & Root Technology Ltd* v. *Sun Alliance & London Assurance Co. Ltd.* (1997), the lease had been assigned, but the assignment (because of unresolved stamp duty problems) had not been registered. It was held that the assignor, who still had the legal estate, remained entitled to exercise an option to break which had been conferred on it personally.

7.3   Leases Made before 1996

7.3.1   Privity of Contract

A pre-1996 lease will usually contain covenants by the original tenant and the original landlord for the whole of the term. So long as the original parties remain landlord and tenant, all the covenants in the lease are therefore enforceable by one against the other through the doctrine of privity of contract. Even after one of the original parties has assigned, he will, through the doctrine of privity of contract, remain liable to the other during the remainder of the term. If, for example, the original tenant, T1, assigns the lease to T2, the original landlord, L, may sue and recover from T1 the rent arrears incurred by T2. An original tenant's liability for rent arrears can include an increase in rent effected after the original tenant assigned, provided that the higher rent was fixed pursuant to a rent-review clause contained in the lease at the time the original tenant assigned (*Centrovincial Estates plc. v. Bulk Storage Ltd.* (1983): see Chapter 11.2).

Formerly, an assignee was considered to stand in the shoes of the original tenant so as to be capable of varying the contract between the landlord and the original tenant. On this basis the original tenant was held liable to pay an increased rent brought about by improvements carried out by the assignee, even though such improvements were contrary to the terms of the lease: *Selous Street Properties Ltd. v. Oronel Fabrics Ltd* (1984). This situation has now been modified by the Court of Appeal decision in *Friends' Provident Life Office* v. *British Railways Board* (1996), which draws a distinction between the contractual obligation undertaken by an original tenant (T1), and obligations attaching to the estate which are enforceable against an assignee (T2). If the latter are varied, then such varied obligations, although binding on T2, will not be binding on T1, whose obligations arise under a prior contract, unless the original contractual obligation in the lease specifically envisages a variation which will bind T1.

In the *Friends' Provident* case, an agreement between the then landlord and an assignee varied the user and disposition covenants in the original lease and increased the rent from a sum of £12,000 per annum payable in arrear to a sum of £32,626 payable in advance. A previous assignee that had entered into a direct covenant with the landlord was held liable to pay only the original rent of £12,000 contemplated by the covenant, not the increased rent agreed in the variation. Adopting four propositions derived from a commentary by Patrick McLoughlin,[2] Slade LJ considered the cases and concluded that the decision in *Centrovincial* might be justifiable, as the increased rent was one contemplated by the rent-review clause in the lease, but that *Selous Street Properties* was a more dubious decision, as the improvements which were responsible for the increased rent were contrary to a covenant in the original lease.

In *City of London Corp* v. *Fell* (1994), the House of Lords held that, unless the lease expressly provides otherwise, the liability of an original tenant who has assigned ends at the expiration of the contractual term, even though the estate is statutorily extended (by the Landlord and Tenant Act 1954, Part II) where the current tenant holds over. The lease did expressly provide otherwise in *Herbert Duncan Ltd.* v. *Cluttons* (1994), where the original tenant had covenanted to pay the rent during the term of the lease, the 'term' being defined to include any period of holding over under the 1954 Act. This was sufficient to make the original tenant liable to pay the contractually agreed rent during the period of holding over, but not for the greater sum resulting from an increase in rent under an interim rent order.

Perpetually renewable leases

The only exception to the rule of continuing liability through privity of contract in pre-1996 leases is on the assignment of a perpetually renewable lease (see Chapter 2.5). Such a lease is statutorily converted into a term of 2,000 years; here the tenant must give notice of any assignment or devolution of the term, but thereafter ceases to be liable: LPA 1922, s.145 & Sch. 15.

7.3.2 Privity of Estate

Where a tenant assigns the remainder of his term, there will be privity of estate between the assignee and the landlord. If the tenant assigns the lease and the landlord assigns the reversion, there will be privity of estate again between the two assignees. There is however no privity of contract other than between the original parties to the lease, unless an assignee enters into a separate covenant on taking the assignment.

The Rule in *Spencer's Case* (1583) allows an assignee of the tenant to enforce against his landlord all those covenants which touch and concern the land. These have been described by Cheshire and Burn as covenants which affect either the landlord *qua* landlord or the tenant *qua* tenant and are 'reasonably incidental to the relation of landlord and tenant'.[3] Such covenants include covenants to pay rent, to repair, and to insure and covenants affecting user and restricting assignment or subletting.

An option for the tenant to renew the lease touches and concerns the land (*Richardson* v. *Sydenham* (1703)); whereas an option to purchase the reversion does not (*Woodall* v. *Clifton* (1905)). The burden of either type of option will bind an assignee of the landlord's reversion, however, if (but only if):

▶ where the title to the reversion is unregistered, the option is protected by registration as an estate contract (i.e. as a land charge Class C(iv)), or,

▶ where the title to the reversion is registered, the option is either protected by notice on the charges register or takes effect as an overriding interest under paragraph 2 of Schedule 3 to the Land Registration Act 2002 (LRA 2002) (i.e. where the tenant is in 'actual occupation').

In *Webb* v. *Pollmount* [1966] Ch 584, a lease contained an option for the lessee to purchase the landlord's freehold reversion. The landlord transferred the reversion (the title to which was registered) to the defendant. Although the option had not at the time been protected by notice, it was held that the option was an interest in land capable of subsisting through different ownerships, and therefore, as the tenant was in actual occupation, the option was protected as an overriding interest under the predecessor to what is now paragraph 2.

The benefit and burden of covenants which do not touch and concern the land will not pass to an assignee of the lease or the reversion. One example of such a covenant, the option to purchase the reversion, has already been mentioned. Another example is a covenant that concerns land other than that demised; so in *Thomas* v. *Hayward* (1869), a covenant in a lease of a public house not to open another within half a mile of the demised premises was held not to run. Similarly, a covenant does not run if it is to pay a sum of money not in any way connected with the demised premises; so in *Hua Chiao Commercial Bank Ltd.* v. *Chiapua Industries Ltd.* (1987), a covenant to repay a security deposit, which was refundable at the termination of the lease, was held not to run so as to bind an assignee of the landlord.

Even a covenant that does not touch and concern (unless it is purely personal to the assignor) will be enforceable by the assignee, however, if it is assigned. Assignment can be express, but in *Griffith* v. *Pelton* (1958) an option to purchase the reversion was held to have been assigned impliedly. In that case the option was conferred on the 'lessee', and the lease defined that term to include the lessee's 'executors, administrators and assigns where the context so admits'. It was held that as the definition so clearly included the lessee's assigns the benefit of the option passed to the assignee on the assignment of the lease, notwithstanding that it was not a covenant that touched and concerned the land.

On an assignment of a lease, the assignor retains the right to sue the landlord for subsisting breaches of covenant: such right does not pass to the assignee. This was held in *City and Metropolitan Properties Ltd.* v. *Greycroft Ltd.* (1987), where the court rejected the argument that, by analogy with LPA

1925, s.141, as interpreted in *Re King* (1963), s.142 (discussed below) operated to pass the right to sue for existing breaches of covenant to the tenant's assignee. It was there held that, after assignment of the lease, the former tenant could still sue the original landlord for damages for breach of a repairing covenant that had caused the former tenant loss (including the former tenant's costs of an abortive auction).

Assignment of the reversion

When the landlord assigns its reversion (which must be effected by deed, as the landlord is disposing of a legal estate) the benefit of covenants in the lease 'having reference to the subject-matter thereof' passes to the assignee under LPA 1925, s.141. Similarly, the burden of such covenants passes to an assignee under section 142 of that Act. Covenants 'having reference to the subject-matter of the lease' are the same as those described in *Spencer's Case* as 'touching and concerning the land', so that all the case law deciding which covenants touch and concern the land are applicable to sections 141 and 142.

On an assignment of the reversion, all such rights attaching to it pass to the assignee, including the right to sue for breaches of covenant which occurred before assignment: *Re King* (1963). Thus in *Arlesford Trading Co Ltd v. Servansingh* (1971), the landlord's assignee was able to recover from the tenant rent which had accrued before the reversion was assigned to him.

The assignee will not, however, be liable for a breach of covenant which occurred before the assignment to him. This point was decided in *Duncliffe v. Caerfelin Properties Ltd* (1989), where a long lease included an express repairing covenant by the landlord. The property had been in disrepair for some thirteen years when the landlord became insolvent and the reversion was assigned. Before the assignment, water damage from the disrepair had caused consequential damage to the tenant's decorations, carpets, furniture and other goods. The assignee was clearly bound by the repairing covenant, which meant that it would effectively have to make good the accumulation of disrepair to the premises that had occurred before assignment. Garland J. decided, however, that s.142 did not make the assignee liable for past breaches. He therefore held, albeit reluctantly, that, as the consequential damage to the tenant's effects had accrued before the assignment, the assignee was not liable for it.

If the title to the landlord's reversion is registered, the assigment of the reversion takes effect in equity until the assignment is registered: LRA 2002, s.27(1),(2)(a). The Court of Appeal has recently held that, in such circumstances, s.141 operates to pass to the equitable assignee all the rights therein mentioned, including (in that case) the right to forfeit: *Scribes West Ltd. v. Relsa Anstalt* (2005). This was a sound result, but the court was apparently not referred to the slightly earlier first-instance decision in *Rother District Investments Ltd. v. Corke* (2004), where the opposite conclusion had been reached.

The benefit of a covenant that does not pass to the assignee of the reversion under s.141 remains with the original landlord, who can therefore (because of privity of contract) bring an action on such covenant against the original tenant even after the assignment of the reversion.

It was held in *Systems Floors Ltd. v. Ruralpride Ltd.* (1995) that a covenant may be so worded as to be personal on one side, and so not run on that side, and yet have reference to the subject-matter of the lease, and so run on the other. In that case, the landlord had given a side letter to the tenant personally, agreeing to accept a surrender of the lease within three months of a rent-review date. Although the benefit was personal to the tenant, it was held that this did not preclude the burden from running on the landlord's side (under LPA 1925, s.142) so as to bind the landlord's assignee.

7.3.3 Recovery Amongst Earlier and Later Tenants *inter se*

If an earlier tenant is made, through the doctrine of privity of contract, to pay the landlord for breaches of covenant committed by the present tenant, the earlier tenant may be able to recover either from the present tenant or from an intermediate tenant. The various actions available are best explained in the context of a lease granted by the original landlord, L, to T1. The lease has been successively assigned to T2, then to T3, and then to the current tenant, T4, who has committed a breach of covenant by failing to pay the rent due. Let us assume that T1, T2 and T3 each covenanted directly with the landlord to pay the rent throughout the term of the lease. In these circumstances, L can sue all or any of them for the rent in default. Let us assume that L sues and recovers from T1. There are three possible actions available to T1 in such circumstances.

(a) *Restitutionary action directly against the current tenant*

To recover the sum paid to L, T1 can bring an action directly against T4. This is a restitutionary claim established in *Moule v. Garrett* (1872), and is designed to prevent the current tenant from being unjustly enriched. In practice, such an action might be more theoretical than real, since if L thought that T4 could pay, he would probably have sued T4 for the rent, rather than bringing an action against an earlier tenant.

(b) *Action against immediate assignee on indemnity covenant*

T1 may be able to recover by way of indemnity from T2, his immediate assignee. The T1–T2 assignment itself may contain an express indemnity covenant under which T2 covenants with T1 to indemnify T1 for any losses that T1 suffers as a result of any breaches of covenant in the lease occurring after assignment to T2. Most assignments contain such an express covenant. Even if no express indemnity has been given, one may be implied by statute if the assignment is for value.[4] It is possible, however, that the implied indemnity covenants impose liability on an assignee only for breaches of covenant occurring while the lease is vested in him.

If T2 is made to indemnify T1 under the T1–T2 indemnity covenant, he may be able to recover from his own immediate assignee, T3, if there was an indemnity covenant in the T2–T3 assignment. If T3 is made to pay T2, T3 may be able to recover from T4 under an indemnity covenant in the T3–T4 assignment. If, therefore, there is a chain of indemnity covenants, liability passes down the line until it reaches the tenant responsible for the default.

It is possible, however, for the chain of indemnities to be broken. This may occur if one of the assignees is a company which is insolvent or has gone into liquidation, or, is an individual who cannot be traced, or is bankrupt, or is deceased and his or her estate has been wound up. If, in the foregoing example, T2 were a company that had gone into liquidation and been dissolved, T1, having been made to pay L, will not be able to recover from T2 under the T1–T2 indemnity covenant. T1 might be able to sue T3 directly under the T2–T3 indemnity covenant, if T2, being in insolvent liquidation, were to assign the benefit of such covenant to T1. T2 cannot, however, be compelled to assign the benefit of such covenant to T1: *RPH Ltd.* v. *Mirror Group (Holdings) Ltd.* [1993] 1 EGLR 74. Alternatively, T1 might consider a direct action against T4 under *Moule* v. *Garrett* (above), or an action against T3 under the principles of subrogation now to be considered.

(c) *Subrogation to rights of landlord*

As T1 has paid L for the breach of covenant, T1 is entitled to stand in L's shoes and recover from anybody else whom L could have sued, provided that, as between T1 and such person, the latter is primarily liable. L could have sued either T2 or T3, as each entered into direct covenants with L to pay the rent through the term. Through subrogation, T1 is entitled to sue either (or both) T2 and T3 and to recover in full from either of them. Subrogation would also enable T2, if he is made to pay, to recover in full from T3. Effectively, liability passes down the line of assignees: *Selous Street Properties Ltd.* v. *Oronel Fabrics Ltd.* (1984).

Subrogation enables T1 to sue T3 directly, which he cannot do under either the law of restitution or under the T1–T2 indemnity covenant. T1 may prefer to sue T3 if T1 is aware that neither T2 nor T4 can pay. The weakness of a subrogated claim, however, is that the defendant can raise against the claimant any defence that he could have raised against the person whose rights are subrogated (L, in this case). If, for instance, L has not served a default notice on T3 (under LT(C)A 1995, s.17, see 7.5.1 below) within the six months' time-limit, T3 will have a defence to a subrogated claim brought by T1. This would not have been a defence to an action against T3 brought on a T2–T3 indemnity covenant.

7.3.4 Surety Covenants

Enforceability

A tenant may be required to provide a surety for the payment of the rent and the performance and observance of the other obligations under the lease. To this extent the surety's liability is that of a guarantor. In a typical surety covenant, however, the surety also enters into independent obligations, including an obligation to enter into a similar lease for the unexpired term in the event that the tenant becomes bankrupt or insolvent and the lease is disclaimed.

If the tenant is a small company, the landlord might often insist that one or more of its directors enter into surety covenants. As only four persons can hold a legal estate in land as joint tenants, if there are more than four partners in a business, the landlord might require suretyships from those who do not become tenants.

A surety enters into a direct covenant with the landlord, which will usually be expressed to last for the same period as the tenant's own covenanted liability (i.e. under a pre-1996 lease, normally the term of the lease). However, where a surety guaranteed the tenant's obligations only 'so long as the term hereby granted is vested in the tenant', it was held that he was not liable for a breach committed by the tenant's assignee: *Johnsey Estates* v. *Webb* (1990).

There is of course never any privity of estate between a tenant's surety and the landlord, so that, on an assignment of the reversion, the benefit of the surety covenant cannot pass to the new landlord under LPA 1925, s.141, although it can pass by express assignment. However, the House of Lords held in *P&A Swift Investments* v. *Combined English Stores Group plc* (1988) that, since a surety is guaranteeing covenants that themselves touch and concern the land, the benefit of a surety's covenants passes at common law to an assignee of the landlord without any express assignment. Lord Templeman said in that case that the tenant's surety 'is a quasi-tenant who volunteers to be a substitute or twelfth man for the tenant's team and is subject to the same rules and regulations as the player he replaces'. Similarly, in *Coronation Street Industrial Properties Ltd.* v. *Ingall Industries*

(1989), the benefit of a surety's covenant to take a new lease (not itself a guarantee) was held to pass.

Although, as a general proposition, the discharge of a debtor discharges his surety, in *Hindcastle* v. *Barbara Attenborough Associates Ltd.* (1994) the House of Lords held that, because of the wording of the Insolvency Act 1986, a disclaimer of a lease by the tenant's liquidator or trustee in bankruptcy does not discharge the tenant's guarantor.

Recovery amongst sureties and tenants *inter se*

A surety who is made to pay the landlord for the default of the tenant whose liability it has guaranteed, has a right of indemnity from that tenant: *Re Fox, Walker & Co, ex p Bishop* (1880).

If two or more persons jointly act as sureties for a tenant, and the landlord recovers from only one of them, that one has a right of contribution from its co-surety or co-sureties, the result being that, as between or amongst themselves, the liability of co-sureties is equal: *Deering* v. *Earl of Winchelsea* (1787).

If a series of successive tenants has each provided sureties, it has been held that a surety for an earlier tenant can, through a subrogated claim (discussed at 7.3.3 above), recover from the surety of a later tenant, so that liability inter se runs down the line: *Selous Street Properties Ltd.* v. *Oronel Fabrics Ltd.* (1984). It would also appear that, by means of subrogation, a surety for an earlier tenant can recover from a later tenant. Similarly, an earlier tenant who had to pay the landlord has been held able to recover against the surety of the later tenant in default: *Becton Dickinson UK Ltd.* v. *Zwebner* (1988).

In principle, a surety for an earlier tenant ought to be able to recover directly from the tenant in default under the rule in *Moule* v. *Garrett* (above).

7.3.5 Assignment of an Equitable Lease or its Reversion

It has already been mentioned (see Chapter 3.5) that on the assignment of a pre-1996 equitable lease or the reversion on it, the benefit of any covenants will pass to the assignee of the term or the reversion. The burden, however, will not pass. The latter point was established in *Purchase* v. *Lichfield Brewery Co.* (1915), where a lease in writing only of a public house was mortgaged by way of assignment of the term. As it was an equitable lease, the assignment transferred only an equitable interest to the mortgagee, who never took possession or attorned tenant of the landlord. There being neither privity of contract nor privity of estate between the landlord and the mortgagee, the latter was held not liable to pay the rent.

7.4 Leases Made after 1995

In a report of 1988, the Law Commission recognised the harshness to the tenant of continuing contractual liability after assignment.[5] The problem was exacerbated by the recession of the early 1990s, which resulted in a number of former tenants being disagreeably surprised to find that they were being held liable to pay rent on leases which they had assigned, in some cases many years earlier, when the current tenant's business failed and he defaulted. This was the catalyst which led to the passing of the Landlord and Tenant (Covenants) Act 1995.

Although qualified in important ways, the basic principles underlying the Act are:

- that leasehold covenants should be enforceable only by and against the landlord and the tenant for the time being; and
- that a tenant should cease to be liable on leasehold covenants when it assigns.

In order to preclude attempts to circumvent the Act, s.25 is an anti-avoidance provision, which states (*inter alia*) that any agreement relating to a tenancy is void to the extent that it would 'have effect to exclude, modify or otherwise frustrate the operation of any provision of this Act': s.25(1)(a).

7.4.1 The Transmission of Leasehold Covenants

Under the Act, a transmissible covenant is either a landlord covenant or a tenant covenant, which means a covenant that falls to be complied with by the landlord or the tenant (as the case may be) of premises demised by the tenancy: s.28(1). Covenant is widely defined to include term, condition, and obligation, and includes a covenant in a collateral agreement: s.28(1).

Section 3 deals with the transmission of leasehold covenants. It provides that the benefit and burden of all landlord and tenant covenants are annexed to, and pass on an assignment of, the premises and the reversion: s.3(1). The effect of s.3(6)(b), however, is that the burden of an option to renew the lease or to purchase the freehold reversion will not bind the landlord's assignee unless protected (if the freehold is unregistered) by registration as a land charge, or (if the freehold is registered) by entry of a notice or through actual occupation.

The assignee does not have any rights or liabilities under the covenant falling before the assignment (s.23(1)), although such rights can be expressly assigned: s.23(2). Tenant covenants are enforceable by, and landlord covenants are enforceable against, the immediate reversioner: s.15. This is similar to the law applicable to pre-1996 leases under *Spencer's Case* (1583) and LPA 1925, ss.141(1) and 142(1), except that, for post-1995 leases, the effect of *Re King* (1963) is reversed. The new provisions effectively endorse the position established in *Duncliffe* v. *Caerfelin Properties Ltd* (1989) and in *City and Metropolitan Properties Ltd* v. *Greycroft Ltd* (1987) (see 7.3.2 above).

Personal and non-personal covenants

The Act abolishes the distinction (applicable to pre-1996 leases) between 'touching and concerning' covenants and others. The Act therefore applies to a landlord and tenant covenant 'whether or not the covenant has reference to the subject matter of the tenancy': s.2(1)(a). The Act provides, however, that s.3 does not operate 'in the case of a covenant which (in whatever terms) is expressed to be personal to any person, to make the covenant enforceable by or (as the case may be) against any other person': s.3(6)(a). If a covenant is personal, the rights and liabilities under it do not pass on an assignment, but remain with the covenanting parties.

It is therefore important to be able to determine precisely when a covenant is personal. In *First Penthouse Ltd.* v. *Channel Hotels and Properties (UK) Ltd.* (2004) (affirmed on an appeal not involving this point in *Channel Hotels and Properties (UK) Ltd.* v. *Tamimi* (2004)), Lightman J. said that

> the tenancy does not have to spell it out in terms that the covenant is to be personal. The intention may be expressed explicitly or implicitly. The intention may be stated in terms or it may be deduced from the language used read in its proper context. In either case the tenancy expresses in a direct or indirect form the required intention.

This comes close to saying that a personal covenant might be inferred from the nature of the covenant itself, in which case the subsection would effectively be preserving in a different guise (i.e. through the personal/non-personal distinction) the essence of the distinction that applies to pre-1996 leases between covenants that do or do not touch and concern. This does not seem to be what the Law Commission envisaged in its 1988 report, but the merit of basing the distinction on the nature of the covenant might be illustrated in the following hypothetical circumstances.

A and B are freehold owners of adjoining premises. A leases his premises to B. In the lease B covenants to maintain a boundary wall that stands on his (B's) adjoining premises. The covenant does not expressly state in so many words that the covenant is personal. B assigns the lease to C. Thereafter B (who retains the freehold of his adjoining premises) fails to maintain the wall.

(i) If the covenant cannot be treated as personal, it is a tenant covenant and B (as is explained below) is released from it on assignment. C is bound by the covenant: s.3(1). A can recover damages from C for breach of covenant in failing to maintain the wall, even though C (because he does not own the adjoining premises) is unable to comply with the covenant. If B entered into an authorised guarantee agreement (AGA) with L on the assignment of the lease to C, L can sue B on it; but, as a guarantor, B is entitled to recover his losses from C. This produces a perverse result.

(ii) If the covenant can be treated as personal, it is not a tenant covenant, so the liability to maintain the wall remains with B. C incurs no liability under the covenant. This is a rational result, but it depends upon the court's being able to infer from the nature of the covenant itself an implicit expression of the intention that the covenant is to be personal.

The fact that an assignor landlord's liability under a covenant is stated in the lease to end on assignment of the reversion does not itself make the covenant a personal covenant: *Avonridge Property Co Ltd.* v. *Mashru* (2006) (see 7.4.3 below).

As already explained (see 7.3.2 above), it has been held that a covenant in a pre-1996 lease could be so expressed as to be personal to the original tenant but binding on assignees of the reversion: *Systems Floors Ltd.* v. *Ruralpride Ltd.* (1995). Although there is no authority as yet on this point as regards post-1995 leases, the wording of s.3(6)(a) appears to admit this possibility.

7.4.2   Liability of Tenant who Assigns

The other main thrust of the Act is to release a tenant, on assignment of the lease, from liability on tenant covenants: s.5(2). The release is not retrospective, so the assignor remains liable for breaches of covenant committed before assignment: s.24(1). Furthermore, if the assignment is what is called an 'excluded assignment', by which is meant that it is unauthorised or takes effect by operation of law (e.g. on death or bankruptcy), the assignor remains liable for breaches of covenant committed after assignment until the next assignment that is not an excluded assignment: s.11(1),(2).

Authorised guarantee agreement

The fact that a tenant is released from liability in respect of tenant covenants on assignment of the lease does not preclude the assignor from entering into an AGA with the landlord under which the assignor guarantees the assignee's performance of the covenants: s.16(1). For the agreement to be an AGA, the lease must contain a covenant against assignment without consent, such consent must be given subject to a condition that the tenant is to enter into an agreement guaranteeing the assignee's performance of the covenants, and the agreement must be entered into in pursuance of that condition: s.16(3). The guarantee can relate only to breaches by the immediate assignee: s.16(4)(a).

The liability of a tenant's guarantor ends when the tenant assigns the lease (unless it is an excluded assignment). What remains unclear, more than a decade after the 1995 Act came into force, is whether the landlord can demand that an assigning tenant's AGA is itself supported by guarantees.[6] If the landlord cannot, it might prefer to insist that persons who would otherwise have provided guarantees for the tenant on the grant of the lease become instead co-tenants under the lease, so that AGAs can be extracted from them when the lease is assigned.

The effect of the decision in *Hindcastle* v. *Barbara Attenborough Associates Ltd.* (1994) (see 7.3.4 above) in the context of the 1995 Act is that the liability of an assignor of the lease under an AGA is not discharged by the disclaimer of the lease by the assignee's liquidator or trustee in bankruptcy.

A former tenant who is required to pay out under an AGA is entitled, under the general law of guarantees, to recover any sums so paid from the assignee in default. As an assignor generally ceases to be liable on the covenants in the lease after assignment, the statutory indemnities available to an assignor of a pre-1996 lease (discussed in 7.3.3 above) do not apply to post-1995 leases. The scope for the rule in *Moule* v. *Garrett* to apply is more restricted in post-1995 leases, as the assignor will generally be liable (under an AGA) only for the default of its immediate assignee. The rule might, however, still be significant in the case of an excluded assignment, where the assignor's liability continues.

Covenants in business leases against assignment without consent

As the provisions of the 1995 Act ameliorate considerably the position of an assigning tenant, who is relieved of what is often a substantial potential liability, it is hardly surprising that the landlord's lobby in Parliament sought to have included in the Act some quid pro quo for landlords to compensate for the loss of continuing tenant liability. The result was the insertion of five additional subsections (1A to 1E) into the Landlord and Tenant Act 1927.[7] The effect of these is to enable a post-1995 lease (other than a residential lease: s.19(1E)) to specify any circumstances in which the landlord may reasonably withhold consent to assign, or any conditions subject to which such consent may be granted: s.19(1A). If the landlord withholds consent on the ground that such circumstances exist, or gives consent subject to such conditions, he is deemed not to be withholding consent unreasonably: s.19(1A). As a result of this provision, many post-1995 business leases specify a range of circumstances and conditions, frequently including the minimum income or profits of any prospective assignee and the condition that the assignor enter into an AGA. By this means, a landlord of a post-1995 business lease can ensure that an AGA is obtained every time the lease is assigned. The new subsections apply only to assignments, and not to sublettings.

7.4.3 Liability of Landlord Who Assigns

Although, as has been seen, a tenant's liability generally ceases on assignment of the lease, it was thought inappropriate that a landlord's liability under landlord covenants should end automatically on the assignment of the reversion. There are two reasons for this: first, whereas landlords can usually control assignments by their tenants, it is rare for tenants to have any control over assignments by their landlords; secondly, most of the important obligations in leases where default is likely to occur (e.g. in the payment of rent) are tenant's obligations.

The Act therefore does not abolish a landlord's continuing covenant liability after assignment of the reversion, but it does provides that a landlord can apply to be released: s.7(2). The landlord must follow the procedure laid down in s.8, under which he must serve a notice on the tenant before, or within four weeks after, the assignment, requesting a release: s.8(1). The landlord will be released unless the tenant serves on the landlord a notice of refusal within a further four weeks: s.8(2)(a). If the tenant serves such a notice, the landlord may apply to the county court for a declaration that it is reasonable that he should be released: s.8(2)(b). If the landlord misses the four-week time limit for service of the original notice on the tenant, he may serve a notice requesting release on any future assignment of the reversion, subject to the same time limits: s.7(2). On being released from any continuing liability under the lease, the landlord also loses the continuing benefit of the tenant's covenants: ss.6(2)(b), 7(1)(a). A release under s.8 releases the landlord only from non-personal covenants: *BHP Petroleum Great Britain Ltd.* v. *Chesterfield Properties Ltd.* (2002).

An easy way for landlords to ensure their liability terminates on assignment of the reversion without having to seek a statutory release is revealed in the decision of the House of Lords in *Avonridge Property Co. Ltd.* v. *Mashru* (2006).[8] In that case, the lease stated that the original lessor's liability under the covenants therein was to end on assignment of the reversion. The House of Lords held that this limitation validly termined the original lessor's liability when it assigned the reversion without its having to obtain a release under s.8. This limitation on liability was not caught by the anti-avoidance provision (s.25(1)), since it did not frustrate the operation of the Act. The majority of their Lordships (Lord Walker dissenting) took the view that s.8 was intended to provide a mechanism by which landlords could seek to terminate their liability on assignment, but that it had not been intended that the Act should deny landlords the right (which exists in pre-1996 leases) to specify that their liability was to end on assignment.

If, as a result of *Avonridge*, it becomes commonplace in leases for lessors to restrict their liability in this way, the protection afforded to tenants by the release procedure in s.8 will be greatly diminished. Furthermore, whilst the decision itself may (as a matter of statutory interpretation) be legally sound, it has undoubtedly made it easier for a dishonest landlord to perpetrate a scam on an unsuspecting tenant.

> The opportunities for a scam can be seen on a more detailed analysis of the facts of *Avonridge* itself. L had granted several leases to T1, who sublet the premises at substantial premiums to subtenants, S. T1 covenanted with S in the subleases to pay the rent under the headlease, but whilst the covenant stated that it was to bind an assignee of T1, it also expressly stated that T1's own liability under it was to end on assignment. T1 assigned its headleases to T2 without seeking a release under s.8. T2 was a man of straw, who disappeared abroad without paying any rent to L under the headlease. S avoided loss of the subleases through forfeiture by paying L the rent due under the headleases. S sued T1 to reimburse them, arguing that T1's liability continued. S failed for the reasons stated above. The lesson for subtenants in such circumstances is not to take a sublease under which it both pays a premium and agrees to the lessor's limiting its liability in this way.

7.4.4   Assignment of an Equitable Lease or its Reversion

The regime of the 1995 Act applies to post-1995 equitable leases because s.28(1) specifically defines a tenancy to include (*inter alia*) 'an agreement for a tenancy'. The term 'covenant' in the Act, as already explained (see 7.4.1 above), is not restricted to a promise in a deed, but includes 'term, condition and obligation'. The benefit and burden of landlord and tenant covenants in an equitable lease therefore pass in accordance with that regime in the same way as in a legal lease.

7.5   Provisions in Landlord and Tenant (Covenants) Act 1995 Applicable to all Leases

Sections 17–20 of the 1995 Act apply to all leases whenever created.

7.5.1   Statutory Default Notice

Section 17 requires a landlord who intends to recover a fixed charge from a former tenant or guarantor, or a tenant who has entered into an authorised guarantee agreement, to serve a notice on him within six months of the sum's becoming due, informing him that the sum is now due and of his intention to proceed against him: s.17(2),(3). The section applies to a landlord's action to recover a fixed charge, which means rent, a service charge, or other liquidated sum: s.17(5). Although the notice must be served within six months, there is no time limit specified for the commencement of an action.

The landlord's failure to serve the notice is a defence to the landlord's claim. Thus in *Bloomfield* v. *Williams* (1999), the landlord sued the original tenant of a pre-1996 lease both for arrears of rent due from a defaulting assignee and damages for breach of a repairing covenant. As the landlord had not served a s.17 notice on the original tenant, it was held that the claim for the rent arrears, being a fixed charge, failed. However, the claim for damages for breach of the repairing covenant, being for an unliquidated sum, succeeded.

In *MW Kellogg Ltd.* v. *F. Tobin* (1999), it was held that a former tenant who paid a landlord before the latter had served him with a s.17 default notice had paid voluntarily, and could not therefore recover from its assignee under an indemnity covenant.

7.5.2 Variation of Lease

Section 18 provides that a former tenant is liable for future defaults under a lease which has been varied only to the extent that the variations were contemplated by the original lease. This section is largely otiose since the Court of Appeal decision in *Friends' Provident Life Office* v. *British Railways Board* (see 7.3.1 above).

7.5.3 Overriding Leases

If a person has paid in full (together with any interest due) a sum which he is required to pay under a s.17 default notice, he can compel the landlord to grant him an overriding lease: s.19. The claim must be made to the landlord in writing within twelve months from the date of payment (s.19(5)), and the landlord must grant an overriding lease within a reasonable time (s.19(6)). The overriding lease will be a reversionary lease of three days longer than that of the lease it will override: s.19(2)(a). The terms of the overriding lease will be essentially the same as those in the lease in respect of which the default has occurred, unless otherwise agreed between the claimant and the landlord: s.19(2)(b). The right to an overriding lease is that of the first person (whether earlier tenant or guarantor) to make a request (unless such request is withdrawn or abandoned) (s.19(7)); except that if two or more requests are made on the same day, a request by a tenant has priority over a request by a guarantor (s.19(8)).

Section 20 contains supplementary provisions relating to overriding leases; notably, it states that an overriding lease is a new tenancy for the purposes of the 1995 Act only if the tenancy which it overrides is itself a new tenancy: s.20(1).

The advantage for the earlier tenant or guarantor in obtaining an overriding lease is that it puts the grantee into the position of being the immediate landlord of the current tenant in possession. Assuming the overriding lease contains a proviso for re-entry, the grantee can seek to forfeit the lease in the event that the current tenant commits further breaches of covenant.

7.6 Enforceability of Covenants where there is a Sublease

If L leases premises to T, and T sublets them to S, there is (while they remain landlord and tenant) privity of estate between L and T, and between T and S, but not between L and S. Similarly, whilst there is privity of contract between L and T, and between T and S, there is no privity of contract between L and S (unless S enters into direct covenants with L on the grant of the sublease). L cannot therefore enforce the covenants in the headlease against S through either privity of estate or (in the absence of a direct covenant) through privity of contract.

7.6.1 Restrictive Covenants in Headlease

There is one type of covenant in the headlease, however, that L can enforce directly against S. This is the restrictive covenant (i.e. a covenant restrictive of the user of the premises), which equity developed, from the case of *Tulk* v. *Moxhay* (1848), into a property right capable of binding those who come to the land, regardless of privity of contract or privity of estate. To restrain S's breach of a user covenant in the headlease, L may obtain an injunction against S, or L may be awarded equitable compensation against S in lieu.

- In unregistered land, a restrictive covenant entered into between landlord and tenant is not registrable as a land charge,[9] but (since *Tulk* v. *Moxhay* (1848)) binds third parties under normal equitable principles i.e. it binds everybody who comes to the land (including sublessees, squatters and mere occupiers) who cannot establish the defence of *bona fide* purchaser of the legal estate for value without notice. As S will have notice of the restrictive covenants in the headlease, it will be bound by them.
- In registered land, a restrictive covenant made between lessor and lessee, so far as relating to the demised premises, cannot be protected by notice.[10] Restrictive covenants in the L–T headlease are binding on S because S's registration as proprietor vests in S a leasehold estate subject to implied and express covenants incident to the estate (which therefore include the restrictive covenants in the headlease).[11]

The foregoing principles are illustrated in *Mander* v. *Falcke* (1891), where the subtenant's father was occupying premises that he was ostensibly using as an oyster bar, but was in fact using as a brothel. This use was in breach of a covenant in the headlease not to cause a nuisance or annoyance to nearby occupiers. The head-landlord was able to obtain an injunction against both father and son.

7.6.2 Forfeiture of Headlease or Action for Damages against T

If S's acts or omissions cause T to be in breach of the covenants in the L–T headlease, L cannot forfeit S's sublease, but it may be able to forfeit T's headlease or to recover from T damages for breach of covenant. For this reason, it is important that T ensures that S covenants with T in the sublease to observe and perform all the covenants in the headlease (other than the covenant to pay rent). If the sublease contains such a covenant, T will be able to bring an action against S (through privity of contract or estate) to restrain the breach, thereby avoiding or reducing its own liability to L, including the risk of forfeiture of the headlease.

Forfeiture of the headlease would terminate the sublease. S may, however, apply for relief in its own right under LPA 1925, s.146(4), and the court has a discretion to grant relief by vesting directly in S a term not exceeding the term of the sublease. If the forfeiture action has arisen because of T's breaches of covenant in the headlease, relief for S is likely to be on condition that S makes good T's breaches, e.g. by paying L the rent due under the headlease. To safeguard its position so far as it can, S should ensure that the grant of the sublease contains a covenant by T with S to pay the rent and to observe and perform the covenants in the headlease.

7.6.3 Mandatory Injunction

An alternative route to forfeiture was revealed in *Hemingway Securities Ltd.* v. *Dunraven Ltd.* (1995). There it was held that a covenant in the headlease against sub-letting without consent was a restrictive covenant for the purposes of *Tulk* v. *Moxhay* (1848), and so binding on a subtenant who had taken a sublease without the head-landlord's consent. The court's alternative reasoning was that in taking the sublease the subtenant had committed the tort of inducing a breach of contract between the parties to the headlease. On either basis, the court awarded the head-landlord a mandatory injunction against the subtenant compelling the latter to surrender the sublease. By this means, the head-landlord was effectively able to destroy the sublease without forfeiture, and so without the subtenant's having a right to seek relief.[12]

7.6.4 Notice Requiring S to Pay Rent due under Sublease Directly to L

If T defaults on payment of the rent under the headlease, L may serve notice on S requiring S to pay the rent due under the sublease directly to L: Law of Distress Amendment Act 1908, s.6.

7.6.5 Termination of Headlease

Although a sublease will necessarily be granted for a term shorter than that of the headlease out of which it was created, the sublease may, if it is protected under Part II of the Landlord and Tenant Act 1954, be statutorily extended beyond the expiration of the headlease. In such circumstances, when T's headlease expires, S becomes a direct tenant of L, and a combination of statutory provisions ensures that the covenants in the (former) sublease are now directly enforceable between L and S.[13] T should ensure that it enforces any covenants in the sublease before its headlease expires, as it will be unable to enforce them after that date.

The potential injustice to a tenant who had failed to enforce an indemnity covenant in the sublease before its headlease had expired was considered in *Electricity Supply Nominees Ltd. v. Thorn EMI Retail Ltd.* (1991). In that case, S had covenanted in the sublease to indemnify T for the payment by T of a service charge due under the headlease to L. T had paid the service charge to L before its headlease expired, but sought to recover the equivalent amount from S only after it had expired. It was held that, on the expiration of T's headlease, the benefit of the indemnity covenant in the T–S sublease had passed from T to L (now S's immediate reversioner). T could not therefore recover from S on the indemnity covenant. The court nevertheless held that, as S would otherwise be unjustly enriched, T was entitled to

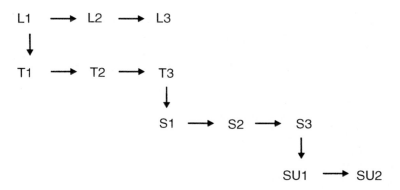

Relationship between the parties: assignments, subleases and subunderleases

recover from S under the principle in *Moule* v. *Garrett* (1872) (see 7.3.3 above).

Assignment of Sublease or the Reversion

If S1 assigns the sublease to S2, or if T1 assigns the reversion on the sublease to T2, the rules relating to the running of the benefit and burden of the covenants in the sublease are the same as those applicable on assignment of a headlease and the freehold reversion. The enforceability of covenants in the sublease therefore depends on whether the sublease is a pre-1996 lease or a post-1995 one: see 7.3–7.5 above).[14]

Notes

▶ **1** This explanation had been supported by what was at that time the latest edition of Megarry & Wade, *The Law of Real Property*, 5th edn, 1984, London, Stevens & Sons Ltd., at p. 667.

▶ **2** [1984] Conv 443.

▶ **3** Cheshire and Burn, *Modern Law of Real Property*, by E.H. Burn, London: Butterworth, 16th edn, 2000, at p. 477.

▶ **4** LPA 1925, s.77 (unregistered title); LRA 2002, s.134 & Sch 12, para 20 (registered title).

▶ **5** *Landlord & Tenant Law: Privity of Contract and Estate* (Law Com. No. 174).

▶ **6** See Cullen and Potterton, 'Must a surety guarantee an AGA?', [1996] 19 Estates Gazette 118, who argue that such a subguarantee would be valid; contrast Adams, 'Another view of AGAs', [1996] 32 EG 68, and Fogel and Slessenger, *The Blundell Memorial Lectures 1996: Current Problems in Property Law*, 1996, RICS Conferences and Training, at 24–28, who take the opposite view.

▶ **7** LT(C)A 1995, s.22.

▶ **8** Noted by Sandi Murdoch [2006] 1 Estates Gazette 97.

▶ **9** LCA 1972, s.2(5)(ii).

▶ **10** LRA 2002, s.33(c).

▶ **11** LRA 2002, s.12(4)(a); LT(C)A 1995, s.3(5).

▶ **12** For criticisms, see Luxton and Wilkie, 'Who needs section 146? Injunctive relief for landlords', [1995] Conv 416.

▶ **13** LTA 1954, s.65(2); LPA 1925, ss.139 and 141.

▶ **14** In the case of post-1995 leases, LT(C)A 1995 expressly provides that a tenancy includes a subtenancy: s.28(1). If the sublease was created before 1996, only the limited provisions in ss.17–20 apply. In no circumstances, however, does the 1995 Act apply to a lease or sublease created as part of a mortgage term: s.28(1).

Summary

- An assignment occurs when the tenant disposes of the whole of the remainder of the term of the lease vested in him. A sublease occurs where the tenant creates a shorter term, retaining a reversion to himself.

- Where an assignment has occurred, the enforceability of covenants in the lease depends on whether the lease was created before 1996 or after 1995.

Pre-1996 leases

- There is privity of contract between an original landlord and an original tenant, making all covenants between them enforceable against each other (except in the case of perpetually renewable leases).

- On assignment of the lease or the reversion, there is privity of estate between the assignee and the original landlord or original tenant, or between assignees of both. All those covenants touching and concerning the land are enforceable between them, but not purely personal covenants.

- On an assignment of the reversion, the right to sue for breach of covenants touching and concerning the land passes to the assignee; but the original tenant may still sue the original landlord for loss suffered owing to the original landlord's breach of covenant.

- On an assignment of the lease, if the original tenant or other assignor is made to pay the landlord for the default of the current tenant, it may recover from (a) the tenant in default through the principle of restitution (*Moule* v. *Garrett*); or (b) from its immediate assignee under an indemnity covenant (express or implied); or (c) from an intermediate assignee or guarantor through subrogation. A guarantor is entitled to recover by way of indemnity from the tenant whose liability it guaranteed, or from the tenant in default (under (a)), or from a later tenant or guarantor (under (c)).

- On assignment of an equitable lease or the reversion on it, only benefits, and not burdens, will pass to an assignee.

Post-1995 leases

- The 1995 Act provides that the benefit and burden of all covenants (except personal ones) pass on an assignment of the lease or the reversion.

- A tenant generally ceases to be liable on the covenants in the lease after assignment, and there can be no contracting out of this provision. Exceptionally, the tenant will continue to be liable after assignment if the assignment was by operation of law, or required the landlord's consent and this had not been obtained. Here, the assigning tenant remains liable until there is an assignment with consent.

- If the lease restricts assignment, the landlord may be able to require a tenant who assigns to enter into an authorised guarantee (AGA), but such guarantee can extend only to breaches committed by that immediate assignee. It remains unclear whether the landlord can require an assignor to provide a guarantor for the AGA.

Summary cont'd

- The 1995 Act amends the Landlord and Tenant Act 1927, s.19(1), as regards commercial leases, by allowing the landlord to stipulate what are to be reasonable grounds for a refusal of consent to assign.

- The statutory indemnity provisions (LPA 1925, s.77, and LRA 2002, s.134 and Sch 12, para 20) are repealed as regards new leases, and *Moule* v. *Garrett* will have only a limited application.

- The lease may provide for the landlord's liability to end on assignment of the reversion. If it does not so provide, the landlord remains liable on landlord covenants after assignment of the reversion unless it obtains a release under s.8.

- On an assignment of an equitable lease created after 1995, the 1995 Act applies, and there pass both benefits and burdens.

All leases

- The Landlord and Tenant (Covenants) Act 1995, ss.17–20, apply to all leases. Section 17 provides that a landlord seeking to recover from an earlier tenant or guarantor must serve notice on him within six months of the sum recoverable falling due.

- Section 19 provides that a person on whom a s.17 notice has been served and who has paid in full may require the landlord to grant him an overriding lease.

Subleases

- There is no privity of contract or estate between a head-landlord and a sub-tenant. The only covenants in the headlease a landlord can enforce directly against a subtenant are restrictive covenants. There is privity of contract between the tenant and subtenant as regards covenants in the sublease. On assignment of the sublease or the tenant's leasehold reversion, there is privity of estate between the landlord of the sublease for the time being and the subtenant for the time being. The regime of the 1995 Act operates in the same way between the landlord and tenant of a sublease and their assignees as it operates between a freehold landlord and its tenant and their assignees.

Exercises

7.1 What is the essential difference between an assignment and a sublease?

7.2 Leslie (a freehold owner) grants a lease for 90 years to Tony, who assigns the remainder of the term to Alan. Alan subsequently assigns the remainder of his term to Bill. Bill subleases to Steven. Steven assigns the sublease to David. Leslie assigns the reversion to Ron. Explain where, between the various parties, there is privity of contract and privity of estate.

Exercises cont'd

7.3 What covenants in a lease are enforceable where there is privity of estate?

7.4 What covenants are enforceable by a landlord against a sub-tenant? Why is it important to include in a sublease all the covenants contained in the headlease?

7.5 In what ways may an assignor of a lease be indemnified by an assignee for breach of covenants in the lease where (a) the lease was made in 1995 and (b) the lease was made in 2006?

7.6 Who is entitled to sue for a tenant's breach of covenant after assignment of the landlord's reversion on a lease made (a) in 1995 and (b) in 2006?

Workshop

1 In 1994 Lisa leased 'The Beeches' to Tom for fifteen years. The lease contained covenants by Tom: (1) to repair 'The Beeches'; (2) to keep tidy the garden of Lisa's neighbouring house 'The Larches'; and (3) not to use 'The Beeches' for business purposes. In 2004, Tom assigned the lease to Andrew, who breached the repairing covenant. Earlier this year, Andrew sub-let 'The Beeches' to Sheila, who is carrying on a mail-order business from there. Lisa subsequently assigned the reversion to Raymond. 'The Beeches' is still out of repair. The garden of 'The Larches' is overgrown.

Consider the possible actions for breaches of the three covenants, and any indemnities, to which this situation gives rise.

2 How would your answer to **1** above differ if Lisa had leased 'The Beeches' to Tom on 1 January 1996?

3 In 1995, Lauren entered into a written agreement with Topsy (which was signed by both of them) to grant Topsy a twenty-one-year lease of 'The Elms'. In the agreement, Lauren agreed to carry out only structural repairs and Topsy agreed to pay the rent. Lauren is in breach of the repairing covenant, and Topsy is in arrears with the rent:

(a) Will either Lauren or Topsy be able to obtain specific performance of the agreement? (See Chapter 3, particularly 3.5).
(b) If Topsy had assigned the lease to Annie and Lauren had assigned the reversion to Ron, would Annie and Ron be able to enforce the covenants for rent and repairs against each other?
(c) How would your answer to (b) differ if the agreement between Lauren and Topsy had been made in 1996?

Chapter 8

Covenants against alienation

Any formal written lease will contain a number of covenants by the tenant and probably some covenants by the landlord. As we have seen in Chapters 5 and 6, there are certain covenants implied by either case law or statute, and in the case of some of the repairing covenants implied by statute on behalf of the landlord, it is expressly enacted that these cannot be modified or abrogated by the terms of the lease. In so far as any express covenant in a lease purports to do this, it will be ineffective.

There is, of course, no limit to the particular covenants which the parties to a lease may choose to include. A lease is a contract, and the parties are free to agree to whatever terms they wish within the constraints of the law. As already mentioned, the general rule of contract law applies, so that an express covenant in a lease will override any implied covenant provided there is no statutory prohibition preventing this.

There are some covenants covering certain aspects of liability which are frequently found in leases, and the purpose of this chapter and Chapters 9–13 is to examine the effect of these covenants in more detail.

8.1 Assignment and Underletting

Before considering the effect of covenants against alienation, it is necessary first to remember the essential difference between an assignment and an underletting (or subletting). This was discussed in Chapter 7.2), and it must be emphasised that it is the effect of the transaction which determines whether it is an assignment or a sublease, and not what any document effecting it describes itself as. It will be a sublease if the tenant retains a reversion, even if it is only a reversion of one day, and an assignment if he disposes of the whole of the remainder of his term. The distinction is very important when considering the enforceability of the covenants contained in the original lease by and against successors in title of the original tenant and the original landlord (see Chapter 7).

A landlord will be understandably anxious about any assignee or subtenant to whom his tenant proposes to dispose of the premises, and the purpose of covenants restricting assignment or subletting is to ensure as far as possible that any such person to whom the property passes is acceptable to the landlord.

8.2 Nature of Covenants against Assignment or Underletting

These covenants are onerous ones, and will be restrictively construed against the landlord, so that a covenant against underletting will not prevent the tenant from assigning – and, vice versa, one against assignment will not prevent the tenant from subletting. The most comprehensive and usual form of covenant is one against assigning, underletting, or parting with the possession of the whole or any part of the premises. In the case of *Akici* v. *L.R. Butlin Ltd.* (2006), the Court of Appeal held that possession had a technical meaning different from occupation, so that where the demised premises were used to run a business by someone other than the tenant, but the tenant called there once a fortnight and all bills were addressed to him, although he was not in occupation, he had not parted with possession. It was conceded on behalf of the tenant in this case that he had, however, shared possession of the premises.

8.2.1 Absolute Covenants

Such covenants may be absolute – that is, they impose a complete prohibition against assignment or underletting. In this case, the tenant may not assign or underlet at all, and any assignment or sublease is a breach of the covenant unless the landlord agrees to waive the covenant on a particular occasion and to allow the assignment or underletting.

8.2.2 Qualified and Fully Qualified Covenants

More usually, the covenants are qualified, and provide that the tenant shall not assign or sublet without first obtaining the consent of the landlord. A qualified covenant of this nature is made fully qualified because it falls within the scope of s.19(1) Landlord & Tenant Act 1927, which provides that any consent required shall not be unreasonably withheld.[1] Section 144 LPA 1925[2] makes it illegal for a landlord to demand a fine or 'sum of money in the nature of a fine' for such consent, and he may require only expenses. Section 144 has been widely interpreted, and in *Gardner & Co Ltd.* v. *Cone* (1928), it was held to include the advantage obtained by a brewery landlord in requiring a covenant making a public house a 'tied' house able to sell only the landlord's beer; the covenant was therefore void.

In the case of a qualified covenant, it is essential for a tenant first to apply for his landlord's consent, and if he assigns or sublets without doing so, he is in breach of the covenant. What is the position, however, where he applies for consent and the landlord refuses? If this happens, a tenant has a choice of actions. He may apply to the court for a declaration that the landlord's refusal of consent is unreasonable. The problem with this procedure is that it must inevitably take time, and the tenant's proposed assignee or subtenant may well have disappeared by the time such a declaration is obtained. An alternative course of action is therefore for the tenant to go ahead with the proposed assignment or sublease and to plead the unreasonable refusal in any action for breach of covenant brought by the landlord.

8.3 Qualified Covenants and the Landlord & Tenant Act 1988

Because the tenant has this choice of action, and he may well lose a possible assignee if the landlord's consent is not forthcoming, it is important for him to know the landlord's reasons for refusing consent so that he may assess whether they are reasonable or not. The Landlord & Tenant Act 1988 was passed to enable a tenant to evaluate his situation and avoids the type of problem which the tenant faced in *Bromley Park Garden Estates* v. *Moss* (1982) (see 8.3.1 below). The Act, which came into force on 29 September 1988 to operate retrospectively as regards leases made before that date, applies to all qualified covenants against assignment, underletting, charging or parting with possession. Section 1(3) places a duty on a landlord who receives a written application from his tenant to serve on the tenant a written notice of his decision within a reasonable time, stating why any consent is withheld or conditions on which it is granted. What amounts to a 'reasonable time' will depend upon the circumstances of the particular case, but it is clear that the landlord should deal with such applications expeditiously. An unreasonable refusal in a letter meant that time ended with the date of the letter and was not extended by subsequent correspondence and negotiations with the tenant.[3] Section 4 of the Act makes it a breach of statutory duty in tort, for which a tenant will have a claim for damages, for a landlord not to comply with the Act. A statement in writing is mandatory, and oral discussions with a tenant as to the suitability or otherwise of a proposed subtenant do not satisfy the section, so that the landlord cannot rely on objections given orally in subsequent court proceedings.[4] The burden of proof to show that any refusal of consent or condition imposed is reasonable, or that notice of his decision was given within a reasonable time, is on the landlord. He does not have to justify his reasons for refusal, but merely to show that he had genuine grounds at the time for believing that the proposed assignee was unsuitable. The grounds relied upon must (as stated above) be stated in writing, however,[5] and the landlord may not rely upon events after his refusal in order to justify it .[6]

In *Design Progression Ltd.* v. *Thurloe Properties Ltd.* (2004), the landlord repeatedly requested further information about the proposed assignee as a delaying tactic to avoid giving consent. The lease had only some eighteen months left to run, and the landlord was trying to put pressure on the tenant to surrender the term, as the rent was well below the market rent for which he could re-let the premises. In addition to damages for the tenant's actual loss, the court awarded exemplary damages of £25,000, being the profit which the landlord would have made from re-letting at a higher rent of £100,000, less the £75,000 premium agreed by the tenant with the proposed assignee which was recoverable by the tenant as part of his actual loss.

On an application to underlet, the Court of Appeal has said that what amounts to a reasonable time under the Act will vary with the circumstances. In a complex case requiring a consideration of the effect of an underlease upon the investment value of the landlord's reversion, three weeks was not excessive (see *NCR Ltd.* v. *Riverland Portfolio No. 1 Ltd.* (2005) in 8.4 below). In *Crestfort Ltd.* v. *Tesco Stores Ltd. & Magspeed Ltd.* (2005), Lightman J. construed a proviso that any underlease must be in the same terms as the headlease as a condition precedent to consent, so that the landlord was under no obligation to even consider an application to underlet where the underlease was substantially different in terms.

8.3.1 When is Refusal of Consent Unreasonable?

It should first be noticed that the form of these qualified covenants where consent must not be unreasonably withheld will also be construed restrictively against the landlord, so that in *Moat* v. *Martin* (1950) a covenant specifying that consent should not be withheld in the case of 'a responsible and reasonable person' did not fall to be tested according to the standards of reasonableness required by s.19(1), and provided a responsible and reasonable person was found the landlord had no further grounds for objecting.

It was held in *Re Smith's Lease* (1951) that it is not possible for the landlord to reserve to himself the right to decide when a consent is reasonable or not and so evade the provisions of s.19(1).[7] This principle has been modified for commercial leases made after 1995, however, by s.22, Landlord & Tenant (Covenants) Act 1995, which has inserted a new s.19(1A) into the 1927 Act allowing the landlord to specify what shall be reasonable (see Chapter 7.4.2). It is likely therefore that post-1995 commercial leases will set out circumstances under which the landlord's refusal of consent to assign is to be deemed to be reasonable. In particular, a landlord may choose to state that it shall be deemed to be reasonable for him to require an assigning tenant to enter into an authorised guarantee agreement with him (see Chapter 7.4.2). The court has refused to allow a landlord to include such a provision in a new lease under the Landlord & Tenant Act 1954, however,[8] taking the view that whether it is reasonable or not to require an authorised guarantee agreement should be considered in relation to each particular assignment, as it clearly relates to the financial standing of the proposed assignee. The Code of Practice for Commercial Leases[9] suggests that a landlord should not ask for an authorised guarantee agreement as a condition for consent to assign unless the proposed assignee is of a lesser financial standing than the assigning tenant.

In *Moss Bros Group plc* v. *C.S.C. Properties Ltd.* (1999) the lease specified that it should be deemed reasonable for the landlord to refuse consent to assign on grounds he thought reasonable, and in particular the distribution of various retail trades within a shopping centre. The tenant's shop was one selling clothes and fashion accessories in part of the centre where there were a number of fashion shops. It was held reasonable for the landlord to refuse consent to assign to a tenant selling computer software, it being the landlord's estate management policy to keep similar shops located together, and it did not matter that there was no formal document setting out the landlord's estate management policy.

The test for 'reasonableness' used to be a very narrow one and in *Houlder Bros. & Co.* v. *Gibbs* (1925) it was said that a reasonable refusal of consent must relate to the personality of the assignee or his proposed use of the premises. The courts have moved away from this narrow interpretation nowadays, however, and other factors may be relevant in determining reasonableness. The Law Commission[10] declined to recommend any statutory guidelines for reasonableness, feeling that it was a matter better left to the courts to deal with in changing social and business circumstances rather than confined within a statutory definition.

Clearly the financial standing of the proposed assignee will be of prime importance to the landlord. In *British Bakeries (Midlands) Ltd.* v. *Michael Testler & Co. Ltd.* (1986) the tenant had furnished six references for the proposed assignee from bankers, solicitors and trade customers, but the unaudited accounts relating to the proposed assignee's previous business did not indicate that they would necessarily be able to meet the rent. The landlord's refusal of consent to assign was therefore held to be reasonable. If a guarantor is offered, then the landlord is also entitled to satisfy himself as to the financial standing of the guarantor.

It is quite clear from the cases that the landlord may refuse consent if it would be prejudicial to his own interests to grant it. In *Bickel* v. *Duke of Westminster* (1977) it was held reasonable for a landlord to refuse consent to assign to an assignee who would have been able to enfranchise under the Leasehold Reform Act 1967 when the original tenant was a limited company and so had no such right. In that case, Lord Denning M.R. said that no one decision creates a binding precedent for future cases, although the totality of decisions should enable practitioners to decide whether a refusal is reasonable or not. The decisions should be tested, however, as propositions of good sense on the particular facts of a case, rather than propositions of law applicable generally.

In *Dong Bang Minerva (UK) Ltd.* v. *Davina Ltd.* (1995) the landlord's refusal to consent to a sublease until the tenant gave an undertaking for costs of £4,500 (which were excessive) was held to be unreasonable and the tenant obtained damages under the Landlord & Tenant Act 1988. Similarly, a dispute as to who was responsible for a comparatively minor repair was not a reasonable reason for refusal of consent to assign.[11]

An underletting at a premium and at a very low rent may be grounds for refusal, as this could make the landlord's recovery of rent difficult if the tenant defaulted.[12] A proposed assignment or sublease necessarily inconsistent with a user clause in the lease may also be one to which the landlord may reasonably refuse consent.[13] Even if the landlord believes that the user of a proposed assignee is likely to be in breach of a user clause, the House of Lords held in *Ashworth Frazer Ltd.* v. *Gloucester CC* (2002) that this was a reasonable ground for refusing consent to assign as the landlord is entitled to avoid the possibility of future litigation for a breach of a user covenant.[14]

A possible conflict between the business interests of any proposed assignee and the landlord, or another tenant of the landlord, may also be relevant. Thus in *Whiteminster Estates* v. *Hodges Menswear* (1974) a refusal to consent to an assignment of premises to a trade competitor of the landlord's where the premises were next door to the shop where the landlord himself was carrying on business was held to be reasonable.[15] Reasonableness does not have to be tested by objective standards, but may be tested by the subjective standards of what is reasonable for the particular landlord.

In *Premier Confectionery (London) Co. Ltd.* v. *London Commercial Sale Rooms Ltd.* (1933) an assignee of the tenants of a tobacconist shop and kiosk sought consent from the landlord to assign the lease of the kiosk separately. The landlord took the view that this would result in the shop and kiosk being in competition with each other and refused: this was held to be reasonable. In *Woolworth (F.W.) & Co. Ltd.* v. *Charlwood Alliance Properties Ltd.* (1987) the landlord of shops in a shopping centre refused consent to assign to a tenant who would be unable to keep a shop open during normal shopping hours. The lease contained a covenant to do this, and it was held that the landlord's refusal was reasonable as closing the store during shopping hours could adversely affect the trade of other shops in the area.

The recession of the late 1980s produced some interesting cases where landlords refused consent to assign or sublet in order to safeguard their own position in a falling property market. In *Olympia & York Canary Wharf Ltd.*

v. *Oil Property Investment Ltd.* (1994) the lease contained a break clause after ten years which was personal to the original tenant. After eight years, the assignee applied for consent to assign the lease back to the original tenant who would then have exercised the break clause. The evidence was that the landlord would only have been able to re-let at a rent of half the rent under the existing lease, and it was held that the landlord's refusal of consent to assign back to the original tenant was in the circumstances reasonable.

In *Hemingway Securities Ltd.* v. *Dunraven Ltd.* (1995) the tenant had sublet in breach of a covenant that the subtenants would first enter into a direct covenant with the landlord and that the form of sublease would be approved. The landlord, who could have commenced forfeiture proceedings, preferred to obtain a mandatory injunction for the immediate surrender of the sublease and damages for breach of contract by the tenant.

It is clear from the cases that the test for reasonableness may take into account the landlord's interests. Is it necessary also to consider the interests of the tenant? In *International Drilling Fluids Ltd.* v. *Louisville Investments (Uxbridge) Ltd.* (1986) it was decided that hardship caused to a tenant by refusal is a factor to be taken into account in exceptional circumstances. In that case, the tenant had vacated the premises and there was only one interested purchaser who wished to use the premises as serviced office accommodation, whereas the lease stipulated use as office accommodation. The landlord refused consent to assign to him. It was held that the refusal was unreasonable and that the hardship to the tenant, who was still liable under the lease, was a factor to be taken into account; the proposed user was sufficiently close to the allowed user. Balcombe L.J. examined the authorities and deduced from them certain propositions:

(1) the purpose of a covenant against assignment is to protect the landlord from an undesirable tenant or user
(2) it follows from this that the landlord cannot refuse consent on grounds which have nothing at all to do with the lease
(3) the onus of proof is on the tenant to show that consent has been unreasonably refused (now reversed by the Landlord & Tenant Act. 1988 and the landlord must show that his refusal is reasonable)
(4) the landlord does not have to justify his refusal if the reasonable man might have refused in the circumstances (also changed by the 1988 Act)
(5) the fact that the proposed tenant intends to use the premises in a way not permitted by the lease does not mean that the refusal is necessarily unreasonable; (modified by the House of Lords decision in *Ashworth Frazer* above)
(6) there is a divergence of authority as to whether the landlord has to have regard to the interests of the tenant, but this may be a relevant

factor if the detriment to the tenant is disproportionate to the benefit to the landlord.

In *Bromley Park Garden Estates* v. *Moss* (1982) some attempt was made to lay down a general principle that the landlord should not seek to obtain from his refusal of consent some advantage which the lease did not originally give to him. In that case, the landlords had purchased the reversions on the leases of a restaurant and a flat over it. The tenant of the flat sought consent to assign her lease and the landlords refused. The lessee of the restaurant was prepared to take a lease of the flat, and the landlords preferred this for their estate management as the restaurant and flat would then be let to the same tenant. The Court of Appeal unanimously found the refusal to be unreasonable, saying that in effect the landlord was trying to impose a condition on the tenant that she would first offer to surrender the lease before assigning. Any such condition should have been contained in the original lease, and the landlord was therefore seeking to obtain an advantage by his refusal of consent to assign which he had not originally reserved to himself. A similar case where the landlord tried to use the Landlord & Tenant Act 1988 to obtain a surrender instead of consenting to an assignment is *Design Progression Ltd.* v. *Thurloe* mentioned in 8.3.

In *Riverland* (8.4 below) the Court of Appeal applied the principles of reasonableness applicable to consent to assign to consent to underlet. The covenant is to protect the landlord's interests, and a genuine concern that an underlease might adversely affect the investment value of the landlord's reversion was sufficient. They applied the principle of *International Drilling Fluids* (above) that hardship to a tenant should only be considered in exceptional circumstances.

If the tenant is in breach of the covenant and there is a proviso for re-entry on breach, then the landlord may forfeit the lease. Although without consent, the assignment is effective and forfeiture proceedings should therefore be against the assignee (*Old Grovebury Manor Farm* v. *Seymour Plant Sales & Hire* (1979). The landlord must first serve a notice under s.146 LPA 1925. In *Scala House & District Property Co. Ltd.* v. *Forbes* (1973) the Court of Appeal ruled that a breach of a covenant against assignment or subletting is irremediable,[16] and the s.146 notice (which has to specify the breach of covenant, require it to be remedied and any compensation) was valid notwithstanding that it gave the tenant only fourteen days to remedy the breach, as it was a breach which could not be remedied anyway.

A landlord may waive his right to forfeiture if he does any act recognising the assignee or subtenant, such as accepting rent from him. The court has a discretion to grant relief against forfeiture on consideration of all the circumstances.

8.4   Conditions Contained in the Lease as to Underletting

A landlord will be anxious to maintain the letting value of his premises, and to this end may take a covenant from the tenant in the lease not to underlet at a rent less than the rent reserved by the headlease. If the rental market has fallen since the lease was granted, this could make it difficult, if not impossible, for a tenant to assign or underlet. The tenant might therefore come to some arrangement with an underlessee to compensate him for the burden of the high rent he is taking on. In *Allied Dunbar Assurance plc* v. *Homebase Ltd.* (2002), a headlease contained a qualified covenant against assigning or underletting, which was subject to a proviso that any underlease should not be at a rent less than the full market rent obtainable with no premium, and that the underlease should contain the same covenants contained in the headlease. The market rent was such, when the lessee wished to dispose of the premises, that an underlessee would not pay the original rent, and the tenant and the underlessee therefore entered into a collateral deed, expressed to be personal to them, whereby the tenant undertook to indemnify the underlessee for the difference in rent and for some of the cost of repairs on more onerous repairing covenants in the headlease. It was held that the underlease had to be read with the deed, and this amounted to a breach of the proviso in the headlease, so that the landlord's refusal of consent was reasonable. As the obligations under the collateral agreement dated 2000 were after the Landlord & Tenant (Covenants) Act 1995 came into force, the landlord could have been required to grant a continuation lease under the Landlord & Tenant Act 1954 Part II on the terms of the underlease, but would have had no recourse on the personal terms contained in the collateral agreement.

Allied Dunbar was applied by Lightman J. in *Crestfort Ltd.* v. *Tesco Stores Ltd. & Magspeed Ltd.* (2005) where Tesco granted an underlease to Magspeed in breach of a requirement that any underlease must include all the same covenants and conditions as the headlease. Lightman J. held that the underlease was a breach of the contractual terms of the headlease of which the underlessee had knowledge, and in accepting the underlease, the underlessee was therefore liable in tort for a wrongful interference with a contract. He therefore made an order for damages against Magspeed and an injunction to surrender the underlease.

In *NCR Ltd.* v. *Riverland Portfolio No. 1 Ltd.* (2005), the rent reserved in the lease, which the tenant had covenanted to reserve in any underlease, was considerably in excess of the market rent obtainable for the property and the tenant was unable to underlet for this rent. He found an underlessee prepared to pay the rent on payment by the tenant to him of a reverse premium of £3 million. The Court of Appeal, reversing the decision at first instance, found that the landlord's refusal of consent to underlet was reasonable and applied the principle of *International Drilling Fluids* (8.3.1 above) that hardship to the tenant should be taken into account only if the hardship far exceeds any benefit to the landlord. The covenant strength of the proposed underlessee was considerably weaker than that of the tenant, but the trial judge took the view that this was irrelevant as the landlord had a direct covenant from the tenant. The underlessee would have been able to require a new lease under the 1954 Act when the lease expired in six years' time however, and the Court of Appeal considered that the trial judge should therefore have had regard to the evidence of the landlord's expert witness that the weaker covenant strength could have considerably depressed the investment value of the landlord's lease. The Court of Appeal also reversed the judge's finding that the landlord, who took three weeks to refuse consent, was in breach of the requirements of the Landlord & Tenant Act 1988. The complexity of the case required this time for the landlord to make an enlightened decision.

Notes

▶ **1 S.19(1) Landlord & Tenant Act 1927**

'In all leases whether made before or after the commencement of this Act containing a covenant condition or agreement against assigning, underletting, charging or parting with the possession of demised premises or any part thereof without licence or consent, such covenant, condition or agreement shall, notwithstanding any express provision to the contrary, be deemed to be subject: (a) to a proviso to the effect that such licence or consent is not to be unreasonably withheld, but this proviso does not preclude the right of the landlord to require payment of a reasonable sum in respect of any legal or other expenses incurred in connection with such licence or consent.'

▶ **2 S.144 LPA 1925**

'In all leases containing a covenant, condition or agreement against assigning, underletting, or parting with the possession, or disposing of the land or property leased without licence or

consent, such covenant, condition or agreement shall, unless the lease contains an express provision to the contrary, be deemed to be subject to a proviso to the effect that no fine or sum of money in the nature of a fine shall be payable for or in respect of such licence or consent; but this proviso does not preclude the right to require the payment of a reasonable sum in respect of any legal or other expense incurred in relation to such licence or consent.'

▶ **3** *Go West Ltd.* v. *Spigarolo* [2003] 1 All ER 141, applying *Norwich Union Life Insurance Society* v. *Shopmoor Ltd.* [1999] 1 WLR 531

▶ **4** *Footwear Corporation Ltd.* v. *Amplight Properties Ltd.* (1998) 25 EG 171

▶ **5** Dictum of Scott V-C in *Norwich Union Life Insurance Society* v. *Shopmoor Ltd.* (section 0.0) and *NCR Ltd.* v. *Riverland*

Portfolio No. 1 Ltd. [2005] EWCA Civ.312 where Carnwath L.J. said that whilst informal exchanges between the parties might be desirable, the legal consequences of failing to comply with the Act were so serious that both the application and the decision should be subject to 'a reasonable degree of formality'.

▶ **6 In *CIN Properties* v. *Gill* [1993] 38 EG 152**, the landlord sought to give evidence of the accounts of a proposed assignee and a winding-up order some nine months after his refusal of consent to assign to it. The dictum of Slade L.J. in *Bromley Park Garden Estates* v. *Moss* was followed, and it was held that evidence relating to subsequent events was inadmissible. In determining the reasonableness of the landlord's refusal for the purposes of s.19(1), Landlord & Tenant Act 1927, the matters to be considered were those affecting the landlord's decision at the time

▶ **7 *Re Smith's Lease* [1951] 1 All ER 346**

A lease contained a covenant not to assign, underlet, or part with the possession of the demised premises without consent 'provided always that any refusal by the lessor . . . shall not be deemed to be an unreasonable withholding of consent by reason only that the lessor . . . may offer to accept from the lessee a surrender of the tenancy thereby created'. It was held that the parties could not curtail the operation of s.19(1) Landlord & Tenant Act 1927 by stipulating circumstances which should be deemed not to be unreasonable, and refusal on the ground that the lessor wanted possession for himself was unreasonable.

▶ **8 *Wallis Fashion Group Ltd.* v. *CGU Life Assurance Ltd.* [2000] 2 EGLR 49**

▶ **9** 'A Code of Practice for Commercial leases in England and Wales', 2nd edition, produced by the Commercial leases Working Group, 2002. The Group comprised members from various Associations and bodies concerned with the commercial property industry.

▶ **10** Law Commission Report No. 141 (1985) and later report, Law Commission Report No. 161 (1987).

▶ **11 *Beale* v. *Worth* [1993] EGCS 134**

A continuing minor breach of a covenant to repair did not justify a refusal of consent to assign. If there was an extensive and long-standing breach of a repairing covenant, the landlord was entitled to be satisfied that the proposed assignee would remedy it before consenting.

▶ **12 *Re Town Investments Ltd. Underlease* [1954] Ch 301**

The tenants had a sixty-three-year lease and proposed to grant a twenty-one-year underlease of part at a rent well below the market value but for a substantial premium. It was held that the landlord's consent was not unreasonably withheld as the underlease was subtracting something from the future value or possible earnings of the premises.

▶ **13 *Wilson* v. *Flynn* [1948] 2 All ER 40**

The covenanted use was for office or professional purposes. It was held that the landlord was not unreasonable to refuse consent to assignment to a commercial undertaking.

▶ **14** The House of Lords decision in *Ashworth Frazer* overruled the previous decision in *Killick* v. *Covent Garden Property Co. Ltd.* [1973] 1 WLR 658. Lord Bingham said that a user clause in a lease is part of a contract to which the tenant has agreed, and it is reasonable for a landlord to seek to avoid an unwanted user and possible consequent litigation which may result from the assignment.

▶ **15** Followed more recently in

Sportoffer Ltd. v. *Erewash B.C.* [1999] EGCS 37

▶ **16** But in *Akici* v. *L. R. Butlin Ltd.* (2006) Neuberger L.J. expressed the opinion that even this breach of covenant might be remediable in certain cases: see Chapter 15.5.1. A breach of a covenant against underletting was dealt with by an injunction to surrender the underlease in *Crestfort Ltd.* v. *Tesco Stores Ltd. & Magspeed*: see 8.4.

Summary

▷ Covenants against assignment or underletting are restrictively construed, so that a covenant against assignment only will not preclude the tenant from underletting, and vice versa.

▷ Such covenants may be absolute or qualified.

▷ Section 19(1) Landlord & Tenant Act 1927 provides that in the case of a qualified covenant consent shall not be unreasonably refused.

▷ If a landlord refuses consent, a tenant may seek a declaration of the court that the refusal is unreasonable, or may go ahead and assign or underlet and plead the unreasonableness of the refusal as a defence in any action brought by the landlord.

▷ The Landlord & Tenant Act 1988 requires a landlord to serve written notice of his decision on a tenant who applies for consent within a reasonable time. The burden of proof to show that his refusal of consent is reasonable is on the landlord, and the tenant may claim damages for breach of a statutory duty if consent is unreasonably withheld.

▷ There is a considerable body of case law on what amounts to an unreasonable refusal of consent. Some of the matters which have been taken into consideration are the character of the proposed tenant, the proposed user of the premises, the business interests of the landlord or other tenants of his, and hardship to the tenant.

▷ There have been some difficult cases on applications to underlet in a falling rental market where a tenant has suffered hardship as he is unable to assign or underlet for the rent required to be reserved by his lease. The same principles as to reasonableness have been applied, however, and the Court of Appeal's most recent decision held that the dictum of *International Drilling Fluids*, whereby hardship to a tenant should be taken into account only in certain circumstances, should apply also to consent to underlet.

Exercises

8.1 How would you distinguish between an assignment and a sublease?

8.2 What is the most comprehensive form of covenant against disposition of the lease?

8.3 Is a landlord permitted to stipulate what amounts to a reasonable ground for refusing consent to assign or underlet?

8.4 Give some examples of reasons for refusal to assign or underlet which have been held to be reasonable.

8.5 What courses of action has a tenant if his landlord refuses consent to assign under a qualified covenant against assignment?

8.6 What particular dilemma of a tenant's does the Landlord & Tenant Act 1988 solve?

Workshop

1 Louise granted a ten-year lease of a flat to Theo. The lease contained a covenant against assigning, underletting or parting with possession of the premises without the consent of the landlord and a covenant to use the premises as a private dwellinghouse only. It also contained a proviso for re-entry on breach of covenant.

Theo wishes to assign the lease to Anton. Louise has told Theo that she will not agree to this as she suspects that Anton will use the flat for business purposes. Advise Theo.

2 Joe is the tenant of an ironmonger's shop under a lease of fifteen years commencing four years ago. He decided to retire earlier this year because of his wife's ill health, but had considerable difficulty in finding an assignee to take on the lease. After about six months, he found a proposed assignee, Errol, who agreed to take an assignment of the lease but wished to sell some garden plants from the shop in addition to the covenanted user of an ironmonger's shop. Joe's application to Jack, the landlord, to assign to Errol also requested consent to this additional user as a subsidiary use as well as the ironmongery.

After two weeks, Jack wrote requesting various financial references for Errol and objecting to the proposed subsidiary user, although he gave no reasons for this. Joe provided these references a week later, but some two weeks later received further requests for accounts relating to Errol's last business. Errol then found alternative shop premises and informed Joe that he no longer wished to proceed with the transaction. Advise Joe as to whether he might have any claim for damages against Jack.

Chapter 9

Repairing covenants

Repairing Covenants Generally

In Chapters 5 and 6 the extent to which covenants relating to the condition and maintenance of the premises will be implied (by statute or case law) on behalf of both the landlord and the tenant was considered. An implied provision may be varied by an express one, except in so far as some of the statutory obligations of a landlord cannot be contracted out of, and any covenant which purports to do this will be void. For example, s.11(1) Landlord & Tenant Act 1985 may be excluded or modified only by an order of the court, but not by agreement between the parties.

The purpose of the present discussion is to examine the effect and scope of an express repairing covenant, and it should be noted at the outset that the obligation it imposes is the same, whether it is the landlord or the tenant who has entered into the covenant. Most formal leases will, of course, expressly provide for repairs, and sometimes the liability may be split, the tenant undertaking decorative and interior repairs and the landlord undertaking structural ones.

There is no limit to the ways in which a repairing covenant may be expressed and the cases display a considerable variety of language. The standard of repair imposed will not differ, however, whether the covenant is one for 'good tenantable repair', 'good repair' or 'excellent repair'. A comprehensive example of a repairing covenant would be one which requires the tenant 'to put into a good state of repair, maintain and deliver up the premises in repair'.

Careful attention should be given to the drafting of a repairing covenant, however, as the courts will give an exact interpretation of each word used. To 'put into repair' is obviously something more than merely to maintain a state of repair, and it is possible to imply from such a covenant that the tenant will undertake repairs which need doing at the commencement of the lease. Thus in the case of *Elite Investments Ltd.* v. *TL Bainbridge Silencers Ltd.* (1986) tenants who had covenanted 'well and substantially to repair, replace, cleanse, paint, maintain, mend and keep the demised premises' were liable for the cost of replacing a roof which had been deteriorating at the date of the lease and subsequently went beyond the stage of repair. In *Credit Suisse* v. *Beegas Nominees Ltd.* (1995) Lindsay J. applied the dictum of Fletcher-Moulton L.J. in *Lurcott* v. *Wakely & Wheeler* (see 9.3 below) that 'the duty of the court is to give a proper and full effect to each word used in repairing covenants', and held that a covenant which included the words (*inter alia*) to 'amend' and 'renew' any 'defect or want of repair' required the landlord to replace the whole of the cladding on a building which was letting in water. Moreover, a covenant to 'keep' in repair differs from a covenant to 'put into repair', and is broken as soon as there is a state of disrepair.

Whilst 'repair' refers only to a physical state, 'condition' connotes a certain amenity value. In *Welsh* v. *Greenwich LBC* (2000), the lease of a ground floor flat contained a covenant to maintain the property in 'good condition and repair'. The flat was badly affected by black spot mould due to there being no insulation system. The installation of such a system would have been outside the scope of a usual repairing covenant (see *McDougall* v. *Easington DC* in 9.3 below), but it was held necessary nevertheless in order to comply with the covenant as to good condition.

The courts have been prepared to apply a criterion of reasonableness in construing repairing covenants. In *Holding & Management Ltd.* v. *Property Holding & Investment Trust plc* (1990) the Court of Appeal was prepared to imply a requirement of reasonableness in interpreting a covenant to do such work as the maintenance trustee 'shall consider necessary to maintain the building as a block of first class residential flats', and held that this did not give the landlord the right to effect unlimited improvements at the tenants' expense. In *Scottish Mutual Assurance plc* v. *Jardine Public Relations Ltd.* (1999) a three-year lease included a covenant by the tenant for 'maintaining, repairing and (if necessary) renewing' the structure of an office building. During the last year of the term the landlord renewed the roof. The court held that, although this was within the scope of the tenant's covenant and so the cost was recoverable from it, the renewal was not reasonably *necessary* for the three-year term, and the tenant was required therefore to pay only 40 per cent of the cost.

In the not unusual situation where the responsibility for repairs is split between the landlord and the tenant, the ideal situation is that there should be a designation of responsibility between landlord and tenant which will cover the whole of the property. In *Holding & Barnes plc* v. *Hill House Hammond Ltd.* (2000), Neuberger J. felt free to interpret conflicting and unclear provisions apportioning responsibility in a common sense way, even though this required the addition of notional words to the landlord's covenant. He relied upon the dictum of Lord Hoffman in *Mannai Investment Co.* v. *Eagle Star Life Assurance Co* (1997) that in a case of ambiguity, words should be construed with a common-sense meaning which a reasonable person with background knowledge would have attributed to them (the 'officious bystander' in contract). In *Delgable Ltd.* v. *Perinpanathan* (2000) the tenant had granted a sublease of the 'first, second and third floors . . . and stairway'. The third floor was the top floor, but the roof was not specifically included in the demise. The subtenant had, however, covenanted to pay a fair proportion of the cost of maintaining the gutters, drains and 'other things the use of which is common' to other adjoining property. This general covenant was held to be wide enough to cover a contribution to the repair of the roof although the roof was not specifically mentioned.

In *Goldmile Properties Ltd.* v. *Lechouritis* (2003), the court had to deal with a conflict between the performance of a repairing covenant by the landlord which conflicted with its covenant for quiet enjoyment. The landlord had scaffolding erected for a six -month period to clean the exterior walls and to repair the seals between the window frames and the walls of a seven-storey building. This seriously disrupted the tenant's restaurant business on the ground floor and basement area. The landlord had postponed the work, however, until after the tenant's busy period at Christmas and had postponed payment of the consequent increase in the service charge. The Court of Appeal held that the landlord had taken all reasonable precautions to avoid disturbance. The landlord's covenant for quiet enjoyment had to be read in conjunction with its repairing covenant, which was for the tenant's benefit, and the reasonable execution of repairs would not amount to a breach of the covenant for quiet enjoyment (Chapter 5.1).

9.2 The Standard of Repair Imposed by a Repairing Covenant

To what standard must a tenant (or landlord) repair premises under a repairing covenant? It was decided in *Proudfoot* v. *Hart* (1890) that the standard of repair must be determined according to the age, character and locality of the building at the date when the lease was granted, and must be such as would make it fit for a reasonably minded tenant of the type who would be likely to take it. Lord Esher said in that case 'nobody could reasonably expect that a house 200 years old should be in the same condition of repair as a house lately built . . . the same class of repair as would be necessary to a palace would be wholly unnecessary to a cottage . . . and . . . the state of repair for a house in Grosvenor Square would be wholly different from the state of repair necessary for a house in Spitalfields'. The relevant date is the date when the lease is granted, and not when it terminates, and this could obviously impose a different standard at the commencement of a long lease from that required at the end, and – even more disturbing – could impose a different standard of repair on an original tenant from that imposed on a subtenant to whom he subleases some years after the commencement of his term.

Because the standard of repair is for the period of the lease which the parties contemplated at the commencement of the term, it is not open to a tenant to subsequently seek to restrict his liability by reference to the 'commercial life' of a building, anticipating that the building will become outdated and unsuitable for its particular use (*Ladbroke Hotels Ltd.* v. *Sandhu* (1995). In *Mason* v. *TotalFinaElf* (2003), even a very onerous covenant which, it was conceded, went beyond the scope of 'repair', was limited by the rule in *Proudfoot* v. *Hart* to the period of the lease, and could not extend to preventative work for a possible future breach after the end of the lease, even though the disrepair was possibly caused in part during the term.

9.3 The Scope of a Repairing Covenant

A more difficult aspect of repairing covenants with which the courts have been concerned is the definition of the word 'repair' itself. At what point does a repair become so extensive that it amounts to the creation of an entirely different structure or building from that which was originally leased? Clearly repair will include the renewal of part of a building, and it was said by Buckley L.J. in *Lurcott* v. *Wakely and Wheeler* (1911) 'Repair always involves renewal; renewal of a part . . . repair is restoration by renewal or replacement of subsidiary parts of a whole.' Repairs should not include the replacement of virtually the whole building at once, however,[1] and nor should it include the reinstatement of the building in a substantially different form from that in which it was originally leased. Thus in *Lister* v. *Lane* (1893) a tenant was not liable under a very comprehensively drawn repairing covenant to rebuild a house which had had to be demolished because its wooden foundations in marshy ground had rotted. To restore the house, the foundations would have had to be rebuilt entirely differently. Another illustration of this is to be found in *Halliard Property Co. Ltd.* v. *Nicholas Clarke Investments Ltd.* (1984) where a tenant was held not liable to reinstate a very unstable and inadequately constructed building at the rear of the premises let which had collapsed. In *Eyre* v. *McCracken* (2000) the insertion of a damp-proof course was held to be an improvement and outside the scope of a repairing covenant. In *New England Properties* v. *Portsmouth Shops* (1993) the court held that a covenant to 'renew or replace' covered the replacement of a badly designed roof with a 22.5 degree pitch which had let in water, with a 30 degree pitch roof with new roof trusses where the cost of the new roof was not substantially more. The roof was still fulfilling its same function, and although an improvement, was not giving the landlord something completely different. The judge felt that the case was a borderline one, but fell just within the category of repair rather than improvement considered by the Court of Appeal in *Holding & Management Ltd.* v. *Property Holding & Trust plc* (1990). There a less expensive but inferior scheme for repairing exterior walls was accepted as being a repair, where a more expensive replacement scheme would not have been. In *Cresta Ltd.* v. *Hammersmith & Fulham LBC* (1998) it was held that a defective underfloor heating system, which it was still feasible to repair, should be repaired rather than an entirely new wall-heating system being installed.

Sometimes a repair will necessarily involve putting right some structural defect to the building which was present when the premises were let. In these circumstances, is a tenant who has covenanted to repair liable not only for the cost of the repair, but also for the cost of correcting the structural defect? This question was answered in the affirmative in *Ravenseft Properties Ltd.* v. *Davstone (Holdings) Ltd.* (1980). Stone cladding was in danger of falling from the facade of a building due to the fact that the stone blocks used had not been tied in to the concrete structure of the building and no expansion joints had been used. At the time when the building was erected, it was not appreciated that this was necessary. The court nevertheless held that the remedying of the structural defect fell within the scope of the tenants' repairing covenants. One of the main factors which influenced the court in this case was the relative cost of the repair (a mere two per cent) to the value of the building as a whole.

This factor was also of significance, although with a contrary result, in *Brew Brothers Ltd.* v. *Snax (Ross) Ltd.* (1970). In this case, seepage from drains damaged the foundations of a building, causing a wall to tilt. The repair of the drains, underpinning of the foundations and rebuilding of the wall would have cost very much the same as the value of the premises if totally rebuilt. It was decided that this work was more akin to renewal than repair and was therefore outside the scope of the tenant's repairing covenant.

The correction of a structural defect which has not actually caused a want of repair will not come within the scope of a repairing covenant. In *Post Office* v. *Aquarius Properties Ltd.* (1987) the basement of a building had been flooded for most of the time between 1979 and 1984, but had not caused any actual deterioration to the building itself. Following *Quick* v. *Taff-Ely B.C.* (see Chapter 5.3.3) the Court of Appeal held that work to remedy the flooding was not within the scope of the tenant's repairing covenant, although expressly reserving the possibility that it might become so in the future if the flooding caused actual deterioration. *Minja Properties Ltd.* v. *Cussins Property Group plc* (1998) can be interestingly contrasted with *Quick* v. *Taff-Ely B.C.* on this ground. In *Quick* steel window frames, which were a bad design, were causing condensation but were not in a state of disrepair, whereas in *Minja* the steel window frames had actually corroded, and the replacement of these with double-glazed units was still within a repairing covenant notwithstanding that it also effected an improvement.

The scope of repairing covenants was reviewed by the Court of Appeal in *McDougall* v. *Easington D.C.* (1989). The Court discerned three guidelines applied in the cases:

(1) Do the alterations affect the whole, or substantially the whole, of the building?
(2) Do the alterations make the building different in character from the building originally let?
(3) Is the cost of the alterations a significant proportion of the value of the previous existing building?

If any of these questions is answered in the affirmative, the alterations may be outside the scope of a repairing covenant.

9.4 Qualification of a Tenant's Repairing Covenant

It is not unusual for a tenant's repairing covenant to be qualified by the words 'fair wear and tear excepted'. Exactly what repairs fall within this exception has been the subject of judicial interpretation and was considered by the House of Lords in *Regis Property Co. Ltd.* v. *Dudley* (1959). The Law Lords were agreed that the words cover damage caused by natural deterioration due to time and weathering and normal use, assuming a reasonable tenant using the premises in a tenant-like manner. They will not therefore include damage caused by the tenant's negligence, or the negligence of his family or friends. But, should such damage due to fair wear and tear occur, a reasonable tenant must take any necessary steps to limit its effect. The example given by Lord Denning in *Regis Property Co. Ltd.* v. *Dudley* is that a tenant would not be liable for a slate falling from the roof, but might well be liable for resulting dampness and damage if he did not take steps to replace the slate, and Viscount Simonds quoted with approval a judgment of Salter J. in the earlier case of *Haskell* v. *Marlow* (1928). He said: 'It does not mean that if there is a defect originally proceeding from reasonable wear and tear the tenant is released from his obligation to keep in good repair and condition everything which it may be possible to trace ultimately to that defect. He is bound to do such repairs as may be required to prevent the consequences flowing originally from wear and tear from producing others which wear and tear would not directly produce.'

9.5 Landlord's Right to Enter and View State of Repair

Where a landlord has a liability to repair, there is an implied obligation on the part of the tenant to allow him to enter and view the state of repair (see Chapter 6.4). The landlord may not be liable for damage resulting from his failure to repair unless he is aware of the want of repair, and this is so whether his repairing obligation is express or implied. It is sufficient notice if the landlord's agent or workmen should have realised the want of repair[2] but the casual mention of a possible defect by the tenant in another context some time previously will not be enough.[3] The landlord's liability under s.4 of the Defective Premises Act 1972 is somewhat wider, however, as there is liability under this section if the landlord knows 'or ought to have known'.[4] Moreover, the case of *Loria* v. *Hammer* (1989) held a landlord to be liable under an express repairing covenant for repairs to common parts of a building retained by him even without notice and this was confirmed by the Court of Appeal in *British Telecommunications plc* v. *Sun Life Assurance plc* (1995).

9.6 Landlord's Remedies for Breach of a Repairing Covenant

9.6.1 Damages

If a tenant defaults on repairs, a landlord will have an action for damages for breach of his covenant just as for breach of any other agreement. The landlord's damages are limited by s.18(1) Landlord & Tenant Act 1927 to the difference in the value of his reversion if the repairing covenant had been carried out, and the value of the reversion if the premises are in their unrepaired state at the end of the lease. If it can be shown, therefore, that the landlord intends to demolish the premises at the end of the term, he will be unable to obtain any damages at all. This will not apply, however, if the premises are demolished under a local authority order owing to the bad state of repair.[5] In *Smiley* v. *Townshend* (1950) Singleton L.J. said that evidence of lack of repair is not conclusive of damage to the reversion, but is *prima facie* evidence of it.

An interesting attempt to invoke s.18(1) in order to avoid damages was made in *Shortlands Investments Ltd.* v. *Cargill plc* (1996) A sub-underlessee of a part of business premises argued that it should not be liable in damages to the landlord underlessee for breach of a repairing covenant because the landlord's reversion value was negative owing to the property recession, and any incoming tenant would in any event require a refit of the premises, making any repairs otiose. A large sum had in fact been offered to a new tenant as an inducement to take the lease. The court held that the want of repair was nevertheless a bargaining point for any new tenant to obtain a reduction in the rent and that the reverse premium offered must reflect this. The landlord was entitled to recover the additional sum paid to the new tenant for the disrepair, even though the reversion was of negative value. Conversely, in *Simmons* v. *Dresden* (2004), a sublease of the premises expired only a short time before the headlease, so that the headlessee did not have time to carry out repairs which would have cost about £73,000. The landlord had sold the building, however, about five months after the lease expired for what the valuers for the parties agreed was a very good price. He could not therefore show that he had suffered any diminution in the value of his reversion.

If the lease is within the Leasehold Property (Repairs) Act 1938, being a lease for at least seven years or more with at least three years unexpired, a landlord cannot claim damages for breach of a repairing covenant without first complying with the formalities laid down by the Act (see 9.6.2 below on forfeiture).

9.6.2 Forfeiture

Damages for breach of a tenant's repairing covenant will usually be claimed in the course of forfeiture proceedings, which is the more usual remedy for breach, provided that the lease contains a forfeiture clause – that is, a proviso for re-entry by the landlord on breach of a covenant.

As with all forfeitures for breach of a covenant other than payment of rent, the landlord must first serve a notice under s.146 LPA 1925 specifying the breach complained of, requiring it to be remedied and requiring any compensation for it. This procedure is dealt with more fully in Chapter 15.5 with regard to forfeiture generally.

As regards forfeiture for repairs, however, the Leasehold Property (Repairs) Act 1938, which applies to leases of at least seven years with three years left to run, places limitations on a landlord where it applies. It requires that when a landlord serves a notice under s.146 LPA he must inform the tenant in the notice of his right to serve a counter notice under the 1938 Act.

For the purposes of s. 146 and the 1938 Act, it was decided in *Smith* v. *Spaul* (2002) (rather surprisingly perhaps, and overruling *Target Home Loans* v. *Iza* (2000)) that the tenant and not his mortgagee in possession is the person on whom a s.146 notice must be served and who has the right to serve a counter-notice under the 1938 Act.

If the tenant serves a counter-notice within twenty-eight days, then the landlord may not proceed further in a claim for either damages or forfeiture without first obtaining the leave of the court. Leave will be granted if one of the five circumstances (a)–(e) in s.1(5) of the Act apply. These are:

(a) that the value of the landlord's reversion has been, or is likely to be, substantially diminished if the repairs are not done;
(b) that the repair is necessary to comply with an order of any authority or local bye-law;
(c) where the tenant does not occupy the whole of the premises, that the repair is necessary in the interests of another occupier;

(d) that an immediate repair will avoid further deterioration leading to more expensive repairs;

(e) that there are any special circumstances making leave to proceed just and equitable.

The hearing is an interlocutory one at which the landlord must prove his case under s.1(5) on a balance of probabilities.

The court decided in *Landmaster Properties Ltd.* v. *Thackeray Property Service* (2003), where the property was burned down before the hearing of the application, that the relevant date for consideration of the circumstances is the date of the application and not the hearing. The tenant had allowed a public house to remain empty and had not taken sufficient steps to prevent vandals from entering it. This was a nuisance to other neighbouring tenants, and the court therefore held that there was a discretion to grant leave to proceed with a forfeiture under s.1(5)(e).

In *Associated British Ports* v. *Bailey plc* (1990) the landlord of a dry dock was seeking to forfeit the lease after serving a s.146 notice for dilapidations of £600,000. The tenant served a counter-notice under the 1938 Act and the landlord applied for leave to continue on the ground of diminution of the value of the reversion under s.1(5)(a). The lease did not expire, however, until 2049 and the tenant argued that by then the dry dock would be useless for modern shipbuilding and was therefore unlikely to be used again for shipbuilding purposes. There were in fact proposals, which were likely to be profitable, to develop the site. The House of Lords decided that the landlord's *prima facie* case was not sufficient to grant leave to proceed and the landlord must show the likelihood of a diminution in value of the reversion on a balance of probabilities, which it was unable to do.

9.6.3 Provision for Landlord to Enter and do Repairs

Some leases may contain an express covenant allowing the landlord to enter and carry out repairs himself, recovering the cost of this from the tenant. The Court of Appeal held in *Jervis* v. *Harris* (1996) that the costs of such repairs are recoverable as a debt from the tenant for work done by the landlord and not as damages, so that the Leasehold Property (Repairs) Act 1938 will not apply. If the landlord is seeking to recover the debt as a fixed sum from any previous tenant or guarantor of the lease, then he must first serve the appropriate notice under s.17 Landlord & Tenant (Covenants) Act 1995 (see Chapter 7.5.1).

If, however, the landlord is suing for *damages* for breach of a repairing covenant, he must first serve notice under the 1938 Act If the lease is one which falls within the Act.

9.6.4   Specific Performance

It was stated in *Hill* v. *Barclay* (1810) that specific performance is not available to a landlord for breach of a tenant's repairing covenant. The original objection to an order for specific performance of a repairing covenant, that the court could not supervise it, has gradually been eroded and the courts have been prepared to grant specific performance of a landlord's repairing covenant since 1974. In *Co-operative Insurance Society Ltd.* v. *Argyll Stores (Holdings) Ltd.* (1997), the House of Lords distinguished between supervision of an ongoing state of affairs and supervision of work to attain a specific result, and in *Rainbow Estates Ltd.* v. *Tokenhold Ltd.* (1998), it was held that the remedy should be available to a landlord in appropriate cases. In that case, extensive repairs were needed to a Grade II listed building, in respect of which the local authority had served notices under the Housing Act 1985 and the Environmental Protection Act 1990. Unusually, there was no provision for forfeiture in the lease, and no right for the landlord to enter and carry out the repairs. The court therefore made an order for specific performance of the repairs by the tenant.

Normally the landlord's right of forfeiture or of entry to carry out repairs will make such an order unnecessary, but in the exceptional circumstances of a case such as *Rainbow Estates Ltd.*, its availability is clearly desirable.

9.7   Tenant's Remedies for Breach of a Repairing Covenant

9.7.1   Damages

Breach of a repairing covenant by the landlord is a breach of agreement for which a tenant can sue for damages. In *Calabar Properties* v. *Stitcher* (1983) the Court of Appeal considered the damage flowing from the breach of a repairing covenant for which a tenant might be able to seek compensation. In that case, the tenant of a long lease had to find alternative accommodation when the property became uninhabitable through dampness owing to the landlord's failure to repair. She was able to recover damages for discomfort, loss of enjoyment, bouts of ill health and the diminution in market value of the premises based on the cost of the repairs. She failed to recover damages for the outgoings on the flat while she was unable to live there. The court indicated that she would have been entitled to the cost of alternative accommodation had she claimed for this. In a later case, however, the Court of Appeal has indicated that damages for the diminution in value of the tenancy are appropriate only where the tenant is selling or subletting.[6] In *McGreal* v. *Wake* (1984) damages were awarded to a tenant for living for some months in an unrepaired house, storage of furniture while the tenant was obliged to live elsewhere and the cost of the temporary accommodation, and of clearing up and making good decorations after the repairs had been carried out.

In *Clarke* v. *Lloyds TSB Bank* (2002), a landlord who had covenanted to provide an effective air-conditioning system for an office building had failed to do so for 1,380 days over a period of six years. The court assessed damages as the differential between the rental value of the building with such a system, and without it, and allowed damages of the differential for the 1,380 days (which amounted to a year's rent!).

A tenant's claim for damages for repairs may be subject to a landlord's right of equitable set-off for arrears of service charges, and like all equitable claims, this will not be barred by the Limitation Act 1980.[7]

In *Marshall* v. *Rubypoint* (1997) the landlord failed to repair securely the exterior door to a town house in which the tenant had a ground floor flat. The door was broken in 1993 and the tenant was burgled on four occasions during the year, and assaulted on one occasion. There had been no previous burglaries, although the tenant had lived there since 1984. It was held that the burglaries were foreseeable and not a *novus actus interveniens*, so that the landlord was liable in damages for personal injuries to the tenant, his stolen goods and loss of enjoyment of the property.

The Secure Tenants of Local Housing Authorities (Right to Repair) Regulations 1994, made under s.96 Housing Act 1985 (as substituted by s.121 Leasehold Reform, Housing & Urban Development Act 1993) (see later) makes limited compensation payable to secure tenants for failure to carry out certain qualifying repairs within a prescribed period.

9.7.2   Specific Performance

The remedy of specific performance was given to a tenant in the case of *Jeune* v. *Queens Cross Properties Ltd.* (1974). As regards dwellings, it is now enacted in s.17 Landlord & Tenant Act 1985. The remedy is available not only for repairs to the tenant's own premises, but also for repairs to other parts of a building, such as common parts of a block of flats or a roof.

9.7.3   Right to Set off Cost of Repairs Against Rent

In *Lee-Parker* v. *Izzet* (1971) it was decided that a tenant has a right to set off the cost of repairs against future rents. This remedy has to be treated with some caution, however, and a wise tenant should probably first submit estimates for the repairs to his landlord. In any event, he should allow the landlord time to do the repairs and warn him that he intends to do the repairs himself if the landlord does not. The common law right to set off is for a liquidated sum but in *British Anzani (Felixstowe) Ltd.* v. *International Marine Management (U.K.) Ltd.* (1980), it was said that an equitable remedy of set off might lie for an unliquidated sum such as damages for a landlord's failure to repair.[7] Moreover, an equitable right of set-off will not be barred by the Limitation Act 1980.[8]

Before exercising a right of set-off, a tenant may obtain a declaration from the court that the landlord is in breach of his repairing covenant, and this would again seem to be a further safeguard for the tenant.

There is no right of set-off if the lease excludes it. A general statement that the rent is payable without deduction will not operate to exclude it, however (*Connaught Restaurants Ltd.* v. *Indoor Leisure Ltd.* (1993)).

9.7.4   Remedies for Disrepair Available to Tenants of Flats on Long Leases

The tenants of flats in a block which are let on long leases have the right, in certain circumstances, to apply for the appointment of a receiver or a manager, although this is not possible where the landlord is a local authority, as it was said by the Court of Appeal in *Parker* v. *Camden London Borough Council* (1985) that this would amount to an abrogation of the local authority's duties as a housing authority under ss.20–26 Housing Act 1985.

In certain circumstances where 90 per cent of the flats in a building are held on long leases, the tenants may also apply for an order for the acquisition of the landlord's interest by a nominated person, who could be a trustee for the tenants (Landlord & Tenant Act 1987, Part II).

9.7.5   Rights to Repair of Secure Tenants of Local Housing Authorities

Section 121 Leasehold Reform, Housing & Urban Development Act 1993 substituted a new s.96 to the Housing Act 1985 empowering the Secretary of State to make regulations under which secure tenants of a local authority can require certain repairs to be carried out. If the repairs are not carried out within certain 'target' dates, compensation may be payable.

The Secure Tenants of Local Housing Authorities (Right to Repair) Regulations 1994 set out the 'qualifying repairs'[9] which a tenant can require a housing authority to carry out. The housing authority should inform their tenants of their right to have such repairs done and must maintain a list of approved contractors who are prepared to do such work.

9.7.6   Legislative Remedies for Disrepair Enforceable by Local Authorities

Local authorities, as housing authorities, have certain legislative powers and duties with regard to property which is in a poor state of repair which a tenant may be able to use to his advantage. A detailed discussion of these is beyond the scope of a book which is primarily concerned with the relationship of landlord and tenant, but a brief reference to them will be made.

(i) Repair notice under S.189 Housing Act 1985 Under this section, a local authority shall serve a repairs notice on a person having control of a house which is unfit for human habitation specifying repairs which will render it fit for human habitation. The person on whom the notice is served must be given a reasonable time (at least twenty-one days) to carry out the repairs. If, however, the local authority are satisfied that the house cannot be made fit for habitation at reasonable expense, then they must make a demolition order (under s.265) or closing order (under s.264) after giving notice under the section to any person with an interest in the house and giving due consideration to any undertaking to carry out work on the house by any person interested. The reasonable expense to make the house fit for habitation is such that the value of the house repaired on the open market will not be less than its present value plus the cost of the repairs. Once a demolition or closing order has been made, then a tenant ceases to be a protected tenant under the Rent Acts and a landlord may obtain possession.

In determining whether a house is unfit for human habitation regard shall be had to the eight criteria set out in s.604, as amended by Part V of Schedule 9 of the Local Government & Housing Act 1989. These are the repair, stability, freedom from damp, internal arrangement, natural lighting, ventilation, water supply, drainage and sanitary conveniences, facilities for the preparation and cooking of food and for the disposal of waste water. The house will be unfit if it is defective and not reasonably suitable for occupation in one or more respects.

(ii) Repair notice under S.190 Housing Act 1985 Where a house is not unfit for human habitation but requires substantial repair to bring it up to a reasonable standard, having regard to its age, character and locality, or its disrepair is such as to interfere materially with the personal comfort of the tenant, then a local authority may, of its own accord or at the instigation of a tenant, serve a repair notice on the person having control of the house. This shall require him to carry out the repairs specified within a reasonable time, not being less than twenty-one days.

A person aggrieved by a notice under either section may appeal to the County Court. If work specified in a repair notice is not done, then the local authority may carry out the work itself and recover the cost from the person on whom the notice was served (s.193 Housing Act 1985). A repair notice under either section is registrable as a local land charge on the property.

(iii) Part VII Housing Act 1985 In housing action areas or general improvement areas, a local authority may serve a notice on a person in control of a house requiring him to carry out improvements to provide

certain basic amenities such as a bath, wash basin and a sink with hot and cold water supplies and an inside water closet. An occupying tenant of a dwelling not within such an area may request the local housing authority nevertheless to exercise their power to serve such a notice.

(iv) Environmental Protection Act 1990, s.79   Where the state of repair of premises makes them 'prejudicial to health', they constitute a statutory nuisance under this Act (which replaces in this respect the Public Health Act 1936), and the local authority can be required to serve an abatement notice on the landlord. If he does not comply with this, either a tenant of the premises or a local authority may apply for a summons in the magistrates' court for an order requiring a landlord to carry out repairs to remedy the nuisance. In *Dover District Council* v. *Farrar* (1982) the Act was applied to condensation, in *McGuigan* v. *Southwark LBC* (1995) to an infestation of cockroaches, and in *Southwark LBC* v. *Ince* (1989) to noise and vibration from traffic. The Noise & Statutory Nuisance Act 1993, s.2, inserted a new subsection 79(1)(ga) into the 1990 Act however from which it is clear that s.79 is not intended to cover traffic noise, and a tenant's summons under s.79 alleging a nuisance prejudicial to health as a result of traffic noise failed. As in *Ince*, the court indicated that magistrates' courts should be wary of abatement notices putting onerous duties on a local authority which might have a large stock of housing but only a limited budget. Also, it was said in *Ince* that local authorities should be careful not to draw up unreasonable abatement notices, bearing in mind that even adequate insulation might not afford complete protection from noise.

In *R.* v. *Bristol City Council ex parte Everett* (1999), it was held that a steep staircase not complying with the Building Regulations was not a nuisance within the section, as the section is intended to cover matters previously within the Public Health Acts and not accident preventative requirements covered by other statutory provisions such as the Building Regulations.

Notes

▶ **1** *Torrens* v. *Walker* **[1906] 2 Ch 166**

The front and back walls of a house were demolished by London County Council after serving a dangerous structure notice. The landlord had covenanted to keep the outside walls in repair. It was held that this was a repairing covenant, to be construed as any other repairing covenant, and the rebuilding of the walls was outside the scope of the repairing obligation, so that the landlord was not liable.

▶ **2** *Sheldon* v. *West Bromwich Corporation* **[1973] P&CR 360**

A plumber employed by the Council was sent to investigate noises in the pipes of a council house. He found some rust and discoloration in the water tank, which was thirty to forty years old. It was held that the landlords were liable for damage caused by the burst tank.

▶ 3 *O'Brien* v. *Robinson* [1973] AC 912

The landlord was liable on the implied covenant under s.32 Housing Act 1961 to keep (*inter alia*) the structure of the leased premises in repair. The tenants had complained in the course of court proceedings some three years earlier that the ceiling was damaged by the dancing activities of the tenants above. Since that time, the dancing had ceased and there was no more apparent damage. The ceiling fell and injured the tenant and his wife. It was held that the landlord was not liable for a latent defect of which the tenant's mention some time earlier did not amount to notice.

▶ 4 *Smith* v. *Bradford Metropolitan Council* (1982) 44 P&CR 171

A tenancy agreement gave the landlord the right (but not the duty) to enter and inspect and carry out repairs. The tenant slipped on a crumbling part of concrete on the patio. It was held that the landlord had an obligation under s.4(4) of the Defective Premises Act 1972 and therefore a duty of care to the tenant under s.4(1) and was liable. (For the text of this section, see Chapter 5, Note 15. For a discussion of liability under the section, see Chapter 5.3.4.)

▶ 5 *Hibernian Property Co.* v. *Liverpool Corporation* [1973] 1 WLR 751

The Corporation who were tenants of a house defaulted on a repairing covenant in the lease. The house was then designated by them as unfit for human habitation and within a clearance area, which meant that under s.18(1) Landlord & Tenant Act 1927 damages were

payable only for the site value. It was held that s.18(1) was inapplicable as (1) it was not shown that the house would be demolished shortly after the end of the lease and (2) s.18(1) contemplates only the landlord's decision to pull down the house.

▶ 6 *Wallace v. Manchester City Council* (1998) EGCS 114

▶ 7 *British Anzani (Felixstowe) Ltd.* v. International Marine Management (UK) Ltd [1980] QB 137

The plaintiff company was lessee of land under a building lease. It was agreed that the plaintiff would build two warehouses and sublet these to the defendant company, and the agreement contained an undertaking by the plaintiff to put right any defects in the buildings within two years. There was a defect in the flooring of the first warehouse within the two years. The plaintiff sued the defendant for unpaid rent and the defendant counter claimed for the defective flooring. It was held that the cost of repairing the defective flooring, although a claim for unliquidated damages under the agreement and not under the sublease itself, could be set off against the rent. There was a close connection between the agreement and the sublease, and the defendant's claim was fair and just and went to the foundation of the plaintiff's claim for rent

▶ 8 *Filross Securities Ltd. v. Midgely* (1998) EGCS 124, where a landlord's claim for unpaid service charges ten years previously could be set off against a tenant's claim for damages for disrepair.

> **9 S.I. 1994/133 (Schedule)**
>
> The defects are (*inter alia*) total or partial loss of electricity, water or gas supplies, space or water heating, blocked flues, blocked or leaking drains, toilet, sink, bath or basin wastes, leaking roof, insecure window, door or lock, loose or detached banister or handrail, rotten flooring or stair tread, non-functioning extractor fans or entry phone.

Summary

- Either landlord or tenant may covenant to repair.

- The standard of repair under a repairing covenant is the same however the covenant is expressed. It is that laid down in *Proudfoot* v. *Hart* (1890) – according to the age, character and locality of the building at the commencement of the lease.

- 'Repair' involves renewal of part but not the whole, and may include a structural repair which was present but latent when the lease was granted. A test which the courts have applied to distinguish 'repair' from 'renewal' is the relative cost of the repair to the value of the building as a whole.

- A qualification of a tenant's repairing covenant by the words 'fair wear and tear excepted' exempts the tenant from liability for damage caused by natural deterioration, but not from damage flowing from this.

- Wherever a landlord is liable for repairs, there is an implied obligation on the part of the tenant to allow him to enter and view the state of repair.

- A landlord may sue a tenant for damages for breach of a repairing covenant, but his damages are limited to the diminution in the value of his reversion.

- If the lease contains a proviso for forfeiture, the landlord may take forfeiture proceedings, but he must first serve a notice under s.146 LPA 1925 and must inform the tenant of his rights under the Leasehold Property (Repairs) Act 1938 if this Act applies,

- A tenant may claim damages from his landlord for the landlord's breach of repairing covenant,

- A tenant may seek an order for specific performance against a landlord. This is available for repairs to common parts of a building as well as repairs to the tenant's own premises.

- A tenant may set off rent against the cost of repairs, even if the claim for repairs is an unliquidated one.

- The Court may appoint a receiver to collect rents and deal with repairs needed to a block of flats. The County Court may similarly appoint a manager. Neither remedy is possible where the landlord is a local authority.

Summary cont'd

▶ Local authorities have a number of powers to require a landlord to carry out repairs:

(a) where a house is unfit for human habitation (s.189 Housing Act 1985),
(b) where a house requires substantial repairs to bring it up to a certain standard (s.190 Housing Act 1985);
(c) in housing action areas, or where a tenant requests a local authority to act in respect of basic amenities (Part VII, Housing Act 1985);
(d) where the state of the premises makes them prejudicial to health (s.92 Public Health Act 1936).

▶ A secure tenant of a local authority may serve a repairs notice on his landlord which his landlord may accept or refuse. If he refuses, the tenant may, if the conditions are satisfied, go ahead with the repairs and recover the cost from the local authority.

Exercises

9.1 What is the standard of repair imposed by a repairing covenant?

9.2 How have the courts defined 'repairs'?

9.3 What is the effect of a qualification to a tenant's repairing covenant of fair wear and tear excepted'?

9.4 What are the limitations to a landlord's claim for damages for breach of a tenant's repairing covenant?

9.5 To what leases does the Leasehold (Property) Repairs Act 1938 apply?

9.6 What must a landlord do before commencing forfeiture proceedings for breach of a repairing covenant?

9.7 In what circumstances may a landlord carry out repairs which his tenant has covenanted to do and recover the cost from his tenant?

9.8 What damages may a tenant recover for breach of a landlord's repairing covenant?

9.9 What would you advise a tenant to do before setting off the cost of repairs under his landlord's repairing covenant against rent?

9.10 Under what circumstances may a local authority take steps to compel a landlord to carry out repairs to leased property?

9.11 What provision has been made for a secure tenant to require his landlord to carry out repairs or carry out the repairs himself in default?

Workshop

1   Lottie granted a ten-year lease of 'The Lodge' to Tina which contained a proviso for re-entry on breach of covenant. The lease contained a covenant by Tina to keep the premises in good repair, fair wear and tear excepted.

   Six months ago, a slate was blown from the roof and there is now extensive damp to a bedroom wall as a result. A jerry-built shed in the garden has collapsed. Advise Lottie as to what remedies she may have.

2   Leo granted Tony a lease for three years of a flat. The lease contained a covenant by Leo to carry out any structural repairs. Two months ago Tony told Leo that the plaster on the bedroom ceiling was badly cracked, but Leo has done nothing. Some plaster has now fallen and the ceiling is dangerous. Advise Tony.

Chapter 10

Covenants restrictive of the user of the premises and covenants against alterations

Types of Covenants as to User

A formal lease will often contain covenants imposing restrictions on the user of the demised premises. These may be positively phrased – for example, to use the demised premises as a private dwellinghouse only – or negatively phrased – such as not to use the demised premises for certain trades. Covenants as to user are liberally interpreted, so that only a slight deviation from a covenant which is largely observed will not amount to a breach.[1] In *St. Marylebone Property Co. Ltd. v. Tesco Stores Ltd.* (1988), Hoffman J. said that in order to constitute a breach of covenant, the sale of prohibited items would have to constitute a distinct trade, but need not be the dominant trade. This was adopted and approved as the test for breach of a user covenant by the Court of Appeal in *Williams v. Kiley* (2003) discussed more fully in 10.3 below.

In *Basildon Development Corporation v. Mactro Ltd.* (1986) it was conceded that the relevant time for interpreting a widely drawn user clause is the date of the lease, although when the case went to the Court of Appeal, Sir Denys Buckley indicated that he would not necessarily regard this as the sole criterion for the interpretation of user covenants.[2]

Occasionally the permitted user of the premises may be defined by reference to a particular Use Class under the Town and Country Planning Acts. This can cause problems if the Use Classes Order is amended as recently (see 10.3) as it is then necessary to ascertain what user was permitted by the Use Class at the date the lease was granted.

User covenants may be absolute or qualified – that is, that no other use will be allowed without the landlord's consent – but there is no statutory provision for user covenants that in the case of a qualified covenant the landlord's consent shall not be unreasonably withheld. S.19(3) Landlord & Tenant Act 1927 does prohibit the landlord from asking for a fine for such consent, however, 'whether by way of increase of rent or otherwise',[3] although he may require payment of a reasonable sum (to be determined by the court in case of dispute) in respect of damage to or diminution in the value of the premises or any neighbouring premises belonging to him. Nor may the landlord seek to obtain an advantage from the granting of consent to change of user which he did not originally reserve to himself in the lease.[4] S.19(3) does not apply to absolute covenants against change of user. Nor does the section apply where the change of user involves structural alterations (see 10.4 below).

10.2   Landlord's Remedies for Breach of User Covenant

A landlord's remedies for breach of a user covenant are damages, forfeiture (assuming that there is a proviso for re-entry on breach of covenant contained in the lease) and an injunction. In *Hampstead & Suburban Properties Ltd.* v. *Diomedous* (1969). Megarry J. was prepared to grant an interlocutory injunction pending trial and said: 'Where there is a plain and uncontested breach of a clear covenant not to do a particular thing, and the covenantor promptly begins to do what he has promised not to do, then in the absence of special circumstances it seems to me that the sooner he is compelled to keep his promise the better . . . I see no reason for allowing a covenantor who stands in clear breach of an express prohibition to have a holiday from the enforcement of his obligations until the trial.' In this case, the landlord granted a licence to assign to new tenants allowing a change of user to a restaurant and the playing of music in the evenings provided that adequate sound-proofing was first carried out to protect his other tenants living above the premises. The new tenant played music without adequate sound proofing and the landlord received numerous complaints from his other tenants. He was able to obtain an interlocutory injunction pending trial.

Where a lease contains a covenant against assignment or underletting, a landlord's refusal of consent to assign or underlet is reasonable if a change of user is a possible result[5] (see the House of Lords decision in *Ashworth Frazer Ltd.* v. *Gloucester CC* (2002) discussed in Chapter 8.3). If the landlord has an estate management policy involving user for a shopping centre however, and has stipulated that it shall be deemed reasonable for him to refuse consent to assign for a user inconsistent with this, then such refusal may be reasonable (see *Moss Bros Group plc* v. *C.S.C. Properties Ltd.* in Chapter 8.3).

A landlord who is leasing a shopping development will sometimes have an 'anchor' store which attracts shoppers to the shopping precinct. This is usually a supermarket or other large store. In order to protect the smaller traders in the precinct, the lease of the supermarket will sometimes include a covenant by the tenant to keep the shop open. The courts have traditionally been reluctant to grant mandatory injunctions for 'keep open' covenants (*F.W. Woolworth plc* v. *Charlwood Alliance Properties Ltd.*). In *Co-operative Insurance Society Ltd.* v. *Argyll Stores (Holdings) Ltd.* (1996), the tenant had covenanted to 'keep the demised premises open for retail trade during the usual hours of business'. The premises were a Safeway supermarket which was the 'anchor' store in the Hillsborough shopping centre. The tenant had made a loss of over £70,000 during the preceding financial year, however, and therefore decided to close the shop despite the 'keep open' covenant. At first instance, the landlord was granted damages. The Court of Appeal, Millett L.J. dissenting, went further and granted an order for specific performance of the covenant, notwithstanding that the tenant had already stripped the premises. The House of Lords reversed the Court of Appeal decision and reinstated the trial judge's award of damages. Lord Hoffman considered that the traditional grounds for refusing an order for specific performance – the difficulty of supervising a positive obligation, which in this case was not sufficiently precisely stated, and the liability of imposing an unquantifiable burdensome loss on the appellants – were grounds for refusing the order. He described both parties as 'sophisticated commercial institutions' who must have appreciated that closure was a commercial risk for which damages would be available.

10.3 Other Restrictions on User

Quite apart from the terms of the lease, a tenant may be restricted as to user of the demised premises by planning permission or restrictive covenants affecting the freehold title.

Planning permission is required for change of user of premises where the use is of a different class, and sometimes even for a change from one use to another in the same class. In *Belmont Riding Centre Ltd.* v. *First Secretary of State* (2003), it was held that a change from a mixed use to part only of the mixed use also required planning consent. A lease will often contain a covenant to comply with any planning consents affecting the property, and if so, then the landlord will have the usual remedies of damages and possible forfeiture if the tenant is in breach of the covenant. The Town & Country Planning (Use Classes) (Amendment) (England) Order 2005 (in force April 2005) has amended the Town & Country Planning (Use Classes) Order 1987 by separating Class A3 into three separate Classes – A3 (restaurants and cafes), A4 (pubs and wine bars) and A5 (hot food takeaways), and planning consent is required to change from A3 to A4 or A5.

A restrictive covenant affecting the freehold title will bind a tenant, subtenant or any other occupier of the premises whether or not it is contained in the lease. Covenants restrictive of user are restrictive covenants and binding on a subtenant or even a squatter (see Chapter 7). A restrictive covenant as to user in leases granted by the same landlord may also give an earlier tenant the right to sue a later tenant for breach of a restrictive covenant if he took with notice of it.[6] The Court of Appeal has recently accepted that a scheme of development, whereby the purchasers of all plots on an estate agree to be bound by identical restrictive covenants and the covenants thereby become enforceable *inter se* as a kind of local law, may also apply to a letting scheme. In *Williams* v. *Kiley* (2003) the Swansea CC leased a small parade of some six shops. Each tenant's lease contained a designated user clause and a covenant by the tenant not to carry on any other specific trades which were designated users for the tenants of the other shops. The tenant of a shop with user as a newsagent, confectioner and tobacconist successfully sued the tenant of an adjoining supermarket (whose lease contained a covenant not to carry on these trades) for infringement of the covenant. The Court of Appeal identified the shopping parade as a defined geographical area, and the leases clearly showed a reciprocity of obligation (essential requirements for a scheme of development). The Court was further influenced by the fact that the leases did not contain any provision for enforcement of the user covenants by the landlord.

In *Kiley*, the Court of Appeal recognised a problem in applying a scheme of development (more usually applicable to restrictive covenants on a residential freehold estate) to a trade development involving leases for ninety-nine years, as clearly trade patterns could change during that time. As with all restrictive covenants, however, it is possible to apply to the Lands Tribunal for their modification or discharge on certain grounds under s.84 LPA 1925 (as amended by LPA 1969), and the Court of Appeal considered that an application under s.84 (which includes *inter alia* obsolescence as a ground) would be adequate to deal with this problem.

A number of conjoined appeals on the validity of a beer tie in the leases of public houses by breweries under Article 81 (previously Article 85) European Community Treaty 1957 was referred by the Court of Appeal to the European Court of Justice, which ruled that a person affected by unfair competition contrary to the Article might be able to recover damages. The House of Lords has now held however that a decision by the European Commission in proceedings relating to other participants in the same market does not bind a national court. Their Lordships restored the decision of Park J. who had held that, on the facts, there had been no breach of Article 81.[7] For a case suggesting that such a tie might be void as distorting competition between Member States in leases granted by a large brewery with 4,500 public houses, but valid against an assignee who was a smaller brewer, see *Passmore* v. *Morland plc* (1999).

10.4 Types of Covenants against Alterations

A lease may contain such covenants in an absolute form, that is, 'not to make any alterations to the demised premises'. Alternatively, and more usually, the covenant may be in a qualified form – namely, 'not to make any alterations to the demised premises without the landlord's consent'. In the case of an absolute covenant, no alterations can be made unless the landlord consents, even though the alterations are improvements to the premises.

A qualified covenant against alterations again requires the landlord's consent, but if the alterations amount to improvements, then s.19(2) Landlord & Tenant Act 1927 will apply,[8] and this provides that the landlord's consent shall not be unreasonably withheld. It also provides, however, that the landlord may require a sum of money for any diminution in the value of the premises or of any neighbouring premises belonging to the landlord, or require an undertaking from the tenant to reinstate the premises at the end of the term, as conditions for granting consent.[9]

In deciding whether an alteration is an improvement or not and so within the scope of the section, the court must consider it from the tenant's point of view. In *Lambert* v. *F. W. Woolworth & Co. Ltd.* (No. 2) (1938) a forty-two-year lease contained a covenant not to erect any other building or make any structural alterations without the previous consent of the landlord. The tenants proposed to take out a back wall of the premises in order to connect the shop to another shop leased by them which belonged to another landlord. The tenants offered to reinstate and to give security. It was held that the proposed alterations were 'improvements' within the section, and that the consent had been unreasonably withheld. In *Haines* v. *Florensa* (1990) a loft conversion of the roof space included in the lease of a top-floor flat in a converted house was held to be an improvement within s.19(2) of the Act.

If the tenant feels that consent has been unreasonably withheld, then he may go ahead with the alterations, but if he does so, he takes the risk of a claim by the landlord for damages and forfeiture should the landlord be able to show that his refusal was in fact reasonable. An alternative course of action for the tenant is to apply to the court for a declaration that the landlord's consent has been unreasonably withheld, or for a ruling on any sum required by the landlord as security for the alterations.

A refusal to give any reason is in itself unreasonable. However, the landlord's reasons may relate to a variety of matters, including his own personal ones. Slesser L.J. in *Lambert* v. *F. W. Woolworth* said: 'Many considerations, aesthetic, historic or even personal may be relied upon as yielding reasonable grounds for refusing consent'. In *Iqbal* v. *Thakrar* (2004), the Court of Appeal took the view that the purpose of s.19(3), like s.19(1), is to protect the landlord's property interests, and that the same principles applicable to s.19(1) should therefore apply to determine what amounted to a reasonable reason for refusal of consent under s.19(3). In that case, the landlord had purchased the reversion of a building, the ground floor of which was let to a tenant who carried on a takeaway food business. He applied for consent to alterations to convert the premises to a restaurant, but the landlord wanted to convert the upper floors to residential flats and took the view that this would be disadvantageous to residential lettings. As with s.19(1), however, the Court of Appeal held that the test is a subjective one and the landlord can take into account his own personal reasons for refusal if these are to protect his business interests.[10] Moreover, the Landlord & Tenant Act 1988 does not apply to s.19((3), so that the burden of proof is on the tenant to show that the landlord will not be adversely affected by his planned alterations. The tenant had failed to do this as he had not ensured that alterations to load-bearing structures would be adequate, but had left it to the builder to decide what would be adequate.

10.5 Statutory Requirements Necessitating Alterations to the Premises

It should be noted that certain statutory requirements contained in Acts such as the Fire Precautions Act 1971, the Factories Act 1961, the Offices, Shops & Railway Premises Act 1963 and the Disability Discrimination Act 1995 Part III (in force on 1 October 2004) impose requirements for the types of premises to which they relate, and these override any covenant in a lease against alterations. The statutes may provide for a variation of the lease, or a requirement for consent to be given to any necessary alterations to comply with the statutes.

Notes

▶ **1** *Calabar (Woolwich) Ltd.* v. *Tesco Stores Ltd.* **[1977] 245 EG 479**

A lease to T Ltd. restricted the user of the premises to that of a supermarket and for the sale of a named range of articles ancillary thereto. The premises were used for the sale of freezers, which constituted fifteen per cent of the business carried on. It was held that 'supermarket' was a technical term and that goods sold were not to be restricted to portable ones.

▶ **2** *Basildon Development Corp.* v. *Mactro Ltd.* **[1986] 1 EGLR 137**

The plaintiffs were lessors of shops in a parade, the largest of which was let as a food and drink supermarket. The lease contained a covenant by the lessees to use the premises for this purpose and the sale of items 'incidental to this main use'. The plaintiffs were anxious to protect the business of the other shopkeepers and sought to restrict the sale of certain types of goods. On appeal, it was conceded by both parties that the relevant date for determining what a 'food and drink supermarket' might legitimately sell was the date of the lease. The Court of Appeal refrained from approving this as the sole test, however. Sir Denys Buckley indicated that he thought other factors might be relevant and O'Connor L.J. indicated that the size of the supermarket might be a factor as to what additional goods they might wish to sell.

▶ **3 S.19(3) Landlord & Tenant Act, 1927**

'In all leases whether made before or after the commencement of this Act containing a covenant condition or agreement against the alteration of the user of the demised premises, without licence or consent, such covenant condition or agreement shall, if the alteration does not involve any structural alteration of the premises, be deemed, notwithstanding any express provision to the contrary, to be subject to a proviso that no fine or sum of money in the nature of a fine, whether by way of increase of rent or otherwise, shall be payable for or in respect of such licence or consent; but this proviso does not preclude the right of the landlord to require payment of a reasonable sum in respect of any damage to or diminution in the value of the premises or any neighbouring premises belonging to him and of any legal or other expenses incurred in connection with such licence or consent. Where a dispute as to the reasonableness of any such sum has been determined by a court of competent jurisdiction, the landlord shall be bound to grant the licence or consent on payment of the sum so determined to be reasonable.'

▶ **4 *Anglia Building Society* v. *Sheffield City Council* [1983] 266 EG 311**

Sheffield City Council had let premises on a lease restricting user to a travel and employment bureau and theatre ticket agency. They refused consent to assign to a Building Society because they wanted the premises to be used as a retail shop rather than for service user which tended to depress rents. It was held that this was an unreasonable refusal, applying the test used in *Bromley Park Garden Estates* v. *Moss* (see 8.3.1) that it was unreasonable for the landlord to seek to obtain an advantage not originally reserved in the lease by refusal of consent.

▶ **5** The House of Lords decision in *Ashworth Frazer* overruled the previous decision in *Killick* v. *Covent Garden Property Co. Ltd.* [1973] 1 WLR 658. Lord Bingham said that a user clause in a lease is part of a contract to which the tenant has agreed, and it is reasonable for a landlord to seek to avoid an unwanted user and possible consequent litigation which may result from the assignment.

▶ **6 *Walker* v. *Arkay Caterers Ltd.*** [1997] EGCS 107, referring *to Holloway Brothers* v. *Hill* [1902] 2 Ch.612 and *Woodfall* on Landlord & Tenant.

▶ **7 *Crehan* v. *Intrepreneur Pub Co. (CPC)* [2006] 2 UKHL 38.**

▶ **8 S.19(2) Landlord & Tenant Act 1927** In all leases whether made before or after the commencement of this Act containing a covenant condition or agreement against the making of improvements without licence or consent, such covenant condition or agreement shall be deemed, notwithstanding any express condition to the contrary, to be subject to a proviso that such licence or consent is not to be unreasonably withheld; but this proviso does not preclude the right to require as a condition of such licence or consent the payment of a reasonable sum in respect of any damage to or diminution in the value of the premises or any neighbouring premises belonging to the landlord, and of any legal expenses properly incurred in connection with such licence or consent nor, in the case of an improvement which does not add to the letting value of the holding, does it preclude the right to require as a condition of such licence or consent, where such a requirement would be reasonable, an undertaking on the part of the tenant to reinstate the premises in the condition in which they were before the improvement was executed.'

▶ 9 In *Westminster CC v. HSBC Bank* [2003] EWHC 393, the tenant had made extensive alterations under various licences, all requiring reinstatement. The landlord served a notice of dilapidations 3 weeks before the end of the term. It was held (applying *Mannai Investment Co. Ltd. v. Eagle Star Life Assurance Co. Ltd.* [1997] 3 All ER 362) that even though the alterations made under licence were not specifically referred to, any reasonable person receiving the notice would have understood it to mean the reinstatements.

▶ 10 The Court of Appeal said that a refusal might not have been reasonable if the landlord had known of the tenant's proposed alterations when he purchased the reversion, or if the refusal would have caused undue hardship to the tenant, as in *International Drilling Fluids Ltd. v. Louisville Investments (Uxbridge) Ltd.* (see Chapter 8.3).

Summary

▶ A covenant restricting user of premises may be absolute or qualified.

▶ In the case of a qualified covenant, Section 19(3) Landlord & Tenant Act 1927 applies to prevent the landlord from requiring payment for consent to change of user, although not a 'reasonable sum' as security against damage to or diminution of the value of the premises or of neighbouring premises of the landlord's.

▶ A landlord's remedies for breach of a user covenant are damages or forfeiture if the lease contains a proviso for re-entry on breach of covenant, or in some cases an injunction.

▶ A tenant's user of premises should also comply with any restrictive covenants affecting the property (even on the freehold title) and planning permissions for the premises.

▶ Covenants against alterations may be absolute or qualified.

Summary cont'd

➧ If there is a qualified covenant requiring the landlord's consent to an alteration which is an 'improvement', s.19(2), Landlord & Tenant Act 1927 provides that the landlord's consent may not be unreasonably witheld, but the landlord may require a sum of money for the diminution in value of the demised premises or any neighbouring premises belonging to the landlord and in certain circumstances an undertaking to reinstate at the end of the lease.

➧ 'Improvement' is widely interpreted as any alteration which is of benefit to the tenant.

➧ In the case of any alterations which have to be made to premises to comply with statutory requirements, the relevant statute will provide for consent to alterations to be given, or variation of the lease to enable this if necessary.

Exercises

10.1 How does s.19(3) Landlord & Tenant Act 1927 affect a qualified covenant against a change of user?

10.2 What are a landlord's remedies for breach of a user covenant?

10.3 What forms may a covenant against alterations take?

10.4 To what alterations does s.19(2) Landlord & Tenant Act 1927 apply?

10.5 What conditions does s.19(2) allow the landlord to impose upon his consent?

Workshop

1 LK Ltd. granted a fourteen-year lease of large corner-site premises in a shopping precinct to TB Ltd. The lease contained a covenant by TB Ltd. to use the premises as a food supermarket and not to sell any goods other than those usually sold by a food supermarket and a proviso for re-entry on breach of covenant. TB Ltd. have started to sell plants and gardening equipment, including lawnmowers. LK Ltd. are concerned as there is a gardening shop nearby. Advise them.

Would your answer differ if the covenant had been not to sell any goods other than those usually sold by a food supermarket without the consent of the landlord?

2 Laura granted a fourteen-year lease of shop premises to Toby. The lease contained a covenant by Toby to use the premises only for the purpose of selling groceries and not to make any structural alterations to the premises without the landlord's consent. It also contained a proviso for re-entry on breach of covenant.

Toby has purchased the freehold of the adjoining premises next door and wishes to break through the wall in order to extend the shop. He proposes to increase the business to sell also meat and greengroceries and some electrical goods from the shop. Laura has refused consent to both the alterations and the change of user. Advise Toby.

Chapter 11

Reservation of rent and rent-review clauses

11.1   Nature of Rent and Entitlement to it

It has already been briefly mentioned in Chapter 6 that payment of rent is an obligation on the part of the tenant which will be implied into a lease even if there is no express reservation. Most leases will in fact expressly reserve a rent, however.

The correct legal name for rent reserved by a lease is 'rent service', as it is an incident of tenure, being payment to the landlord for the estate held by the tenant. It must be paid to the tenant's immediate landlord, and payment to someone else for a period of twelve years had the effect of barring the reversioner's right to recover the reversion under the Limitation Act 1980. Similarly, non-payment of rent for twelve years by a periodic tenant whose lease was not in writing, or a tenant at will after the termination of the tenancy at will, was effective to bar the landlord reversioner's right of recovery of the premises if he had taken no steps during that time to recover rent or possession. Under the Land Registration Act 2002, adverse possession is regarded as inconsistent with a registered title; a squatter who is acquiring a title may apply to register his title after ten years. The Registrar must then serve notice on the registered proprietor of the estate which the squatter is claiming, and on the proprietor of any superior registered estate, who may object. This effectively means that the Limitation Act 1980 will only apply to a lease not exceeding twenty-one years granted before 13 October 2003 which is an overriding interest, the title to which is not registered.

Although rent will usually be a money payment, it need not necessarily be so, and rent may be payable in kind[1] or, more usually, in service, where the tenancy is known as a 'service tenancy'. It may be that part of the rent will have been capitalised into a lump sum payment (technically known as a fine or premium) and that only a small amount of rent is payable in instalments for the duration of the lease. This is then usually referred to as a 'ground rent'. Sometimes a gratuitous occupation is granted and a merely nominal rent reserved to preserve the nature of a lease. This is known as a 'peppercorn rent'. Although traditionally payment of rent had to be proffered in coins of the realm, there are many other acceptable methods of payment nowadays. If payment by cheque has been the accepted method of payment, then acceptance of a cheque for arrears shortly before the hearing of a forfeiture action for arrears of rent will cause the hearing to be adjourned to see if the cheque clears on presentation, even though the ground for possession is mandatory (*Coltrane* v. *Day* (2003)).

Whatever the nature of the rent, it must be either quantified or ascertained, or capable of ascertainment. There is no objection, of course, to a provision that the rent should be fixed by a third party, and indeed this is a common form of agreement in rent review clauses, considered in 11.3 below. S.4 of the Landlord & Tenant Act 1985 requires a landlord to provide a residential tenant with a rent book.

Rent is payable in arrears unless the lease specifically provides (as most leases do) for payment in advance. In a periodic tenancy, the rent will be calculated and payable by the period. A fixed term tenancy or yearly tenancy will usually specify when the rent is payable – e.g. monthly in advance. Payments of rent are apportionable, so that rent is payable for any proportionate part of a term at the commencement or termination. In *Beer* v. *Bowden* (1981) the rent on the extension of a lease was to be 'such rent as shall thereupon be agreed between the landlord and the tenant'. The landlord and the tenant failed to reach any agreement and it was argued on behalf of the landlord that the lease was void for want of certainty. Although Foster J. found that there was a complete hiatus as to what rent was payable under the lease, he concluded that it was clear that some rent was intended, and therefore ordered that a rent should be fixed by the Master on hearing expert evidence for both sides. The approach is similar to that subsequently adopted by the House of Lords in *Sudbrook Trading Estate Ltd.* v. *Eggleton* (1983) in directing the court to hear evidence and determine a purchase price for the landlord's reversion in an option (see Chapter 13.4); and both cases illustrate the courts' reluctance to allow what they regard as essentially a valid contract to fail for uncertainty of a particular term.

Rent, being originally an incident of tenure, is payable for the land and not for the premises built upon it. If the premises are destroyed by fire, it follows that the rent is nevertheless still payable. Most leases provide that the landlord will insure the premises and will expend any insurance monies received on their destruction in rebuilding and reinstatement. This does not suspend the tenant's liability for rent, however, and in the absence of a clause in the lease to the contrary, the tenant would still be bound to pay the full rent. It is incumbent upon a tenant's legal adviser therefore to ensure that this eventuality is expressly provided for in the lease.

In the lease of a flat above the ground floor in a block, it is airspace rather than ground which is leased, and reinstatement is impossible without reinstatement of the floors beneath. Most leases will, of course, expressly provide for reinstatement, but it is not clear what the position would be in the absence of any such provision. It is possible that the courts might be prepared to regard such a lease as terminated by frustration. Frustration has always been recognised as a way in which a contract may be terminated, but the courts have been reluctant to apply it to leases, as leases were contracts creating an estate in land. In *National Carriers Ltd.* v. *Panalpina (Northern) Ltd.* (1981),[2] however, the House of Lords did accept that the doctrine might apply to a lease, and this would seem to be in keeping with the general tendency of the courts nowadays to emphasise the contractual nature of a lease rather than its tenurial nature.

Generally, money payable under a mistake of law was not recoverable, but the House of Lords' decision in *Kleinwort Benson Ltd.* v. *Lincoln C.C.*(1998) held that money paid under a void interest swap contract was recoverable. Following this decision, it has recently been held at first instance in *Nurdin &. Peacock plc* v. *D.B.Ramsden & Co. Ltd.* (1999) that rent paid under a mistake of law (namely, that it would be recoverable by the tenant if subsequently found not to be payable on a rent review) could be recovered. This represents an important departure from a well-established principle, which may conceivably give rise to a number of claims in the furture, which will not necessarily be statute barred as time only begins to run under the Limitation Act 1980 when a mistake is discovered.

11.1.1   Tenancy Deposit Schemes

Short leases of residential premises commonly require the tenant to pay a deposit as security against non-payment of rent or breaches of covenant. In some instances, tenants have had difficulty recovering such deposits from dishonest landlords. Sections 212–15 of the Housing Act 2004 (expected to be in force in April 2007) are designed to strengthen the position of a tenant who pays a security deposit under an assured shorthold tenancy. The landlord must enter into one of two schemes (schedule 10). Under the *insurance* scheme, the landlord retains the deposit but pays an insurance premium to the administrator of an authorised scheme and gives an undertaking to pay the administrator all or any part of the deposit if so directed. Under the *custodial* scheme, the landlord pays the deposit itself to a scheme administrator who, at the end of the lease, applies the deposit as the parties agree. Failing agreement, the deposit can be dealt with only under a court order.

11.2   Rent on Assignment of the Lease and the Reversion

In a lease created before 1996, a tenant who assigns his lease nevertheless may be liable to the landlord for payment of the rent as there is privity of contract between them (see Chapter 7.3.1). The rent will, of course, be primarily recoverable from the assignee, but this is an uncomfortable position for the original tenant if the assignee becomes insolvent, as an indemnity from his assignee will then be of little use.

Moreover, it was held that an original tenant could be liable not only for the rent reserved in the lease, but also for any increases under a rent review clause contained in the lease. In the case of *Centrovincial Estates plc* v. *Bulk Storage Ltd.* (1983) the original tenant paid a rent of £17,000 per annum. After assignment of the term, the assignees agreed a new rent with the landlords of £40,000, but subsequently failed to pay. The landlords were able to recover six months' arrears of the increased rent from the original tenant. The scope of this decision was happily restricted by the Court of Appeal decision in *Friends' Provident Life Office* v. *British Railways Board* (1995) which limits any increased liability of the tenant to that actually contemplated by the lease (see Chapter 7.3.1), The ratio of the decision was also given statutory force in s.18, Landlord & Tenant (Covenants) Act 1995, which applies to both pre-1996 and post 1995 leases.

In commercial leases a landlord will often require a guarantor for the rent, and a guarantor may remain similarly liable for rent, including any increase in rent, after the assignment of the lease by the tenant for whom he has stood as guarantor. The House of Lords decided in *P. & A. Swift Investments* v. *Combined English Stores Group plc* (1988) that a surety's covenant was one which had reference to the subject matter of the lease and that the benefit passed with the reversion without express assignment.. Moreover, the guarantor will remain liable even where the lease has been disclaimed by the tenant's trustee in bankruptcy (*Hindcastle* v. *Barbara Attenborough Associates Ltd.* see Chapter 7.3.4).

Since 1 January 1996, before a landlord can recover rent from a prior tenant, assignee or guarantor, he must first serve a notice on him under s.17 Landlord & Tenant (Covenants) Act 1995 within six months of the sum becoming due. Failure to serve such a notice within the six months will be a defence to the landlord's claim (see Chapter 7.5.1). This entitles the person served to request an overriding lease (see Chapter 7.5.3). As regards leases made on or after 1 January 1996, the landlord will usually only have recourse for unpaid rent against a tenant's immediate assignor under an authorised guarantee agreement (see Chapter 7.4.2).

On an assignment of the reversion, rent is payable to the landlord's assignee, but only after the tenant has received notice of such assignment (s.151(1) LPA 1925).

11.3 Rent-review Clauses

The courts' tendency to regard a lease basically as a contract between the parties rather than a form of tenure is reflected also in the courts' attitude to the payment of rent, and the modern approach is to regard this more as a contractual obligation than as an incident of tenure. During periods of high inflation, landlords have been understandably reluctant to grant long leases without some provision for increasing the rent after a certain time, and the courts have had to consider a number of rent-review clauses.

11.3.1   Procedure under a Rent-Review Clause

Such clauses were originally strictly construed against the landlord and time was of the essence in them, so that if the landlord failed to give notice within the stated time of a rent review, then he was unable to do so subsequently. Since the House of Lords case of *United Scientific Holdings* v. *Burnley Borough Council* (1978),[3] however, it will be presumed that time is not of the essence in such clauses, unless there are contra-indications from which it may be inferred that the parties intended time to be of the essence. In *Trustees of Henry Smith's Charity* v. *A.W.A.D.A* (1984), a rent-review clause specifying a very detailed procedure with time limits for each step was held to infer that time was to be of the essence .[4] If the rent review is tied in with a tenant's break clause allowing the tenant to terminate the lease within a certain time after review, then this will infer that time is of the essence in the rent review. In the Court of Appeal case of *Starmark Enterprises Ltd.* v. *CPL Distribution Ltd.* (2001), it was held (reversing the majority decision of the Court of Appeal in *Mecca Leisure Ltd.* v. *Renown* (1984)) that a deeming provision that the new rent should be that specified in a notice served by the landlord unless a counter-notice was served by the tenant within a specified time, was held to make time of the essence, and the tenant's counter-notice served after the specified time of one month was too late.[5] Obviously each rent-review clause will fall to be construed ultimately on its own wording, but the *Starmark* decision seems likely to encourage parties to argue against the presumption in *Burnley* wherever there is a possibility of a reference to a time limit being construed as making time of the essence.[6]

Even where it is clear that the presumption in *Burnley* that time is not of the essence applies, it is still open to either party to serve a notice on the other making time of the essence.

11.3.2   Formulae for Ascertaining Rent under a Rent-review Clause

Various formulae have been used in rent-review clauses for fixing a new rent and because a rent review will usually involve a large sum of money, they have frequently led to litigation. It is important therefore to define a method of rent review as precisely as possible. A rent-review clause will usually provide that the new rent shall be the best rent obtainable for the premises from a hypothetical willing tenant on the open market. The terms of the hypothetical lease are taken to be those of the actual lease under which the tenant holds unless there is a clear indication to the contrary; but it is recognised that this may operate unfairly. It would be unfair to a tenant, for instance, if improvements made by him were not to be disregarded as he would then be paying again for the benefit of the improvements in an increased rent; and it could be unfair to a landlord to assume only the particular user of the tenant when the user clause in the lease is wider than this. To deal with these possibilities, many rent-review clauses will include certain assumptions and disregards. Because of the considerable sum at stake on a rent review, the parties are often all too willing to argue for a favourable construction of a rent-review clause wherever there is any possible ambiguity, sometimes asserting quite fanciful interpretations of assumptions or disregards in the hypothetical lease. It must be emphasised that each individual clause is subject to its own construction, and that even a slight variation in wording may lead to a different construction. The courts have clearly indicated, however, that they will generally prefer an interpretation which is realistic and commercially viable to one which is purely hypothetical and unrelated to the actual circumstances of the case.[7]

Most rent-review clauses provide for resolving a difference between the landlord and the tenant by reference to an arbitrator or an expert. The functions of the two are different. An arbitrator hears evidence from both sides and adjudicates between them, whereas an expert applies his own experience and knowledge to fix what he considers to be an appropriate rent.

Although most rent-review clauses provide that the new rent shall be the rent fixed on review or the existing rent whichever is the higher, thus precluding the possibility of a downward rent review, if there is no such clause, then it is open to an arbitrator to reduce the rent on a rent review.

11.3.3   Assumptions and Disregards

For the reason mentioned above, most rent-review clauses will require a disregard of tenant's improvements, unless the improvements are made in pursuance of an obligation to the landlord for which the landlord may then have allowed the tenant consideration. If it is not specifically stated as a disregard, however, then the improvement must be taken into account on fixing the new rent.[8] It is usual also to provide for disregard of the tenant's goodwill and the tenant's occupation, assuming that the premises are to be let with vacant possession.

A requirement to have regard to all the terms of the tenancy 'other than as to rent' has given rise to disputes as to whether this includes a disregard of *all* provisions as to rent, including any future rent reviews, or whether it is intended to refer only to the amount of the rent written into the lease. In *British Gas Corporation* v. *Universities Superannuation Scheme Ltd.* (1986) a thirty-five-year lease provided for five rent reviews, one factor in the rent review being what the premises could be expected to be let for on an open market by a lease containing the same provisions 'other than as to yearly rent'. The arbitrator was directed by the court not to exclude the provisions for rent review from the hypothetical lease as it would give the landlord an advantage not necessarily intended. Sir Nicholas Browne-Wilkinson V.C. said that wherever possible an interpretation consistent with commercial efficacy, taking into account rent reviews, should be inferred. But in the later case of *Equity & Law Ltd Assurance Society plc.* v. *Bodfield Ltd.* (1987) the Court of Appeal emphasised that each clause should be construed on its merits, and that although commercial efficacy might tend towards a construction which would take account of rent reviews in a hypothetical lease, this could be negated by an express exclusion.

A landlord leasing premises to a new tenant will sometimes allow him a rent-free period for fitting out. It is common for a rent-review clause expressly to provide that rent is to be agreed on the assumption that any rent-free period has expired (which is essentially fair, as the tenant will have already fitted-out by the time of rent review). During the recession, however, rather than letting commercial premises at a lower rent (which would reduce the value of the landlord's reversion), landlords were sometimes prepared to offer a reduction in rent to a new tenant by allowing him a rent-free period at the commencement of the term, unrelated to fitting out. The landlord would, however, make up this loss by correspondingly increasing the rent payable over the rest of the term. Such higher rent is known as a 'headline rent', since it is higher than the obtainable open-market rent. A direction in a rent-review clause to assume that any rent-free period had by then expired could be construed to allow the landlord to argue for a rent review based on the headline rent rather than the market rent. The Court of Appeal heard four conjoined appeals on these grounds.[9] The commercially realistic approach of the Vice-Chancellor in *British Gas Corporation* was again adopted in these cases by Hoffmann L.J., who was able to find that, in all but one of them, the assumption of a rent-free period having expired (amounting to a reduction in rent) was not intended to allow the landlord to take advantage of fixing a new rent by reference to a headline rent. In *Broadgate Square plc.* v. *Lehman Brothers Ltd.* (1995), however, the open-market rent at review was to be that which would become payable *after the expiry* of a rent-free period. This wording clearly rebutted the presumption that the inducement of a rent-free period had already been enjoyed, and the reviewed rent was therefore held to be the headline rent.

A restriction on the user of premises in the lease may well operate to depress the rent which a landlord can obtain on review. In *Plinth Property Investments Ltd.* v. *Mott, May & Anderson* (1979) the lease stated that the rent review was to be on the basis of the terms of the lease granted, one of which was not to use the demised premises otherwise than as offices in connection with the lessee's business of consulting engineers. It was held that the arbitrator was right to take the restriction into account when fixing the new rent as the landlord could demand a considerable sum to waive it. A landlord may seek to lessen the effect of a user restriction by providing that for the purposes of rent review the hypothetical lease shall assume a different or wider user. The landlord's unilateral authorisation of uses which the tenant has not requested in order to justify an increase in rent will not be taken into account in a rent-review clause, however.[10] Nor will the courts take into account an actual illicit user of premises in contravention of planning permission, such as residential premises used partly for office purposes. If the user and assignment clause in the actual lease is totally restrictive however, then it may have to be completely disregarded for the purposes of the hypothetical lease. Thus in *Law Land Co. Ltd.* v. *Consumers' Association Ltd.* (1980) the rent review clause referred to a hypothetical tenant paying a market rent, but there was a clause restricting user to the Consumers' Association and associated organisations for office purposes. The user clause here was held not to affect the hypothetical tenant paying a market rent.

Nevertheless, the courts have intimated that the postulated hypothetical user should be taken to be the actual user so as to give commercial reality to the rent review unless there is a very clear indication to the contrary. In *Basingstoke & Deane B. C.* v. *Host Group Ltd.* (1988) the Council had leased a vacant site with use restricted to a public house. The Council reserved a ground rent which was to be reviewed on the basis of a vacant site (discounting the public house built on it at the tenant's expense) with no user restrictions. The Court of Appeal held that review of the ground rent should be as the parties had agreed as a vacant site valuation, but the restriction of user to a public house in the lease should be taken into account and there should not be an assumption that the site, being vacant, was available for any lawful use. Nicholls L.J. applied the dictum of Sir Nicholas Browne-Wilkinson V.C. in *British Gas Corporation* (*supra*) that the courts should favour a commercially realistic interpretation of assumptions in rent review clauses wherever possible.

In *Bovis Group Pension Fund Ltd.* v. *G. C. Flooring & Furnishing Ltd.* (1984) a rent-review clause directed the arbitrator to have regard to the use of the premises as offices although planning permission for this user had not yet been obtained. This was a clear and unequivocal agreement as to user for the purposes of rent review and it was held that the arbitrator must assume that planning permission had been granted and not determine the rent on the actual use of the premises at the time. In *Beegas Nominees Ltd.* v. *Decca Ltd.*

[2003] 33 EG 62, the demised premises were on a new business park. The rent-review clause required the arbitrator to fix the rent as if the premises were on two established business parks elsewhere. The tenant's argument that this was not in accordance with reality was rejected, as the direction was very specific and clearly contemplated that the business park would become well established in time.

The general trend in interpreting user covenants in rent-review clauses has been to accept a wide interpretation of the covenant not necessarily restricted by a requirement for the landlord's consent to any change of user[11] or a prohibition against assignment necessarily restricting user to a particular purpose.[12]

A case where a tenant argued unsuccessfully for a realistic interpretation of a rent-review clause which would have operated unfairly on the landlord was *Jefferies* v. *O'Neill* (1983). Solicitor tenants added to their own freehold premises by taking a lease of adjoining next-door premises at first-floor level, breaking through from their own premises for access. They argued that the rent-review clause should take account of the fact that a tenant could gain access only at first-floor level, and the premises could therefore be let only to them. The argument was rejected and the court decided that these circumstances should be disregarded in determining what rent a hypothetical 'willing tenant' would pay.

Where a rent-review clause directs an arbitrator to have regard to the length of the term of the lease, should the arbitrator regard the term of the lease as that originally granted, or should he regard it as the unexpired residue of that term as at the date of the rent review? It seems that this must again depend upon the construction of the particular clause in each case. Where possible, the courts will generally favour a realistic approach and regard the length of the hypothetical term as the unexpired residue of the actual term.[13] However an individual clause may lead to another construction.[14]

11.4   Mesne Profits

Where a tenant remains in possession after the termination of his lease (e.g. after a notice to quit has expired or a fixed-term tenancy has come to an end) the landlord may claim mesne profits. Mesne profits are a sum payable for the occupation and enjoyment of the premises, and will usually be the same amount as rent. It is important that a landlord should refer to any claim he has for such use and occupation as a claim for mesne profits, because a claim for rent may imply a further tenancy or waiver of any termination by forfeiture or notice to quit.

11.5   Landlord's Remedies for Non-payment of Rent

11.5.1   Distress

This is a very old remedy available to a landlord. It allows him to enter the demised premises and seize the tenant's goods with the ultimate object of selling them and recovering the arrears of rent from the proceeds of sale. He must, however, give the tenant five days after seizure before selling. The seizure, which is usually done by the bailiff, may be actual and the goods removed from the premises, or notional, where the goods are impounded but left upon the premises and the tenant is not allowed to interfere with them. In these circumstances, it has been held that the bailiff cannot forcibly enter the premises to remove the goods on a subsequent default by the tenant.[15]

Certain goods are exempt from a landlord's right to distrain. These are tenant's fixtures, clothing, bedding and tools of trade up to the value of £50, loose money and perishable goods.

There is protection available for goods belonging to third parties under s.4A Law of Distress Amendment Act 1908 and on hire purchase under the Consumer Credit Act 1974.

11.5.2   Forfeiture

Forfeiture is the much more usual remedy for non-payment of rent, provided that there is a forfeiture clause in the lease. Most leases include a proviso for re-entry on non-payment of rent or breach of any other covenant contained in the lease.

The procedure for forfeiture for non-payment of rent differs from forfeiture for breach of other covenants in that it is not necessary first to serve a notice under s.146 LPA 1925. For forfeiture for breach of any other covenant, the s.146 procedure must first be complied with.

Before the landlord may start proceedings for forfeiture for non-payment of rent, he must first make a formal demand for the rent, attending at the premises between sunrise and sunset to do so. Happily, most leases dispense with this requirement, providing for forfeiture for non-payment of rent 'whether formally demanded or not'. A formal demand is not necessary either if there is six months' rent in arrears and not sufficient distress upon the premises (s.210 Common Law Procedure Act 1852).

A landlord's right of forfeiture is waived and thereby lost if he or his agent does any act which recognises the continuance of the tenancy, such as demanding or accepting a payment of rent after he has commenced proceedings. He will, however, be able to claim mesne profits for the period of occupation between the commencement of forfeiture proceedings and the time when he actually gets possession of the premises.

Mesne profits are assessed on the market value of the premises, and are therefore usually the same sum as the rent would have been.

11.5.3   Relief Against Forfeiture

In the High Court   Where the Common Law Procedure Act 1852 applies and there is more than six months' rent in arrears, the tenant has an automatic right to relief against forfeiture if he pays all arrears and costs into Court at any time before judgment is given. Thereafter, he has an equitable right to relief, on payment of arrears and costs, within six months after the landlord's re-entry. Being equitable, the right is discretionary and will not be exercised if it would be unjust to do so – for example, if the landlord has re-let the premises to a third party. Where the Common Law Procedure Act does not apply, there is no time limit on the availability of the equitable relief, although as with all other equitable remedies, it will not be exercised if the tenant is guilty of an undue delay or it would be unfair to a third party.

In the County Court   Where there is a statutory tenancy under the Rent Acts, the landlord must also apply to the court to terminate this as well as forfeiting the contractual tenancy. The County Court has exclusive jurisdiction to terminate the statutory tenancy under s.98 Rent Act 1977, so that forfeiture proceedings for most statutory tenancies will be brought in the County Court to avoid duplicating proceedings.

Relief against forfeiture in the County Court is governed by s.138 County Courts Act 1984. Under this section, a tenant has an automatic right to relief against forfeiture if he pays arrears and costs into court up to five days before the return date for the summons for possession. If the tenant does not do this and the matter proceeds to trial, the court has a discretion as to when it orders possession, being not less than four weeks after the date of the order. The tenant will be granted relief if he pays all arrears and costs before the date fixed for possession, but thereafter he used to be 'barred from all relief' (s.138 County Courts Act). The Court of Appeal decided in *Di Palma* v. *Victoria Square Property Co. Ltd.* (1985) that there was no inherent jurisdiction in the High Court either to grant relief after the date for possession fixed by the County Court, as the words 'barred from all relief' included relief in the High Court as well as in the County Court. This was amended by s.55 Administration of Justice Act 1985, which added a new subsection to s.138 providing that the tenant has a right to relief against forfeiture within six months after the landlord re-enters.

11.5.4   Relief for Subtenants

A subtenant who derives his title from the lessee's lease will automatically lose any interest he has if that lease is forfeited. S.146(4) provides that a subtenant may apply to the court for relief in any proceedings for the forfeiture of the headlease, and the court has a discretion to vest a term not exceeding the term of the sublease directly in the subtenant. Relief under this subsection is also available to a mortgagee of the lease, whether the mortgage is by way of a sublease or a legal charge.[16]

The relief available to subtenants is discussed more fully in Chapter 15.5.2.

Notes

▶ **1** *Pitcher* v. *Tovey* **(1692) 4 Mod 71**

A lease reserved rent and twelve bottles of canary wine each year. It was held that the wine was recoverable by action as well as the rent.

▶ **2** *National Carriers Ltd.* v. *Panalpina (Northern) Ltd.* **[1981] AC 675**

A warehouse was leased for ten years from 1974 and the lessee covenanted to use the premises only as a warehouse. In 1979, the street was closed by the local authority for demolition of a dangerous building opposite, making access to the warehouse impossible and thereby rendering it useless. The anticipated time for this was twenty months. It was held by the House of Lords that the doctrine of frustration could apply to leases as to any other contract. In this case, however, the lease was not terminated by frustration, as the time of closure of the street was only a short part of the period of the lease and not enough to frustrate it.

▶ **3** *United Scientific Holdings* v. *Burnley BC* **[1978] AC 904**

There is a presumption that the time stated in a rent review clause is not of the essence of the clause. A lease provided that the landlord should give notice of a rent review and a new rent should be agreed upon or the matter should go to arbitration during the last year of a ten-year period. There was no agreement or arbitration within the time. It was held that this was not fatal as time was not of the essence, and a new rent should be determined and backdated to the review date.

▶ **4** *Trustees of Henry Smith's Charity* v. *A.W.A.D.A. Trading & Promotion Services Ltd.* **(1984) 47 P&CR 607**

A lease set out a clear timetable for a sequence of steps in the process for a rent review. On service of notice of review by the landlord, a counter-notice was to be served by the tenant within one month. If the rent was not agreed within a further month, then the landlord was to appoint a surveyor. If no agreement or surveyor was appointed after two months from counter-notice, then rent would be that specified in the counter-notice. It was held that the landlord was out of time as the parties had set out a clear procedure which did make time of the essence.

Also, in *Mammoth Greeting Cards Ltd.* v. *Agra Ltd.* **[1990] 29 EG 45**

A rent-review clause provided that if the tenant failed to serve a counter-notice on the landlord within two months, then the rent was to be 'conclusively' fixed as in the landlord's notice. It was held that the finality of the wording made time of the essence and the rent stipulated in the landlord's notice was binding.

▶ 5 **Starmark Enterprises Ltd. v. CPL Distribution Ltd. [2002] 4 All ER 264**

A rent-review clause provided that the tenant should be 'deemed' to have agreed to pay the new rent specified in the notice served on him by the landlord, unless the tenant served a counter-notice within one month of the receipt of the landlord's notice. The landlord's notice was served on 30 March 1999, but the tenant's counter-notice was not served until 16 June 1999. The Court of Appeal held that an express deeming provision was sufficient to displace the presumption that time was not of the essence, and the tenant's notice was therefore out of time.

▶ 6 In *First Property Growth Partnership LP v. Royal & Sun Alliance Property Services* [2003] 1 Au ER 533 (CA), a rent-review clause provided that a landlord could serve a rent notice not more than twelve months before the rent review date 'but not at any other time'. This was held to make time of the essence, and a notice served after the rent-review date was too late.

▶ 7 E.g. Browne-Wilkinson V.C. in *British Gas Corporation v. Universities Superannuation Scheme Ltd.* [1986] 1 EGLR 120, and Hoffmann L.J. in *Broadgate Square plc v. Lehman Brothers Ltd.* [1995] 1 EGLR 97

▶ 8 *Ponsford v. H.M.S. Aerosols Ltd.* [1979] AC 63

A rent-review clause provided for a reasonable rent to be assessed. The premises were burned down and rebuilt. It was held that a reasonable rent was the rent for the premises as rebuilt and improved, even though the tenant had paid for the improvements.

▶ 9 *Co-operative Wholesale Society Ltd. v. National Westminster Bank plc.; Scottish Amicable Life Assurance Society v. Middleton Potts & Co.; Broadgate Square plc v. Lehman Brothers Ltd.; Prudential Nominees Ltd. v. Greenham Trading Ltd.,* all at [1995] 1 EGLR 97.

▶ 10 *C. & A. Pensions Trustees Ltd. v. British Vito Investments Ltd.* [1984] 272 EG 63

▶ 11 *Mars Security Ltd. v. O'Brien* [1991] 2 EGLR 281

Limitation of change of user only with the landlord's consent did not include that possibility being taken into account in rent review.

▶ 12 *Post Office Counters Ltd. v. Harlow DC* [1991] 2 EGLR 121

The lease included an absolute covenant against assignment and a clause limiting user to that of a branch Post Office, but required rent review on the basis of a hypothetical letting. The court concluded that the arbitrator's 'notional' redrafting on this basis to fix a new rent for a hypothetical tenant, not necessarily using the premises as a branch Post Office, was correct.

▶ 13 *Lynnethorpe Enterprises Ltd. v. Sidney Smith (Chelsea) Ltd.* [1990] 2 EGLR 131.

A hypothetical tenancy for a 'term of years equivalent to the said term' was held to be the term running from the date of the original lease and not the rent-review date.

▶ **14** In *Canary Wharf Investments (Three) v. Telegraph Group Ltd.* [2003] 3 EGLR 31, the rent-review clause required the parties to assume, for the grant of the hypothetical lease, the grant of a lease for the actual term of twenty-five years. Neuberger J. held that the clear intention of the assumption was that the tewnty-five-year term should run from the review date, and not from the date of the original grant.

▶ **15** *Khazanchi v. Faircharm Investment Ltd.* (1998) EGCS 46.

▶ **16** *Grand Junction Co. Ltd. v. Bates* [1954] 2 All ER 385

A tenant mortgaged his leasehold interest by way of legal charge. It was held that the mortgagee had all the same rights as a mortgagee by way of subdemise, including the right to relief against forfeiture of the headlease under s.146(4) LPA 1925.

Summary

▶ Rent will usually be a money payment but may be payable in kind. It is payable for the land, and may still be payable even if the premises are destroyed.

▶ The original tenant of a lease made before 1 Janaury 1996 remains liable to the original landlord for rent even after assignment of the lease.

▶ Time is not of the essence in rent-review clauses, unless the parties make it so.

▶ The interpretation of rent-review clauses must depend upon the construction of the particular clause, but generally a user clause in a lease will be a relevant factor in determining a new rent,

▶ The same applies to clauses which direct an arbitrator to have regard to the terms of the lease 'other than as to rent'. Commercial practice would suggest that the rent-review clause is taken into consideration when determining a new rent under such a clause, but the construction of the clause may preclude this.

▶ A landlord may claim mesne profits for the use and occupation of premises from a tenant who remains in possession after a lease has been terminated.

▶ A landlord may distrain against certain goods of the tenant's on the premises for unpaid rent.

▶ A landlord may take forfeiture proceedings for non-payment of the rent provided there is a forfeiture clause in the lease. He must first make a formal demand for rent unless the lease dispenses with the necessity for this or the Common Law Procedure Act 1852 applies,

▶ In the High Court, the tenant has an automatic right to relief against forfeiture in certain circumstances and an equitable right thereafter.

▶ In the County Court, the tenant has an automatic right to relief against forfeiture under s.138 County Courts Act 1984 if he pays rent and costs into

Summary cont'd

court up to five days before the hearing date, and a discretionary right up to six months after re-entry by the landlord.

▶ A subtenant may apply for relief against forfeiture of the headlease during the forfeiture proceedings under s.146(4) LPA 1925.

Exercises

11.1 What provision with regard to rent, in the event of the premises being destroyed by fire, would you advise a tenant to include in his lease?

11.2 What provision with regard to a rent-review clause and repairs would you advise a tenant to include in his lease?

11.3 Should a covenant restricting user affect the decision of an arbitrator appointed to determine a rent review?

11.4 What is the effect of a direction to an arbitrator on rent review to have regard to the terms of the lease 'other than rent'?

11.5 Against what goods may a landlord distrain for unpaid rent?

11.6 What is the procedure for forfeiture for non-payment of rent, and how does it differ from forfeiture for breach of any other covenant?

11.7 What relief against forfeiture for non-payment of rent is available to a tenant, (a) in the County Court and (b) in the High Court?

Workshop

1 In 2001 Paul leased shop premises to John for twenty years with a provision that the rent should be reviewed every four years upon the landlord giving notice of his request for a review six months before the end of the four-year period. In 2003 John assigned the lease to Jake who has carried out extensive improvements to the premises. At the beginning of 2006, the landlord gave notice of a rent review to Jake and proposes to take into account the improvements made by Jake in assessing the new rent. Advise Jake.

2 Annie is the assignee of a lease made nine years ago for a term of twenty-five years. The lease provides for a rent review every five years on the assumption that the lease is for a term of twenty-five years and that the user is that of a restaurant. The user was changed with the landlord's consent to that of a takeaway food shop some four years ago. Advise Annie:

   (i) as to when the twenty-five year hypothetical term should be deemed to start for the purposes of the rent review

   (ii) as to the user which should be applicable to the premises for the purposes of rent review.

Chapter 12

Service charges and insurance

12.1 What is Covered by a Service Charge?

It is quite usual for demised premises to be part of a larger building, such as a flat in a block, a shop in a shopping precinct, or an industrial unit on an industrial estate. In these circumstances, ownership of the common parts will remain with the freeholder, who may be the original developer or an assignee from him. He will be responsible for repairs and maintenance of the common parts, and in some cases, the provision of services for the tenants.

The extent of the landlord's liability for repairs will depend upon the terms of the leases. For example, in the leases of offices in an office block, has the landlord included in the leases the outside walls, ceilings and floors, or has he retained the structure of the building? If they are included in the demise to the tenant, then there is likely to be a repairing covenant by the tenant making him liable for their repair. If, however, they are part of the structure which the landlord undertakes to repair along with the retained common parts, then he will want to recover the cost of this from the tenant as part of a service charge.

The common parts of any building, such as stairs and landings, will require cleaning and lighting. The leases of residential flats usually designate a dustbin area and provide for maintenance of drives and gardens; the malls and lifts in a shopping centre have to be cleaned and maintained, as do the roads and signs on an industrial estate. In the case of a block of flats or offices, the landlord may supply additional services, such as a hot water boiler and central heating. The landlord will deal with all these matters and then recover the cost from the tenants as part of a service charge.

As regards commercial leases, an IRCS Code of Practice, entitled *Service Charges in Commercial Property*, is to come into force on 1 April 2007. A Joint Sub-Committee of the Law Society and the Royal Institution of Chartered Surveyors on Model Clauses in commercial leases has suggested that provisions in leases for service charges should be made as flexible as possible to allow for additional units (for example, if an office is split into two), and new services, such as a CCTV system introduced for security.

As regards residential leases, the control of service charges is highly regulated by ss.18–30, Landlord & Tenant Act 1985, as amended by the Landlord & Tenant Act 1987 and the Commonhold & Leasehold Reform Act 2002. Service charges are defined by s.18(1)(a) of the 1985 Act as 'amounts payable directly or indirectly for services, repairs, maintenance, improvements or insurance or the landlord's costs of management'. The procedures for the control of these service charges is dealt with more fully in Chapter 17.2.

12.2   Apportionment of Service Charges

Various formulae are used for the apportionment of service charges between tenants. The most usual and straightforward ones are a contribution based on the area of the demised premises or on the rateable value. Whilst this may be suitable for offices and flats, it may not be as suitable for shops or industrial units. On an industrial estate, one tenant may have a much greater use of the services than another, and if insurance is to be effected by a block policy, one tenant may have much higher insurance risks than another. All these matters will require consideration on any apportionment. In the event of there being no specification as to what the service charge should be, it was held in *Finch* v. *Rodriguez* (1976) that it must be a fair and reasonable charge for reasonable services. The House of Lords has held[1] that any variation of a service charge in a new lease under the Landlord & Tenant Act 1954, Part II, must also be fair and reasonable, and the burden of showing that it is so lies with the party seeking the variation.

With residential flats, the landlord is required to give the tenants certified accounts for each year, showing how the service charge has been spent, and to produce receipts for inspection by the tenants if required. Any dispute with regard to service charges can be referred to a Leasehold Valuation Tribunal. The landlord of commercial premises will similarly produce accounts (although the accounting period may be for less than a year) and there should be a provision in the lease for dispute resolution by a third party. In both cases, the service charge is usually estimated and payable for a year in advance and then an adjustment made for the amount actually spent at the end of the year (or other accounting period) on the next statement of account.

12.3   Reserve Fund for Large Expenditures

To avoid presenting the tenants with a particularly high bill for a year when a major repair or redecoration is carried out, the landlord will usually include in the service charge a sum to go into a reserve account to be kept for such expenditures. The reserve fund should be kept in a separate account and held by the landlord as trustee for the tenants. This means that the fund will not be available for distribution to the landlord's creditors in the event of his insolvency. Even if no trust has been formally set up, it may be possible to imply one if the fund is held in a separate account.[2] In residential tenancies, s.42, Landlord & Tenant Act 1985 requires any service charges held by a landlord to be held on trust for the tenants, and the landlord must show on each statement of account the amount held for each tenant. Should the tenant assign his lease, then any such sum is credited to the assignee who should repay the tenant, but this is a matter for the tenant to negotiate with his assignee.

12.4 Recovery of Service Charges

Service charges are usually reserved as additional rent payable under the lease. This is to enable the landlord to distrain or to forfeit the lease for non-payment without having to follow the forfeiture procedure under s.146, LPA1925. The landlord may use the forfeiture procedure for non-payment of the rent instead (see Chapter 15.5). A landlord cannot distrain for a service charge, however, if any part of it is disputed.[3]

12.5 Liability to Insure and Reinstate

Any formal lease will usually deal specifically with requirements to insure the buildings. In the case of flats or units in a larger building, insurance of the whole building is usually effected by the landlord, who can choose the insurance company,[4] and the lease will charge each lessee with a proportion of the insurance premium, often based on the proportionate rateable values of the flats in the building. This is often made payable as part of the service charge or an additional rent which gives the landlord the remedies available for recovery of rent in default of payment. The tenant will usually covenant not to do anything which vitiates the insurance policy. In commercial leases, one tenant may carry more risk than others – for example, due to an industrial process – and the apportionment of the insurance premiums should obviously reflect this. It may therefore be preferable to make insurance premiums recoverable separately from service charges. The Code of Practice[5] for commercial leases recommends that a tenant who occupies a whole building should be allowed to choose his own insurance company, and that any insurance by a landlord should be on 'competitive terms'.

A provision that the landlord will expend any insurance monies on rebuilding or reinstating the premises should they be destroyed should also be included. In the absence of any such provision, the landlord is not obliged to do so, unless there is an element of insurance premium paid by the tenant in his rent, as in *Mumford Hotels Ltd.* v. *Wheler* (1964).[6] In *Vural* v.

Security Archives (1990) it was held that reinstatement need not be an exact replacement but must not be appreciably less in standard. The landlord was obliged to replace a wooden parquet floor with a similar floor and not with linoleum. The Code of Practice for commercial leases points out that the effect of this decision may be too restrictive in not allowing for more modern replacements available due to technological advancements, and suggests that a reinstatement clause should be worded to allow for modernisations whilst allowing the tenant some discount if appropriate.

The tenant is able to demand production of the last receipt for premiums and a copy of the policy, and to require that his insurable interest be noted on the policy.

Where the tenant is required to insure, the landlord may specify the insurance company. If the tenant is taking a mortgage to buy the property, this may result in the property being insured twice over as the mortgagees may insist upon insuring themselves with another company.

12.6   Claims to Insurance Monies

If the premises are not reinstated for any reason, then it will have to be decided to whom the insurance monies belong. In *Re King* (1963), premises were insured by the lessee against fire at her expense in the joint names of herself and the landlord. In 1944 the premises were destroyed by fire but could not be rebuilt because it was wartime. The Council then compulsorily purchased the site and built a housing estate. It was held that the insurance monies belonged to the tenant as she had paid the premiums. The joint names in which the monies had been held were merely to ensure that the monies were expended on rebuilding. Diplock L.J. said that the measure of the tenant's loss is the full value of the premises and not his own leasehold interest. Denning L.J. dissenting, however, said that insurance in joint names insured the interests of both the landlord and the tenant and the monies should therefore be divided between them according to their interests.

It is possible, in view of the more recent case of *Beacon Carpets Ltd.* v. *Kirby* (1984), that Denning L.J.'s dissenting judgment may now prevail. In that case, a lease contained a covenant by the landlord to insure a warehouse in the joint names of the landlord and the tenant and to expend the insurance monies on reinstating the premises should they be destroyed. The tenants were required to pay the insurance premiums as additional rent. The sum insured was not enough to rebuild after the premises had been destroyed by fire. The landlord obtained planning permission for a smaller building, but the tenants said they did not wish to re-occupy this. The site was therefore left vacant and the insurance monies held in a joint account. It was held that the lease contemplated that the insurance policy should be for the benefit of both parties, and the insurance monies should therefore belong to the parties according to their interests.

Notes

▶ 1 *O'May v. City of London Real Property Co. Ltd.* [1983] 2 AC 726

▶ 2 *Re Chelsea Cloisters Ltd.* (1981) 41 P & CR 98

▶ 3 *Concorde Graphics Ltd. v. Andromeda Investments SA* [1983] 1 EGLR 53

The service charge must be agreed or 'otherwise ascertained' (which requires a determination by someone other than the landlord's surveyor) for the landlord to distrain.

▶ 4 *Berrycroft Management Co. Ltd. v. Sinclair Gardens (Kensington) Ltd.* [1996] EGCS 143

The landlord has an unrestricted right to choose the insurer for a building, and the management company and tenants are protected by the requirement that the landlord should insure with a company of repute.

▶ 5 See Chapter 8, Note 9.

▶ 6 *Mumford Hotels Ltd. v. Wheler* [1964] Ch 117

A lease provided that the tenant should pay insurance premiums as additional rent but did not include any covenant by the landlord to reinstate the building in the event of its being destroyed. It was held that the landlord must use the insurance monies to reinstate the building if required to do so by the tenant. The relevant question was not whether any such covenant was implied into the lease, but whether the landlord should be treated as having insured for her own and the tenant's benefit, or purely for her own benefit.

Summary

▶ Where demised premises are part of a building or an estate, the landlord will retain ownership of the common parts and will charge the tenants with a proportionate part of the maintenance and upkeep as part of a service charge.

▶ There are a number of different ways of apportioning service charges, the most usual being according to the rateable value or the area of the demised premises.

▶ The landlord must produce certified accounts of his expenditure each year, and in residential tenancies, comply with the statutory regulations for the service of notices to be served with the accounts.

▶ The landlord will usually include in each year's service charges a sum towards capital replacement of equipment or expensive repairs. These sums should be held by the landlord in a separate account on trust for the tenants.

Summary cont'd

- A service charge is usually reserved as an additional rent.

- The landlord will insure a demised building or precinct which consists of different demised units, but the tenants' interests should be noted on the insurance policy. The tenants can demand to see the policy and the receipt for the last insurance premium.

- A lease should specifically provide that the landlord will reinstate the premises in the event of their destruction by an insured risk. If it does not, the landlord is not obliged to do so unless the terms of the lease imply that insurance has been effected at the tenant's expense for the benefit of both landlord and tenant.

- If the premises cannot be reinstated, it is possible that the insurance monies will be held to belong to the tenant alone (*Re King* (1963)), but it may be that they will belong to the landlord and the tenant according to their interests.

Exercises

12.1 What might a service charge cover on (a) a domestic flat in a block of flats and (b) an industrial unit on an industrial estate?

12.2 Why might an additional method of apportioning insurance premiums separately from service charges be used for industrial units but not for residential flats?

12.3 What can a residential tenant do about a service charge which he believes to be excessive?

12.4 How should a landlord deal with any reserve fund which he holds for future service charges?

12.5 Why is a service charge usually reserved as an additional rent in a lease?

12.6 What provision is usually made for the insurance of a flat in a block of flats?

12.7 To ensure that insurance monies are spent in reinstating a building which is destroyed by an insured risk, what covenant by the landlord should be included in the lease?

12.8 To whom do insurance monies belong if the building cannot be reinstated for any reason?

Workshop

Ravinder is the landlord of a block of light industrial units, two of which are let on fifteen-year leases to Tom and Josh. Under the terms of all the leases, Ravinder insures the block of units and recovers the insurance premiums from the tenants as part of the service charges.

Two months ago, the units were destroyed by fire. Advise on the following situations:

(i) Tom would like his unit rebuilt with a reinforced floor and a different better-quality floor covering.

(ii) Josh is refusing to pay rent while his unit is unusable.

(iii) It has been discovered that the cause of the fire was a soldering accident due to the negligence of an employee of one of the tenants.

Chapter 13

Options to renew the lease, break clauses and options to purchase the reversion

13.1 Option to Renew the Lease

A lease will sometimes contain an option for the lessee to renew it for a further term. The lessee will not be able to take advantage of the option unless he has complied strictly with all the covenants and conditions in the lease. In *West Country Cleaners* v. *Saly* (1966) the tenants were given an option to renew the lease provided there had been due observance and performance of all the covenants in the lease. The lease contained a covenant to paint, paper and whitewash every third year. The tenant did not comply strictly with the covenant although the premises were well kept and the landlord, who often visited, never complained. It was held nevertheless that the landlord's silence did not amount to a waiver of the breach of the covenant, that the option to renew the lease was a privilege and the tenant was disqualified from exercising it by reason of the breach of the covenant, even though it was a trivial breach.

The option to renew the lease is an agreement which touches and concerns the land so that, in a pre-1996 lease, the benefit passes to an assignee of the lease under the rule in *Spencer's Case* and the burden to an assignee of the reversion under s.142 LPA 1925. In a post-1995 lease, the benefit and burden would also pass under the Landlord & Tenant (Covenants) Act 1995 (see Chapter 7.4.1). To be binding on an assignee of the reversion, however, the option also requires registration as a class C(iv) land charge in unregistered title. In registered title, it will be binding if it is noted on the register as a minor interest, or will be binding as an overriding interest if the lessee is in actual occupation under Schedule 3, para.2, LRA 2002 in the same way as an option to purchase the reversion.[1] Given that the new stamp duty land tax (SDLT) will tax the total rent payable under a lease, causing a substantial increase in duty payable on longer commercial leases, it is possible that there will be a trend towards granting shorter leases with an option for the tenant to renew.

13.2 Provision for Rent under New Lease

Any such option will usually also provide for a new rent to be fixed. In *Lear* v. *Blizzard* (1983) the court decided that improvements made by either party should be taken into account in fixing a new rent.[2]

In *Newman* v. *Dorrington Developments Ltd.* (1975) the parties agreed that an arbitrator should determine a new rent which should be a 'commercial yearly rack rent'. Because s.46 Rent Act 1968 did not permit scarcity value to be taken into account when determining the rent limit, the arbitrator's valuation produced a rent which was higher than the permissible rent under the Rent Acts. It was held that as the landlord was affected by the legislation, the rack rent was subject to the limit which the Acts imposed. This was then the best rent obtainable, and it did not invalidate the option.

13.3 Break Clauses

A lease may contain a proviso that either party may determine it after a certain period. For example, a twenty-one-year lease may provide for this after seven years and fourteen years. The right to terminate is usually exercisable by notice. It may also be made dependent upon the tenant's performing all covenants and paying all rent due.

The House of Lords decision in *Mannai Investment Co. Ltd.* v. *Eagle Star Life Assurance Co. Ltd.* (1997) considered whether a six months' notice to terminate a lease 'on the third anniversary' of the commencement of the term was good when the six months' notice was to terminate on 12 January 1995 and the term had commenced on 13 January 1992. Reversing the Court of Appeal decision by a majority of three to two, the Lords took the view that an objective test should be applied to notices such as break notices, namely, would a reasonable recipient have understood the notice in its context and been left in no doubt as to its intention? The decision overrules the requirement for technical accuracy in such notices established in *Hankey* v. *Clavering* (1942) and was intended as a guidance to the courts in determining the validity of such notices in future.[3]

The benefit and burden of a break clause will generally pass with the term and with the reversion, but its wording may make it specifically exercisable by the original tenant only (see *Olympia & York Canary Wharf Ltd.* v. *Oil Property Investment Ltd.* and other cases in Chapter 8.3.1).

If the tenant is a secure tenant under statute, the effect of a landlord's serving notice under a break clause is to terminate the contractual tenancy but not any statutory-protected tenancy. In times of recession, a tenant might well consider that the rent he is paying under his lease is higher than the premises' current market rent. If a business tenant has the benefit of a break clause, he could serve a contractual notice to break; but this would terminate his basic rights to a continuation tenancy and to a new lease under the Landlord & Tenant Act 1954. In *Garston* v. *Scottish Widows Fund* (1996) the tenant, instead of serving a valid break notice, merely served a s.26 request for a new tenancy. The tenant argued that, under the 1954 Act, it was entitled to serve such a request as the tenancy 'could be brought to an end by notice to quit given by the tenant' (s.26(2)), and that a break notice ranked as a notice to quit for this purpose (s.69(1)). The court rejected this argument: but the reasoning is not convincing, and the point cannot yet be regarded as settled.

13.4 Options to Purchase the Reversion

A lease may contain an option for the lessee to purchase the landlord's freehold reversion. To be valid, the option should specify clearly how a price for this is to be determined. In *Sudbrook Trading Estate Ltd.* v. *Eggleton* (1983) the price for the reversion was to be agreed by two valuers appointed by the landlord and the tenant, and if they failed to reach agreement, by an umpire appointed by them. The landlords refused to appoint a valuer. The House of Lords took the robust view that the court itself could hear evidence and decide upon a reasonable price, either because the parties had waived their contractual rights to do so (per Lord Diplock) or because the actual valuation was a subsidiary part of the agreement and should not be allowed to defeat it (per Lord Fraser).

An option to purchase the reversion is not an agreement which runs with the land under a pre-1996 lease. It may not be a purely personal covenant so that the benefit and burden will pass under the Landlord & Tenant (Covenants) Act 1995 in a post-1995 lease (see Chapter 7). Even in a pre-1996 lease, such an option was held to have been assigned along with the term of the lease in *Griffith* v. *Pelton* (1958).[4] In *Re Button's Lease* (1964) it was said that such an option is a form of property which may be assigned by the tenant provided that it is not made personally exercisable by him alone, and could possibly be assigned separately from the lease. S.9(1) of the Perpetuities & Accumulations Act 1964 provides that options exercisable during the period of the lease and within one year after its termination will not be void under the rule against perpetuities, which is a rule against the remoteness of vesting of future interests, provided that they are exercisable only by the lessee or his successors in title.

In order to bind a purchaser for money or money's worth of the freehold reversion, an option to purchase must be registered as a class C(iv) land charge in unregistered title, and even actual notice of it will not make it binding if it has not been registered.[5] In registered title, it will be binding if it is either noted on the register as a minor interest or takes effect as an overriding interest under Schedule 3, para. 2, LRA 2002, where the tenant is in occupation.[1] In *Ferrishurst Ltd.* v. *Wallcite Ltd.* (1998), a sublease of part only of demised premises contained an option for the sublessee to purchase the leasehold reversion on the whole of the demised premises. It was held to be binding as an overriding interest under s.70(1)(g), Land Registration Act 1925, against a purchaser of the leasehold reversion as regards the whole of the property contained in the lease and not merely the part occupied by the sublessee. This decision has been reversed, however, by the wording of Schedule 3, para. 2, Land Registration Act 2002, which replaces s.70(1)(g), and which limits the overriding interest to the land actually occupied.

Notes

▶ **1** *Webb* v. *Pollmount Ltd.* **[1966] Ch 584**

A lease contained an option for the lessee to purchase the reversion. The reversion was conveyed by the landlord to the defendant. The plaintiff lessee sought to exercise the option. It was held that the interest created by the option was one capable of subsisting through different ownerships, and was therefore an overriding interest under s.70(1)(g) of the Land Registration Act 1925 (now replaced by Schedule 3, para. 2, Land Registration Act 2002) and binding on the defendant.

▶ **2** *Lear* v. *Blizzard* **[1983] 3 All ER 612**

A tenancy of a garage contained a covenant not to make alterations without the landlord's consent. The tenant built a tune-up bay, carwash and carport, to which the landlord subsequently consented. Both the lease and the reversion were assigned, and the assignee of the lease subsequently exercised an option to renew it. The option provided that a new rent was to be fixed by an arbitrator. It was held that the arbitrator should take into account the improvements made by the tenant.

▶ **3** The application of such a test is necessarily uncertain as it depends in each case upon an objective assessment of the facts and so is open to argument. A tenant used the principle successfully in *Peer Freeholds Ltd.* v. *Clean Wash International Ltd.* [2005] EWHC 179(Ch.) where the date stated in a letter to the landlord, to be treated as notice to break, was the rent review date in August instead of the break date in November. In the case of *Akici v. L.R. Butlin Ltd.* (2006) Neuberger L.J. accepted that the principle could apply to a notice of breach of covenant under s.146(1), Law of Property Act 1925, although it did not cure the particular fault in the notice in that case.

▶ **4** *Griffith* v. *Pelton* **[1958] Ch 205**

See section 7.3.2.

▶ **5** *Midland Bank Trust Co. Ltd.* v. *Green* **[1981] AC 513**

The tenant of a farm was the son of the freeholder and the lease contained an option to purchase the reversion. This had not been registered as an estate contract under the Land Charges Act 1972. The father conveyed the farm, which was worth about £40,000, to the mother for £500 with the express intention of defeating the son's option to purchase. It was held that the mother was a purchaser for money or money's worth and the purchase by her defeated the option, notwithstanding that she had actual knowledge of it.

Summary

▶ An option to renew the lease and a break clause are agreements which touch and concern the land, the benefit and burden of which pass to an assignee of the lease or the reversion. To bind an assignee of the reversion, an option to renew the lease must also be registered as a Class C(iv) land charge (an estate contract) in unregistered land or a minor interest in registered land. In registered land it may, however, be an overriding interest under Schedule 3, para. 2, Land Registration Act 2002.

▶ An option to purchase the reversion is a personal covenant but the benefit may pass to an assignee of the lease or possibly even be assigned separately. It will bind an assignee of the reversion only if registered in the same way as an option to renew the lease, or may be an overriding interest in registered title under Schedule 3, para. 2 LRA 2002

▶ A break clause may be exercisable by either the landlord or the tenant after a certain period during the term of a lease. Time is of the essence in giving notice of an intention to exercise it.

Exercises

13.1 What is

(a) A break clause?
(b) An option to renew the lease?
(c) An option to purchase the reversion?

13.2 When may a landlord refuse to allow a tenant to exercise a right to terminate a lease under a break clause?

13.3 In what circumstances will (b) and (c) be exercisable against an assignee of the reversion?

Workshop

1 Patsy leased a flat to Ameet for fourteen years from 1 January. The lease contained an option for either party to terminate it after seven years on giving six months' written notice to the other. It also contained an option for the tenant to purchase the reversion. Last year, Patsy assigned the reversion to Rita and Ameet assigned the lease to Tim.

It is now August in the seventh year of the lease and Rita wishes to terminate it. Advise her.

Tim wishes to purchase the reversion. Advise him.

Chapter 14

Title to leasehold property and enforceability of a lease against a purchaser of the freehold reversion

14.1 Registered and Unregistered Title

As most readers will be aware, the 1925 property legislation was intended to make radical changes in the process of conveyancing. Its main purpose was to simplify the whole procedure and, to this end, the Land Registration Act 1925 (LRA 1925) extended an existing (but little used) system of registration of title to land. The system has been further extended by subsequent Land Registration Acts, and registration of title at local Land Registries was finally extended to the whole country in 1990. The Land Registration Act 2002 (LRA 2002), part of which brought into force extensive and significant changes on 13 October 2003, furthers the ultimate aim of registered title, which is that the register will be a mirror of the title to the land and will contain everything which a purchaser needs to know.

Registration of title is effected by the purchaser's solicitor on completion of the first transaction with the land after the date on which registration was introduced for the area in which the land is located. Registration was introduced for many urban areas fairly early on, so that there are probably very few unregistered titles remaining in an area where registration of title was compulsorily introduced in, say, the 1950s or the 1960s, but there may still be a number of unregistered titles in areas where it was more recently introduced. There must also be a number of unregistered titles to public buildings, such as schools, universities and hospitals where there has never been any dealing with the land for many years. The LRA 2002 has speeded up the process of registration by introducing a number of 'triggering' transactions. In particular as regards leases, the grant of a lease exceeding seven years, or the assignment of a longer lease with over seven years left to run, or the grant of a reversionary lease (of any length) which is to take effect in possession more than three months after its grant, must now all be registered substantively with their own title number.[1] A lease with an absolute prohibition against its assignment may also be registered substantively. This reduces the number of legal leases which are not on the register, but nevertheless binding on a purchaser of the freehold reversion as overriding interests, to legal leases (other than the reversionary leases described above) not exceeding seven years (see Schedule 3, para. 1, LRA 2002). Reversionary leases which do not take effect in possession for more than three months after they are granted, whether granted out of registered title or unregistered title and for any length of time, are registrable interests and are not binding on a purchaser of the land unless registered. An equitable lease may be binding on a purchaser of the reversion if it is registered as a minor interest, or if the equitable lessee has an overriding interest as a person in occupation under Schedule 3, para. 2, LRA 2002 (see Chapter 3.3 and 3.4).

14.2 Title to Leasehold Property

14.2.1 Unregistered Title

It will be apparent from section 14.1 that leases with unregistered title will be drastically reduced. It is envisaged that registrable leases will eventually include all leases exceeding three years, so that virtually all legal leases, other than periodic leases, will be registered.

The title offered to a lessee and their assignee in unregistered land could be far from satisfactory. This was because, under an open contract, a lessee or their assignee were precluded by s.44 Law of Property Act 1925 from calling for the freehold title, and could therefore find themselves bound by restrictive covenants affecting the freehold title of which they were totally unaware. A new s.44A has now been added by the LRA 2002, which changes this situation and allows a lessee or their assignee to insist upon seeing the freehold title. The grant or assignment of leases will in many cases now be a transaction which triggers registration, and as the lessee or assignee will now be able to call for the freehold title as well as the leasehold title and deduce both titles to the Registrar, all leases which are registered substantively should in future be registered with a title absolute. The "Good Leasehold" title, which was granted when the Registrar had seen and was satisfied as to the leasehold title but had not seen the freehold title out of which the lease was derived, will gradually disappear.[2]

As already mentioned, the grant of a reversionary lease (of any length) in unregistered title to take effect more than three months after its grant must also be registered substantively with its own title number. The freehold reversionary title on such a lease will similarly be available, and it should therefore qualify for an absolute title.

14.2.2 Registered Title

Access to the Land Register was opened to the public by the Land Registration Act 1988, so that for many years now it has been possible for any lessee, sublessee or their assigns to see the freehold and any superior leasehold title from which the lease (or sublease) derives. They should, of course, try to insist on production of office copy entries for the relevant freehold title and any superior leasehold title. Assuming these to be in order, they will then be able to register a lease (or sublease) exceeding seven years with a title absolute. An assignment of a longer lease with over seven years left to run must be similarly registered, even if there is an absolute prohibition against its assignment.[1]

As already mentioned, reversionary leases to take effect more than three months after the date of the grant must also be registered.

14.3 Enforceability of a Lease against a Purchaser of the Freehold Reversion

14.3.1 Unregistered Title

A lease which is created by deed, or which is within s.54(2) LPA 1925 is a legal lease (see Chapter 3.2). It is a legal estate in the land binding on everyone, irrespective of notice, and a purchaser of the freehold reversion from the landlord is bound by it. Being legal, it is not registrable under the Land Charges Act 1972, the purpose of that Act (which replaced the Land Charges Act 1925) being to introduce a more certain method of protecting *equitable* interests instead of the somewhat uncertain doctrine of notice. A prospective purchaser of land is likely to discover the existence of any leases anyway by reason of the tenant's occupation of the premises.

An equitable lease is one which is enforceable in equity because there is a contract to grant a lease of which equity will grant specific performance (see Chapter 3.3). It is, of course, binding as an enforceable contract between the parties to it. Either party may obtain specific performance of the agreement so that he will then have a valid legal lease, unless his conduct has been such that the court will not exercise its discretion in his favour (see Chapter 3.5). If, however, the lease remains an equitable one, either because neither party seeks specific performance or because the court is unwilling to grant it, what is the position of the lessee as regards a third party who purchases the freehold reversion'?

Such a lease is an equitable interest and will bind a purchaser of the freehold reversion from the landlord only if it is registered as a class C(iv) land charge (an estate contract) in the Land Charges Register at Plymouth, set up to register equitable interests under the Land Charges Acts 1925 and

1972. Where an interest is registrable under the Land Charges Act, the sole factor which determines its enforceability against a purchaser is registration, so that even if a purchaser has actual knowledge of the lease, or the tenant is in occupation, it will not be binding on him unless it is registered.[3]

14.3.2   Registered Title

It has been explained in 14.1 that many more legal leases have now become registrable substantively, and when so registered will bind any purchaser of the freehold reversion. A note of the grant of the lease will be made on the Property Register of the freehold title.

A legal lease not exceeding seven years (which is not registrable substantively) is an overriding interest under Schedule 3, para. 1, LRA 2002, and is therefore binding on the registered proprietor of the freehold title and any transferee from him. All periodic tenancies, which are legal leases within s.54(2), LPA 1925 are within this category of overriding interests.

Equitable leases (see Chapter 3.3) are not registrable substantively or overriding, however. They are minor interests and will not be binding on the registered proprietor or a transferee from him unless they are noted on the Register as minor interests. They may, however, become binding as overriding interests if the tenant is in occupation under Schedule 3, para. 2, LRA 2002 (formerly under s.70(1)(g) LRA 1925) and the conditions of that para. are satisfied.[4]

14.4   Short Form of Model Lease

We are including a short form of model lease below, but this should not be used as a precedent. A lease is a contract, and the contract will necessarily vary according to the property leased and the individual requirements of the parties.

As regards commercial leases, the Land Registry have prescribed a format for a table with fourteen specified clauses which must be included at the front of every lease to be registered after 19 June 2006. The clauses cover all the matters which are relevant to the disposition, the title or encumbrances (such as easements or restrictive covenants) and which therefore require to be entered on the register. Many commercial leases are very lengthy documents, and the purpose of this is to make it easier for the Land Registry staff to extract and register this important information, which will affect anyone dealing with the registered property. For various reasons, the trend more recently has been to grant shorter commercial leases; many commercial leases are for seven years or less and so will not be affected by this requirement.

THIS LEASE made the 22nd day of May Two Thousand and Three BETWEEN LENNIE LANDLORD of 6, Laburnum Avenue, Clifftop-on-Sea (hereinafter called 'the Lessor') of the one part and TERRY TENANT of 23, Willow Lane, Clifftop-on-Sea (hereinafter called 'the Lessee') of the other part WITNESSETH as follows:

1. IN CONSIDERATION of the rent and covenants hereinafter reserved and contained the Lessor HEREBY DEMISES unto the Lessee ALL THAT first floor flat (including the ceilings and floor joists and windows thereof) known as 12A, Hollybush Lane, Clifftop-on-Sea (hereinafter called 'the Flat') in the building (hereinafter called 'the Building') known as 12, Hollybush Lane, Clifftop-on-Sea TOGETHER WITH the easements and rights set out in the First Schedule hereto but EXCEPTING AND RESERVING the easements and rights set out in the Second Schedule hereto TO HOLD the same unto the Lessee for the term of TEN YEARS from the 1st day of June Two Thousand and Three YIELDING AND PAYING therefor from the 1st day of June 2003 the yearly rent of Seven Thousand Pounds to be paid in advance by equal quarterly instalments on the usual quarter days

2. THE LESSEE for himself and his assigns HEREBY COVENANTS with the Lessor as follows:

(1) To pay to the Lessor:
  (i)   the rent hereby reserved as herein required;
  (ii) one half of the water rate payable on the Building;
  (iii) one half of the cost of insuring the Building against loss or damage by fire, storm or tempest;
  (iv) one half of the cost of maintaining and repairing the structure and services and of maintaining, repairing and redecorating the exterior of the Building payable annually on the 1st day of April each year in arrear.*

And the said sums shall be payable annually in advance on the 1st day of April each year and in the case of default shall be recoverable from the Lessee as rent in arrear.

---

* A more usual provision for this on a block of flats is to include this in a service charge (see Chapter 12.1). The landlord's managing agents will prepare an estimate of costs in advance and adjust this as necessary in the estimate for the following year. Also, items (ii), (iii) and (iv) above are often made payable as part of an apportioned service charge, and there may be a further schedule to the lease to state what the service charge covers – particularly for leases of shops in a precinct or industrial units on an estate where the landlord is likely to provide a number of other services.

(2) To paint and redecorate the interior of the Flat in the sixth and last year of the term hereby demised.

(3) To permit the Lessor and his agents and workmen (upon giving reasonable notice in writing of their intention so to do) to enter the Flat at reasonable times during the daytime for the purpose of viewing the condition and state of repair thereof.

(4) Upon receipt of written notice by the Lessor, within two months to repair and make good any defects or want of repair to the Flat.

(5) Not to assign or underlet or part with the possession of the whole or any part of the Flat without the written consent of the Lessor.

(6) Not to use the Flat for any purpose other than that of a private dwelling in single occupation only.

(7) Not to make any structural alterations to the Flat without the Lessor's consent in writing.

(8) Not to cause any nuisance or annoyance to the Landlord or any other tenants of the Landlord.

(9) Not to do any act or thing which may render void any policy of insurance on the Flat or the Building or any part thereof or which may cause an increase in the premium payable in respect thereof.

(10) To pay all expenses incurred by the Lessor incidental to the preparation and service of a notice under s.146 LPA 1925 notwithstanding that forfeiture is avoided (see Chapter 15.5).

(11) At the determination of the tenancy to yield up the Flat and all additions and fixtures thereto in good and tenantable repair.

3. PROVIDED THAT if the rent hereby reserved shall be twenty-one days in arrear (whether the same shall have been lawfully demanded or not) or the Lessee shall fail to observe or perform any of the covenants on his part herein contained then it shall be lawful for the Lessor at any time thereafter to re-enter the Flat or any part thereof in the name of the whole whereupon this demise shall absolutely determine but without prejudice to any right of action of the Lessor in respect of any breach by the Lessee of any covenant herein contained.

4. THE LESSOR hereby covenants with the Lessee:

(1) Subject to the payment of the contributions hereinbefore provided, to maintain and repair the structure, drains, water pipes (etc.) of the Building and to redecorate the exterior of the Building every three years.

(2) To keep the Building insured against loss or damage by fire, storm or tempest to the full value thereof and to cause all monies received in respect of any such insurance to be paid out in rebuilding and reinstating the Building or any part thereof.

(3) To produce to the Lessee on demand a copy of the policy of insurance and a receipt for payment of the last insurance premium.

(4) To pay the water rates charged on the Building.

(5) The Lessee paying the rent and performing the covenants on his part herein contained shall peaceably hold and enjoy the Flat without any interruption by the Lessor or any person lawfully claiming through or under him.

5. The provisions of s.196 LPA 1925 shall apply to any notice served under this Lease.[5]

IN WITNESS whereof the parties hereto have hereunto set their hands.

Signed as a deed by the said LENNIE }
LANDLORD in the presence of }

Signed as a deed by the said TERRY }
TENANT in the presence of }

FIRST SCHEDULE

Rights and privileges hereby granted to the Lessee.

(1) The right for the Lessee and all persons authorised by him at all times by day or night to pass and repass over and along the entrance of the Building and the paths giving access thereto and the stairs to the flat.

(2) The free and uninterrupted passage of water, soil, gas and electricity through the pipes conduits and drains which pass through the Building.

(3) The right to support shelter and protection from other parts of the Building.

SECOND SCHEDULE

It is hereby excepted and reserved to the Lessor and his assigns (including the lessee or lessees for the time being of any other part of the Building): –

(1) The right for the owner and his assigns and any persons authorised by him at all times by day or by night to pass and repass over and along the entrance of the Building and the paths giving access thereto.

(2) The free and uninterrupted passage of water, soil, gas and electricity through the pipes conduits and drains which pass through the Building.

(3) The right to support shelter and protection from other parts of the Building.

Notes

▶ 1 Section 3, Land Registration Act 1986, amending s.8(2) LRA 1925, made such leases registrable if granted after the commencement of the Act (1 January 1987) or if assigned (with consent) when a term of twenty-one years is left. Since 13 October 2003, the LRA 2002 makes an assignment of such a term with more than seven years left to run registrable substantively (s.4(2), LRA 2002).

▶ 2 A lessee, sublessee, or assignee would usually expressly exclude the operation of s.44, LPA 1925 by providing in the contract that the freehold and leasehold titles should be deduced, so that "Good Leasehold" titles have always been rare. Presumably they will now be limited to those existing before 13th October 2003, and it is likely that, on any dealing with them, any proposed sublessee or assignee will take the opportunity to upgrade the title to an Absolute one by requiring production of any superior title, as they are now able to do by reason of the amendment to s.44, Law of Property Act 1925.

▶ 3 *Midland Bank Trust Co. Ltd.* v. *Green* [1981] AC 513.

▶ 4 In keeping with the idea that the register should be a mirror of the title, the general policy of the LRA 2002 was to make more estates and interests registrable and to reduce the overriding interests by which a purchaser could find himself bound. Schedule 3, para. 2 is therefore narrower than the previous 'occupation' section, s.70(1)(g), LRA 1925. A person who was 'in receipt of the rents and profits', which could include a lessee who had sublet, was covered in s.70(1)(g) but is no longer included in para. 2, and there are other conditions stipulated for the para. to apply which were not applicable to s.70(1)(g).

▶ 5 Section 196, LPA 1925 provides for methods of serving notices which can be made applicable to the service of notices in leases if the section is applied by the lease. This is highly desirable, as service would otherwise have to be personal, which could be very difficult in the case of an absent tenant. For the text of this section, see Chapter 15, Note 6. Also see Luxton 'Service of notices in Business Tenancies by recorded delivery' [2004] JBL 564.

Summary

▶ The effect of the LRA 2002 is to extend the substantive registration of leases to:

(a) legal leases exceeding seven years;
(b) a longer legal lease with more than seven years left to run on assignment;
(c) a reversionary lease, however long, to take effect in possession more than three months after its grant.

▶ In unregistered title, because of the amendment to s.44, Law of Property Act 1925, it will be possible for a lessee, sublessee, or assignee to insist on seeing the freehold title and any superior leasehold title out of which his lease (or sublease) is granted.

▶ In registered title, this has been possible since the register became a public document with open access under the Land Registration Act 1988.

▶ This means that titles to leasehold estates registered substantively in the future should be Absolute rather than Good Leasehold, and the Good Leasehold category of title should gradually disappear.

▶ In unregistered title, a legal lease will be binding on a purchaser of the reversion in any event, but an equitable lease will be binding only if it is registered as a Class C(iv) land charge (an estate contract) under the Land Charges Act 1972.

▶ In registered title, a lease may be:

(i) registrable substantively if it is one of the three leases in Note 1 above;
(ii) an overriding interest within Schedule 3, para.1, LRA 2002 (a legal lease not exceeding seven years).

Both these categories of leases are binding on a purchaser of the reversion.

▶ In registered title, equitable leases are minor interests and binding if registered as such. They may, however, become overriding interests binding under Schedule 3, para. 2. LRA 2002 if the lessee is in occupation.

Exercises

14.1 How will title to a lease be deduced in (a) unregistered land and (b) land with registered title?

14.2 Why should a lessee, sublessee, or assignee insist upon seeing the freehold title and any superior leasehold title from which his lease is granted?

14.3 In unregistered title, is a legal lease:

(a) registrable under the Land Charges Act 1972;
(b) binding on a purchaser of the freehold reversion?

14.4 Answer (a) and (b) in 14.3 in relation to an equitable lease.

14.5 What provision is made for legal leases in registered title?

14.6 In what ways may an equitable lease be binding on a purchaser of the reversion in registered title?

Workshop

1 Lucy granted by deed a six year lease of 'Rose Cottage' (the title to which is unregistered) to Tom. Tom took possession two years ago and has paid rent yearly. Rudy has recently purchased the reversion from Lucy. Advise Rudy as to whether Tom's lease is binding on him or not.

(a) How would your answer differ if the title to 'Rose Cottage' were registered?
(b) How would your answer differ if the lease had been granted by an agreement in writing only?

2 Sam, a student, was granted a legal lease of a flat by John in May for the following academic year, to commence in September and to finish in July the following year. Three months later, in August, John sold the freehold reversion to Peter. Advise Peter as to whether he is bound or not by Sam's lease. Would your answer be the same whether the title to the property is registered or unregistered?

Chapter 15

Termination of a lease

On the termination of the contractual tenancy between the parties, a statutory protected tenancy will arise if the property falls within the limits prescribed by the Rent Act 1977 or Housing Act 1988 (see chapters 16, 17 and 18). If the demised premises are commercial premises, then the tenant may have a right to a continuation tenancy under s.24 Landlord & Tenant Act 1954, Part II. In these circumstances, the landlord will not be able to obtain possession unless he can prove he has one of the grounds for doing so (see Chapter 19).

This chapter considers the ways in which the contractual tenancy between the parties may be terminated. The grounds for possession under the legislation are considered in Part II of this book.

15.1 Effluxion of Time

A lease for a fixed term will terminate automatically on expiry of the term. A fixed term lease may be terminated before the end of the period if it contains a 'break' clause, although notice must be served to take advantage of a break clause. The House of Lords decision in *Mannai Investment Co. Ltd. v. Eagle Star Life Assurance Co. Ltd.* (1997) (dealt with in detail in Chapter 13.3) is likely to be helpful to practitioners in that the requirement for absolute accuracy in these notices would seem to be no longer essential. A lease may also terminate before its full term if it is made terminable upon the happening of some prior event (a determinable lease). It will not terminate automatically on the occurrence of the event and notice must be given.[1] A fixed term lease may also be terminated prematurely by forfeiture (see 15.5 below). It is a matter of construction as to whether a term in the lease is a condition causing it to terminate automatically or a covenant for which a right of re-entry on breach must be reserved.

A tenant holding over at the end of a fixed term tenancy will be a tenant at sufferance, but may become a periodic tenant by implication if he pays rent regularly by reference to a period. So, for instance, if he continues to pay rent monthly as he has done during the tenancy, he will become a monthly periodic tenant.

15.2 Notice to Quit

Either party to a periodic tenancy may serve a notice to quit on the other party and any provision abrogating this right will be void (see Chapter 2.2).

In the absence of any express stipulation as to the period of notice required, the notice must generally be for one full length of the period, expiring on the last day of the period. Thus a monthly tenancy would be terminated by a month's notice to terminate at the end of the month. A yearly tenancy is an exception to this rule, however, and is terminable by six months' notice to expire at the end of the year. A notice which purports to terminate the tenancy at any time other than the expiration of the period is void,[2] although the *Mannai* decision may give some scope for slight inaccuracies in these notices too.

The Protection from Eviction Act 1977 s.5(1) prescribes the form which any notice to quit a dwellinghouse must take. It must be in writing and give at least four clear weeks' notice. It must also contain certain prescribed information informing the tenant of his possible rights.[3] Notices terminating business tenancies should be in a prescribed form, setting out details of the tenant's rights.[4] Notice to terminate agricultural holdings must comply with ss.25–33 of the Agricultural Holdings Act 1986 or Agricultural Tenancies Act 1995, respectively.

A notice to quit must be served by the landlord for the time being on the tenant for the time being. In *Lower* v. *Sorrell* (1963) the parties to a yearly tenancy of an agricultural holding were negotiating for a new lease which was to commence on 29 September 1961. The landlord served a notice to quit the new tenancy on 27 September 1960, and this was held to be bad. Donovan L.J. said: 'a notice to quit is a notice given by an existing landlord to an existing tenant, and, if that view be right, it follows that a person cannot give a valid notice to quit before he has become a landlord and the recipient of the notice his tenant, or before legal relations exist between them which otherwise permit such a notice.'

A notice served by one of two landlords will be valid, as will a notice served by one of two joint tenants, even though the tenancy is a secure tenancy. This is because the automatic renewal of a periodic tenancy, which occurs at the end of each period, cannot happen unless both tenants agree to it. In *Hammersmith & Fulham L.B.C.* v. *Monk* (1992) the House of Lords confirmed an earlier decision that a notice to quit given by one joint tenant without the knowledge or consent of the other was nevertheless effective to terminate the joint periodic tenancy. The House of Lords accepted that the two joint tenants held on trust for sale under s.36(1) LPA 1925, but held that giving notice in these circumstances did not amount to a breach of the requirement to consult beneficiaries imposed by S.26(3) LPA 1925 as that section referred only to positive acts done by trustees and the notice to terminate a periodic tenancy was a negative act. The position remains the same as regards trusts of land under the Trusts of Land & Appointment of Trustees Act 1996.[5] This was followed in *Crawley L.B.C.* v. *Ure* (1995), where the Court of Appeal declined to find that the local authority, which advised the joint tenant who had left the premises to serve a notice to quit, had induced a breach of trust. In *Harrow L.B.C.* v. *Johnstone* (1997) where a husband and wife were joint tenants of a council house and the wife left, the husband obtained an injunction against her to prevent her from excluding, or attempting to exclude him, from the property. The wife subsequently served notice to quit on the council, which then sought possession of the property. The House of Lords held that the council was not in contempt of court for breaching the injunction as it was seeking possession in pursuit of its housing policy.

In *Harrow LBC* v. *Qazi* (2003), Mr and Mrs Qazi were secure tenants under the Housing Act 1985. Mrs Qazi left the property and gave notice terminating the tenancy, whereupon Harrow LBC brought proceedings to recover possession of the property. Mr Qazi alleged that these proceedings were a violation of his right to a home under Article 8(1) of the Human Rights Act 1998. The House of Lords held that although he had a right under Article 8(1), the domestic proceedings brought by Harrow LBC were justifiable under Article 8(2) as proceedings in pursuance of their housing policy, as they were required under Article 8(2) to have regard to (*inter alia*) the rights of others; this was confirmed by the European Court of Human Rights. *Qazi* was recently approved and followed by the House of Lords in *Kay* v. *Lambeth LBC* (8 March 2006) after a review of the cases heard by the European Court of Human Rights since *Qazi* was decided. Most importantly for housing authorities, the House of Lords said that it is not necessary for local authorities to plead in every eviction case that the domestic law is compatible with Article 8, and that they should proceed in such actions on the assumption that the domestic law is compatible. It will only be in exceptional cases where the occupier can show that he has a seriously arguable case that the county courts should have to consider it, and they should in the majority of cases be able to decide the issue themselves without referring proceedings to the High Court.

The notice may be served by an agent, and often managing agents will serve a notice on behalf of a landlord. The tenant should receive the notice before the period starts to run. Many leases specifically incorporate s.196 LPA 1925 with regard to the service of any notices.[6] This provides for service of notice by registered post or recorded delivery, or by affixing the notice to the demised premises. The latter means of service is helpful if the tenant has disappeared. The section will not apply, however, unless the lease includes a clause specifically stating that it shall apply.

An upwards notice to quit served by a tenant on his landlord will automatically terminate any subleases granted by the tenant,[7] unlike surrender where the sublease survives (see 15.3).

15.3   Surrender

This occurs where the immediate tenant surrenders his interest to his immediate landlord. It will not terminate any subleases granted by the tenant but will have the effect of making the subtenant a tenant of the landlord on the terms of the sublease. S.150 LPA 1925 allows a headtenant to surrender his lease and to take a new lease without in any way affecting any subleases granted, which continue 'as if the lease out of which the underlease was derived had not been surrendered' (s.150(4)). Surrender by a statutory tenant will destroy any rights he has granted, however, as a statutory tenant has no estate in the land but only a right of occupation.[8]

A clause in a lease providing that a tenant who wishes to assign or underlet his lease will first offer to surrender the term to the landlord is valid and will not be regarded as an infringement of s.19(1) Landlord & Tenant Act 1927 and therefore void.[9]

Surrender involves the transfer of a legal estate and so should be by deed if it is an express surrender. The usual rule as to enforceable contracts in writing will apply, however, and surrenders by operation of law or those which may be effected without writing are specifically exempted from the necessity of a deed. A surrender by operation of law may be implied from the conduct of the parties, as where a tenant gives up possession or takes a new lease, but the tenant's conduct must be unequivocal.[10]

Any surrender by operation of law must also be accepted by the landlord, and this requires a positive act and not merely acts of omission, such as failing to make a demand for rent or service charges. In *Proudreed Ltd.* v. *Microgen Holdings plc* (1995), there was no surrender of a lease by operation of law when the landlord accepted the keys of the premises from the tenant on the understanding that the sureties would take a new lease of the premises as they were bound to do under the terms of the lease. The landlord's intention was very clearly not to accept a surrender until the new lease was granted. In *Bellcourt Estates Ltd.* v. *Adesina* (2005), Mrs Adesina signed a lease of some dilapidated property in August 2000 and started redecoration. She changed her mind, however, and had vacated the property and demanded back her deposit by November 2000. The landlords carried out a roof repair and reminded Mrs Adesina that she still owed the balance of a £5,000 deposit, but otherwise took no action at all. They made no demand for the December instalment of rent or for any service charges, but then brought forfeiture proceedings in November 2001 claiming arrears of rent. Longmore L.J. found that there had been no positive act of acceptance of the purported surrender of the lease and so there could not have been a surrender by operation of law. He referred to *Woodfall*, March 2002, para. 17.020, which allows for a surrender by the tenant in circumstances making it 'inequitable for the tenant to dispute that the tenancy has ceased', and regretted that the amendment of the paragraph suggested in *Proudreed* to include also 'circumstances such as to render it inequitable for the landlord to dispute that the tenancy has ceased' had not been made.

Another case in which the tenant tried to argue (unsuccessfully again) that there had been a surrender by operation of law is *Representative Body for the Church in Wales v. Newton* (2005). Here the original tenant had assigned the lease, but the assignee returned the keys to the tenant instead of the landlord, although he wrote to the landlord informing him. When the keys were returned, the original tenant allowed a third party (B) into occupation. Although the landlord at first thought that B was simply managing the business for the tenant, it soon became obvious that he was trading on his own account. The landlord accepted rent from B and negotiated with him for an assignment of the lease. All negotiations were 'subject to contract' however. It was held that at no time had the landlord done anything inconsistent with the continuation of the lease and he could therefore sue for forfeiture and arrears of rent.

A substantial variation of an existing lease might operate as a surrender by operation of law and regrant of it. In *Friends' Provident Life Office* v. *British Railways Board* (1996) the Court of Appeal considered the type of variation which might effect this, and decided that it would have to be a variation either in the term of the lease, or as to the extent of the demised premises.

15.4 Merger

One of the essential elements of a lease is that the landlord and the tenant must be two different persons. Where a tenant acquires his immediate landlord's reversion, a merger occurs extinguishing the lease. It will not apply if a subtenant acquires the reversion, however, as the headtenant's term is then still outstanding.

A deed of purchase of the reversion will usually expressly declare that the term and the reversion are thereby merged, but if it does not do so, this may be presumed from the circumstances. Conversely, the deed may expressly, provide that the term shall not be merged where, for instance, it is desired to keep the covenants in the lease enforceable for any reason.

The Leasehold Reform Act 1967 gives a tenant the right to acquire the freehold reversion on a lease of over twenty-one years in certain circumstances (see Chapter 17).

Section 153 LPA 1925 provides for the enlargement into a freehold of a term of not less than 300 years with not less than 200 years left to run at a peppercorn rent.

15.5 Forfeiture

Most leases include a proviso for re-entry on non-payment of the rent or breach of any other covenant contained in the lease. The proviso must be expressly stated and will not be implied. A right of forfeiture exists only where there is such a proviso.

The forfeiture proceedings for non-payment of rent differ from those for breach of any other covenant in the lease, and have already been dealt with in Chapter 11.5.2. A forfeiture action for non-payment of service charges will fall within a forfeiture for non-payment of rent if the service charges have been reserved as additional rent, but will be within the procedure under s.146, LPA, described below, if not. In any event, in a residential tenancy, a landlord cannot seek forfeiture for a disputed service charge until fourteen days after a determination of the amount owed by a leasehold valuation tribunal, or an admission of this amount by the tenant.[11]

As in forfeiture for non-payment of rent, any waiver by the landlord of his right to forfeit for breach of any other covenant will bar his right, but whereas strict principles apply to the demand and acceptance of rent (*Yorkshire Metro Properties Ltd.* v. *Co-operative Retail Services Ltd.* (2001)), waiver for breach of other covenants is not susceptible of 'a rigid and precise taxonomy of principles' (Robert Walker LJ in *Ballard (Kent) Ltd.* v. *Oliver Ashworth Holdings Ltd.* (1999)).[12]

For forfeiture for breach of any other covenant, the landlord must first serve a notice under s.146 LPA 1925 on the tenant and on any mortgagee in possession, who would of course be at risk of losing his security if the lease were forfeited (*Target Home Loans Ltd.* v. *Iza Ltd.* (2000)).

The notice must :

(a) specify the particular breach complained of; and
(b) if the breach is capable of remedy, require the lessee to remedy the breach; and
(c) in any case, require the lessee to make compensation in money for the breach.

Where the landlord is seeking to forfeit a long residential lease exceeding twenty-one years, the Commonhold and Leasehold Reform Act 2002, s.168(1) and (2) now require the landlord to obtain a determination from a leasehold valuation tribunal that a breach of covenant has in fact occurred before issuing a s.146 notice. The lease will be reinstated if forfeiture proceedings under s.146 are discontinued or dismissed (*Mount Cook Land Ltd.* v. *Media Business Centre Ltd.* (2004)).

15.5.1   Relief against Forfeiture

The purpose of serving a notice under s.146 is to allow the tenant an opportunity of making good his breach of covenant, and a reasonable time should be given for this in the notice before forfeiture proceedings are started. Some breaches of covenant, such as covenants against assignment or underletting, or bankruptcy or liquidation of a company where the landlord expressly reserves a right of re-entry on this, are deemed to be irremediable, and in such cases a s.146 notice will still be valid even if it does not allow the tenant sufficient time to remedy the breach.[13] A breach which appears to be irremediable because the time for performing a positive covenant has passed may not necessarily be so, however, and the notice will be bad if it fails to give the tenant sufficient time to remedy the breach. In *Expert Clothing Service & Sales* v. *Hillgate House* (1985), the lease contained a covenant to reconstruct premises by 29 September 1982 or as soon as possible thereafter. A s.146 notice was served in October 1982 alleging that the failure to do so was an irremediable breach of covenant. It was held that it was not irremediable and that the tenant should be allowed a reasonable time for the reconstruction. In this case, Slade L.J. said that the test of whether a breach of covenant was remediable or not was whether it did irreparable harm to the landlord. This test was approved by Aldous L.J. in *Savva* v. *Hussein* (1997), where a negative covenant was held to be remediable,[14] and by Neuberger L.J. in *Akici* v. *L.R. Butlin Ltd.* (2006), where he expressed the opinion that most breaches of covenant should be remediable, including possibly even a breach of a covenant against assignment if the circumstances were such that the court could order a re-assignment.

Illegal or immoral use by a tenant has been held to be irremediable,[15] but if the immoral use is by a subtenant and the tenant himself was not aware of it, it may be remediable.[16] If the landlord does not want compensation for the breach, the notice will not be bad if it fails to ask for compensation.[17]

Section 146(2) LPA 1925 allows the court to grant relief to a tenant against forfeiture having regard to 'the proceedings, and conduct of the parties . . . and to all the other circumstances'. Relief may be granted on conditions which the court may impose, such as compensation or an injunction to restrain further breach. It was accepted implicitly in *Fivecourts Ltd.* v. *J.R. Leisure Development Co. Ltd.* (2001) that it would be open to the court to vary the conditions. If, however, the parties reach an agreement as to the conditions which are embodied in a consent order, then although the court may well have jurisdiction to vary the conditions, they should be reluctant to do so, as this would vary a contract made between the parties.

In the case of *Hyman* v. *Rose* (1912) which was a case concerning the court's right to grant relief against forfeiture under s.14(1) Conveyancing Act 1881, being the forerunner of s.146 LPA 1925, the House of Lords indicated that rigid rules for when, and upon what terms, relief will be granted are not appropriate. Earl Loreburn L.C. said in that case: 'Now it seems to me that when the Act is so express to provide a wide discretion . . . it is not advisable to lay down any rigid rules for guiding that discretion. I do not doubt that the rules enunciated by the Master of the Rolls in the present case are useful maxims in general, and that in general they reflect the point of view from which judges would regard an application for relief. But I think it ought to be distinctly understood that there may be cases in which any or all of them may be disregarded. If it were otherwise, the free discretion given by the statute would be fettered by limitations which nowhere have been enacted.' Generally the court will be prepared to grant relief if the landlord's interests will not be damaged thereby. One relevant factor in granting relief is the value of the property to be forfeited.

In *Cremin* v. *Barjack Properties Ltd.* (1985) relief was granted even after numerous delays in carrying out work required by a covenant as the value of the property was £45,000. The court approved a statement from *Woodfall on Landlord and Tenant* that 'The court will consider the conduct of the tenant, the nature and gravity of the breach (or breaches) and its relation to the value of the property to be forfeited'. Hardship to an innocent third party to whom the landlord has re-let would be a reason for not exercising the discretion to grant relief. In *Fuller* v. *Judy Properties Ltd.* (1992) the Court of Appeal granted relief to an assignee when the landlord had re-let, but avoided hardship to the new tenant by making the assignee's lease a reversionary lease on the tenant's new lease, so that the assignee was the new tenant's landlord. The general view is that the statutory relief given to a lessee under s.146(2) excludes any equitable rights (which apply to the procedure for forfeiture for non-payment of rent) and only in circumstances such as fraud or mistake would a lessee who failed to apply for relief under s.146(2) be able to apply for relief in reliance upon the court's inherent jurisdiction. For relief against forfeiture for non-payment of rent where equitable relief may be available, see Chapter 11.5.2.

In *Billson* v. *Residential Apartments Ltd.* (1992), the landlord had peaceably re-entered the premises for four hours after the service of a s.146 notice, but before a court order was obtained. The landlord then argued that the peaceable re-entry was a forfeiture in itself, so that the tenant's right to relief under s.146(2) was barred. The House of Lords rejected this argument and interpreted the wording of the section (where the landlord 'is proceeding by action or otherwise') to include any action by the landlord up to the time he re-enters in pursuance of a court order. As the landlord was still *proceeding*, the tenant was able to obtain relief under s.146(2). In this case, Lord Templeman said that the statutory provisions for relief in s.146, LPA, (originally conferred in s.14, Conveyancing Act 1881) were enacted to supplement the equitable right to relief, which was available only for the non-payment of rent or in circumstances where equity may intervene, such as mistake or fraud.

Two High Court decisions have held that a landlord's right of forfeiture by peaceable re-entry is not the enforcement of a security for the purposes of s.10(1) and s.11(3) Insolvency Act 1986, and will therefore be valid notwithstanding the presentation of an administration petition or order for the administration of a company.[18]

| 15.5.2 | Relief Available to a Subtenant on Forfeiture for Non-payment of Rent and for Breach of any other Covenant |

Forfeiture of a headlease automatically results in the forfeiture of any sublease deriving from it. S.146(4) therefore provides that a subtenant may apply to the court in the course of the forfeiture proceedings for relief against forfeiture of the headlease, whether the forfeiture is for non-payment of rent or for breach of any other covenant in the headlease. The court has a discretion to vest directly in the subtenant a term which should not exceed the term of the sublease. The relief may be on conditions such as the execution of a deed or provision of security and a condition as to payment of a lump sum to cover costs has been held to be valid. The special rules for subtenants discussed in Chapters 16 and 20 should also be noted. It has already been mentioned that a mortgagee of leasehold property, whether his mortgage is by way of subdemise or legal charge, has a right of relief against forfeiture for non-payment of rent under s.146(4) (see Chapter 11.5(b)) but it is uncertain whether this right extends to an equitable mortgagee.[19]

If forfeiture is for non-payment of rent, a mortgagee is within the definition of 'lessee' (from whom he derives title) in s.138 County Courts Act 1984 and so may apply for relief under that section. If the forfeiture action is in the High Court, then he has a parallel right of relief under s.38 Supreme Court Act 1981 and the Common Law Procedure Act 1852 (see Chapter 11.5). These statutory rights of relief are automatic if the arrears of rent and costs are paid within six months of re-entry by the landlord, but are not available after the six-month period (*United Dominions Trust Ltd.* v. *Shellpoint Trustees Ltd.* (1993)). In *Escalus Properties Ltd.* v. *Dennis* (1995), s.138 County Courts Act 1938 did not apply as the action was additionally for recovery of service charges as well as rent and there was no provision in the lease that the service charges were to be treated as rent. It was held, however, that the mortgagee was still entitled to relief under s.146(2), LPA

1925, being within the definition of 'lessee' in S.146(5)(b). Even the grant of a new lease by the landlord will not necessarily be a bar to relief against forfeiture under the sections and the court may order that the mortgagee be granted a reversionary lease on the new lease granted by the landlord.[20]

Relief granted under s.146(2), LPA and for non-payment of rent is the reinstatement of the original lease, and the mortgagee sublessee is liable to pay any rent not paid, but relief under s.146(4) is the grant of a new lease, and the mortgagee would not be liable for unpaid arrears unless this were made a condition for the granting of the new lease.

In *Abbey National Building Society* v. *Maybeech* (1984), which was an action for forfeiture for non-payment of a contribution to maintenance costs; it was held that the court had an equitable jurisdiction to grant relief to a subtenant in addition to the statutory power. In that case, the Building Society were unaware that the landlord had taken forfeiture proceedings, but they were granted relief subsequently under the court's inherent jurisdiction to grant relief to a subtenant which, it was said, was not displaced by s.146(4). A judgment creditor with a charging order over the assets of a tenant has merely equitable rights however and not proprietary or possessory rights and has no claim to relief (see the cases on this already referred to in Note 19). The inherent jurisdiction does not apply to relief from forfeiture on the grounds of bankruptcy, however, and in that case the statutory relief under s.146(10) is exhaustive. In the case of forfeiture on the grounds of the tenant's bankruptcy, or liquidation in the case of a limited company, there is a right to relief against forfeiture if the leasehold property is sold within a year, and the tenant has a year within which to apply for relief if it is not sold (s.146(10)). There is no subsequent right to grant equitable relief.[21]

In the case of a forfeiture by peaceable re-entry, as the wording in s.146(4) granting a right of relief to subtenants is the same as that in s.146(2), the principle of *Billson* could presumably be applied to grant relief before a possession order is made to a subtenant under s.146(4), so that a subtenant would not have to rely on the inherent jurisdiction claimed in *Maybeech*.

15.5.3 Landlord's Waiver of his Right of Forfeiture

A landlord waives his right to forfeit if he does any act, even if unintentional, which recognises the continuance of the tenancy, such as accepting rent, after the right has arisen. Moreover, he cannot do some act consistent with the continuation of the lease and at the same time preserve his position by stating that he is acting 'without prejudice' to his right to forfeit. Where a purchaser of the reversion whose title had not been completed by registration at the Land Registry peaceably re-entered and re-let premises which had been vacated, he was unable subsequently to recover unpaid rent for the period after re-entry as his acts amounted to an estoppel which was later fed by his subsequent registration of title.[22] He must, however, know of his right to forfeit in order to waive it. The degree of knowledge necessary to effect a waiver is by no means certain, and it may be that reasonable grounds for suspecting that the tenant is in breach of covenant will be sufficient, even though the landlord does not know all the relevant facts.[23] The knowledge of his agent may be imputed to the landlord, or if the breach of covenant has continued openly for some time, he may be deemed to have knowledge of it.[24] The landlord's right to forfeit revives if there is a fresh breach of covenant, and it is important therefore to distinguish between a breach which is once and for all – such as breach of a covenant against assignment or underletting, which once waived cannot be revived – and a continuing breach, such as breach of a repairing covenant, for which a landlord may subsequently forfeit even though he has in the past waived it.

15.6 Disclaimer

A trustee in bankruptcy, or liquidator of a company may disclaim an onerous lease thereby terminating it and accelerating the reversion on it. Disclaimer operates to terminate the insolvent tenant's liability under the lease. As to the liability of the tenant's surety and previous tenants, see Chapter 7.4 and 7.5 and *Hindcastle* v. *Barbara Attenborough Associates Ltd.* (1994).

A landlord can claim damages under s.178(6), Insolvency Act 1986 for losses arising on disclaimer, although any such claim will usually be fruitless as the tenant is insolvent. In *Christopher Moran Holdings Ltd.* v. *Bairstow* (1999) however, the liquidator of a *solvent* tenant disclaimed a lease on which the rent was over four times the rental value of the premises. The House of Lords held that the damages should be assessed in the same way as for breach of contract, which was the difference between the contractual rent and the market rent with a discount of 8.5 per cent for immediate payment rather than payment by future instalments. The case is significant because the discounting may make it financially worthwhile for a company tenant to escape from an onerous lease in this way, giving such a tenant added bargaining power with its landlord.

15.7 Frustration

The contractual nature of a lease has led the House of Lords to indicate that frustration, which is one of the circumstances which will terminate a contract, may also apply to terminate a lease. In *National Ltd.* v. *Panalpina (Northern) Ltd.* (1981) (for the facts, see Chapter 11, Note 2) the House of

Lords nevertheless declined to find, in the circumstances of that particular case, that the lease had been frustrated. Nevertheless, the decision would seem to leave open the possibility of a court finding that a lease has been frustrated, and Yates and Hawkins suggest as a possibility the destruction of an upper-floor flat, which in effect is a lease of air space (see Chapter 11.1).

15.8 Repudiatory Breach

In *Hussein* v. *Mehlman* (1992) the court again recognised the contractual nature of a lease by accepting that there could be a repudiatory breach of a tenancy agreement. The landlord had let the premises for three years and was therefore liable to repair under s.11 Landlord & Tenant Act 1985. The property became uninhabitable and the tenant moved out and returned the keys. It was held that the landlord's clear intention not to be bound by the covenant implied by s.11 abrogated the purpose of the letting. It amounted to a repudiatory breach which the tenant had accepted.

In *Chartered Trust plc* v. *Davies* (1997) the Court of Appeal accepted the trial judge's finding that a landlord's breach of covenant of non-derogation from his grant amounted to a repudiation of the lease (see Chapter 5.2). In *Nynehead Developments Ltd.* v. *R.H. Fibreboard Containers Ltd.* (1999) however it was held in the Chancery Division that breaches of parking covenants by tenants on an industrial estate were not sufficient to deprive a neighbouring tenant of 'substantially the whole benefit' of its lease, and gave rise to a claim for damages rather than repudiatory breach.

15.9 Tenant's Fixtures

When a lease terminates and the tenant leaves the demised premises, he may take with him any personal belongings and chattels, but any fixtures will remain as part of the demised premises. Fixtures are determined by two tests. First, an item will be a fixture *prima facie* if it is attached to the premises or the land. Fitted furniture, shelving and central heating radiators will be fixtures under this test, whereas something merely resting on the land such as a greenhouse[25] will not be. There is a second test which may override this, however, and that is the purpose for which the attachment was made. If it was for the better enjoyment of the chattel itself rather than the improvement of the building, then it will remain a chattel.[26] Conversely, objects not affixed but which form part of the landscaping may become fixtures.[27] In *Elitestone Ltd.* v. *Morris & Another* (1997) the House of Lords adopted a threefold classification: chattels, fixtures and objects which became part of the land. In that case, a bungalow had been erected some fifty years previously which did not have foundations but merely rested on brick piers on the land. It was impossible, however, to remove it without demolishing it, and it was held that it was not merely a fixture but had become part of the land itself. This classification was also applied in *Wessex Reserve Forces* v. *White* (2006) where a pre-existing stone shed was held to be part of the land, certain huts erected by the tenant with foundations, piers and perimeter walls were tenant's fixtures and as such had become part of the land, and a Portakabin and other sheds easily removed remained as chattels.

It was appreciated that the rule as to fixtures could operate unfairly against a tenant who had installed trade fixtures, for instance. The rule that fixtures are part of the property and may not be removed has therefore been relaxed for tenants, and a tenant is allowed to remove certain tenants' fixtures at the end of his lease unless there is any agreement in the lease to the contrary. These are domestic fixtures of ornamental and utility value, any trade fixtures, and fixtures of any sort where the tenancy is of an agricultural holding. He must give the landlord notice of his intention to remove them, and must do so before the end of the tenancy, or within two months after the end of the tenancy in the case of an agricultural holding. A tenant who remains in possession under a statutory tenancy may remove fixtures during the statutory tenancy, however.[28] A tenant who removes fixtures must make good any damage which he causes, and failure to do so will amount to waste (see Chapter 6.3.1).

Notes

▶ **1** *Bashir* v. *Commissioner of Lands* **[1960] AC 44**

A lease of a town plot in Nairobi was subject to a number of 'special conditions', including the building of an hotel, which had not been done. It was held that the conditions had a dual character of conditions and covenants, and it was therefore necessary to serve notice as for breach of covenant.

▶ **2** *Bathavon R.D.C.* v. *Carlile* **[1958] 1 QB 461**

The tenant was a weekly tenant who entered into possession on a Monday, the tenancy being terminable by either party giving one week's notice in writing before noon on a Monday. The Council gave the tenant notice to quit 'by noon on Monday'. It was held that the notice

was bad as the tenancy terminated at midnight on Sunday.

▶ **3** The Notices to Quit (Prescribed Information) Regulations 1988.

▶ **4** Landlord and Tenant Act 1954, Part II (Notices) Regulations 2004.

▶ **5** Although the statutory trust for sale under s.36(1) LPA 1925 became a trust of land under s.5, Trusts of Land & Appointment of Trustees Act 1996 (TLATA), and the obligation to consult is contained in s.11, TLATA, the changes made by TLATA have not affected the decision in this case (*Notting Hill Housing Trust* v. *Brackley* [2001] EWCA Civ.601)

▶ 6 S.196(2)

'Any notice required or authorised by this Act to be served on a lessee or mortgagor shall be sufficient, although only addressed to the lessee or mortgagor by that designation, without his name, or generally to the persons interested, without any name, and notwithstanding that any person to be affected by the notice is absent, under disability, unborn, or unascertained.'

S.196(3)

'Any notice required or authorised by this Act to be served shall be sufficiently served if it is left at the last-known place of abode or business in the United Kingdom of the lessee, lessor, mortgagee, mortgagor, or other person to be served, or, in case of a notice required or authorised to be served on a lessee or mortgagor, is affixed or left for him on the land or any house or building comprised in the lease or mortgage.'

S.196(4)

'Any notice required or authorised by this Act to be served shall also be sufficiently served, if it is sent by post in a registered letter addressed to the lessee, lessor, mortgagee, mortgagor, or other person to be served, by name, at the aforesaid place of abode or business, office or counting house, and if that letter is not returned through the post-office undelivered; and that service shall be deemed to be made at the time at which the registered letter would in the ordinary course be delivered.'

This was amended to include recorded delivery by the Recorded Delivery Service Act 1962.

▶ 7 *Pennell* v. *Payne* [1995] 6 EG 152

For a discussion of this Court of Appeal case, see [1995] Conv. 263.

▶ 8 *Solomon* v. *Orwell* [1954] 1 All ER 874

A protected tenant had sublet three rooms with a right to share a kitchen. He surrendered his tenancy by moving out and giving the keys to the landlord. It was held that the subtenants had no rights of possession.

▶ 9 *Bocardo S.A.* v. *S. & M. Hotels Ltd.* [1979] 3 All ER 737

A lease provided that before applying for consent to assign or underlet under a qualified covenant against assignment or underletting a tenant would first offer to surrender his term to the landlord. It was held that s.19(1) Landlord & Tenant Act 1927 did not invalidate the provision. The section did not purport to limit the freedom of contract of the parties, and there were no policy reasons for invalidating the covenant.

▶ 10 *Chamberlain* v. *Scally* [1992] EGCS 90

A tenant who lived at the property moved out but kept a key, returning each week to visit two cats and look after her possessions left at the premises. It was held that her actions were equivocal and there was no surrender by operation of law.

Conversely, in *John Laing Construction Ltd.* v. *Amber Pass Ltd.* (2004) 17 EGCS 128 (Ch), the tenant exercised its right to break the lease under a break clause and vacated the premises. The landlord was concerned about vandalism, and the tenant therefore put in security guards and barriers. The court held that the tenant had nevertheless yielded up the premises effectively.

▶ **11** Housing Act 1996, s.81(1) and (2) as amended.

▶ **12** *Ballard (Kent) Ltd. v. Oliver Ashworth Holdings Ltd.* [1999] 2 EGLR 25 at 27A.

▶ **13** *Scala House & District Property Co. Ltd.* v. *Forbes* [1974] QB 575

A s.146 notice for breach of a covenant against assignment allowed the tenant only fourteen days to remedy the breach. It was held that as the breach was irremediable, the notice was good.

▶ **14** In *Savva* v. *Hussein* (1997) 73 P&CR 150, the Court of Appeal said that although it was accepted law that a breach of a covenant against assignment was irremediable, most other breaches would be remediable, whether negative or not. A covenant not to put up signs or to make alterations was remediable, and the s.146 notice which did not allow time for remedying it was therefore bad.

▶ **15** *Rugby School* v. *Tannahill* [1935] 1 KB 87

▶ **16** *Glass* v. *Kencakes Ltd.* [1966] 1 QB 611

The subtenant was using the premises for immoral purposes, but the tenant did not know this. It was held that this was remediable by the tenant as he could take forfeiture proceedings against the subtenant.

▶ **17** *Factors (Sundries) Ltd.* v. *Miller* [1952] 2 All ER 630

▶ **18** *Re Lomax Leisure Ltd.* (1999) EGCS 61 and *Clarence Café* v. *Colchester Properties Ltd.* (4.11.98, unreported).

▶ **19** In *Bland* v. *Ingram Estates Ltd.* [1999] 25 EG 185, Peter Leaver Q.C. decided that an equitable mortgagee, by

reason of a charging order in respect of a lease, had no right to claim relief against forfeiture of the lease under the court's inherent jurisdiction as he was not a person with any rights of possession. He had merely an equity rather than an equitable interest. In the earlier decision of *Ladup Ltd.* v. *Williams & Glyns Bank plc* (1985), however, Warner J. refused to strike out an application for relief by an equitable chargee by reason of a charging order and opined that the court's inherent jurisdiction might well be wide enough to encompass such a person.

For a recent Court of Appeal decision holding that a person with a charging order was 'a person with an interest under a lease of land derived . . . from the lessee's interest therein' and so within s.138(9C), County Courts Act 1984, see *Croydon Unique Ltd.* v. *Wright & Crombie* [1999] 3 EGLR 28.

▶ **20** *Bank of Ireland Home Mortgages* v. *South Lodge Developments* [1996] 1 EG 91

The landlords obtained an order for possession of a flat in 1991 and peaceably re-entered in March 1992. They informed the mortgagee in April 1992, and in July that year the mortgagee wrote to the landlords undertaking to pay arrears of rent and claiming relief, for which they applied to the County Court on 10 August. On 11 August, the Land Registry cancelled the leasehold title and a new lease was granted on 19 August. The Court of Appeal held that this was not an absolute bar to relief against forfeiture. The landlords had acted unreasonably and the mortgagee was granted a reversionary lease on the new lease.

The landlords were ordered to pay the premium of £48,000 on the new lease to the mortgagee.

This followed the earlier Court of Appeal decision in *Fuller* v. *Judy Properties Ltd.* [1992] 14 EG 106 where relief was granted to an assignee by way of a reversionary lease on a new lease granted by the landlord.

▶ **21** *Official Custodian for Charities* v. *Parway Estates Developments Ltd.* **[1984] 3 All ER 679**

A lease provided for forfeiture on liquidation of the tenant company. Notice of its liquidation appeared in the *London Gazette* in 1979, but the landlords did not see it and continued to accept rent until they learned of the liquidation in 1981. It was held that publication in the *London Gazette* did not amount to notice of the liquidation to the landlords, and they had not therefore waived their right to forfeit by accepting rent subsequently. As relief under s.146(9) and (10) was comprehensive however and there was no right to grant relief in equity, it was too late to grant relief at all.

▶ **22** *Rother District Investments Ltd.* v. *Corke* **[2004] 1 EGLR 47**

▶ **23** For cases on what amounts to sufficient knowledge of a breach of covenant to effect a waiver of the breach, see *Chrisdell* v. *Johnson* (1987) 54 P&CR 257, *Van Haarlam* v. *Kasner* [1992] 2 EGLR 59, and *Cornillie* v. *Saha* (1996) 28 HLR 561.

▶ **24** *Metropolitan Properties Co. Ltd.* v. *Cordery* **(1979) 39 P&CR 10**

A lease of a flat in a block belonging to the landlord contained a covenant against assigning or underletting. In May 1975 the tenant sublet and the sublessee lived in the flat openly. For a period of some eighteen months, she had dealings with the porters over a leak in the flat. In 1978 the landlords instituted forfeiture proceedings for breach of the covenant against underletting. It was held that, as part of the porters' duty was to inform the landlords of any change of occupiers, the landlords had imputed notice of the subletting after a reasonable time for communication of a change in occupation by the porters. The right to forfeit had therefore been waived.

▶ **25** *H. E. Dibble Ltd.* v. *Moore* **[1970] AC 157**

▶ **26** *Leigh* v. *Taylor* **[1902] AC 157**

Tapestries affixed to a wall were held to be chattels as the purpose of affixing them was to enjoy them as chattels.

▶ **27** *D'Eyncourt* v. *Gregory* **[1866] LR 3 Eq 382**

Garden ornaments and seats forming part of the landscaping of the gardens and two statues of lions on pedestals in a large hall were held to be fixtures although not attached to the land and merely resting on it.

▶ **28** Authority for this is the Court of Appeal case of *New Zealand Government Property Corporation* v. *H.M.&S. Ltd.* [1982] 1 All ER 624

Summary

▶ The circumstances discussed in this chapter terminate the contractual relationship between the parties and the estate created by it. In many cases, however, a statutory tenancy will arise on its termination.

▶ A lease for a fixed term terminates automatically when its term expires. Some leases may specifically provide for termination on the happening of a specified event during the term, or may contain a 'break' clause (see section 8.7).

▶ Periodic tenancies, which continue automatically from period to period, are terminable by notice to quit given by either party. Any undue restriction on the right to serve a notice to quit will be void. The notice is generally for the period of the term, Notice served by one of two landlords, or one of two tenants, will be sufficient to terminate a periodic tenancy.

▶ A lease may be terminated by the tenant surrendering his term to his landlord, or by his immediate landlord acquiring the tenant's term so that it merges into the landlord's reversion. An express surrender or merger should be by deed to comply with s.52 LPA 1925, as it involves the transfer of a legal estate, but a surrender may be implied by operation of law and will be exempt from this rule.

▶ Forfeiture proceedings for non-payment of rent involve a different procedure from forfeiture proceedings for breach of any other covenant and have been dealt with in Section 8.2. Forfeiture proceedings for breach of any covenant other than payment of rent must be commenced by service of a notice under s.146 LPA 1925, the purpose of which is to allow the tenant to remedy or compensate for his breach of covenant. A landlord may lose his right to forfeit if he waives a breach of covenant unless it is a continuing breach.

▶ Section 146(2) gives the court a wide and unfettered discretion to grant relief against forfeiture to a tenant, and s.146(4) a right to grant relief to a subtenant whether the forfeiture of the headlease is for nonpayment of rent or breach of any other covenant. There is also an inherent jurisdiction to grant relief to a subtenant in addition to the statutory power under s.146(4), except in cases of bankruptcy or liquidation where the right to relief specified in s.146(10) is comprehensive.

▶ A lease maybe terminated by a trustee in bankruptcy disclaiming it and damages on disclaimer will be assessed as damages for breach of contract.

▶ The contractual doctrines of frustration and repudiatory breach may also apply to terminate leases.

Exercises

15.1 In the absence of any express provision, what period of notice should be given to terminate:

(a) a monthly tenancy, and
(b) a yearly tenancy?

15.2 Distinguish between the termination of a lease by surrender and by merger. In what circumstances will a surrender by operation of law be implied?

15.3 What are the requirements of a valid s.146 notice? Have the courts relaxed these requirements in certain circumstances?

15.4 What is the significance in forfeiture proceedings of a continuing and non-continuing breach of a covenant?

15.5 What rights of relief has a subtenant if the headlease out of which his sublease is derived is forfeited? Do these rights extend to a mortgagee of the lease?

15.6 What are tenant's fixtures?

Workshop

1 John and Jane took a weekly tenancy of a flat which started on Saturday. Consider the validity of the following:

(a) an agreement by the landlord not to serve a notice to quit unless he required the flat for his own use (see Chapter 2.2);
(b) seven days' notice to quit by the landlord served on Friday evening;
(c) twenty-eight days' notice to quit served by the landlord on Saturday evening;
(d) seven days' notice to quit served by John alone on the landlord on Friday evening.

2 Two years ago Kyle granted a seven-year lease to Tom which includes a proviso for re-entry on breach of covenant. The lease contains a covenant not to assign or sublet without the landlord's consent and to use the premises only as a private dwellinghouse.

Six months ago, Tom assigned the lease to Joe without consent. Joe is carrying on a mail-order business from the premises. Advise Kyle as to:

(i) whether he may forfeit the lease;
(ii) if so, the procedure for forfeiture.

3 Four years ago Cameron granted a ten-year lease of a flat to Teri, and two years ago Teri sublet to Susy for three years.

(i) Teri has defaulted on payment of the rent and Cameron has commenced forfeiture proceedings. Advise Susy.
(ii) Cameron has discovered that Susy is using the premises for immoral purposes contrary to a covenant in the lease. Advise Cameron and Teri.

Part II

Leases: the statutory codes

Chapter 16

Private residential accommodation

Introduction

Although this is the area of law most frequently associated with landlord and tenant, it has come to affect a dwindling number of people – despite attempts by successive governments to reinvigorate the private rented sector. The first Rent Act (known as the Increase of Rent and Mortgage Interest (War Restrictions) Act) was passed in 1915 in order to prevent landlords (most particularly in Glasgow) from raising rents to exploit the increased wages of munitions workers. As its title suggests, the Act was intended as a temporary measure but it was followed by a succession of Rent Acts which variously reduced security and rent control (in 1923 and 1933), restored it (in 1939), withdrew it (in 1957) replaced it again (in 1965), and extended it to most lettings without resident landlords (in 1974). The last act in this long line is the Rent Act 1977 – a consolidating act – to which around 80,000 tenancies are still subject. The different rationales behind the various Acts all failed to halt the decline of the private sector from 90 per cent of total stock in 1914 to 11 per cent in 1981 and 7 per cent in 1991. However, subject to a very few exceptions, no new Rent Act tenancies have been created since 15 January 1989 and the changes made by the Housing Acts of 1988 and 1996 have led to a slight increase so that the private rented sector today accounts for around 10 per cent in Great Britain (Office of the Deputy Prime Minister, *Housing Statistics 2003*).

In September 1987, the government published a White Paper (Department of the Environment, *Housing: The Government's Proposals*, Cm 214) in which it set out proposals for deregulating new lettings by private landlords with the aim of regenerating the private rented sector. Its proposals were incorporated in the Housing Act 1988. The 1988 Act applies only to tenancies created on or after its commencement date, 15 January 1989. Thousands of tenants continue to be bound, therefore, by the Rent Acts, whose philosophy is very different from that of the 1988 Act. Whereas the Rent Acts provide indefinite security of tenure to all who fall within them, together with rent control and control of premiums, the Housing Act 1988 gives much more limited security, and at market rents. The changes were, and are, intended to encourage potential landlords to enter the market because the returns on their investment will be better and they will be able to recover possession more easily. As the figures above indicate, the changes made by the Housing Act 1988 (which itself has been amended by the Housing Act 1996) have been marginally successful, with many people using private renting either as a first step on their way to join the 70 per cent of households in Great Britain who are owner occupiers or on their way down the property ladder from owner occupation, often as a reuslt of relationship breakdown. This chapter will consider tenancies created under the Rent Act 1977 and the Housing Acts of 1988 and 1996.

It should be noted that the Law Commission has recently undertaken a comprehensive review of the legal framework for regulating the provision of rented homes. Observing that 'the current position is extremely complex', it has proposed that there should be only two statutory housing 'statuses': type I agreements (which would be periodic agreements only) providing a high degree of security of tenure and type II agreements (which could be either fixed-term or periodic) with a low degree of security. The Commission anticipates that social landlords would usually use the type I agreement and private landlords the type II. Were the Commission's recommendations to be put on a statutory footing, they would apply not only to all new housing agreements but should also, as far as possible, embrace existing tenancies and licences. However, as the Commission points out, 'any decision as to whether or not the Bill the Commission finally produces is introduced into Parliament is wholly a matter for Government' (Law Commission, *Renting Homes* (Law Com No 284 2003)) and it remains to be seen whether it will ever find its way onto the statute book. In the meantime the Government has expressed its commitment to the 'present structure of assured and assured shorthold tenancies' which it describes as 'working well' and has made it clear that there is no question of rent controls being re-introduced in the 'deregulated market' (ODPM, *Quality and Choice: A Decent Home for All, The Housing Green Paper* (2000), para 5.2).

16.2 Concepts Applicable to All Residential Tenancies

16.2.1 A Dwellinghouse Let as a Separate Dwelling

Although each type of residential tenancy has its own special preconditions governed by its respective piece of legislation, one condition applies to them all, including long leases. It has its origins in the Rent Acts and is to be found in s.1 of the 1977 Act which requires there to be 'a tenancy of a dwelling house ... let as a separate dwelling'. Similar wording is to be found in s.1(1) of the Housing Act 1988, and in s.79 of the Housing Act 1985 – the latter provision governing secure tenancies, which are discussed in detail in Chapter 18. This commonality, together with exhaustive judicial interpretation of almost every word in the section, merits closer examination before exploring in detail the types of tenancy currently existing and the security enjoyed by the tenants – who may, of course, be sole occupants or joint tenants as recognised in s.1(1) of the 1988 Act and s.81 of the 1985 Act.

16.2.2   'Dwellinghouse'

There is no statutory definition of 'dwellinghouse'. The term covers anywhere immobile which 'constructed or adapted for use as, or for the purposes of, a dwelling' (*Ashridge Investments Ltd.* v. *Ministry of Housing and Local Government* (1965)). A dwellinghouse was formerly viewed as a place where the tenant could carry on all the 'ordinary activities of daily existence': sleeping, cooking and eating. If one or more of the ordinary activities of daily existence could not take place on the premises, they could not amount to a dwellinghouse and a tenancy of them was not, therefore, protected under the Rent Acts (*Curl* v. *Angelo* (1948)) or assured under the Housing Act 1988. However, in *Uratemp Ventures Ltd.* v. *Collins* (2001), the House of Lords held that a room without any cooking facilities could be a 'dwellinghouse'. Lord Millett summarised the position as follows: If the subject-matter of the tenancy agreement is a house or part of a house of which the tenant has exclusive possession with no element of sharing, the only question is whether it is the tenant's home. If so, it is his dwelling. The presence or absence of cooking facilities is irrelevant. In reaching their decision, their Lordships were mindful of the social changes which had taken place (including the growth in the number of single person households and the proliferation of 'self-service cafeteria, sandwich shops, takeaway shops, home delivery services and other fast food outlets') which made it necessary to interpret the legislation 'in the world of today.' Lord Bingham of Cornhill voiced his reluctance to regard as a dwellinghouse a room which was 'so small and cramped as to be unable to accommodate a bed' but Lord Irvine even went so far as to suggest that 'one could live in a room, which is regarded and treated as home, although taking one's sleep, without the luxury of a bed, in an armchair, or in blankets on the floor.' The time at which it has to be judged whether premises are entitled to protection is when the proceedings are brought (*Prout* v. *Hunter* (1924)) so that it is irrelevant, for example, that the premises were originally let unfurnished.

A degree of permanence would also appear to be necessary. In *Elitestone* v. *Morris* (1997) a wooden bungalow, resting by its own weight on concrete pillars which were attached to the ground, was held by the House of Lords to be part of the land and to be a dwelling-house because it could only be removed by being demolished. By contrast, a moored houseboat, which could easily be removed from its position and detached from its connections to utility supplies, did not constitute a dwellinghouse because it was not annexed to the land to the extent that it had become part of the land (*Chelsea Yacht & Boat Co Ltd.* v. *Pope* (2000)).

Caravan dwellers may fall within the Rent Act 1977 or Housing Act 1988 if their homes have become permanent fixtures, for example with wheels removed and solid bases constructed (*Makins* v. *Elson* (1977); cf *R* v. *Rent Officer of the Nottingham Registration Area ex p Allen* (1985)). Such major alterations are unlikely, however, and security will more probably depend on whether or not the site they occupy is 'protected' and whether or not they own or occupy their caravan. This area is more fully considered below in 16.7.

16.2.3 'Let'

The use of this word emphasises that the premises must be the subject of a lease, not a licence (although it should be noted that the Housing Act 1985 specifically extends protection to 'a licence to occupy a dwellinghouse' (s.79(3)). In the context of private residential occupiers the lease/licence division will have a significant impact on security of tenure and rent control. Attempts to circumvent the protection which the legislation affords to them have manifested themselves in a variety of ways, including agreements whereby the landlord retains a right to enter and/or occupy at will, agreements calling themselves licences, or the grant reserving a right to the landlord to add extra occupiers at will. The continuing difficulties of classifying interests into leases or licences were considered in Chapter 1. Suffice to say, the courts should take into account the agreement itself and the circumstances surrounding its creation, and should be astute to ascertain its true character.

16.2.4 'As'

The interest must have been created for *residential purposes*. If the user becomes mixed the courts will examine the degree and frequency of the business use (*Cheryl Investments* v. *Saldanha, Royal Life Saving Society* v. *Page* (1977)) in order to discover whether the letting has lost the security of the relevant legislation. The status of mixed residential and business lettings is considered further at Chapter 19.2.5. Additionally or alternatively, of course, the landlord may consider seeking possession under the forfeiture provisions of the Law of Property Act 1925 s.146 (discussed at Chapter 15.5) on the basis of breach of an express user covenant.

16.2.5 'A'

The Rent and Housing Acts apply only to lettings of one unit. Thus the lessee of a house divided into bedsitters will be able to claim security only for that area which he or she occupies and not for the whole house, even though it may all be used for residential purposes. It should be noted, however, that two or more physically separate units, demised together, may together constitute a single dwelling (see, e.g., *Whitty* v. *Scott-Russell* (1950)).

16.2.6 'Separate'

Most tenants will have exclusive possession of all the accommodation they use – being totally separate from other occupiers although, as was explained in Chapter 1, two or more people may together enjoy exclusive possession as joint tenants provided that the 'four unities' are present.

Sometimes, however, the tenant will enjoy exclusive possession of 'separate' accommodation (usually a bedroom) but will share living accommodation, such as a kitchen or bathroom, with other tenants. Section 22 of the Rent Act and s.3(5) of the 1988 Act (but not the 1985 Act) provide that the tenant will have a protected or assured tenancy of his 'separate' accommodation in spite of the sharing element. No order can be made for possession of the shared accommodation unless a similar order is (or has been) made in respect of the separate accommodation. Thus a tenancy can be protected (or assured) even though the tenant has to share a kitchen or bathroom with other tenants.

Problems will occur when the landlord is in residence: this will reduce the pre-15 January 1989 tenant to the holder of a restricted contract, and the post-14 January 1989 tenant to a tenant without protection.

16.2.7 Rateable Value Limits

Until the abolition of rates, and their replacement by Community Charge and then Council Tax, a crucial factor dictating whether private sector tenancies had any security of tenure was whether their rateable values exceeded the limit applicable on the appropriate day: only if it did not could they claim protection. Removal of rating for individual properties in 1990 necessitated a review of the process. The present position is as follows:

(a) The appropriate day is 23 March 1965 if the property was registered for rating purposes on that day (s.25(3) Rent Act 1977).

(b) But if it was not so registered on that day, the appropriate day is the date on which it was registered.

(c) The rateable value limits for (a) and (b) above are £1,500 in Greater London and £750 elsewhere in England and Wales.

(d) For the purpose of both the Rent Act 1977 and the Housing Act 1988, properties whose rateable value on the appropriate day as defined above exceeded the limits could not claim any of the benefits of the legislation as protected tenants, assured tenants or assured shorthold tenants. The Rent Act 1977 s.5 and Housing Act 1988 Schedule 1, Paragraph 3, further provide that no security exists if the occupier pays no rent or rent is less than two-thirds of the rateable value.

(e) With the abolition of rateable values, leases commencing on or after 1 April 1990 can only claim protection if the rent is below £25,000 per annum *and* over £1,000 per annum in London (£250 elsewhere). Rent does not include sums for rates, services, repairs, maintenance or insurance unless it could have been regarded by the parties as so payable as part of the rent.

(f) The changes made in (c) above are made under powers contained in the Local Government and Housing Act 1989, s.189 and apply to the Landlord and Tenant Act 1954, the Leasehold Reform Act 1967 and the Housing Act 1988.

16.3 Excluded Lettings

Some interests are excluded from full protection under the Housing Act and the Rent Act. This section lists the exclusions and indicates their effect.

(a) Tenancies of properties which exceed the rateable value or rental limits, as explained above in section 16.2.

(b) Tenancies let at a low rent: that is less than two-thirds of the rateable value or granted since 1 April 1990 at a rent of below £1,000 per annum in London or £250 per annum elsewhere, or tenancies where there is no rent (s.5 Rent Act; Sch 1, para 3, Housing Act). Many of the interests in this heading or in (a) above will be long leases and therefore within the law discussed in Chapter 18. If the latter does not apply, the only protection afforded to these tenants will be under the Protection from Eviction Act 1977: that is notice to quit and possession only through judicial process (see 16.8 below). The relationship between rent and rateable value is highlighted when the tenant carries out some services for the landlord and suggests that, if these were taken into account, she or he would acquire some protection. While the courts have accepted that services or payment of bills can be taken into account, they must be capable of quantification, as through scrutiny of records such as bills, bank statements or such like (*Barnes* v. *Barratt* (1970)).

(c) Business lettings, including premises licensed for the sale of liquor, all of which are dealt with in Chapter 19.

(d) Agricultural tenancies, which are discussed in Chapter 20.

(e) Lettings to students by educational institutions, whether the students are studying at the leasing institution or not. The occupants will be eligible for protection under the Protection from Eviction Act.

(f) Holiday lettings (s.9 Rent Act; Sch 1, para 9 Housing Act). There will, of course, be no difficulty when the occupier wants the premises only for a short break from the trials and tribulations of life. More complicated, however, are the arrangements where the 'holiday-maker' has lived in the premises for some time and perceives it as his or her home, perhaps leaving from the address each day in order to go to work. So-called 'holidays lets' were another mechanism used by landlords to circumvent the Rent Acts. The leading case is *Buchmann* v. *May* (1978) in which Mrs May, a ballet dancer from New Zealand, agreed with her landlord to take a further three month letting of premises in Norbury which she, her husband and child had occupied for about two years under a series of short lets. The tenancy agreement stated that the letting was 'solely for the purpose of the tenant's holiday in the London area.' At the end of the period, she refused to vacate, claiming that she had a protected tenancy. The Court of Appeal turned to the dictionary definition of 'holiday' as 'a period of cessation from work or a period of recreation' and held that, where the tenancy is stated to be for a holiday, the onus is on the tenant to prove that the provision has been inserted in the agreement so as to derpive him or her of statutory protection. Given the more rigorous approach advocated by the House of Lords in *Street* v. *Mountford* and the requirement that the courts look at the realities of the situation, *Buchmann* v. *May* might well be decided differently today. A holiday letting granted after 15 January 1989 is an excluded tenancy (see section 16.8) so that the court order and four-week notice to quit rules contained in ss.3 and 5 of the Protection from Eviction Act 1977 do not apply. It is lawful, therefore, for the landlord to recover possession once the tenancy has expired, with or without a court order.

(g) Tenancies with resident landlords (s.12 Rent Act; Sch 1, para 10 Housing Act). The purpose of this exemption is to encourage resident owners with spare accommodation to let it, secure in the knowledge that they can recover it without difficulty and sell with vacant possession (*O'Sullivan* v. *Barnett* (1995)). Both the Rent Act, Schedule 2 and the Housing Act 1988, Schedule 1 set out specific requirements for resident landlords, in that

– the premises must not be a purpose-built block of two or more flats, one of which is occupied by the landlord. It is therefore possible to apply the resident landlord exception to properties where the tenant occupies self-contained extensions or additions to the original building (*Wolff* v. *Waddington* (1989)) or where a large house is converted into separate, self-contained dwellings, one of which is occupied by the landlord;

– the shared accommodation must be the landlord's only or principal home, the test being one of fact and degree; thus in *Palmer* v. *McNamara* (1990) a landlord only occupied his share of the house during the daytime. He was unable to cook so had no cooker: he was unable to dress or undress himself, so spent each night with a friend. It was held that he was resident because he was in occupation as much as he was able;

– tenancy must not have originally been an interest granted to a tenant with a non-resident landlord who moves in and then grants a new lease. In this situation, the original protection continues.

The status of these occupiers will vary depending on whether their lease was created before or after the 1988 Act came into force. Where, but for the resident landlord exemption, the occupier would have a protected tenancy (the agreement was entered into before 15 January 1989) the occupier will have a restricted contract (unless the rent is varied after that date, as such variation will be deemed to have given rise to a new contract – which is not restricted). Restricted contract holders enjoy limited rights of rent control and security of tenure. The jurisdiction for assessing and registering 'reasonable' rents is conferred on the Rent Tribunal (the Rent Assessment Committee in another guise) which has a duty to maintain a register of reasonable rents and cannot re-consider an application for the registering of such a rent until the expiry of two years from the previous application unless certain exceptional circumstances apply (s. 80(1) Rent Act 1977). Once a reasonable rent has been registered, the landlord cannot recover more from their tenants than the registered sums (s.81 Rent Act 1977). Holders of restricted contracts granted between 28 November 1980 and 15 January 1989 are entitled to 4 weeks' notice to quit in the prescribed form (s.5 Protection from Eviction Act 1977) and the county court has the power to stay or suspend the execution of an order for possession for up to 3 months after making the order (s. 106(A)(2) and (3) Rent Act 1977). A tenancy or other contract entered into after 15 January 1989 is incapable of being a restricted contract unless it was entered into in pursuance of a contract made before the commencement of the 1988 Act (s.36 Housing Act 1988).

(h) Crown tenancies, tenancies of the Duchies of Cornwall and Lancaster, and tenancies granted by government departments continue to be outside the legislation (s.13 Rent Act; Sch 1, Para 11 Housing Act), although Crown tenants may create assured etc. subtenancies within the terms of their individual leases. Crown tenants are protected by the Protection from Eviction Act 1977, as amended, and discussed at 16.7 below. Sections 27 and 28 of the 1988 Act, which are also discussed at 16.7 do not apply to these lettings (s.44).

The National Health and Community Care Act 1990 s.60 provides that lettings by Health Authorities on or after 1 April 1991 are no longer excluded from the Housing Act 1988 Schedule 1.

(i) Public sector tenancies, including transitional lettings in that sector, which are discussed in Chapter 18.

(j) Where the dwelling-house was let in good faith at a rent which included payments in respect of board and attendance, the tenancy will not be protected under the Rent Act (s.7 Rent Act). The onus is on the tenant to show lack of *good faith* (so see again Chapter 1 on licences). Substantiality apparently has a low threshold given the House of Lords decision in *Otter* v. *Norman* (1989) in which the grantor let a bedsitter for a weekly rent which included a continental breakfast served in a communal dining-room. The breakfast amounted to two bread rolls with butter and marmalade, unlimited coffee or tea with milk and sugar, milk for cornflakes (provided by the tenant) and a glass of milk which the tenant drank in his room. The Lords upheld the county court and Court of Appeal decisions that board had been provided since anything more than *de minimus* excluded the tenancy from protection; even though the meal was a modest one, its regularity of serving prevented any finding of bad faith. Attendance has been defined as 'service personal to the tenant performed by an attendant, provided by the landlord in accordance with his covenant for the benefit or convenience of the individual tenant in his use or enjoyment of the demised premises' (*Palser* v. *Grinling* (1948)). The essence of 'attendance' is its personal nature such as cleaning and tidying or changing linen in the particular flat; it does not therefore include services common to others: for example, cleaning common parts, provision of utilities, or piling up everybody's post in a central collection point. In *Nelson Developments Ltd.* v. *Taboada* (1992) the parties' oral agreement included an arrangement by which the grantor provided cleaning, laundry, refuse removal, hot water, window cleaning, lighting and heating of common parts, and a non-residential housekeeper. On receiving notice to quit the tenant asserted that provision of linen was not attendance so he was entitled to statutory protection. The Court of Appeal held that (i) provision of linen could be included in attendance, and (ii) an acceptable test of substantiality was whether the services amounted to 20 per cent or more of the rent. Here they did, so the letting carried no protection. An occupier who is provided with board and attendance will have a restricted contract.

No such exclusion applies to tenancies granted on or after 15 January 1989 so that a letting which includes payments in respect of board and attendance can be an assured tenancy so long as all the other conditions are satisfied.

16.4 The Transitional Provisions

The erratic changes in direction and policy resulting from different legislation have meant that protection has had to be preserved for those whose tenancies were granted under previous, repealed, statutory provisions. The mechanism for that protection has been transitional provisions which, as time goes on, apply to an ever-decreasing number of tenants.

The most important current transitional provision is s.34 of the Housing Act 1988 which states that no protected or restricted contracts can be created after the Act came into force. However, the same section goes on to recognise that protected tenancies may still be granted

- in pursuance of a contract made before the commencement of the Act; or
- where, before the grant of the tenancy, an order was made against the tenant on the ground of suitable alternative accommodation (see section 16.5) and the court has directed that the gant of an assured tenancy would not afford the required security; or
- to a person who was a protected or statutory tenant of the landlord immediately before the grant. It would be prudent in the latter situation for the new lease to contain a clause confirming that the parties agree that the new tenancy is protected under the Rent Act pursuant to s.34. In *Secretarial and Nominee Co Ltd.* v. *Thomas* (2005) it was made clear that the purpose behind s. 34 is to extend Rent Act protection to a person who was a Rent Act tenant when the Housing Act 1988 came into force and not to 'parties who become tenants of the landlord after the commencement of the new regime'. Thus, although the grant of joint tenancies – after 15 January 1989 – to the protected tenant and others would have resulted in protected tenancies, the grant of further joint tenancies after the protected tenant's departure to people who had been joint tenants with him under earlier tenancies did not suffice to confer protected status upon them.

16.5 Lettings under the Rent Act 1977

16.5.1 Security of Tenure

To recover possession of a property let on a protected tenancy, any contractual tenancy must first be brought to an end at common law, by notice to quit (in the case of a periodic tenancy) or effluxion of time or forfeiture (in the case of a fixed term tenancy). Once the contractual tenancy has been terminated, a statutory tenancy arises (s.2).

16.5.2 Statutory Tenancies

At Common Law, the expiry or termination of a contractual tenancy brings the tenant's rights of occupation to an end. However, when a Rent Act protected tenancy is determined (for example, a fixed term expires or a periodic tenancy is ended by notice to quit) the former protected tenant will be a statutory tenant 'if and so long as he occupies the dwelling-house as his residence' (s.2(1)(a), Rent Act 1977). The statutory tenant will hold on the same terms as the original contract of tenancy in so far as they are consistent with the requirements of the Act (s.3(1)). Protected tenancies and statutory tenancies are together known as 'regulated' tenancies.

A statutory tenant may surrender his tenancy or, subject to s.5, Protection from Eviction Act 1977 (see 16.8 below), bring it to an end by giving the notice to quit specified in the original lease. If no notice is specified (that is, where the protected tenancy was a fixed term tenancy), not less than three months' notice must be given (s.3(3)). The landlord cannot lawfully recover possession from a statutory tenant unless he obtains a court order which will be granted only if he can provide suitable alternative accommodation for the tenant or establish one of the grounds for possession contained in Sch.15, Rent Act 1977. No notice to quit need be served before possession is sought from a statutory tenant (s.3(4)) but it may be in the landlord's best interests to serve such notice or to send the tenant a 'letter before action' if the landlord is seeking to recover possession on one of the discretionary grounds contained in the 1977 Act.

Statutory tenants under the Rent Act are not tenants in the true sense of the word since they have no estate or interest in the premises, no existing contract of tenancy and no right at common law to retain possession. What they have instead is a statutorily protected 'status of irremoveability' (*Keeves* v. *Dean* (1924)); in other words a right as against the whole world to remain in possession until an order of the court is obtained. They can therefore bring an action in trespass against anyone who enters the premises without their permission. Generally speaking, a statutory tenancy is not assignable (*Keeves* v. *Dean* (1924)) and cannot be transmitted by will (*John Lovibond &*

Sons v. *Vincent* (1929)). However, up to two statutory transmissions may take place in favour of the spouse and/or members of the family of the deceased tenant (see below). Furthermore, the landlord may agree to a transfer of a statutory tenancy to a third party (Sch.1, para.13, Rent Act 1977) and the court may, during divorce proceedings or on the separation of cohabitants, vest protected or statutory tenancies in the non-tenant spouse or cohabitant (Sch.7, Family Law Act 1996).

16.5.3 Residence

For the purposes of a Rent Act protected tenancy, the tenant need never live in the property (*Horford Investments* v. *Lambert* (1976)). Residence is an essential ingredient, however, of a statutory tenancy. For a statutory tenancy to exist,

(a) the tenant must hold over from a contractual tenancy which has terminated by expiry of a fixed term, notice to quit, or forfeiture;
(b) the tenancy must have been a protected tenancy at the date of its termination;
(c) the tenant must have been occupying the premises as a residence at the date of termination (regardless of whether or not he or she was living in the premises throughout the contractual period of the tenancy); and
(d) he or she must continue to occupy the dwelling-house as his or her residence (s.2(1)(a), Rent Act 1977).

If a statutory tenant ceases to occupy the premises as his residence, the protection of the Rent Act is lost completely and a landlord bringing possession proceedings need only prove ownership of the premises, the termination of the contractual tenancy and the fact that the tenant no longer resides there. The following points should be noted:

– A limited liability company can be a protected tenant within the Rent Act 1977, but it cannot 'reside' in a dwelling-house personally and is incapable, therefore, of becoming a statutory tenant (*Hiller* v. *United Dairies (London) Ltd.* (1934)). Not surprisingly, the company let was a device often used by landlords to limit the effect of the Rent Acts, the landlord usually requiring the tenant to acquire an 'off-the-shelf' company with which the agreement to occupy would then be made (e.g. *Hilton* v. *Plustitle Ltd.* (1989)).
– 'The tenant cannot be compelled to spend twenty four hours in all weathers under his own roof for three hundred and sixty-five days in the year' (per Asquith L.J. in *Brown* v. *Brash and Ambrose* (1948)). An absent

tenant will still be regarded as occupying the premises as his residence within the meaning of s.2(1)(a) provided that he can show both (a) a continuing physical presence and (b) an intention to return. The former requires some outward and visible evidence of the tenant's intention to return, such as furniture or occupation (as a licensee) by a relative. The latter must be 'a real hope, coupled with the practical possibility of its fulfilment within a reasonable time' (per Ormerod L.J. in *Tickner* v. *Hearn* (1960)). What is a reasonable time depends on the circumstances. In *Brickfield Properties Ltd.* v. *Hughes* (1988), in which a statutory tenant of a flat in London (in which he kept books and furniture) lived most of the time with his wife in a cottage in Lancashire. Between 1978 and 1987 he did not visit the flat at all but it was occupied by his three adult children and a son-in-law. The tenant's wife was in poor health and the tenant intended to return to London if her health deteriorated or she died. Because there was a real possibility of the tenant's return to the flat within a reasonable time, the landlord's application for possession was dismissed.

– A tenant may occupy two properties at the same time, maintaining Rent Act protection in either or both. Comparatively short periods of occupation in one home may suffice as in *Bevington* v. *Crawford* (1974) where the tenants lived mainly in Cannes and spent approximately two to three months each year in their rented accommodation in Harrow. However, in *Hampstead Way Investments Ltd.* v. *Lewis-Weare* (1985) the statutory tenant married and moved into a nearby house. The tenant kept his flat, sleeping there five times a week so that he did not disturb his wife when he returned home early in the morning from his job at a night club. He kept his work clothes at the flat, his mail was delivered there and he paid the rent and all other outgoings. He did not eat there, however, nor entertain his friends there. The House of Lords held that the tenant's limited use of the flat, and the fact that one essential activity of daily life, i.e., eating, was not carried out there, meant that his occupation was insufficient to make it his second home. There was not therefore the required residence and thus no security of tenure.

Secure tenants and assured tenants can only obtain protection as to their only or principal homes (s.81, Housing Act 1985 and s.1, Housing Act 1988).

16.5.4 Possession Proceedings

Once the contractual tenancy has been determined, the landlord can commence court proceedings. By s.98(1), a court cannot make an order for possession of a dwelling-house which is let on a protected tenancy or subject to a statutory tenancy unless it considers it reasonable to make such an order and either (a) it is satisfied that suitable alternative accommodation is available for the tenant or will be when the order in question takes effect; or (b) the circumstances are as specified in any of the Cases in Part 1 of Sch.15 to the Rent Act 1977 (the discretionary grounds). By s.98(2) the court must make an order for possession if the circumstances of the case are as specified in any of the Cases in Part II of Sch.15 (the mandatory grounds).

16.5.5   Reasonableness

Reasonableness is not an issue if a landlord is seeking an order of possession by establishing a mandatory ground for possession but it must always be considered if the landlord is pleading one of the discretionary grounds for possession or, alternatively, seeking to establish, in the case of a Rent Act regulated tenant, that suitable alternative accommodation is available. Even where a ground or case itself in terms involves a requirement of reasonableness, the general issue of reasonableness must itself be separately considered. Failure by the court to consider reasonableness (even where the tenant does not enter an appearance or serve any defence) means that the order can be set aside (*Peachy Property Corporation Ltd.* v. *Robinson* (1967)).

The onus is upon the landlord to convince the court that it is reasonable to order possession. In *Cumming* v. *Danson* (1942), Lord Greene MR explained that

> the judge is to take into account all relevant circumstances as they exist at the date of the hearing . . . in . . . a broad commonsense way as a man of the world, . . . giving such weight as he thinks right to the various factors. Some factors may have little or no weight, others may be decisive, but it is quite wrong for him to exclude from his consideration matters which he ought to take into account.

The 'relevant circumstances' might include such matters as the health of the parties (*Briddon* v. *George* (1946)), their ages (*Battlespring Ltd* v. *Gates* (1983)), the financial consequences if an order for possession were to be made (*Williamson* v. *Pallant* (1924)), the public interest (*Cresswell* v. *Hodgson* (1951)), loss of amenities (*Siddiqui* v. *Rashid* (1980)), and the conduct of the parties (*Yelland* v. *Taylor* (1957)). The judge must look at the effect on each party of the court making or withholding the order (*Cresswell* v. *Hodgson*).

16.5.6   The Discretionary Cases

Case 1   The tenant is in breach of covenant or is in rent arrears. The effect of the exercise of judicial discretion here is that an offer to pay the arrears (provided there is evidence of the money being available), or an undertaking to remedy or not to repeat the breach will very likely lead to a refusal of possession (*Central Estates* v. *Woolgar* (1972)).

Case 2 The tenant, or anyone else residing or lodging with him, or any subtenant, has been guilty of conduct which is a nuisance to adjoining occupiers, or has been convicted (not just warned or accused) of using or allowing the dwelling to be used for immoral or illegal purposes. Again the discretion manifests itself in it being open to the tenant to undertake not to repeat the transgression. The term 'adjoining owners' is widely interpreted to include anyone sufficiently close to be affected (*Cobstone* v. *Maxim* (1984)). As regards conviction for immoral or illegal purposes, the landlord must show that the premises themselves were connected with the crime; it is 'not enough that the tenant has been convicted of a crime with which the premises have nothing to do beyond merely being the scene of its commission' (*Schneiders & Sons* v. *Abrahams* (1925)). If the tenant has been convicted of the possession of drugs but the drugs were merely found in the tenant's pocket or handbag, this would not amount to using the premises. It would be different if the premises were used as storage or as a hiding-place (*Abrahams* v. *Wilson* (1971)).

Case 3 Deterioration of the dwelling-house owing to acts of waste by, or the neglect or default of the tenant, or any person residing or loding with him, or any subtenant.

Case 4 Deterioration of any furniture provided for use under the tenancy owing to ill-treatment by the tenant, or any person residing or loding with him, or any subtenant. Neither of these last two Cases is often used owing to their technical meaning and their obvious overlap with the wider Case 1.

Case 5 The tenant has given notice to quit and the landlord has acted in reliance upon that notice, e.g. by undertaking to sell with vacant possession.

Case 6 The tenant has assigned or sublet the premises without consent. Statutory tenants will lose protection if they assign or sublet since they will have ceased to occupy the dewlling-house as their residence, so this Case is relevant only for protected tenants whose lease does not contain any prohibition against assignment etc.

Case 7 The tenancy is an off-licence and the tenant has, by offences under the Licensing Acts, prejudiced his chances of renewing the licence. This case has been repealed.

Case 8 The tenant was an employee of the landlord, the employment has ceased, and the landlord wants the premises for another employee. This Case deals only with service tenants, not service occupiers. The latter are those obliged to live in the premises in order to do their jobs properly and are classified as licensees. The trend of decisions has been towards widening the group of service licensees (*Torbett* v. *Faulkener* (1952)) with a consequent reduction in scope of this Case.

Case 9   The landlord acquired the property by purchase before the relevant date and reasonably requires the premises for himself or herself, spouse or civil partner, any child over the age of eighteen, or a parent or parent-in-law. In reaching a decision on this category the court must weigh up where the greater hardship lies, taking account, for example, of any alternative accommodation available to either party, together with its cost and security of tenure that would be acquired.

Case 10   The tenant has sublet the premises for a rent greater than that registered with the Rent Officer.

16.5.7   The Mandatory Cases

All the mandatory cases under the Rent Act 1977 require the landlord to serve written notice upon the tenant not later than 'the relevant date' stating that possesssion may be recovered under the case in question. In most cases the relevant date will be the start of the tenancy. The court may dispense with the notice requirement in relation to cases 11, 12, 19 and 20 if it is of the opinion that it is just and equitable to do so.

Case 11   The premises were acquired after the appropriate date, the owner had occupied them as his or her residence before the lease in question, and they are now required for one of the following:

(i)   a residence for the owner or any member of his family who resided there with the owner when he or she last lived there. The court needs to be satisfied that the landlord has a genuine intention to occupy, so any hardship the tenant might suffer from having to move is irrelevant (*Kennealy* v. *Dunne* (1977)). In contrast is *White* v. *Jones* (1994) in which at the start of the tenancy in 1972 an oral indication was given of possible return by the landlord. A year later a letter indicated the tenant could stay provided the rent was paid and the property kept clean and tidy. In 1988 the landlord indicated the possibility of returning from Bermuda and in 1992 possession proceedings were started under Case 11 on the basis that the landlord needed a *pied à terre* for three months each year. The court balanced that need with the effect on tenant of possession: loss of home, need to sell furniture, dogs having to be put down, and found against the landlord. Last, *Lipton* v. *Whitworth* (1994) decides that obtaining occupation with a view to sale does not conflict with possession under Case 11.

(ii) The owner has retired from regular employment and requires the dwelling-house as a residence.

(iii) The owner has died and a member of the deceased's family who lived with the former owner at time of death requires the premises; the purpose of obtaining possession is irrelevant for this condition.

(iv) By the deceased owner's successor in title for residential or other purposes.

(v) By a mortgagee who wants to exercise a power of sale and sell with vacant possession.

(vi) By an owner who wishes to sell in order to obtain somewhere more suitable to his or her needs.

It should be noted that prior residence by the landlord is required although it need not be in his or her capacity as freeholder. Furthermore, the Court of Appeal held in *Mistry* v. *Isidore* (1990) that it was not necessary for the landlord to show that he had occupied the premises as a home but merely as a residence and that such occupation could be temporary or intermittent Here, the tenancy was of a first-floor flat in premises where the landlord and his brother ran a newsagent's, confectioner's and dry-cleaning business on the ground floor. For some eight or nine weeks prior to the letting, the landlord had slept at the flat for five to six nights a week, spending the other night(s) in his brother's home where he kept most of his belongings. The flat contained no washing or cooking facilities. The Court of Appeal held that the landlord had occupied the flat as his residence within the meaning of Case 11. An owner-occupier seeking possession of his house under Case 11 need not show that he reasonably requires to occupy the house; merely that he genuinely wants and intends to do so as a residence for himself or for members of his family (*Kennealy* v. *Dunne* (1977)).

Case 12 The property was acquired by the landlord and let after 14 August 1974 with a view to occupation on retirement. Possession will be granted if: (i) the owner wants to occupy the property as a residence on retirement, or (ii) any of conditions (ii)–(vi), listed under Case 11, apply. Unlike Case 11, there is no requirement that the owner previously occupied the premises as his or her residence.

Case 13 Premises which within the last twelve months have been the subject of a holiday letting have been let for a fixed term of up to eight months. This Case provides for recovery at the end of long winter lets so that the landlord can gain access to the more lucrative summer holiday market.

Case 14   The premises belong to an educational institution which normally lets them to students, but the institution wishes to let for a fixed term of up to twelve months. This Case covers vacation lettings, although it is not clear why the fixed term needs to be for so long.

Case 15   The premises were let to a minister of religion and are now required for another minister.

Cases 16, 17, 18   Apply to premises which were formerly agricultural tied properties, which are no longer used as such and are not occupied by the former tied tenant (on which see Chapter 20.5), provided that the present occupier was given notice of possible recovery under these Cases.

Case 19   The letting was a protected shorthold tenancy. The protected shorthold tenancy (PST) was a creation of the Housing Act 1980. Such tenancies had to be for a fixed term of between one and five years and, at the end of the term, provided landlords with a mandatory ground for possession in addition to all the other Cases. Since no new PSTs have been created since 15 January 1989, all PSTs existing at that date will by now have run their course. If, however, on or after that date, a landlord grants a tenancy to a tenant who, before the grant, held a PST, the new tenancy will be an asured shorthold tenancy (s.34(3), Housing Act 1988).

Case 20   The owner is a member of the Armed Forces, began letting after 28 November 1980 and requires possession: (i) for use as a residence for himself/herself, or (ii) any of conditions (ii)–(vi) listed under Case 11 apply.

16.5.8   Suitable Alternative Accommodation

Landlords may offer alternative accommodation as a negotiating ploy in the process of obtaining possession, but the Rent Act 1977, the Housing Act 1988 and the Housing Act 1985 all allow for formal offers of suitable alternative accommodation to be made as a way of obtaining possession. If the provision of suitable elternative accommodation is established, the tenant will have the choice of accepting the accommodation on offer or becoming homeless. For the sake of convenience, suitable alternative accommodation – as it applies to all three statutes – is dealt with in this section.

Although the conditions are broadly similar in all three statutes there are some significant differences: the Housing Act 1985 does not include 'character' as a factor to be taken into account when assessing the suitability of the alternative. Again, the 1985 and 1988 Acts specifically include suitable alternative accommodation within the list of Grounds, while the Rent Act presents it as a totally separate way of obtaining possession. Finally, a landlord who successfully obtains possession on this Ground under the 1988 Act is obliged to pay reasonable removal expenses.

So far as availability is concerned, it was held in *London City Properties* v. *Goodman* (1978) that the tenant's own (empty) property can be 'available accommodation'. In *Amrit Holdings Co. Ltd.* v. *Shahbakhti* (2005) the landlords sought to recover possession on the ground that, in accordance with s 98(1), suitable alternative accommodation was available for the tenant in the form of one of his five investment properties which was currently occupied under an assured shorthold tenancy, the contractual term of which had expired. The Court of Appeal held that the alternative accommodation would be available only if it was reasonable to expect the owner to take steps to recover it. They also held that, in considering the reasonableness of making the order, the judge had been entitled to take into account the financial implications of requiring a tenant to reorder his affairs in order to accommodate his landlord. Although the landlords had a legitimate financial interest in getting a higher rent from the premises than they were getting from the tenant, he would lose his investment in his own flat and would have the expense and trouble of bringing proceedings against his tenants.

The criteria for the 1977 and 1988 Acts are contained in Schedule 15, Part IV and Schedule 2, Part III respectively. They are:

(a) Irrespective of anything which follows, the Local Authority has certified that it will provide suitable alternative accommodation by a date stated in the certificate. If the authority does this, its offer is conclusive proof of suitability – although objection could still be made on the grounds of the unreasonableness of having to move at all.

(b) The offered accommodation must be let under an assured or protected tenancy (depending on when the original tenancy was created). This provision also means that the new accommodation:
   - must fall within s.1 of the 1977 or 1988 Act, as the case may be;
   - must not be governed by one of Grounds 1–5 or Cases 11 or 20, all of which are mandatory;
   - must not be an assured shorthold;
   - must give broadly equivalent security to that offered by the relevant piece of legislation. In *Laimond Properties* v. *Al-Shakarchi* (1998) the Court of Appeal concluded that an assured tenancy would provide sufficient security. It would be binding on the head landlord on

expiry of the intermediate landlord's interest to the same extent as would be a protected tenancy, and that would afford sufficient protection to the tenant.

(c) The proposed accommodation must be reasonably suitable as regards proximity to work (which includes voluntary work, on which see *Dakyns* v. *Pace* (1948)) for both the tenant and the tenant's family. 'Family' has the same definition as in the succession cases (see below). In addition, the accommodation must either:

(i) be similar in rent and size to that provided by the Local Authority (again a certificate from the latter will be conclusive on this point), or

(ii) must be reasonably suitable for the means and needs of the tenant as regards extent and character. 'Means' allows account to be taken of eligibility for housing benefit. 'Extent' raises difficult questions when the offer is for fewer rooms in the same premises; the courts will look to whether the tenant uses all the rooms at present and thus needs them or whether one or more lies empty (*McDonnel* v. *Daly* (1969) and *Mykolyshyn* v. *Noah* (1970)). 'Character' allows comparisons to be made between the present and proposed environment. An alternative dwelling on a main road close to shops and other services is not a suitable alternative to a quiet flat with a garden situated in a side road (*Redspring* v. *Francis* (1973)). Loss of friends and society because the new premises are some distance away is not part of character (*Siddiqui* v. *Rashid* (1980)), nor is loss of paddocks and outbuildings (*Hill* v. *Rochard* (1983)). The weight to be given to the various relevant factors is for the trial judge (*Dawncar Investments* v. *Plews* (1994)).

(d) If furniture is provided in the existing assured/protected tenancy, then it must also be provided in the new letting.

(e) The new premises must not be overcrowded within the Housing Act 1985, Part X.

It should be noted that the suitable alternative accommodation provisions are sufficiently general to allow wide judicial discretion. The landlord who offers extras as part of the deal, such as redecoration or reduced rent for some fixed term, might therefore be able to convince the court that borderline accommodation is in reality suitable.

16.5.9 Suspension or Postponement of Possession Orders

Where possession is sought on a discretionary ground, the court may adjourn proceedings for possession for such period as it thinks fit, or, on the making of a possession order or, at any time before its execution, stay or suspend execution of the order or postpone the date of possession for such period as it thinks fit (s.100(1)(2), Rent Act 1977). On any such adjournment, stay, suspension or postponement, the court must impose conditions as to the payment of any rent arrears or mesne profits, or such other conditions as it thinks fit, unless it considers that this would cause exceptional hardship to the tenant or would otherwise be unreasonable (s.100(3), Rent Act 1977). Where the tenant complies with conditions which have been imposed, the court may, if it thinks fit, discharge or rescind the possession order (s.100(4)). The court commonly exercises its discretion to suspend the operation of a possession order, especially where possession is sought on the basis of rent arrears so long as the tenant pays the current rent and a specified amount off the arrears.

The powers exerciseable under s.100 do not apply to the mandatory grounds for possession. In such cases, s.89 of the Housing Act 1980 provides that any postponement (whether by the order or any variation, suspension or sty of execution) can be for no more than fourteen days after the making of the order unless exceptional hardship would be caused by requiring possession to be given up by that date. In such circumstances it shall not be postponed beyond six weeks from the making of the order.

A spouse or former spouse with rights of occupation under the Family Law Act 1996 who has remained in occupation of a dwelling-house let on a protected tenancy or subject to a statutory tenancy has the same rights in relation to the adjournment of proceedings etc. (s.100(4A) and (4B), Rent Act 1977). This provision is useful if, for example, the remaining spouse had no knowledge of mounting rent arrears, believing perhaps that the other spouse was still paying sums due.

16.5.10 Succession

Although the general rule is that the rights of statutory tenants are personal to them and therefore cannot be assigned, an exception exists on death when the tenancy can be transmitted to a surviving member of the tenant's family. A statutory tenancy cannot be devised by will nor will it pass under the intestacy rules. Instead, it is transmitted solely by virtue of the Act. Needless to say there are conditions which must be complied with before transmission can occur. These are set out in the Rent Act 1977, Schedule 1, Part 1 (as amended by the Housing Act 1988).

Under the Rent Act 1977, as originally enacted, a maximum of two transmissions was possible to spouses and members of the deceased's family. A spouse was entitled to succeed if he or she was 'residing in the dwelling-house immediately before the death of the original tenant'. A member of the tenant's family was entitled if he or she had resided with the tenant for at least six months prior to the tenant's death. In *Foreman* v. *Beagley* (1969) the Court of Appeal held that 'residing with' requires some factual community of living and companionship. The tenant spent the last three years of her life in hospital. Her son visited her flat to air it and he lived there for the year immediately preceding her death. The Court of Appeal held that he had not been 'residing with' the tenant as he had only moved in as caretaker without any indication of establishing a joint household. There had never been any 'community of living' with his mother. Had he lived with her before her admission to hospital and continued to live in the flat during her absence, the residence requirement would doubtless have been satisfied.

None of the Rent Acts has included a definition of the word 'family'. In *Brock* v. *Wollams* (1949) Cohen L.J. said that the court should ask itself if an 'ordinary man' would answer 'yes' or 'no' to the question of whether or not the claimant to the tenancy was a member of the family. It has been said that the term 'family' requires 'a broadly de facto familial nexus' which may be 'found and recognised as such by the ordinary man' where the link would be 'strictly familial had there been a marriage, or where the link is through adoption of a minor, de jure or de facto, or where the link is 'step-', or where the link is 'in-law' or by marriage' (per Russell L.J. in *Ross* v. *Collins* (1964)). It has been held to include brothers and sisters (*Price* v. *Gould* (1930)), and a grandchild (*Collier* v. *Stoneman* (1957)) but not first cousins who were living together for reasons of convenience rather than because they were related (*Langdon* v. *Horton* (1951)). In *Carega Properties SA* v. *Sharratt* (1979), the House of Lords made it clear that the only de facto relationships which were recognised for succession purposes were the 'common law' spouse and the 'parent/child' relationship where the child had joined the tenant's household at a young age but had never been legally adopted (cf *Brock* v. *Wollams* and *Sefton Holdings Ltd.* v. *Cairns* (1988)).

For deaths, and hence transmissions, after the Housing Act 1988 came into force, succession to a tenancy for members of the tenant's family is more restricted than weas formerly the case:

▶ Members of the tenant's family must have resided with the tenant throughout the last two years of his or her life in order to qualify;
▶ On the death of a protected tenant on or after 15 January 1989, the second successor must be a member of the original tenant's family and a member of the first successor's family;
▶ The second successor takes as an assured periodic tenant (as explained in section 16.6 below), unless the potential second successor has become a joint tenant with the first successor, in which case the landlord may

be estopped from denying the existence of a statutory tenancy (*Daejan Properties Ltd.* v. *Mahoney* (1995)).

The word 'spouse' is not defined in the Rent Acts but, until the amendments made by the Housing Act 1988, was taken to mean a person who had gone through a legal ceremony of marriage with the tenant. An unmarried cohabitee could not be a spouse and, in order to become a statutory tenant by succession, had to prove that he or she was a member of the tenant's family. The first occasion on which the Court of Appeal was faced with this issue was in *Gammans* v. *Ekins* (1950) in which the defendant had lived with the tenant for 20 years or so 'in close, but unmarried, association'. He had taken her name and posed as her husband. The couple had no children. The court obviously disapproved of the relationship, Asquith L.J. stating that it was 'anomalous' that a person could acquire 'a 'status of irremoveability' by living or having lived in sin.' In *Dyson Holdings* v. *Fox* (1976), the Court of Appeal departed from *Gammans* v. *Ekins* and found for the claimant (who had lived with the tenant as his wife for 21 years until his death but had borne him no children) on the ground that the popular meaning of 'family' had changed. Bridge L.J. spoke of the 'complete revolution in society's attitude to unmarried partnerships' which had occurred between 1950 and 1975. The amendments made to the 1977 Act by the Housing Act 1988 now allow cohabitees to succeed, stating that 'a person who was living with the tenant as his or her wife or husband' is to be treated as the tenant's spouse (Sch 1, para 2(2) Rent Act 1977 inserted by sch 4, para 2, Housing Act 1988). Where the successor is the spouse or a cohabitant, he or she is entitled to a statutory tenancy under the Rent Act 1977.

In *Fitzpatrick* v. *Sterling Housing Association Ltd.* (2001) the House of Lords was called upon to decide whether the homosexual partner of a protected tenant had lived 'with the original tenant as his or her wife or husband' or was 'a member of the tenant's family' for the purposes of the Rent Act 1977. The tenant (who had a Rent Act protected tenancy) and his partner, Mr Fitzpatrick, had lived together in a 'close, loving and faithful, monogamous' homosexual relationship for 18 years. Eight years before his death, the tenant suffered a stroke and Mr Fitzpatrick gave up his work to nurse him full-time. Having reveiwed the statutory scheme, together with Parliament's intention in extending the definition of 'spouse' in 1988, the House of Lords held that a 'spouse' did not include a same sex partner. Living as 'husband and wife' were gender-specific words which connoted a relationship between a man and a woman. Thus the man was required to show that the woman was living with him as 'his' wife, and the woman had to show that the man was living with her as 'her' husband. However, by a majority, their Lordships decided that a same sex partner was capable of being a member of the tenant's family. They made it clear that such a person would have to establish the necessary characteristics of the word 'family' as used in that provision, namely a mutual degree of inter-dependence, the sharing of lives in a single family unit, living in one house, caring and love, commitment and support. Thus a transient superficial relationship would not be sufficient even though it was intimate; nor would mere cohabitation by friends as a matter of convenience.

Fitzpatrick was decided before the Human Rights Act 1998 came into force (on 1 October 2000). In *Mendoza* v. *Ghaidan* (2004) (a post-Human Rights Act case, the facts of which were, in all material respects, identical to those of *Fitzpatrick*) the House of Lords held (by a majority) that to grant a statutory tenancy to the survivor of a heterosexual relationship when the survivor of a same sex relationship was entitled only to the less beneficial assured tenancy amounted to discrimination on the ground of sexual orientation contrary to the non-discrimination provisions of Article 14 of the European Convention on Human Rights (now incorporated into the Human Rights Act). Their Lordships held that the breach could be remedied by construing the words 'as his or her wife or husband' in Sch. 1 para. 2(2) to mean 'as if they were his or her wife or husband'.

Now, as a result of the Civil Partnership Act 2004, the Rent Act succession provisions have been amended so as to allow for transmission of the tenancy to the tenant's 'surviving civil partner'. This will include 'a person who was living with the original tenant as if they were civil partners'. In deciding whether such a relationship exists, the courts may well apply *Southern Housing Group* v. *Nutting* (2005), in which it was held that there must be a relationship of mutual lifetime commitment between the partners, which is openly and unequivocally displayed to the outside world.

The courts may settle disputes as to eligibility, for example between a spouse and a cohabitant, or two children, and may also decide, whether the claimant was actually residing with the deceased.

16.5.11 Rent Control

Under the Rent Act 1977, rent control was achieved through the imposition of a 'fair rent' on regulated tenancies, or the very similar 'reasonable rent' standard on restricted contracts. Assured tenancies within the 1988 Act are let at 'market rents' (see 16.6 below) so this difference between the two types of tenancy is significant and the evidence needed to sustain assertions of scarcity must be carefully assembled (*BTE Ltd.* v. *Merseyside & Cheshire RAC ex p. Jones* (1992)).

With the ending of any opportunity to create new protected tenancies, the fair rent regime will in time disappear. Nevertheless, the continuing presence of a significant number of tenancies whose rents are assessed by very different criteria from assured tenancies makes some mention of their standards of control essential. It should be noted that, if no rent is registered for a dwelling-house subject to a regulated tenancy, the parties are free to agree on whatever rent they like, but either the landlord or the tenant, or both jointly, may apply at ay time for the registration of a fair rent.

The formula for fixing a fair rent is contained in s.70(1) Rent Act 1977, which directs that: 'in determining . . . what rent is or would be a fair rent regard shall be had to all the circumstances (other than personal circumstances) and in particular to (a) age, character, locality and state of repair of the dwelling . . . and (b) any furniture provided (whether or not it remains or even arrives on the premises).' The controversial subsection (2) then follows, requiring rent officers to make their determination on the assumption that 'the number of persons seeking to become tenants of similar dwelling-houses in the locality . . . is not substantially greater than the number of dwelling-houses in the locality which are available for letting'. In other words, local scarcity is to be disregarded. 'Locality' in subsection (2) has been interpreted as being 'a really large area, an area that really gives . . . a fair appreciation of the trends of scarcity and their consequences' (*Metropolitan Properties* v. *Finegold* (1975)). Finally, subsection (3) requires disregard of disrepair or defects attributable to the tenant, tenant's improvements and local amenities arriving after the last registration or after the lease began.

The registration process is by application to the Rent Officer with appeal to the Rent Assessment Committee. The Rent Assessment Committee comprises three members: a legally qualified chair and two valuers. The same group would meet in another guise as the Rent Tribunal to assess 'reasonable rents' on an application by either party in respect of a restricted contract (s.77) were any application still to be made. Proceedings of the Rent Assessment Committee and of the Rent Officer are intended to be informal. They are usually preceded by a visit to the premises followed by a hearing, although in London the reverse order is followed. Once a fair rent has been determined, details thereof must be entered in an area register which is available for public inspection (s.66 Rent Act 1977).

Where a rent for a dwelling-house is registered, the rent recoverable under any regulated tenancy of the dwelling-house is limited to the registered rent (s.44(1), s.45(1) Rent Act 1977). If a regulated tenant has paid more than the registered rent, he or she can recover the excess by proceedings in the county court or by deducting it from future payments of rent (s.57 Rent Act 1977). If the rent is lower than the registered rent, the tenant is bound only to pay the amount which has been contractually determined. If the tenancy agreement provides for an increase in rent, the landlord will have to follow the requirements of the lease and, in addition, serve a notice of increase in the prescribed form (s.49(2) Rent Act 1977). The effect of serving such a notice will be to bring a protected tenancy to an end and to replace it with a statutory tenancy (s.49(4)).

A registered rent normally lasts for two years although an application for a different rent can be made before the expiry of the two year period if there has been such a change in (a) the condition of the dwelling-house (including the making of any improvements), (b) the terms of the tenancy, (c) the qantity, quality of condition of the furniture, or (d) any other circumstances, as to make the registered rent no longer a fair rent (s.67(3)). Once a fair rent is registered, it remains the recoverable rent for the dwelling house in respect of which rent is payable until either the demised premises undergo such a change in their structure as to render them no longer the dwelling house referred to in s.44 or there is a new registration consequent upon s. 67 (*Rakhit* v. *Carty* (1990)).

The Rent Officer or Rent Assessment Committee may adopt any method of ascertaining a fair rent provided that it is not unlawful or unreasonable (*Mason* v. *Skilling* (1974)). A popular method has been the registered comparables test, in which regard is had to the recently registered rents of comparable properties in a locality. The relaxation of controls by the Housing Act 1988 (especially the introduction of the assured shorthold tenancy) has reduced scarcity in the private rented sector with the result that there is a greater number of tenancies (albeit created under the Housing Act 1988) with which comparison can be made. In a series of cases the Court of Appeal made it clear that the preferred method for setting fair rents was no longer to be by comparison with registered fair rents but should be by reference to the open market rents at which comparable properties were being let on assured tenancies (including assured shorthold tenancies) under the 1988 Act. As Auld L.J. observed in *Curtis* v. *London Rent Assessment Committee and others* (1998):

> It now seems to be accepted that if there are market rent comparables enabling the identification of a market rent as a starting point there is normally no need to refer to registered fair rent comparables at all, still less to engage in an arid exercise of verifying or reconsidering their soundness as current indicators of an adjusted market rent . . . it can only cause confusion to attempt to use the two regimes of market and fair rent comparables calibrating one against the other to determine a fair rent.

Not surprisingly, this practice resulted in a steep increase in registered rents, over and above inflation, in the years immediately after the coming into force of the 1988 Act. In England, the average annual rate of increase on re-registration between 1989 and 1995 ranged from 18 per cent to 25 per cent (Department of the Environment, *Housing and Construction Statistics 1985–1995*, HMSO, 1996: Table 11.6). Having pledged before the 1987 general election that it would take steps to stem escalating fair rents for Rent Act tenants, the Government introduced the Rent Act (Maximum Fair Rent) Order 1999. Since the intention of Parliament in enacting the 1988 Act was that existing regulated tenants would continue to enjoy security of tenure, succession rights and fair rents under the Rent Act 1977, it was felt unfair that such tenants (many of them elderly) should face large increases in rent. The Order places a limit on the amount of rent which Rent Officers and Rent Assessment Committees are able to register for regulated tenancies and secure housing association tenancies where a fair rent has previously been registered on the property. The limits are RPI + 7.5 per cent for the first registration after the limit came into force and RPI + 5 per cent for the next and all subsequent registrations. Additional increases are permitted where the landlord has carried out major works to the dwelling.

An application for the determination of a fair rent may be made as a way of checking whether the parties' arrangement is a lease or not, thereby forcing a landlord who objects to jurisdiction being taken to initiate possession proceedings. This rather convoluted process is cheaper than a declaration from the county court as to the nature of the agreement, given that a successful application there would require a further application for a fair rent. The same short-cut could presumably be used in the event of doubt as to whether an agreement is a licence or an assured letting.

16.5.12   Premium Control

Section 128 of the Rent Act 1977 defines a premium as '(a) any fine or other like sum and (b) any pecuniary consideration in addition to rent and (c) any sum paid by way of deposit, other than one which does not exceed one-sixth of the annual rent and is reasonable in relation to the potential liability in respect of which it is paid.' Part IX of the Act declares illegal the process of requiring or receiving a premium as a condition of granting, renewing, continuing or assigning a protected tenancy (ss.119 and 120), or a restricted contract (s.122). It is also illegal to require purchase of furniture, fixtures or fittings at an unreasonable price as a condition of granting, renewing, continuing or assigning either a protected tenancy or a restricted contract (ss.123 and 124). Although ss.119–24 permit recovery by criminal process, s.125 classifies the arrangements as illegal contracts, thereby allowing, as an alternative, civil actions for recovery of money paid. Section 120(3)(*a*) permits an assignor to recover the reasonable cost of structural alterations or of landlord's fixtures from the assignee.

The premium control provisions have always been important as a way of controlling excessive deposits, and preventing landlords charging excessive rents by circuitous routes. Precedents show a readiness to explore the substance of a transaction in order to ascertain whether a landlord, or a former tenant (*Farrell* v. *Alexander* (1976)), had obtained more than they were entitled to receive. There were, of course, problems – such as how to assess an unreasonable charge for furniture – and provisions which allowed legal premiums, such as the provision in s.128 allowing up to two months' rent to be charged as a deposit. It is notable that there are no similar controls of assured and assured shorthold tenancies.

16.6 Lettings under the Housing Act 1988

16.6.1 Assured Tenancies

The Housing Act 1988 creates two varieties of tenancy: the assured tenancy and the assured shorthold tenancy, both of which must comply with the general conditions set out in 16.2 above and must have come into existence on or after 15 January 1989. The differences between them turn on the form of rent control to which they are subject and the amount of security of tenure which each of them confers. The overall result of the post 1988 Act shorthold regime and the amendments made by the Housing Act 1996 has been a steady rise in the number of assured shortholds at the expense of assured tenancies. In 2000/2001, assured shorthold tenancies accounted for 56 per cent of all private sector tenancies (1.2 million) (ODPM, *Survey of English Housing Live Tables*, Table S510 (A5.2)). Now – because of the long-term security they confer – assured tenancies are likely to be granted only by housing associations.

16.6.2 1988 Act Assured Tenancies

Assured tenancies may be for a fixed term or may be periodic; they can be brought to an end during their term only by a court order or by surrender (s.5(5)). Possession during the currency of the fixed term can only be sought if the terms of the tenancy make provision for it to be brought to an end prematurely by a right of re-entry by way of forfeiture, determination by notice or otherwise and even then only on certain grounds, i.e., Grounds 2, 8 or 10–15 (s.7(6) Housing Act 1988). A landlord will nearly always reserve a right of re-entry for the tenant's breach of covenant. Should the tenant remain in occupation after the end of a fixed term then, provided no new fixed term comes into existence (s.5(4)), a statutory periodic tenancy will arise. This last will continue until a new periodic or fixed-term assured tenancy is created, or until possession is granted to the landlord. If the immediate landlord's interest comes to an end, all of his rights and obligations will pass to his successor (s.18(1)) thereby affording protection to subtenants with assured tenancies. The only, but major, proviso is that the new relationship must not be one of those excluded under Schedule 1 (s.18(2)); that list has been considered at 16.3 above.

During the statutory tenancy, the original terms and conditions will all prevail, although either party may within 12 months of the end of the contractual tenancy serve a notice in the prescribed form proposing new terms (s.6). Any dispute about that variation may be referred to the Rent Assessment Committee within the next three months. The Committee will consider whether the disputed clause(s) might reasonably be expected to be found in an assured tenancy and will determine the date from which any amendment it requires is to come into effect, unless the parties mutually agree an alternative. If no reference is made to the Rent Assessment Committee, the new terms set out in the notice will automatically take effect within three months.

16.6.3 Rent Control

In contrast to the Rent Act 1977, the policy of the Housing Act 1988 is to allow feedom of contract to prevail and to limit the degree of statutory intervention. It is left to the parties, therefore, to agree on the level of rent and make provision for rent reviews in appropriate cases. The only external influences provided for by the 1988 Act operate through the s.13 review procedure for assured periodic tenancies and via referrals to the Rent Assessment Committee by assured shorthold tenants. The aim of these provisions is not to limit rents but to set rents at a market level.

The parties to a fixed-term tenancy may agree on whatever rent they like. Unless there is a rent review clause, a landlord who wishes to increase the original rent will have to wait until the fixed-term tenancy ends and a statutory periodic tenancy arises. The landlord will then be able to serve a notice of increase under s.13.

Subject to any agreement that the parties may themselves reach, the landlord may increase the rent of a periodic or statutory periodic assured tenancy by serving notice under s.13. The landlord must serve a notice in the prescribed form, proposing a new rent to take effect as from a 'new period of the tenancy specified in the notice' (s.13(2)). The increase cannot take effect any earlier than

(a) the minimum period after the date of service of the notice; and
(b) the end of the first anniversary of the date in which the first period of the tenancy began (s.13(2)(b)). The 'minimum period' from which the new rent is payable is:

- six months' time if the tenancy is yearly;
- one month if the tenancy is monthly;
- the period of the tenancy in any other case.

These periods are extended if the lease is less than twelve months old, or if there has been a previous increase by notice (s.13(2)). In these two alternative instances the twelve months must expire, or there must be a twelve-month gap between notices, respectively.

The new rent will apply from the proposed date, any disputes being referred by the tenant to the Rent Assessment Committee. The Committee resolves the matter by fixing a *market rent* achieved by considering the amount for which the 'dwellinghouse might reasonably be let in the open market by a willing landlord under an assured tenancy' starting at the same time on the same terms. The following matters must be disregarded (s.14(2)–(4)):

- the presence of a sitting tenant (a rule which applies equally to an application to vary terms (s.6(6));
- any improvements carried out by the tenant as assured tenant within the twenty-one years prior to the adjudication;
- any deterioration caused by the current (that is not predecessor) tenant's omissions;
- service charges.

The Committee will take account of payments made by the tenant for furniture, and will assume that the tenant is responsible for the payment of council tax (s.14(4)).

The Rent Assessment Committee's decision will take effect from the date specified in the original notice unless this would impose hardship on the tenant, in which case there is a discretion to delay for such period as the Committee thinks fit (s.14(7)). Section 14(6) allows for the Rent Assessment Committee to hear an application for variation of terms under s.6 at the same time as an application for an increased rent.

16.6.4 Implied Terms

Section 15 of the 1988 Act implies into assured periodic tenancies a covenant not to assign, sublet or part with possession of all or part of the dwelling without the landlord's consent (s.15(1)), unless the parties agree to the contrary or unless a premium is payable on grant or renewal (s.15(3)). 'Acceptable premiums' are defined in s.15(4) as being fines, pecuniary consideration in addition to rent or deposits of up to two months' rent. Section 19 of the Landlord & Tenant Act 1927 and s.1 of the Landlord and Tenant Act 1988 (see Chapter 8.2.2 and 8.3) do not apply (s.15(2)). This means that, in relation to the implied term, the landlord can unreasonably withhold consent and is not under a duty to reply in writing, or within a reasonable time.

Section 16 implies into all assured tenancies a right of access and all reasonable facilities to the landlord for carrying out repairs.

16.6.5 Security of Tenure

Although the assured statutory tenancy could exist indefinitely, it is open to the tenant to terminate it by giving notice of intention to leave. Alternatively, the landlord may serve a notice of seeking possession under s.8 (a 's.8 notice') alleging one of the Grounds referred to in s.7 and listed in Schedule 2, and specifying the earliest date upon which proceedings can start (s.8(3)(*b*)).

A s.8 notice must comply with certain requirements:

▶ It must be in the prescribed form, or a form substantially to the same effect (Assured Tenancies and Agricultural Occupancies (Forms) Regulations 1988);

▶ It must inform the tenant that the landlord intends to bring possession proceedings;

▶ It must state which ground or grounds the landlord intends to rely and also give particulars thereof. If the Ground alleged is any of 1, 2, 5–8, 9 or 16, the date cannot be earlier than two months from service or, if the tenancy is periodic, the earliest date on which a notice to quit will expire: that is the contractual period of the tenancy. It makes no difference to the validity of the notice that the lease changes from fixed-term to periodic during the subsistence of the notice, or that the notice refers to misdemeanours during the fixed term that ended before the notice was served (s.8(5)). However, no order for possession on one of the Grounds can be made to come into effect during the fixed term (s.7(6)), so if early possession is needed the landlord will have to use powers of recovery (provided they were reserved in the lease) under s.7(6). These powers do not permit the tenant to apply for relief since the jurisdiction is not forfeiture under s.146 Law of Property Act 1925 as explained in section 15.5. Once served, no further notice is needed for twelve months although it is not clear what impact an invalid notice will have on the twelve months: will they start to run anyway? That question acquires even more significance with s.8(1)(*b*) allowing the court to dispense with a notice if it is just and equitable to do so. The scope of that provision is illustrated by *Kelsey Housing Association* v. *King* (1996) in which the landlord sought to recover possession from the tenant on the basis of alleged nuisance, annoyance, threatening and abusive behaviour and assault. The tenant contended that the notice with which he had been served did not comply with s.8 because it did not contain sufficient particulars of allegations made against the family and that the judge had wrongly exercised his discretion in deciding that it was just and equitable to dispense with the requirements of the notice. The Court of Appeal held that the tenant had had ample opportunity to rectify any or all of the breaches: he had not done so and must take the consequences of an inadequate notice.

It is permissible to serve a notice on only one tenant in shared accommodation, in which case only that tenant's interests will be terminated or modified (s.10).

Landlords who obtain possession after misrepresentation or concealment of material facts may be ordered to pay compensation, irrespective of the Ground alleged (s.12).

16.6.6   Mandatory Grounds

Ground 1   The landlord occupied the premises at some time as his only or principal home and, having given notice of possible intention to return, now requires the premises as the principal home for himself, his spouse or civil partner. The court can waive absence of notice if it seems just and equitable. Successors in title may also use this Ground provided they did not acquire the reversion for money or money's worth. This Ground is similar to Rent Act Case 11 above, but not identical because there is no obligation on the landlord to want to occupy the premises once he obtains possession. In *Boyle* v. *Verrall* (1996) the landlord had intended to create an assured shorthold tenancy but had served an incomplete and invalid s.20 notice. The result was the creation of an assured tenancy which was terminable only on one of the grounds specified in Schedule 2 to the 1988 Act. Recovery of possession on Ground 1 depended on it being 'just and equitable' to dispense with the service of written notice on the tenant, at the time when the tenancy was created, that the landlord might require the property back for her own or her husband's use. The Court of Appeal held that all the circumstances of the case should be considered. The giving of oral notice might be an important factor favouring dispensation but was not necessarily a prerequisite of dispensation. Nor, if oral notice was absent, was dispensation restricted to 'exceptional cases'.

Ground 2   A mortgagee of the property wishes to obtain possession in order to exercise a power of sale and sell with vacant possession. Notice must have been given to the tenant unless the court considers it to be just and equitable to dispnse with service of such notice.

Ground 3   The same as Rent Act Case 13.

Ground 4   The same as Rent Act Case 14 .

Ground 5 The same as Rent Act Case 15.

Ground 6 This Ground is similar to one well-established under the Landlord and Tenant Act 1954, in that it allows recovery of possession if the landlord intends to demolish or reconstruct the whole or a substantial part of the dwelling, or to carry out substantial works on the dwelling or on some part of it. There is room for negotiation with the tenant over reduced use of the premises or modification of the terms of the lease during the works, but if the negotiations are unsuccessful the landlord can require possession. Alternatively, the tenant can defend an action on the basis that he would be prepared to modify his use. A proviso prevents a landlord purchasing the premises currently occupied by assured tenant(s) and then embarking on major works in order to obtain vacant possession; the proviso operates by excluding subsequent purchasers from the Ground. There are uncertainties in the operation of this Ground in its 1954 Act guise and these are discussed in Chapter 19. The uncertainties have been replicated in the 1988 Act, and and there is the potential therefore for disputes over, for example, the genuineness of the landlord's intention, or whether the works are sufficiently substantial to fall within the Ground.

If the landlord does recover possession under this Ground or Ground 9, there is an obligation to pay the tenant's reasonable removal costs (s.11 Housing Act 1988), with the opportunity for judicial resolution of any disputes and recovery of unpaid sums through the civil process.

Ground 7 The periodic tenancy devolved on testacy or intestacy of a former assured tenant, that is not through transmission or after the only permitted transmission has taken place – and possession proceedings were begun within a year from death (or later if the court agrees, for example if the landlord has only just discovered the death), irrespective of whether rent was accepted or not. This Ground cannot be used against a surviving spouse or civil partner.

Ground 8 Arrears of rent are owed which exceed eight weeks if the rent is paid weekly or fortnightly, two months if it is paid monthly, or three months if yearly, or one quarter if it is paid quarterly. The arrears must exist at both the notice of proceedings and at the hearing. The original period of three months (13 weeks) was reduced to two (8 weeks) by the Housing Act 1996. Often the reason behind the build-up of rent arrears is 'failure in the administration of housing benefit, rather than any unwillingness on the part of the occupier to pay the rent' (Law Commission, *Renting Homes 1: Status and Security* (Law Com Consultation Paper No 162)). While a decision on a housing benefit claim should be made by the relevant authority within 14 days of receiving all the necessary information or as soon as reasonably practicable thereafter, it was recently reported that 'the average time taken to process housing benefit claims in 2003–04 was 49 days compared to 55 days in 2002–03' (HC Deb, vol 423, col 876W, 12 Jul 2004). Tenants who are entitled to housing benefit can easily therefore fall foul of Ground 8.

16.6.7   The Discretionary Grounds

Ground 9   Suitable alternative accommodation is available.

Ground 10   There are rent arrears which do not amount to the figures set out in Ground 8. Section 19 does allow arrears of rent to be recovered by distress, but only with leave of the court.

Ground 11   Persistent delays have occurred in payment of rent. There is a similar provision to this in s.30(1)(b) of the Landlord and Tenant Act 1954. The word 'persistent' implies two possibilities: either a long history of rent arrears, or one or two instalments in arrear for a long period. This discretionary basis of this Ground allows for the all too frequent problem of arrears being beyond the control of the tenant, owing for example to delays in housing benefit payment or assessment.

Ground 12   There has been some breach of obligation by the tenant. This is, of course, a truncated version of Case 1 under the Rent Act.

Ground 13   This is the same as Rent Act Case 3 above, with the addition of liability for common parts.

Ground 14   This ground and 14A are identical to Grounds 2 and 2A that apply when possession is sought of secure tenancies (see Chapter 18). They were introduced by the Housing Act 1996 s.148 as part of a number of changes intended to facilitate possession when occupiers or those for whom they have some responsibility commit anti-social behaviour. The possession application will allege that the tenant, a co-resident, or a visitor has been guilty of one or more of the following: carrying out conduct causing or likely to cause nuisance or annoyance to a resident, visitors or anyone engaged in lawful activities in the locality; has been convicted of using the property for illegal or immoral purposes; has been convicted of carrying out an arrestable offence (defined in the Police and Criminal Evidence Act 1984) on the property or in its locality. The wide terminology, notably 'visitors' and those engaged in lawful activity in the 'locality' means that the Ground's scope is broader than the old Case 2 which it is designed to replace. If this Ground is alleged there is no need for the landlord to wait until expiry of the notice before initiating proceedings (Housing Act 1988 s.8A, introduced by the Housing Act 1996). Nevertheless, the Ground is discretionary so the extent to which a person is to blame, or to which there have been attempts to control children or visitors, will be relevant. The interests of neighbours who would otherwise be deprived of relief will be considered as well as those of the tenant . If the court is considering whether it is reasonable to make an order for possession on ground 14 it must consider, in particular (a) the effect that the nuisance or annoyance has had on persons other than the person against whom the order is sought; (b) any continuing effect the nuisance or annoyance is likely to have on such persons; and (c) the effect that the nuisance or annoyance would be likely to have on such persons if the conduct is repeated (s. 9A, Housing Act 1988).

Ground 14A Also added by the Housing Act 1996 s.149, it allows recovery of possession when one partner has left as a result of domestic violence and the court is satisfied that the victim is unlikely to return because attempts to serve notice on that person have all been unsuccessful. This ground is available only where the landlord is a registered social landlord or a charitable housing trust.

Ground 15 Furniture has been ill-treated. This is similar to Rent Act Case 4 above.

Ground 16 The tenant was a service tenant who has left the employment of the landlord. This is similar to Rent Act Case 8, with the difference that here there is no need for a replacement employee wanting the accommodation.

Ground 17 (Introduced by the Housing Act 1996.) The tenancy must have been created as a result of a false statement made knowingly by the tenant or by someone acting on his behalf. There is a similar provision relating to public sector lettings (see Ground 5 in Chapter 18).

16.6.8 Suspension and Postponement

Section 9 of the Housing Act 1988 gives the court wide powers, when dealing with possession actions based on *discretionary* grounds, to adjourn the proceedings, or to stay, suspend or postpone any order it makes. If the court does make a suspended possession order it is obliged to impose conditions, e.g. as to payment of rent, unless to do so would cause exceptional hardship (s.9(3)). In practice, judges will expect the tenant to offer to pay the current rent and express a readiness to begin to clear accumulated arrears by regular instalments. Should there be a further breach or default, possession will be almost inevitable. Where the tenant complies with conditions which have been imposed, the court may discharge or rescind the possession order (s.9(4)). A spouse of the tenant who has remained in the tenanted matrimonial home may claim similar s.9 protection.

The court has no power to adjourn etc where the landlord has been able to prove a *mandatory* ground in Schedule 2, Part 1, or if the tenancy is an assured shorthold (s.9(6)). In these situations the reasonableness (or otherwise) of making the order is irrelevant and possession is potentially instantaneous unless the court can be prevailed upon to exercise its inherent powers to postpone.

In *Coltrane* v. *Day* (2003) the tenant became entitled to housing benefit but the housing benefit authority took several weeks to process his claim. When 11 weeks' rent was outstanding, the landlord served a valid section 8 notice, stating her intention to start proceedings to recover possession of the flat on ground 8 which, as stated above, requires that the rent be unpaid both when the s.8 notice is served *and* at the date of the hearing. A cheque for the full amount due was delivered by the tenant to the landlord's solicitor shortly before the hearing of the landlord's claim for possession and the solicitor handed it to their client at the hearing. Although the cheque was not cleared until after the hearing, it was cleared at first presentation. The Court of Appeal held that the debt was discharged at the date the cheque was delivered, and was thus not unpaid at the date of the hearing. Given that the judge could not be sure at the date of the hearing that the landlord was entitled to possession, he had jurisdiction to adjourn the claim to see whether the cheque would be paid.

In *North British Housing Association Ltd.* v. *Matthews* (2005) the Court of Appeal confirmed that only in exceptional circumstances should a hearing be adjourned to enable a tenant to reduce the outstanding rent arrears below the ground 8 threshold. An example might be where a computer failure prevented the housing benefit authority from paying the arrears of benefit until after the date of the hearing. Pointing out the 'sad feature of contemporary life that housing benefit problems are widespread', Dyson L.J. concluded that maladministration on the part of the housing benefit authority was not an exceptional circumstance.

Accelerated possession of assured and assured shorthold tenancies is possible when (unusually) there is no application for money in addition to possession.

16.6.9   Succession

Unlike the Rent Act 1977, the Housing Act 1988 makes no special provision for succession to fixed-term tenancies. When a fixed-term assured tenant dies, the remainder of the term will pass to whoever is entitled under the tenant's will or on intestacy. That person will become the assured tenant provided that the requirements of an assured tenancy are satisfied, e.g. the dwelling-house is occupied as the tenant's only or principal home.

In the case of a periodic assured tenancy (be it contractual or statutory), s.17 of the 1988 Act provides for a single transmission of the tenancy to a spouse or civil partner who, immediately before the tenant's death, was occupying the dwelling-house as his or her only or principal home. A spouse includes a person living with the tenant as his or wife or husband or as if they were civil partners (s.17(4)). That transmission may occur through succession by will, on intestacy, or succession on the death of another joint tenant. Provided there has been no succession by the tenant's spouse, civil partner or cohabitee, a periodic tenancy can devolve under the tenant's will or intestacy. Where it passes to someone other than the deceased tenant's spouse, civil partner or cohabitee, the landlord can use mandatory Ground 7 to commence proceedings for possession not later than twelve months after the tenant's death or the date upon which the landlord became aware of the tenant's death. Ground 7 further provides that the landlord's acceptance of rent from a new tenant after the death of the original tenant shall not be regarded as creating a new periodic tenancy unless the landlord agrees in writing to a change in the amount of the rent, the period of the tenancy, the premises which are let or any other term of the tenancy.

16.6.10   Assured Shorthold Tenancies

As originally enacted, an assured shorthold tenancy was for a fixed term of at least six months. There was no upper limit to its duration. By s.20 a notice which both described the lease as a shorthold and was in the prescribed form had to be served by the landlord on the tenant before the beginning of the lease (which was held to include the first day of the lease: *Bedding* v. *McCarthy* (1994)). Failure to serve a valid s.20 notice resulted in the creation of an assured tenancy although in *Ravenseft Properties Ltd.* v. *Hall* (2002) the Court of Appeal held that where the s.20 notice contains errors, the sole question is whether, despite any errors or omissions, it is substantially to the same effect as a correct notice in that it fulfils the statutory purpose of informing the prospective tenant of the special nature of an assured shorthold tenancy. The Government's White paper described the 'procedures' which the landlord had to go through to create a valid assured shorthold tenancy as 'a trap for inexperienced landlords' which might 'deter owners of empty properties from putting them to use' (Department of the Environment, *Our Future Homes: Opportunity, Choice Responsibility* (Cmnd 2901), 1995). The Housing Act 1996 therefore removed the requirement to serve prior notice.

Section 19A of the Housing Act 1988 (inserted by s.96 of the Housing Act 1996) provides that, unless the landlord specifies otherwise, all assured tenancies (oral or written) entered into after 28 February 1997 will automatically be assured shortholds. No longer is there any requirement that the tenancy is for a fixed term or that prior notice be served. The previous position, regarded as unjust to landlords who had overlooked the provision out of ignorance and had then found themselves with tenants who had indefinite security, is thus reversed.

There are exceptions set out in the 1996 Act, Schedule 7, which adds Schedule 2A to the 1988 Act:

- the landlord serves a notice on or after the start of the tenancy stating that it is not an assured shorthold, or there is an express provision to that effect in the lease. The landlord can also choose to grant greater security after the tenancy has been entered into. Assured tenancies are most likely to be used by registered social landlords.
- the tenancy is the result of application of the succession provisions of the Rent Act 1977. Thus, the first succession to a member of the tenant's family and all second successions will continue to take effect as fully assured rather than assured shorthold tenancies.
- the tenancy was formerly secure (see Chapter 18) and became assured on transfer from a Local Authority to a registered social landlord;
- the tenancy was formerly a long lease within the 1954 Act Part I (see Chapter 17) but became assured at its end;
- the tenancy is an assured agricultural occupancy (see Chapter 20).

Once an assured shorthold has come to an end, any new agreement between the same parties is automatically an assured shorthold. Where an assured shorthold has come to an end and a statutory periodic tenancy has arisen by virtue of s.5(2), the statutory periodic tenancy will also be an assured shorthold tenancy (s.20(4)).

The court cannot make an an order for possession in respect of an assured shorthold tenancy created before 28 February 1997 unless the fixed term has come to an end (unless there is provision for forfeiture or re-entry and one of the grounds of possession for an assured tenancy can be relied upon). As there is no requirement of a fixed term of at least six months for assured shorthold tenancies created since 28 February 1997, s.21 has been amended to prevent possession being ordered until at least six months has elapsed from the grant of the tenancy (s.21(5)–(7)). The six months runs from the grant of the original tenancy and not the start of any replacement tenancy whether this arises by virtue of an agreement with the landlord or as a statutory periodic tenancy under s.5 of the Housing Act 1988.

An assured shorthold tenancy may be terminated in the same ways (i.e., using the same grounds for possession) as any assured tenancy but s.21 contains what is, in effect, an additional mandatory ground for possession enabling the landlord (or at least one of them in the case of a joint tenancy) to recover possession by giving the tenant not less than two months' written notice stating that he or she requires possession of the dwelling-house (s.21(1)(b), 21(4)(a) Housing Act 1988). The court cannot use its discretion to consider the issue of reasonableness, nor to suspend the execution of an order for possession.

Section 22 Housing Act 1988 provides that an assured shorthold tenant may apply to the Rent Assessment Committee to determine the rent 'which, in the committee's opinion, the landlord might reasonably be expected to obtain'. Where the tenancy was granted after 28 February 1997, the tenant cannot refer the rent if more than six months have elapsed since the beginning of the tenancy (s.22(2)(aa), as amended by s.100(1), HA96) or, in the case of a replacement tenancy, since the beginning of the original tenancy. The tenant cannot in any case refer the rent if a rent has previously been determined under s.22 (s.22(2)(a)).

The Rent Assessment Committee can only make a determination if, by s.22(3) they consider that

(a) there is a sufficient number of similar dwelling-houses in the locality let on assured tenancies (whether shorthold or not); and

(b) the rent payable under the assured shorthold tenancy in question is 'significantly higher' than the rent which the landlord might reasonably be expected to be able to obtain under the tenancy, having regard to the level of rents payable under the tenancies of similar dwelling-houses in the locality.

The rent, as determined by the Rent Assessment Committee, takes effect from whatever date the Committee directs, but no earlier than the date of the application (s.22(4)(a)). The landlord cannot serve notice of an increase of rent under s.13(2) until after the first anniversary of the date on which the determination takes effect (s.22(4)(c)). Given the lack of security anyway after six months and the rigorous terms of the test, it is reasonable to assume that few tenants will attempt to challenge their landlords.

Because all assured shorthold tenancies were formerly for a fixed term and notice had to be served before the tenancy was entered into, nearly all assured shorthold tenancy agreements were in writing. Now that no prior notice need be served and no fixed term is required, an assured shorthold tenancy can be created orally. Section 20A (inserted by s.97 Housing Act 1996) imposes a duty on landlords to provide a written statement of certain terms of the assured shorthold tenancy within twenty-eight days of the tenant's request for such a statement. Failure to do so without reasonable excuse constitutes a criminal offence. The terms in question are:

(a) the date the tenancy began or came into being;
(b) the rent payable and the dates on which it is payable;
(c) any term providing for an express rent review; and
(d) if the tenancy is for a fixed term, its length (s.20(A)(2)).

16.7 Mobile Homes

Mobile homes (otherwise known as park homes) have been described as 'usually factory-built, single-storey dwellings installed on a concrete slab and connected to mains services . . . [which] are used as a relatively cheap form of accommodation by many people' (M. Partington, *Landlord and Tenant* (1980), p. 464). Some resemble bungalows while others are closer to traditional caravans. There are an estimated 100,000 mobile homes in England and Wales on more than 1,700 sites. The sites vary in size and quality, from small fields with a handful of mobile homes, to large parks with shopping and leisure facilities. Most mobile homes are owner-occupied (and subject, therefore, to the Mobile Homes Act 1983) but a minority are rented along with the pitch. In the latter case, if the caravan is immobilised, the tenancy agreement may be subject to the Rent Act 1977 or the Housing Act 1988 (see *Makins* v. *Elson* (1977)). Typically, residents who own ther mobile homes enter into an agreement to keep their home on site, and pay the site owner a pitch fee, which includes utilities and maintenance.

The Mobile Homes Act 1983 applies 'to any agreement under which a person ('the occupier') is entitled –

– To station a mobile home forming part of a protected site; and
– To occupy the mobile home as his only or main residence' (s.1(1)).

A mobile home is defined as any structure designed or adapted for human habitation which is capable of being moved from one place to another (whether by being towed, or by being transported on a single motor vehicle or trailer) and any motor vehicle so designed or adapted (s.5(1)). A motor vehicle is only 'adapted' for human habitation where some physical alteration has been carried out: the mere act of furnishing a van with a bed and other furniture does not turn it into a caravan even though someone lives in it (*Backer* v. *Secretary of State for the Environment* (1983)). A protected site is any site in respect of which a site licence is required under the Caravan Sites and Control of Development Act 1960, or would be required if there were no exemption for land occupied by local authorities, and provided that the relevant planning permission or site licence is not granted for holiday use or subject to such conditions that there are times of the year when caravans may not be stationed on the land for human habitation (s.5(1)).

Where a mobile home is to be sold by the site owner, s.1 of the Mobile Homes Act 1983 requires the site owner to give the proposed homeowner the details of the site agreement in a written statement not later than 28 days before the agreement for the sale of the mobile home is made or, if there is no such sale agreement, not later than twenty-eight days before the site agreement is entered into (s.1(3)). The parties may agree to a shorter period than 28 days. The written statement must include the following information (s.1(2)):

- the names and addresses of the parties and the date of commencement of the agreement
- particulars of the land on which the occupier is entitled to station the mobile home sufficient to identify it
- the express terms of the agreement
- the terms implied by the s.2(1) of the 1983 Act, and
- any other requirements prescribed by regulation.

Express terms usually include rules about pitch fees and other charges, and the responsibilities of the home owner and the site owner. If any express term is contained in an agreement to which this Act applies, but was not set out in a written statement given to the proposed occupier, it will be unenforceable (s.1(5)) unless, within six months, a court considers it reasonable to include it (s.2(3)).

Certain terms are implied into every agreement to which the 1983 Act applies, and any express terms take effect subject to these implied terms (s.2(1)), and Sch.1, Part 1). Most importantly:

- Every agreement to which the Act applies will continue indefinitely until
  (a) the agreement is validly terminated by either the home owner or the site owner; or
  (b) the site owner's lease or planning permission expires. If either is extended, the agreement will be extended accordingly (Sch.1, para.2).

- The agreement can be terminated by the home owner by giving at least four weeks' notice in writing (Sch.1, para.3).
- The site owner can only terminate the agreement with the leave of the court and only on three grounds:
  (a) the court is satisfied that the occupier has breached a term of the agreement and, after service of a notice to remedy the breach, has not complied with the notice within a reasonable time, and the court considers it reasonable for the agreement to be terminated (Sch.1, para.4); or
  (b) on the application of the owner, the court is satisfied that the occupier is not occupying the mobile home as his only or main residence (Sch.1, para.5); or
  (c) on the application of the owner, the court is satisfied that, having regard to its condition, the mobile home is having a detrimental effect on the amenity of the protected site or is likely to have such an effect before the end of the next relevant period. 'Relevant period' means a period of five years beginning with the commencement of the agreement and each succeeding period of five years (Sch.1, para.6(2)).

Within six months of the provision of the written statement, either party may apply to the court for an order that certain further terms be implied (s.2(2)); these may include the right of the occupier for quiet enjoyment, the sums payable by the occupier and the times at which they are to be paid, the yearly review of the sums payable and the maintenance and repair of the protected site by the site owner. On any such application, the court must make such provision as it thinks just and equitable (s.2(4)).

A homeowner who wishes to sell his home and assign his agreement must give notice in writing of the prospective homeowner to the site owner. The site owner must respond in writing within 28 days, giving or withholding approval of the prospective homeowner. Approval cannot be unreasonably withheld (Sch.1, paras. 8 and 9). If the approval is withheld, the reasons must be given in writing. If the site owner does not issue a decision in writing within 28 days, or withholds approval unreasonably, the homeowner can apply to the court and claim damages. The homeowner can also seek an order from the court declaring that the prospective homeowner is approved. If the court grants a declaration, the site owner must allow the sale. When a mobile home is sold on site and the agreement is transferred, the site owner is entitled to receive a commission, currently set at a maximum of 10 per cent of the sale price (Sch.8, para. 2 and the Mobile Homes (Commission) Order 1983, SI 1983/748).

Where an occupier dies at a time when he is occupying the mobile home as his only or main residence, the agreement operates for the benefit of, and is binding on, his widow, widower or surviving civil partner residing with him at that time or, in default of such person, any member of his family who was so residing. This includes those who were living with the homeowner as husband and wife or as if they were civil partners (s.5(3)). A person is a member of the deceased's family if he is a parent, grandparent, child, grandchild, brother or sister, uncle or aunt, nephew or niece. Any relationship by marriage is treated as a blood relationship and any relationship of the half blood is treated as one of the whole blood. A stepchild of any person is treated as his child and an illegitimate child is treated as the legitimate child of his mother and reputed father (s.3(3)(a)). If there is no-one residing with the deceased occupier at his death, the agreement may pass under the deceased's will or intestacy (s.3(3)(b)). Where this happens, the implied terms enabling or requiring such a person to occupy the mobile home will not apply.

Caravan dwellers who have a licence or contract to occupy someone else's caravan and/or site have limited security under the Caravan Sites Act 1968 provided that the site is 'protected', that is, it has a site licence under the Caravan Sites and Control of Development Act 1960 (which excludes holiday sites). Such caravan dwellers must be given four weeks' notice to quit (s.2), are protected against unlawful eviction and harassment (s.3), and may request the court to suspend any possession order against them, for up to twelve months initially, renewable on application (s.4).

16.8 Other Forms of Protection

There are a number of other ways of protecting tenants, and sometimes licensees too, which have little or nothing to do with the security of tenure already discussed. Instead, they concentrate on ensuring that occupiers are properly informed of their rights, are entitled to remain in the property undisturbed, and can only be evicted after due process.

16.8.1 Rent Books

All weekly tenants, except those who are provided with board, must be given a rent book (s.4 Landlord & Tenant Act 1985). The rent book must contain certain information (s.7 Landlord & Tenant Act 1985):

- the address of the property;
- the identity and address of the landlord, and of their agent if relevant;
- the amount of rent due, as well as whether it is inclusive or exclusive of council tax, and information about housing benefit;
- some indication of the nature of security of tenure;

– suggestions as to agencies which might provide help in the event of a dispute.

These useful provisions are of limited effect, however, in that they apply only to weekly tenants and not to other tenants or to licensees, and failure to comply carries only a criminal sanction – there is no absolution from paying rent (*Shaw* v. *Groom* (1970)).

16.8.2   Harassment and Unlawful Eviction

Since 1964 it has been a criminal offence to harass or unlawfully to evict an occupier who is legally entitled to be on the premises. The Protection from Eviction Act 1977 is the principal statutory provision in this area, although Part I of the Housing Act 1988 made a number of important changes: it amended the existing offence of harassment and introduced a new offence of harassment as well as a civil action for damages which can be used by wrongfully evicted occupiers, although an actionable civil wrong need not exist before criminal proceedings are initiated (*R.* v. *Burke* (1990)).

The offence of unlawful eviction occurs where 'any person unlawfully deprives the residential occupier of any premises of his occupation of the premises or any part thereof, or attempts to do so, . . . unless he proves that he believed, and had reasonable cause to believe, that the residential occupier had ceased to reside in the premises' (s.1(2), Protection from Eviction Act 1977). Generally, an unlawful eviction occurs where the occupier is evicted without the proper procedure for terminating the right of occupation having been followed. A 'residential occupier means 'a person occupying premises as a residence, whether under a contract or by virtue of any enactment or rule of law giving him the right to remain in occupation or restricting the right of any person to recover possession of the premises' (s.1(1) Protection from Eviction Act 1977).

The offence of harassment takes place where 'any person with intent to cause the residential occupier of any premises

(a) to give up occupation of the premises or any part thereof; or
(b) to refrain from exercising any right or pursuing any remedy in respect of the premises or part thereof,
     – does acts likely to interfere with the peace or comfort of the residential occupier or members of his household, or
     – persistently withdraws or withholds services reasonably required for the occupation of the premises as a residence' (s.1(3), Protection from Eviction Act 1977, as amended).

Two changes were made by the Housing Act 1988 which, theoretically, should have made prosecution more readily achievable. First, as regards the existing offence, the word '*likely*' was substituted for the word '*calculated*' by the Housing Act 1988. The offence is now easier to establish, but still requires an intent to cause occupiers to give up their occupation or to refrain from exercising their rights. Secondly, for the purposes of establishing harassment, it had been difficult for the prosecution to prove that the landlord specifically intended to cause the occupier to leave, rather than just make life unpleasant in the hope that he or she might decide to go. To counter these problems the 1988 Act introduced s.1(3A), creating an offence which can be committed only by certain individuals, i.e., the landlord of the residential occupier concerned ('landlord' being defined as including any superior landlord (s.1(3C))), or an agent of the landlord. The actus reus is identical to s.1(3); the only difference is the mental state. Whether or not the landlord intended to cause the occupier to leave is not relevant; what matters is whether a reasonable man (having at his disposal the facts known to the landlord) would believe the occupier to be likely to give up possession as the result of the landlord's behaviour. This lowering of the evidential burden, however, has not led to any noticeable increase in the number of prosecutions. There is a defence where the accused proves that 'he had reasonable grounds for doing the acts or withdrawing or withholding the services in question'.

Local authorities are given specific powers to prosecute offences by s.6 of the 1977 Act but have no powers of arrest. Where the police or local authority are unwilling to initiate proceedings, the individual occupier may bring a private prosecution. Prosecutions are infrequent, possibly owing to a combination of a desire on the part of local authority officers to negotiate rather than prosecute and the high standard of proof in criminal proceedings. In addition, because there is a need to prove 'acts' rather than omissions, general allegations of malice are insufficient. A person found guilty of an offence under s.1(2), s.1(3) or s.1(3A) is subject to a maximum penalty of six months' imprisonment or a £2,000 fine or both. If convicted on indictment, imprisonment may be for up to two years and/or an unlimited fine my be imposed (s.1(4)). In *R v. Brennan and Brennan* (1979) (in which the landlord accompanied by a 'very large man and an Alsation dog' evicted a group of students from their rented premises), it was said that 'loss of liberty should be the usual penalty where landlords use threats or force, in the absence of unusual mitigation'.

Note should also be taken of s. 6, Criminal Law Act 1977 which makes it an offence for a person without lawful authority (such as a bailiff executing a warrant of possession) to use or threaten violence for the purpose of securing entry to premises upon which, to his knowledge, someone is present who is opposed to the entry. Even an excluded tenant or licensee (see below) or a trespasser cannot be evicted whilst actually within the premises. Eviction can only occur through a bailiff or sheriff and with a court order. The landlord or the licensor can, however, wait until the occupier leaves the premises, e.g. to go to work, and then remove his or her belongings and change the locks. Displaced occupiers who are tempted to organise their own re-entry should also take care not to fall foul of s.6.

The difficulties experienced in using the criminal law and the inadequacy of its remedies for the harassed or displaced occupier have meant an increasing interest in civil remedies. There will have been a breach of the implied covenant of quiet enjoyment when the ordinary and lawful enjoyment of the demised premises is substantially interfered with by the acts or omissions of the landlord or those lawfully claiming under him. Although the traditional view is that the tenant must have suffered physical interference with his enjoyment of the property, it has been said that a breach of covenant will occur when anything is done which is an invasion of the tenant's right to remain in possession undisturbed even if it caused no direct physical interference (*Kenny* v. *Preen* (1963)).

Since neither exemplary nor aggravated damages can be awarded for breach of contract, it may be to the tenant's advantage to bring an action in tort. The landlord may have committed trespass (to the person, land or personal property) and possibly assault and/or nuisance. A new statutory tort was created by s.27 of the Housing Act 1988 which gives the residential occupier evicted after 9 June 1988 a right to sue his landlord, or any person acting on the landlord's behalf, for committing an act which amounts to a criminal offence under s.1 of the Protection from Eviction Act 1977 and which has caused the occupier to give up occupation of the premises as a residence. There does not need to have been a prosecution for the occupier to pursue this course of action. Although this remedy can be regarded as a significant disincentive to enthusiastic developers, it does have its limitations. There is no liability at all if the occupier has been reinstated or is to be reinstated by the court (s.27(6)), although as Lord Donaldson pointed out in *Tagro* v. *Cafane* (1991) 'reinstatement does not consist in merely handing the tenant a key to a lock which does not work and inviting her to resume occupation of a room which has been totally wrecked'. Alternatively, it is a defence for the landlord to show that a reasonable belief that the occupier had ceased to reside on the premises or that it was reasonable to suspend services (s.27(8)).

If damages are awarded, they will be assessed on the increased value of the vacant possession acquired by the landlord assuming that there could be a sale on the open market, that neither the occupier nor any member of his family wishes to buy, and that any demolition or reconstruction would be illegal (s.28(1),(3)). The amount of the award might vary depending on the status of the occupier (licencees getting less than assured shorthold tenants, who will in turn receive less than assured tenants). Other factors might be the length of the interest remaining and the severity of the breach.

If liability is established, damages can be mitigated if the occupier had behaved unreasonably or if the former occupier received a reasonable offer of reinstatement prior to start of proceedings, whether or not that occupier had already obtained alternative accommodation (s.27(7)). Mitigating conduct (s.27(7)(*a*)) by the former occupier could include actions such as removal of belongings during the subsistence of the tenancy, only occasional residence, or omissions such as failure to pay rent or allowing rent arrears to accumulate (*Regalgrand Ltd.* v. *Dickerson & Wade* (1997)).

If an action is brought under s.27 for loss of occupation, damages can only be ordered under that section for that cause: exemplary and general damages cannot be awarded in addition, on which see again *Nwokorie* v. *Mason* (1994) (p. 34). Nor can damages be awarded under s.27 if they have already been awarded under s.28. If exemplary damages are awarded, some account must be taken of any successful criminal prosecution against the landlord, the landlord's means, and the advantage to him of having obtained vacant possession (*Francis* v. *Brown* (1997)).

The Protection from Harassment Act 1997, prompted by the need to provide protection from stalkers, is wide enough to provide some security for tenants. It prohibits any course of conduct (defined in s.7 to include speech, but subject, whatever its form, to the proviso that the conduct must have taken place on at least two occasions) which a reasonable person would perceive as harassment (s.1(1)and (3)). The imposition of an objective standard would seem to rule out actions that are less than unreasonable, malicious or aimed at causing worry, distress and the like. Victims within the terms of the Act may take civil proceedings to recover damages and/or may seek an injunction to prevent further repetition (s.3).

16.8.3 Notice to Quit

At Common Law the rule was that notice had to be for the same period as that for which rent was paid (with the exception of yearly tenancies where six months' notice was sufficient) and must expire on a rent day. The parties could contract out of the Common Law provided the lease so indicated clearly and explicitly. Common Law has been modified in different ways for different tenancies, with s.5 of the Protection from Eviction Act 1977 providing a basic rule for tenancies of premises let as separate dwellings that there must be four weeks' notice in writing. The notice must contain information that the landlord can obtain possession only after judicial process and must indicate organisations which can provide the tenant with advice; the information and the organisation are detailed in the Notice to Quit (Prescribed Information, etc.) Regulations 1975. Non-compliance will make the notice invalid.

Section 5(1A), added in 1988, extends the notice requirements to licences (whenever granted), but s.5(1B) removes from the jurisdiction of s.5 all 'excluded' lettings – as listed in s.3A and set out below.

16.8.4   Court Order

Section 3 of the Protection from Eviction Act 1977 requires that all tenants and licensees be evicted only after due process: i.e. court proceedings followed by bailiff's warrant for execution, if necessary. Its scope has been reduced, however, by s.30 of the Housing Act 1988, which introduces subsections 3(2B) and (2C) to the 1977 Act. These two subsections apply only to post-Housing Act 1988 tenancies, and create a class of excluded tenancies and licences, to which s.3 does not apply. The 'excluded' interests listed in s.3A are:

– accommodation shared with the landlord or his/her family provided it is part of the landlord's main residence;
– accommodation in the same block as the landlord's principal residence;
– temporary accommodation for which a licence was granted, i.e. licensed squats;
– holiday accommodation;
– hostel accommodation provided by a public sector landlord; a typical example, of course, being homeless persons' bed and breakfast accommodation (*Mohamed* v. *Manek & RB Kensington & Chelsea* (1995)).

This provision thus firmly recognises that tenants and licensees are entitled to judicial process, but then denies groups who may be in the position of alleging sham agreements a right of access to the courts, in the event of their eviction.

16.8.5   The Accommodation Agencies Act, 1953

Section 1 of the above Act, as interpreted in *Saunders* v. *Soper* (1974) declares that agencies can charge prospective tenants for their services only if suitable accommodation is found *and* occupied. Thus charging for searching, supplying a list of possible addresses, or registering an applicant on books, is a criminal offence.

Summary

▶ There are two major pieces of legislation affecting private residential rented property which is not the subject of a long lease. These two statutes are the Rent Act 1977 and the Housing Act 1988, as amended by the Housing Act 1996.

▶ Interests created under the Rent Act 1977 are protected tenancies or statutory tenancies (together known as regulated tenancies) or restricted contracts. Interests created under the Housing Act 1988 are assured or assured shorthold tenancies.

▶ Various lettings are excluded from the two main Acts. These interests will either be licences or will be covered by other protective legislation, or will have the minimal protection referred to in 9 below.

▶ No new tenancies can be created under the Rent Act 1977 after 14 January 1989, but transitional provisions protect those tenants whose interests were created prior to that date. The transitional provisions encourage the conversion of Rent Act tenancies into Housing Act tenancies. Restricted contracts, in particular, will have disappeared quickly.

▶ The Housing Act 1988 was intended to provide a boost to the private rented sector by dramatically changing security and rent control.

▶ There are certain common features running through all tenancies whether they fall within the Rent Act 1977 or the Housing Act 1988. These common features are that the letting must be of a dwellinghouse let as a separate dwelling, and that the property must fall within the relevant rateable value or rental limits.

▶ Tenancies within either of the two pieces of legislation will have security of tenure, the benefit of varying degrees of rent control, and, in the event of the tenant dying while still in residence, the possibility of transmission of the tenancy to a spouse or relative who was living with the deceased at his or her death. Protected tenancies are also subject to premium control provisions.

▶ When a protected tenancy, or an assured tenancy, or an assured shorthold tenancy comes to an end, it will continue on the same terms and conditions, and will be known as a statutory tenancy. Statutory tenancies will continue indefinitely unless brought to an end by the landlord proving one of the Rent Act Cases or the Housing Act Grounds or, in the case of an assured shorthold tenancy, by s. 21 notice.

▶ The Cases and Grounds of possession are either discretionary or mandatory. Alternatively the landlord may offer suitable alternative accommodation to the tenant, in which case the tenant does not become homeless in the event of possession being ordered.

▶ There are several significant forms of protection applicable to tenancies, irrespective of whether they fall within or outside of the two main Acts dealt with in this chapter. They are, *inter alia*, the requirement that there be a notice to quit and the need for there to have been judicial proceedings before obtaining possession. Certain tenancies and licences are excluded from these provisions. There may alos be criminal or civil liability in cases of unlawful eviction and harassment.

Exercises

16.1 How do assured tenancies differ from assured shorthold tenancies?

16.2 How has the Housing Act 1988 brought about changes in the private rented sector?

16.3 Must a tenant be actually living in the rented accommodation in order to claim security of tenure under

(a) the Rent Act 1977 and (b) the Housing Act 1988?

16.4 How important is a formal description of an interest in an agreement in its ultimate classification? For example, if the arrangement is described as 'holiday' or 'shorthold', is that the final answer?

16.5 What difference has the Housing Act made to existing protected tenants or holders of restricted contracts?

16.6 What rights will an assured statutory tenant have?

16.7 How do market rents differ from fair rents?

16.8 Explain the difference between the discretionary and mandatory Grounds of possession contained in the Housing Act 1988 in the specific context of non-payment of rent.

16.9 Will it be easier or harder for a landlord to obtain possession using an offer of suitable alternative accommodation, as against alleging one of the Grounds or Cases?

16.10 Why is the lease/licence distinction important in the Rent Act or Housing Act context?

16.11 What legal restrictions are there on landlords which prevent them removing their tenants at any time?

16.12 What legal difference does it make if a landlord is resident?

Workshop

1 Chris has just acquired a large house with vacant possession in an urban area where sales of property, in any condition, are slow. His ultimate intention is to convert the premises for resale but for the moment he is prepared to let the property, provided vacant possession can be recovered at short notice. Advise Chris as to how he might do this.

2 Ellie rents a flat which is intended for residential occupation. Ellie is an interior designer by trade so uses the flat as a place to entertain and meet clients, although it is still also his home. Ellie's landlord has just found out how Ellie uses the premises and wants to know if he can recover possession.

Note: This question could usefully be reviewed again after you have read Chapter 19.

3 Simone occupies a furnished bedsitter with cooking facilities in a house owned by Liam who lets the house as bachelor service apartments: a housekeeper cleans the rooms and provides weekly linen. Simone has been given notice to quit. Advise Simone.

4 When Melanie arrived home yesterday after spending the morning shopping, she found all her possessions in the front garden, the locks on the front door changed so that she could not gain access and a note from the landlord pinned to one of the boxes saying: 'I have found somebody to rent your flat who will pay a higher rent'. Melanie had been given notice to quit four weeks ago but had ignored it because she wanted, and still wants, to stay. Advise Melanie on the alternative bases that she is:

(i)   an assured tenant;
(ii) an assured shorthold tenant;
(iii) a licensee.

5 Paula rents a small property on the outskirts of a seaside town. The property was originally built as a beach house (there are steps leading from the front door down the cliff to the beach) and as a result it is not very substantial in construction. Paula's agreement calls itself a holiday letting, but Paula has lived in the house for some while and works in the town. There is electricity but no running water. Paula's landlord has decided that Paula must leave so that the property can be rented out to summer visitors. Advise Paula.

6 Helen entered the employment of Frank two months ago, whereupon Frank mentioned that he owned the house next door to where Helen was to work and that Helen could rent it if she so wished. Helen has just been told that her probationary term of employment is not to be confirmed so she must leave both job and home. Does she have security of tenure?

Chapter 17

Private residential accommodation: long leases

Introduction

Long leases (ie those for a term certain exceeding twenty-one years) are usually outside the scope of the Rent Act 1977 and of the Housing Act 1988. Both Acts exclude from protection leases subject to a 'low rent' (s.5, 1977 Act; Schedule I, para. 3, 1988 Act) and because a long lease will normally be granted (and subsequently assigned) at a premium, the rent payable therefor will be typically much lower than that chargeable on lettings falling within Chapter 16. In addition, because long leases change hands for sums which reflect their market value, there is no restriction on premiums. Nor is there any rent control, although with the low rents involved this would anyway be unnecessary. Instead, the legislation concentrates on:

(a) protecting tenants against exorbitant service charges;
(b) giving security of tenure where long leases come to an end by effluxion of time. (It is worth noting however that in practice relatively few long leases expire of their own accord. Usually the tenant will have negotiated a new lease with the landlord before the expiry date or will have become statutorily entitled to extend the term of the tenancy or to purchase the landlord's interest.)
(c) enabling tenants to enforce the landlord's management obligations by giving them rights of pre-emption, and powers of compulsory purchase and the appointment of a receiver;
(d) giving tenants of flats the right to take over the management of the building in which their flats are situated without having to prove shortcomings on the part of the landlord and without having to pay him compensation;
(e) giving tenants the opportunity of enlarging their interests either by acquiring a new and/or longer interest or by purchasing the freehold (a process known as enfranchisement).

The law relating to long leases has been the subject of five principal statutes: Part I of the Landlord and Tenant Act 1954, the Leasehold Reform Act 1967, the Local Government and Housing Act 1989, the Leasehold Reform, Housing and Urban Development Act 1993 and the Commonhold and Leasehold Reform Act 2002. Although they all apply to long leases of residential property, there are important differences as to their qualifying requirements and the situations to which they apply. Depending on when they were created, the few long leases for which rents are payable which are not low will be subject to the Rent Act 1977 or Housing Act 1988, bearing in mind that since 15 January 1989 the strict controls on premiums have been relaxed (see Chapter 16.6).

17.2 Control of Service Charges

Tenants are usually called upon to pay service charges, i.e., 'amounts payable directly or indirectly for services, repairs, maintenance, improvements or insurance or the landlord's costs of management' (s.18(1)(a) Landlord and Tenant Act 1985). The landlord (or sometimes a management company which is party to the lease) provides the services, while the leaseholders pay for them. The landlord will generally make no financial contribution, but will sometimes have to pay in advance for the works or services before recovering the cost thereof from the leaseholders via the service charge.

Details of what the landlord can (and cannot) charge for and the proportion of the charge to be paid by the individual leaseholder will be set out in the lease. It may contain specific terms obliging the landlord to carry out certain works or provide certain services and, if a service charge is to be payable, it must contain a power for the landlord to recover the cost of those works or services from the tenant. It must specify whether the charge is recoverable in advance or in arrears of the provision of works or services and whether it is to be collected on a regular basis, perhaps annually or on a specified quarter-day, or whether it is to be levied as costs arise. The lease may be very specific in its wording, setting out quite precisely the works or services to be chargeable; alternatively the clauses may be very general, simply referring to costs of the repair and maintenance of the structure of building. The terms of charging clauses may need to be carefully considered in order to decide whether or not the cost of an item can be passed on to the tenant under the provision in question. Typically, disputes will centre on whether the terms include major works. In such circumstances guidance must be sought from authorities on the scope of repairing covenants as considered in Chapter 9.

Charges may vary dramatically from year to year as various works become necessary on the demised property and – not surprisingly perhaps – disputes frequently arise between landlords and tenants over the cost of, and sometimes even the need for, works to be carried out. Sections 18–30 of the Landlord and Tenant Act 1985 (as amended by the Landlord and Tenant Act 1987, the Housing Act 1996 and Part II of the Commonhold and Leasehold Reform Act 2002) impose important restrictions on landlords' powers in this regard. While their procedures should usually be used where the tenant alleges excessive works and/or costs and either refuses to pay or offers a smaller amount, it was held in *Bounds* v. *Camden LBC* (1999) that in an appropriate case the court has jurisdiction grant an injunction restraining a landlord from carrying out work prior to the hearing by the LVT of an application under s.19(2B) as to whether, if the costs were incurred, they would be reasonable.

The provisions contained in the 1985 Act, as amended, should be read in conjunction with Part II of the Landlord and Tenant Act 1987 and the the Commonhold and Leasehold Reform Act 2002 (see below) whereby an unreasonable demand for a service charge may give rise to a tenant seeking the appointment of a manager for the premises or exercise the right to manage themselves.

17.2.1   Demands for Service Charges

Section 47 of the 1987 Act provides that any written demand for service charges given to the tenant must contain prescribed information, including the landlord's name and address and, where the given address is not in England and Wales, an address in England and Wales at which notices (including notices in proceedings) may be served on the landlord by the tenant. If any of the prescribed information is omitted, the amount claimed is deemed not to be due from the tenant until such time as it is provided (This provision does not apply where a court has appointed a receiver or manager whose duties include the collection of service charges.) Section 48 similarly provides that a landlord of residential premises must give notice to his tenant of an address in England and Wales at which notices may be served on him. Again, failure to give such a notice has the effect that any rent or service charges otherwise due from the tenant shall be treated for all purposes as not being due, until the default is remedied. The proviso in respect of a court-appointed receiver or manager also applies.

Normally the lease will provide for the service charge to be demanded in advance, but the demands may sometimes be issued after completion of the works or provision of the service. In these cases the landlord must issue the demand within 18 months of his incurring the cost (s.20B of the 1985 Act). If the demand is provided later than this, the landlord cannot recover the costs at all, unless a notice is served during the 18 months stating that costs have been incurred and that the tenant will be required to contribute to them by payment of a service charge.

17.2.2   Reasonableness

Although service charge expenditure may go up or down from year to year, s.19 imposes a general requirement of reasonableness. The costs of the service charge must be reasonably incurred and, where they are incurred in the provision of services or the carrying out of works, the services or works must be of a reasonable standard. If works or services are not of a reasonable standard, there may be a proportionate reduction. A charge may be recovered before the costs are incurred so long as the amount is reasonable. This is subject to a requirement for adjustment after the expenditure has been incurred. An application may be made to a LVT or a court as to whether the charge is reasonable. Likewise there may be an application for a determination as to whether future costs would be reasonable if incurred, or whether fuure works or services would be of a reasonable standard, or what amount payable before costs are incurred would be reasonable.

Since the relevant provisions of the Commonhold and Leasehold Reform Act 2002 came into force, application may also be made to the LVT for a determination of whether a service charge is payable and, if it is, as to the person by whom and to whom it is payable, the amount which is payable, the date at or on which it is payable and the manner in which it is payable (s.27A(1)). The LVT may also consider service charge disputes where a tenant has already paid the sum in dispute. No application may be made where the issue has been agreed or admitted by the tenant, or determined by a court or referred to arbitration or determined by arbitration. Any reference to arbitration must be with the tenant's agreement following the dispute. Any clause in a lease or any other agreement which appears to commit the tenant to arbitration in advance of a dispute arising is deemed to be void and will not bind the tenant nor prevent an application to the LVT. The repayment of any money found not to be payable can only be ordered by the county court (s.27A(2)). By s.20C application may be made to the court or an LVT that court, tribunal or arbitration costs are not relevant costs to be added to a service charge.

17.2.3   Estimates and Consultation

As of 30 October 2003 the landlord's responsibilities with regard to the duty to consult with tenants before works are started have been substantially altered by the Commonhold and Leasehold Reform Act 2002. The old provisions continue to apply, however, where the works were carried out before 31 October 2003.

Under the old rules, where the relevant costs incurred in carrying out building works were in excess of £50 multiplied by the number of tenants or £1,000 per block (whichever was the greater), the landlord had to satisify various requirements. A failure to do so would limit the amount recoverable to the prescribed amount. The requirements depended upon whether the tenant was represented by a recognised tenants' association. If the tenant was not so represented, the landlord had to obtain two estimates, one from a person wholly unconnected with the landlord. A copy of the estimates had to be notified to the leaseholders and displayed so as to be likely to come to their attention. It had to described the proposed works and invite observations within one month. If the tenants were represented by a tenants' association, at least two estimates had to be obtained (as above) and the secretary given a detailed specification of the proposed works and a reasonable period allowed for the association to put to the landlord names of persons from whom, in its view, estimates should be obtained. A copy of the estimates had to be given to the secretary and each tenant given a summary or copy of the estimates and invited to make observations within, at least, one month. Each tenant must have had reasonable facilities for free inspection and copies of estimates, although the costs incurred in carrying this out could be added to the management costs. The landlord must have had regard to any observations which were made. Finally, the landlord must not have begun works earlier than the date specified in the notice unless they were urgently required. Where the Leasehold Valutation Tribunal was satisfied that the landlord had acted reasonably they could dispense with any of the requirements for consultation. In *Heron Maple House Ltd.* v. *Central Estates* (2002) the freeholder owned a large building which consisted of a mixture of offices, residential and commerical accommodation. It had spent considerable sums of money on improving the structure of the property and sought to recover the costs via the service charge provisions contained in both the headlease and the subleases. However, neither the freeholder nor Central Estates complied with the procedural requirements of s.20, claiming that because the demised premises included non-residential as well as residential premises, s.20 did not apply. The court held that s.20 must be followed wherever there was a tenant of a dwelling, even if the tenant also leased other non-residential premises. As a result, the service charge of £17,000 could not be recovered. In *Martin* v. *Maryland Estates Ltd.* (1999) the landlord had given the tenants notice of proposed works as required. The landlords then proceeded with the works but also carried out some additional works identified by the builders but of which the tenants had not been told. Whilst the tenants did not dispute the original works they did contest their liability to pay for the additional works. The Court Appeal agreed and dismissed the landlord's claim because the latter had acted unreasonably in failing to consult the tenants over the additional works.

The Commonhold and Leasehold Reform Act 2002 has introduced a new s.20 and an additional s.20ZA which contain considerably more detailed and onerous consultation requirements than those contained in the original s.20 and apply where there are 'qualifying works' or a 'qualifying long-term agreement'. Qualifying works are works on a building or any other premises and which of the two consultation regimes applies will depend on whether or not they take place under long term agreements.

Where works are to be carried out (other than under a long term agreement) for which any tenant will be required to pay more than £250, the landlord must give a Notice of Intention to each tenant (and on the secretary of any recognised tenants' association, if there is one) of his intention to carry out qualifying works. The notice must

(a) give a general description of the proposed works or details of the time and place when a description can be inspected. (Facilities to inspect the description of the proposed works must be provided free of charge although this does not prevent the landlord recovering the costs through the service charge.);

(b) explain why the landlord considers it necessary to carry out the works;

(c) invite observations in relation to the proposed and state where they should be sent, stating that they should be delivered within 30 days of the notice and the date when the 30 day period expires;

(d) invite proposals within the 30 day period for people from whom the landlord should try to obtain an estimate. The landlord is obliged to have regard to the observations. This means he must consider them but does not have to accept them.

The landlord must then supply the tenant with a second notice – the notice of proposals – setting out the details of the proposed works and the likely costs. The landlord must supply at least two estimates (at least one of which must be from a wholly unconnected person), a summary of the observations received in response to the first notice and his response to them. Once again, he must invite observations and allow 30 days for them to be made. The landlord must serve a further notice within 21 days of entering into a contract unless the estimate chosen was made by a nominated person or was the lowest. This further notice must include the landlord's reasons for awarding the contract or a place and time when such reasons can be inspected and a summary of any observations and his response to them.

The landlord must also consult the tenants before proceeding where there is a 'qualifying long-term agreement' (i.e., the agreement under which the works will be carried out is for a period of more than 12 months) and the contribution from any tenant will exceed £100 per annum. The consultation provisions are a simplified version of those set out above. Once again, the landlord must serve a Notice of Intention on each tenant, inviting observations. If a tenant or the association nominates an alternative contractor, the landlord must try to obtain an estimate from that contractor. He must then serve a further notice on the tenants or the association setting out the estimates but also including a statement which

(a) identifies the proposed contractor;
(b) identifies any connection between the contractor and the landlord;
(c) where reasonably practicable, sets out the estimate of cost to the tenant;
(d) where the proposed agreement relates to the appointment of a managing agent, indicates whether the agent belongs to a profession body or trade association and whether he subscribes to a code of practice or voluntary accreditation scheme.

Again, the notice must invite observations and state the address and timescale (minimum 30 days). As with major works, the landlord must have regard to the observations and, where observations or nominations were received from the tenants or a recognised tenants' association

A recognised tenants' association is defined in s.29 of the 1985 Act as one which is recognised (for the purpose of the 1985 Act only – that is not in the context of other parts of the private sector or in the public sector) either by written notice from the landlord to the secretary or by a certificate from the local Rent Assessment Committee. The scope of this provision was considered in *R. v. London Rent Assessment Panel, ex parte Trustees of Henry Smith's Charity* (1988). The landlord had converted a terrace of eight houses into five separate blocks of flats. Each flat was leased and each block had slightly different service charge arrangements. An association was set up for all five blocks and was recognised by a certificate from the Rent Assessment Committee. The landlord successfully challenged the formal recognition, on the basis that each block was a separate entity; each block therefore needed its own association, although they could federate if they so wished. Section 30B permits a recognised tenants' association to insist on consultation before appointment of managing agents. Alternatively, if agents have already been appointed, the landlord must inform the association as to the scope of the agents' obligations. Recognised associations are given the further right to appoint surveyors to assist and advise on questions relating to service charges, the surveyors also having a right of access to relevant documents and premises (Housing Act 1996 s.84 and Schedule 4).

17.2.4 Statements of Account

By s.21, the landlord must, within six months of the end of the accounting period, supply a written statement of account to each tenant by whom service charges are payable. He must also supply (a) a certificate of a qualified accountant that, in the accountant's opinion, the statement of account deals fairly with the matters with which it is required to deal and is sufficiently supported by accounts, receipts and other documents which have been produced to him, and (b) a summary of the rights and obligations of tenants of dwellings in relation to service charges (s.21(3)).

17.2.5 Administration Charges

The 2002 Act introduces controls on administration charges. These are defined in para. 1 of Schedule 11 as 'an amount payable by a tenant as part of or in addition to rent, which is payable directly or indirectly for:

(a) the grant of approvals under the lease or applications for such approvals;
(b) the provision of information or documents by or on behalf of the landlord;
(c) costs arising from non-payment of a sum due to the landlord;
(d) costs arising in connection with a breach (or alleged breach) of the lease.'

Any administration charge levied by the landlord must be reasonable in order for the landlord to recover the charge.

The remedy available to the tenant depends on whether the charge is variable or fixed. Where the charge is variable, the tenant may make an application to the LVT for a determination of reasonableness, as with service charges. A variable administrative charge is one where the amount of the charge is not specified in the lease or calculated according to a formula specified in the lease. Where the charge is fixed by the lease or a formula in the lease, the tenant may apply to the LVT to vary the lease, on the grounds that the amount specified is unreasonable or that the formula is unreasonable. If the LVT is satisfied, it may make an order to vary the terms of the lease, to substitute a reasonable amount or to amend the formula, either as requested by the tenant or as the Tribunal finds appropriate.

17.2.6 Restrictions on Forfeiture for Arrears of Service Charge

The final sanction for a landlord faced with a tenant in breach of covenant because of a failure to pay the service charge or ground rent is to take steps to forfeit the lease and to recover possession of the property in question. The first step in the repossession process usually involves the service of a notice under s.146 of the Law of Property Act 1925. In practice landlords have often served s.146 notices with the intention of scaring tenants into compliance, rather than of securing possession. The reforms contained in s.168 of the Commonhold and Leasehold Reform Act 2002 modify s. 81 of the Housing Act 1996 to prohibit the commencement of forfeiture proceedings, including the issue of a notice under s.146, in respect of non-payment of service charges or administration charges. Now, a landlord cannot serve a s.146 notice unless (a) the tenant has admitted the breach or (b) the breach has been determined by the LVT, a court or arbitration. The s.146 notice may not be served until after the expiry of 14 days of the final date of the determination.

Further, s.167 of the 2002 Act provides that a landlord under a long lease of residential premises may not forfeit the lease for failure by a tenant to pay an amount comprising rent, service charges or administration charges (or any combination of them) unless the unpaid amount either exceeds the prescribed sum (£350) or consists of or includes an amount that has been payable for more than the prescribed period (three years). (The prescribed sum and the prescribed period have been set by the Rights of Re-Entry and Forfeiture (Prescribed Sum and Period) (England) Regulations 2004 (SI 2004 No 3086)).

17.3 Landlord & Tenant Act 1954 Part 1

Around the middle of the nineteenth century, long leases were used as a common means of developing land in certain urban areas – notably in South Wales, Merseyside, Tyneside and London – as well as in certain smaller towns which were often situated in a surrounding area of predominantly freehold tenure, e.g., Eastbourne and Bournemouth. Usually, the tenant would pay a premium at the beginning of a 99-year term and a ground rent throughout the duration of the lease. He would also be required to deliver up the premises at the end of the term in good repair. The original tenant might assign the lease during the term but if he chose not to do so, the remainder of the term would pass on his death under the principles of succession. Long leases presented no difficulties at the beginning of the term. However, by the mid-1950s (after many of the original 99-year leases had run their course), problems had started to arise. Tenants were not only faced with losing their homes but also, because of the original repairing obligation, they incurred the (often considerable) expense of renovating dilapidated housing which they would no longer be able to occupy. To meet these problems, Part I of the Landlord and Tenant Act 1954 was enacted, giving long leaseholders Rent Act protection when their tenancies came to an end by effluxion of time and providing, in certain circumstances, for relief from repairing obligations. However, because – subject to a few limited exceptions – s.34 of the Housing Act 1988 prevents the creation of any new Rent Act tenancies on or after 15 January 1989, the Local Government and Housing Act 1989, s.186 and Schedule 10 – which applies to long leases at low rents entered into on or after 1 April 1990 – provides for their protection on expiry of the initial fixed term as assured tenancies. Long leases at a low rent existing on 1 April 1990 continued to be subject to Part I of the 1954 Act until 15 January 1999 (this being ten years from the introduction of the assured tenancy regime) but as of that date all 1954 Act tenancies were converted into 1989 Act tenancies. The exception was leases which had reached the end of their term before 15 January 1999 but had continued by virtue of s.3 of the 1954 Act. There may be some – though admittedly few – such tenancies still in existence which means that the time has not yet arrived to consign Part I of the 1954 Act to the dustbin of legal history.

In order to claim the benefit of the 1954 Act, a tenancy must satisfy three conditions: it must be a long lease; it must be at a low rent; and it must satisfy the qualifying condition. As has already been noted, a long lease is one which is for a term certain exceeding twenty-one years. An option to determine earlier than twenty-one years does not infringe this prerequisite, nor does the fact that a subtenant has taken over the interest of the leaseholder during the lease. Reference should be made to 16.2 for what a low rent entails. The qualifying condition means that the circumstances (as regards the property comprised in the tenancy, the use of that property and all other relevant matters) are such that on the coming to an end of the tenancy, the tenant would be within the protection of the Rent Act 1977 if the tenancy had not been at a low rent. In other words, s.1 of the 1977 Act, as discussed in Chapter 16, must be complied with.

17.3.1   The Procedures under Part I of the Landlord & Tenant Act 1954

By s.3 of the 1954 Act, the tenancy will automatically continue after the end of its term, at the same rent and on the same terms as before. Either the landlord or the tenant must take positive steps to bring this continuing arrangement to an end. The tenant may do so at any time by giving one month's notice to expire on or after the contractual term date (s.5). Two alternative courses of action are available to the landlord. He can either suggest that a new tenancy be granted of the premises or he can seek to recover possession on certain limited grounds. Either way, he must issue a notice in the prescribed form, specifying the premises to which it applies, giving between six and twelve months' notice that the tenancy is to end, and either containing the proposals for a new tenancy or, alternatively, stating that if the tenant does not give up possession, the landlord will apply to court for a possession order. The tenant must reply to this notice within two months of receipt. If he fails to do so, he is taken to have accepted it and will lose his right to object.

If the landlord opts for the grant of a new tenancy, his notice must include details of the rent to be paid, of any initial repairs to be carried out and the repairing obligations under the new lease. If the tenant objects to these proposals, the landlord may apply to the court for a determination of the terms. If a new tenancy is granted it will be a statutory tenancy under the Rent Act 1977 qand will enjoy the normal security of tenure associated with such a tenancy.

If, on the other hand, the landlord wishes to recover possession and the tenant serves a counter-notice under s.4(4), the landlord can only recover possession with leave of the court (s.13). The grounds on which he can recover possession are limited by s.12 and Schedule 3. All of them are discretionary. They are as follows:

(a) the landlord proposes to demolish or re-construct the whole or a substantial part of the relevant premises;
(b) suitable alternative accommodation will be available to the tenant;
(c) the tenant has failed to comply with any term of the tenancy as to payment of rent or as to insuring the premises;
(d) the tenant, sub-tenant or anyone authorised by him has been guilty of conduct causing annoyance or nuisance to adjoining occupiers or has been convicted of immoral or illegal user with respect to the premises; and
(e) the premises are reasonably required by the landlord for occuaption as a residence for himself or for a member of his family.

If the landlord is able to establish one or more of the grounds, the court will grant possession. If on the other hand the landlord is unsuccessful, then under s.14 the landlord will have one month to propose a statutory tenancy. The unsuccessful outcome will therefore be the same as if the landlord had not objected in the first place to the grant of a statutory tenancy.

Section 10 of the 1954 Act confirms that the tenant's liability under the former lease – for example to pay rent and rates and to insure – continues after the beginning of the statutory tenancy. Responsibility for rent includes liability for all payments under the instrument of letting such as board, and services: the latter may be considerable if they include the cost of rectifying dilapidations (*Blatherwick (Services) v. King* (1991)).

17.3.2 The Procedures under the Local Government and Housing Act 1989, s.186 and Schedule 10

Many of the provisions of the 1989 Act are very similar to those of the 1954 Act. Again, the 1989 Act applies only to long tenancies at a low rent and the qualifying condition must be satisfied. Here, however, the circumstances must be such that if tenancy was not at a low rent, it would qualify as an assured tenancy under the Housing Act 1988 (i.e. it is not excluded and complies with the requirements of s.1 of the 1988 Act).

The tenancy authomatically continues on the expiry of the initial fixed term (s.3) and either party is able to bring it to an end using exactly the same procedure and subject to the same time limits as under the 1954 Act. The grounds of oppostion – which are set out in paragraph 5 of schedule 10 – are

(a) Ground 6 and – except for Ground 16 – those in Part 2 of Schedule II to the Housing Act 1988;
(b) The landlord proposes to demolish or reconstruct the whole or a substantial part of the premises for the purposes of redevelopment after the termination of the tenancy;
(c) The landlord reasonably requires the premises or part of them for occupation as a residence for himself or for his adult son or daughter or his parents or parents-in-law.

If the tenant opposes repossession, application must be made to the court. If the court refuses to order possession, an assured tenancy under the Housing Act 1988 comes into existence.

17.4 Landlord & Tenant Act 1987

The Nugee Committee of Inquiry on *The Management of Privately Owned Blocks of Flats*, which reported in 1986, found that the problems commonly experienced by long leaseholders included excessive delay in carrying out repairs and maintenance, difficulties in enforcing landlords' obligations, poor quality of service, and unexpected bills, excessive delay in obtaining information, and the level of service charges. The Committee's report led to the enactment of the Landlord and Tenant Act 1987 which confers upon long leaseholders:

(a) The right of first refusal should the landlord decide to dispose of the property;
(b) The right to apply to the Leasehold Valuation Tribunal (LVT) for the appointment of a receiver or manager; and
(c) The right collectively to acquire ownership of the landlord's interest.

17.4.1   Right of First Refusal (Part I, ss.1–20)

The 1987 Act provides that no landlord shall make a relevant disposal of premises unless he has first given the qualifying tenants of the flats contained in those premises a right of first refusal in respect of the interest of which he wishes to dispose. Breach may be restrained by means of an injunction. A 'relevant disposal' includes a disposal of any estate or interest including any such interest in the common parts but it excludes the grant of a tenancy of a single flat, disposals on bankruptcy, on liquidation or on divorce (s.4(2)). The premises must consist of the whole or part of a building containing two or more flats held by 'qualifying tenants' where the number of flats held by those tenants exceeds 50 per cent of the total number of flats contained in the premises (s.1(2)). A 'flat' is defined in s.60 as premises forming a horizontal part of a building constructed or adapted for use as a dwelling. 'Qualifying tenants' are tenants of flats other than protected shorthold tenants, assured tenants (including assured shorthold tenants), business tenants within the 1954 Act Part II, or those whose tenancies are terminable on cessation of their employment (s.3). The landlord against whom the right is to be exercised must be immediately superior to the qualifying or the first in the chain with an interest greater than seven years (s.2). Certain landlords are excluded from the operation of the Act. The most important of these are local authorities, certain housing associations (these are exempt landlords under s.8(1)) and resident landlords (s.1(4). A resident landlord is a landlord who lives in part of the building (not being a purpose-built block of flats) and who occupies a flat in the premises as his only or principal home and has done so for at least 12 months.

Where the requisite conditions are satisfied, the landlord must serve an 'offer notice' on the qualifying tenants (s.5). This must contain particulars of the principal terms of the proposed disposal including the price and must state that it consitutes an offer to sell the interest should a majority of the qualifying tenants wish to purchase. Such a majority is determined on the basis of one vote per flat let to qualifying tenant. The landlord is deemed to have complied with his obligations if he serves the notice on not less than 90 per cent of the qualifying tenants or, where there are fewer than ten such tenants, on all but one of them. Tenants wishing to accept the offer must serve an acceptance notice on the landlord within the period stated in the offer notice, which must not be less than two months (s.6). If more than 50 per cent of the qualifying tenants accept the offer, they are then given a further two months to nominate a person who will purchase the landlord's interest on the tenants' behalf (s.6(2)(a)). If a person is so nominated, completion of the transfer must take place within a further three months (s.6(2)(b)). If any of these time limits is not complied with, the landlord is free to proceed with the disposal elsewhere (s.7(1)). If the sale is to be by auction, one month is allowed to appoint a nominated purchaser. The tenants may elect to be notified of the sale price within seven days of the auction, after which they have 28 days to decide whther to buy at this price.

By s.7, instead of serving an acceptance notice in reply to the landlord's offer notice, the qualifying tenants may serve a counter-offer which the landlord may then accept, reject outright (in which case the landlord is free to make a disposal within 12 months of the expiry of the specified acceptance period), or reject and make a fresh offer (s.9).

A landlord commits a criminal offence if, without reasonable excuse, he fails to serve a s.5 notice or contravenes any of the restrictions or requirements in ss.6–10 (s.10A) The maximum fine is £5000. Directors of a landlord company may also be guilty if the company commits the offence with their consent or connivance or owing to their neglect.

Supporting provisions deal with situations where there is a contract to sell or an actual disposal to a new landlord in contravention of the above requirements, the purchaser ultimately being required to sell to the qualifying tenants if they could have successfully applied (ss.5, 11–16). The Leasehold Valuation Tribunal adjudicates on any dispute as to price.

Prospective purchasers may serve notice on the qualifying tenants, under s.18, informing them of the proposed disposal in order to ensure that rights of first refusal do not arise subsequently. In *Kay Green and Others* v. *Twinsectra* (1996) the Court of Appeal emphasised the need to take a pragmatic approach to the interpretation of the notice provisions. The requisite majority of tenants had failed to include one flat of four in the purchase notice but had included buildings outside the scope of the Act. They had not invalidated its provisions because the underlying principle was that a new landlord served with a purchase notice by tenants who had not been given first refusal had to give effect to it.

Part I of the 1987 Act has been described as a 'legislative lemon' which, although it is 'notoriously difficult to comply with', can be squeezed by a majority of tenants to extract for themselves 'very large windfall gains', e.g. by disposing of non-residential parts of the premises and granting themselves very valuable extended leases. Given the extensive rights to enfranchise and to manage conferred by 1993 and 2002 Acts, there is some doubt as to whether the right of first refusal is still required (P. Kenny, 'A bully's charter' [2002] Conv 517).

17.4.2   Appointment of a Receiver or Manager (Part II ss.21–4)

Although s.37 Supreme Court Act 1981 allows for the appointment of a receiver to collect rents and service charges and carry out repairs, that jurisdiction has been effectively superseded by the more detailed provisions of the 1987 Act. Section 24 (as amended by the Housing Act 1996 s.85) permits the Leasehold Valuation Tribunal (LVT) to appoint a manager to control the flats (as defined above) if any relevant person

(a) is in breach of an obligation which is owed to the tenant and relates to management, or
(b) is making or proposing to make unreasonable service or administrative charges, or
(c) has failed to comply with a Code of Management Practice

and it would be just and convenient in all the circumstances to make the order.

A further 'sweeping up' provision (in s.24(2)(6)) permits the LVT to appoint a manager in other circumstances if it is just and convenient to do so. These rights are not available in the case of a local authority or housing association landlord or where the premises are not purpose-built and the landlord is a resident landlord as defined in s.58(2) (s.21(3)(a)).

The jurisdiction might typically be used where the landlord of a large block of flats neglects his repairing obligations with regard to common parts, having lost interest in them perhaps because returns have become too low. The application would seek the appointment of a manager to collect rents and service charges and carry out such repairs as are or have become necessary. Guidance on the appointment of a receiver (and equally, it is submitted, a manager) when the landlord claims after such an application that the work is about to start, is to be found in *Blawdziewicz* v. *Diadon Establishment* (1988) where it was stated that 'if the landlord has shown a disinclination to fulfil his repairing obligations . . . a Court [c]ould appoint a receiver because the balance of convenience would be in favour of taking such a step. It would protect the interests of the tenants without causing any loss to the landlord' (per Hoffman J.).

Detailed provisions require the tenants to serve the landlord with a preliminary notice which must specify the grounds on which the LVT would be asked to make an order and the matters on which the tenants would rely on to to establish them. Where those matters are capable of remedy, the notice must also require him – within such reasonable period as is specified in the notice – to take specified steps to remedy them. The LVT may dispense with the need for a notice where it is satisfied that it would not be reasonably practicable but when doing so, it may direct that such other notices are served, or such other steps are taken, as it thinks fit (s.22(3)). No application may be made to the LVT therefore unless

(a) a s.22 notice has been served and the reasonable period for remedy of a breach has expired, or the breach was not capable of remedy; or
(b) service of the s.22 notice has been dispensed with and any directions made by the LVT as to further steps or notices have been complied with.

The order can make provision for can grant the manager any relevant powers, including the ability to borrow money. In addition, the manager will acquire the power to collect rent as well as to carry out repairs. The tribunal can also order remuneration of the manager by either the landlord or the tenant, or both (s.24). This will undoubtedly console the manager, but still may not provide sufficient money to pay for all the works that the manager deems to be necessary and which may have caused the tenants to instigate proceedings.

17.4.3   Compulsory Acquisition (Part III ss.25–34)

In extreme cases, where the appointment of a manager has proved unsuccessful or is regarded by the court as an insufficient remedy, Part III of the Act allows the court to make an acquisition order, the effect of which will be to deprive the landlord of his interest in the property without his consent. An order will be made where:

(a) the landlord has broken obligations relating to management, or
(b) there has been a management appointment in force on the date of application and throughout the period of two years prior to the application being made.

The right of compulsory acquisition applies to premises which consist of the whole or part of a building containing two or more flats held by qualifying tenants and in which the total number of flats held by such tenants is not less than two-thirds of the total number of flats contained in the premises. The qualifying tenants are tenants under long leases. Business tenants to which Part II of the Landlord and Tenant Act 1954 applies are expressly excluded, as is a qualifying tenant who is a long lessee of two or more other flats.

Part III does not apply to premises if:

(a) any part or parts of the premises is or are occupied or intended to be occupied otherwise than for residential purposes; and
(b) the internal floor area of that part or those parts (taken together) exceeds 50 per cent of the internal floor area of the premises (taken as a whole);

and for the purposes of this subsection the internal floor area of any common parts shall be disregarded.

Before an application can be made to the court for an acquisition order a preliminary notice must be served on the landlord effectively warning him or her of the tenants' intention to apply for an order in respect of the spcified premises. This may be dispensed with if the court accepts it would not be reasonably practicable (s.28, s.27 (3)), e.g., if the landlord cannot be traced (s.33). Once the order has been made, the tenants acquire the landlord's interest subject to any conditions imposed by the court. The parties may agree the detailed term of transfer between themselves: if they cannot, the Leasehold Valuation Tribunal will do so (s.31). The acquisition price will be the open market price, assuming a willing seller and purchaser and full vacant possession (s.31).

17.4.4 Variation of the Terms of a Lease (Part IV ss.35–40)

Any party to the lease of a flat (as defined in s.60 above) may apply for variation by the court of the terms of the lease relating to:

- repair or maintenance of the flat or building;
- insurance – for this term only of flats and of other long leases (s.40);
- repair or maintenance of installations or provision of services reasonably necessary for the enjoyment of a reasonable standard of accommodation, account being taken of safety, security and condition of common parts;
- computation of service charges when the landlord is likely to recover more than he paid out;
- recovery of expenditure incurred by one party from the other (s.35(2)–(4)).

These provisions might typically be used by tenants wishing to vary 'onerous' clauses.

If the court does make the order requested, it has power to depart from the application if appropriate, to order variation of the lease by the parties instead of making an order, to order endorsement on the lease of a memorandum of variation, and to order compensation by one party to the other for loss suffered in consequence of the order (s.38). No order can he made that prejudices substantially the respondent or a third party, nor can the landlord lose entirely the right to nominate an insurer (s.38).

17.5 The Right to Manage

The right to manage (RTM) introduced by the Commonhold and Leasehold Reform Act 2002 gives tenants of qualifying blocks of flats the right to set up a RTM company which can take over the management of the residential common parts of the premises. There is – in contrast to Part II of the Landlord and Tenant Act 1987 – no requirement to show any default by the freeholder or manager . Furthermore, no compensation need be paid, and there is no requirement to make an application to a tribunal or the court. The RTM reflects the fact that, because the freeholds of blocks of flats can often be acquired for a few thousand pounds but the flats themselves may be worth hundreds of thousands of pounds, the leaseholders usually have by far the greatest financial interest in the building The RTM provides an alternative option to collective enfranchisement. In some cases, the shortness of the leases or the retention by the landlord of rented flats or commercial parts of the block makes enfranchisement too expensive. Alternatively, some leaseholders may wish to have the opportunity to try managing the building before they commit themselves to buying the freehold.

17.5.1   Qualifying Requirements

By s.72(1) of the 2002 Act the requirements which need to be met for the exercise of the RTM mirror those used for the right to collective enfranchisement under the Leasehild reform, Housing and urban Development Act 1993 (see below). The right must be exercised by a RTM company (a private company limited by guarantee, the Memorandum and Articles of which are to be prescribed by regulations). The number of long leaseholders participating through membership of the RTM company must equal at least half the total number of flats in the building – except where there are only two flats in which case both long leaseholders must participate.

17.5.2   Exclusions

The following are excluded from the RTM:

(a) Properties in mixed residential and non-residential use where the internal floor area of the of the non-residential parts exceeds 25 per cent of the total internal floor area of the property, disregarding common parts;

(b) Any premises which have been converted into flats (or a mixture of flats and other units used as dwellings e.g. bedsits), if the converted building contains no more than four units and the landlord (or an adult member of his family) lives in one of those units and has done so for the previous twelve months;

(c) Any premises where the landlord is a local authority. Local authority tenants already have a separate right to manage (which encompasses all tenants, including long leaseholders).

(d) Any premises where a RTM company loses the right to manage a property for any reason. In such circumstances, the block in question will be excluded from any exercise of RTM for four years from the date that the body ceased its management duties, unless the permission of a LVT is obtained.

(e) Any property which is already subject to the RTM in accordance with the 2002 Act.

Individual leaseholders will be excluded from the RTM if:

(a) They have sub-let their flat on a long lease; or
(b) They have a business lease.

17.5.3 Claim to Exercise RTM

By s.78(1), before making a claim to acquire the RTM any premises, a RTM company must give 'notice of invitation to participate' to each person who at the time when the notice is given

(a) is the qualifying tenant of a flat contained in the premises, but
(b) neither is nor has agreed to become a member of the RTM company.

Section 78(2) provides that he notice of invitation to participate must

(a) state that the RTM company intends to acquire the right to manage the premises;
(b) state the names of the members of the RTM company;
(c) invite the recipients of the notice to become members of the company, and
(d) contain such other particulars (if any) as may be required by regulation to be contained in such notices.

Section 78 presupposes that an RTM company will have already been formed by a group of leaseholders who will have decided that the RTM is a worthwhile move having presumably considered the matter at a meeting to which all the leaseholders will have been invited. The purpose of s.78 is to ensure, so far as is possible, that all leaseholders who could participate are given the opportunity to do so.

By s.79, the RTM company claims to acquire the RTM by means of a 'claim notice' served on the landlord, on any managing company or agent of the landlord, or, if relevant, on any manager appointed under LTA 1987. A claim notice cannot be given unless all the qualifying leaseholders (except those who are or have agreed to become a member of the RTM company) have been given a notice of invitation to participate (s.79(2)). If at the date the notice is given there are two qualifying tenants then both must be members of the RTM Company (s.79(4)). Otherwise the membership of the RTM company must include tenants who are qualifying tenants in at least half the total number of flats in the premises (s.79(5)).

Section 80 sets out the contents of a claim notice. It must specify the premises and contain a statement of the grounds on which it is claimed that they are premises which fall within the Act. Other information which must be given includes the full name of each person who is both (a) the qualifying tenant of a flat contained in the premises, and (b) a member of the RTM Company. Within the time specified in the claim notice (a minimum period of one month must be allowed) the landlord or other person to whom the claim notice was given may respond with a counter-notice (s.84) in which the right to acquire the RTM is, or is not, admitted. If there is no dispute between the parties, the date on which the RTM Company will acquire the right to manage will be specified in the claim notice under s.80 and will be four months or so after the date of the claim notice (s.90).

The RTM re-allocates the responsibility for many of the landlord's functions under the lease, such as landlords' repairing obligations under s.11, Landlord and Tenant Act 1985 and their obligations to consult tenants about service charges. 'Management functions' are defined by s.96(5) as 'functions with respect to services, repairs, maintenance, improvements, insurance and management'. However, landlords are entitled to carry out functions which apply only to a non-qualifying flat (e.g. premises subject to a business tenancy which falls under Part II of the Landlord and Tenant Act 1954) and retain the right to forfeit, not only for non-payment of rent but also where there is breach of other tenant obligations (s.96(6)). Because the landlord's relationship with the property will be more distant once the RTM Company takes over its management function, s.101 imposes an obligation on the RTM Company to keep under review whether tenant covenants of leases of the whole or any part of the premises are being complied with, and to report to the landlord any failure to comply within three months from the day the failure comes to its attention (s.101(3)).

The RTM Company will deal with consents ('grants of approval') which are required for such matters as assignment, improvement or alteration and change of use (s.98). However, the RTM Company cannot grant an approval without having given 30 days' notice in writing to the landlord. In the case of other matters requiring landlord approval, the period of notice is 14 days. If the landlord objects, the RTM Company cannot grant the approval without the landlord's written agreement or without applying to the LVT.

17.6   Leasehold Extension and Enfranchisement

Although Part I of the Landlord and Tenant Act 1954 gave tenants a measure of security on the expiry of their leases, the fact that the landlord could recover possession on certain specified grounds meant that tenants were still vulnerable. Even where there were still a number of years remaining on the tenancy, tenants who wanted to dispose of the remainder of the term were often unable to do so because institutional lenders were not prepared to grant loans to prospective purchasers. The value of the tenancy would drop at an ever-increasing rate, providing tenants with little incentive to repair or maintain the property. The Leasehold Reform Act 1967 sought to address such problems by giving tenants the right to buy the freehold of the houses they occupied on long leases or to obtain extended leases. Quite clearly, the Act was – and is – of limited application as it applies only to houses. The legislative gap was filled – somewhat belatedly – by the Leasehold Reform, Housing and Urban Development Act 1993 which confers similar rights on long leaseholders of flats.

17.6.1   The Leasehold Reform Act 1967

The Leasehold Reform Act 1967 gives far greater rights to long leaseholders than the Landlord and Tenant Act 1987, in that it allows them to enfranchise (i.e. purchase the freehold of their property), or alternatively to extend the lease for a further fifty years. In *James* v. *United Kingdom* (1986) an unsuccessful challenge was mounted against the 1967 Act on human rights grounds. It was argued that the Act constituted an infringement of Article 1 of the First Protocol which provides that 'every natural or legal person is entitled to the peaceful enjoyment of his possessions.' The right is qualified in that it allows for deprivation of a person's possessions where it is 'in the public interest and subject to conditions provided for by law', the State retaining an overarching right 'to enforce such laws as it deems necessary to control the use of property in accordance with the general interest'. The ECHR held that a taking of property effected in pursuance of legitimate social, economic or other policies may be 'in the public interest', even if the community at large has no direct use and enjoyment of the property taken.

Whether to enfranchise or to extend the lease is entirely for the tenant as the qualifying conditions and procedure are exactly the same. The tenant who opts for enfranchisement but then is unable or unwilling to buy the freehold at the designated price (whether or not determined by the Leasehold Valuation Tribunal) has a right to withdraw from the transaction. He must serve written notice under s.9(3) within one month of the price being fixed. He will then be liable for all the landlord's costs, and will not be able to make another claim for enfranchisement within the next 12 months although he may, of course, apply for an extended lease instead.. Where the tenant chooses the second option (perhaps because he cannot afford the capital sum payable for enfranchisement), the 50 year extension runs from the date on which the existing tenancy would come to an end. This means that the new tenancy is effectively for the unexpired residue of the existing term plus 50 years. The terms of the new lease will be generally the same as under the existing one (s.15(1)). However, after the expiry date of the original lease, the rent will be replaced by a modern ground rent for the site only, and a rent review clause exercisable every 25 years may be inserted if the landlord wishes. Only one extension can be granted; once granted neither the grantee, his subtenants nor assignees can make any further claim.

The tenant need not wait until the expiry of his lease to enfranchise or to obtain an extended lease but if the landlord has issued a notice under the Landlord and Tenant Act 1954 Part I the tenant must take action to exercise any rights under the 1967 Act within the next two months (Schedule 3). A tenant who has given notice under the Landlord and Tenant Act is precluded from exercising any rights under the 1967 Act. Tenants of certain types of landlord have no right to enfranchise. These include the National Trust (s.32), the Crown (s.33) and, subject to certain conditions, local authorities and housing associations (s.140 Housing Act 1980). Also excluded from the 1967 Act are are tenancies of houses in designated rural areas, where the freehold is owned together with adjoining land which is not used for residential purposes (s.1AA(3)).

The scope of the 1967 Act has been significantly extended (so far as enfranchisement is concerned) by the Housing Act 1996 and the Commonhold and Leasehold Reform Act 2002. With effect from 26 July 2002, the following prerequisites must be met to claim the benefits of the Act:

(a) The property must be a house. Long leaseholders of flats will qualify, if at all, undeer the Leasehold Reform, Housing and Urban Development Act 1993 (see below). A 'house' includes, according to s.2(1), 'any building designed or adapted for living in and reasonably so called notwithstanding that [it] is not structurally detached, or was or is not solely designed or adapted for living in, or is divided horizontally into flats or maisonettes'. The section goes on to exclude horizontal or vertical division of the whole property in order to ensure that the acquisition of the freehold of a 'house' does not result in flying freeholds above freeholds belonging to another. The scope of this provision was explored in *Sharpe* v. *Duke Street Securities* (1987), in which a tenant who had acquired the leases of both an upper and lower maisonette in the same property and had lived in them both was held to be living in a 'house'. Again, in *Malpas* v. *St. Ermin's Property Co. Ltd.* (1992) the premises, which looked from the outside like an Edwardian house, had been built as two horizontally divided maisonettes. The tenant held a lease of the whole building and lived in the upper part. A sub-tenant held a long lease of the downstairs maisonette. The Court of Appeal held that enfranchisement of the whole was available on the basis that the lease referred to it as a dwelling-house and a visitor would have been entitled to regard it as a house, even though there were two front doors and two back doors. *Malekshad* v. *Howard de Walden Estates Ltd.* (2003) provides a more recent illustration. Here, a large, terraced residential building in Harley Street was linked by a basement to a mews cottage behind. Together, they had been used as a single residential unit from 1775 to sometime in the 1930s, the mews building having originally been stables serving the property. The premises were all held under a single lease. The tenant claimed to be entitled to enfranchise either the whole as a single 'house' or the main house (excluding the mews cottage) as a single 'house'. The Court of Appeal held that the whole constituted a single 'house' and could be enfranchised. The House of Lords overturned this view. It might be correct to say that both the main house and the mews cottage constituted a single 'building'; but it was not correct in terms of the Leasehold Reform Act 1967 to call both of them together a 'house'. However, the claim to enfranchise the main house (which included the basement extending beyond the vertical boundary of the house) was valid.

The premises must normally be used for residential purposes (s.1), although in *Tandon* v. *Trustees of Spurgeon's Homes* (1982) (in which the premises consisted of a shop with living accommodation above), the House of Lords decided that mixed business and residential accommodation could fall within the Act.

Where the qualifying conditions have been satisfied, a claim under the Act may be made in respect of the 'house and premises.' 'Premises' means any garage, outhouse, garden, yard and appurtenances which are let to the tent with the house and are occupied with, and used for the purposes of, the house or any part of it by him or by another occupant (s.2(3)). In *Methuen-Campbell* v. *Walters* (1979), it was held that 'appurtenances' should be construed to include land within the curtilage of the house, and that a paddock which adjoined the garden of the house and was an amenity enjoyed with the house, was not an 'appurtenance' because it had always been separated therefrom by a fence.

(b) The lease must originally have been for over twenty-one years (s.3).

(c) The tenant must, at the time he serves the appropriate notice exercising his rights (see below), have been tenant of the house (or part of it) under a long tenancy for the last two years or for an aggregate of two years out of the last ten years (s.1(2). Under the original scheme the tenant would qualify only if he had occupied the house as his residence for the last three years or for periods amounting to three years in the last ten immediately preceding the relevant date. The residence requirement was abolished by the Commonhold and Leasehold Reform Act 2002 which means that the right to enfranchise may now be exercised by a non-resident tenant (as in *Hareford Ltd.* v. *Barnet LBC* (2005) in which the property – a shop on the ground floor and, above, a maisonette which was let on an assured shorthold tenancy – was held by the tenant company under a ninety-nine-year lease). If the tenant dies before exercising his rights and the tenancy passes to a member of his family, the successor will, in certain circumstances, be treated as having been tenant during any period when he was resident in the house and it was his only or main place of residence (s.7). Member of the family includes spouse or civil partner, step-children, parents and parents in law (s.7(7)).

There are several ways in which an otherwise valid application to extend or enfranchise may be defeated. When the tenancy is extended, or the tenant claims an extension, the landlord may apply to the court for possession on the grounds that he intends to redevelop the whole, or a substantial part of the house and premises (s.17(1)). Such a claim cannot be made more than 12 months before the term date of the original tenancy. A claim for extension or enfranchisement can be defeated if the landlord can prove that all or part of the property is or will reasonably be required for occupation as his only or main residence or that of an adult member of his family (s.18). The court will only make an order for possession on this ground if, having regard to all the circumstances of the case, including the availability of alternative accommodation for the landlord or the tenant, it is satisfied that greater hardship would be caused by refusing an order for possession. Local authorities and various public bodies (such as universities and regional health authorities) can prevent claims to enfranchise or extend if a Minister certifies that the premises are required for development within the next ten years (s.28). Section 23 contains provisions to prevent parties contracting out of the 1967 Act, although it cannot protect a tenant who has surrendered his lease and subsequently discovers the benefits he has lost through doing so.

17.6.2　Procedure

The tenant must serve written notice of his wish to enfranchise or extend (a desire notice)(s.5). The desire notice is personal to the tenant and not assignable to third parties. However, if the tenant assigns the lease, he can assign the benefit of the desire notice at the same time to the assignee of the lease and the assignee can then proceed with the acquisition of the freehold (s.5(2)). It is important that the tenant includes all the material information in the prescribed form. In *Speedwell Estates Ltd.* v. *Dalziel* (2002), the long leaseholders conceded that their notices had not been correctly completed but argued that they had nonetheless conveyed all the information which they needed to since the landlords had been aware of the facts required to be specified. The Court of Appeal found that there had been no serious attempt to provide the relevant information required by the statutory scheme and the omissions included essential information required by relevant boxes in the form. There was nothing optional about the information required in a tenant's notice and if the tenant wanted his notice to be valid, he must comply with the mandatory requirements. The purpose behind the provision of particulars in the prescribed form was to inform the landlord of the nature and basis of the tenant's claim and as to the basis upon which any price was to be assessed. The fact that the landlord might already know that information was not an answer to the question. The non-inclusion of this information could not be covered by any acceptable means of construction or interpretation.

The notice is deemed to be an estate contract and should, therefore, be protected by appropriate registration under the Land Charges Act 1972 or the Land Registration Act 2002. The landlord must, within two months of service of the notice, serve a notice in reply admitting or objecting to the tenant's claim. If after two months the landlord has not complied with his duty to serve a notice in reply, the tenant may apply to the court to enforce his right (Sch.3, para.7). When by his notice the landlord admits the tenant's claim, he is deemed to have accepted that the tenant is qualified to enfranchise (i.e. he has a long tenancy and has been a tenant for the requisite period). If the landlord refuses to admit the tenant's claim, he must state the grounds on which he does so. The tenant will then be able to commence proceedings in the county court to determine whether he is entitled to enfranchise, or to what property the right extends. The Act sets out complex formulae for the calculation of the purchase price. If the parties cannot agree the application of the relevant formula the dispute will be resolved by the Leasehold Valuation Tribunal (s.21). An appeal may be made from the Leasehold Valuation Tribunal, on a question of law only, to the Court of Appeal. In addition to the price, the tenant is responsible for paying the landlord's legal and other professional fees (s.14(2)).

17.7   Leasehold Reform, Housing and Urban Development Act 1993

This Act is an extensive piece of legislation, which came into force 1 November 1993. The Act allows many long leaseholders or 'qualifying tenants' in the private sector to enfranchise collectively or to acquire extended leases of their properties and thereby to protect what would otherwise be a depreciating asset. The condition of their property will tend to deteriorate as the lease wears on, its value to potential purchasers decline because there is less to buy. Service charges – which may be perceived as excessive – are a constant irritant, and failure to consult before works are carried out may encourage further mistrust of the landlord. The 1993 Act did further strengthen the hand of lessees but how many bother, or are able, to claim its benefits is another matter. Co-operation with other tenants is necessary, the cost (including valuation) can be considerable, the process is complex (notices and counter-notices must all be issued within specific time limits), and the outcome will at best be a share of the freehold, not the whole freehold. Many may prefer to opt for a ninety-year extension knowing that it can be further extended and realising that they will in effect be acquiring a freehold at a peppercorn rent. Whichever route current tenants take, though, the Act almost certainly signifies the end of the long lease as an investment because of the risk that tenants will wrest it from the freeholder.

17.7.1   Qualifying Requirements

By s.3(1) the requirements which need to be met for the exercise of the right to collective enfranchisement are that:

(a) The premises must consist of a self-contained building (or part of a building);
(b) The building contains two or more flats occupied by qualifying tenants. In this context a building is self-contained if it is 'structurally detached' A part of a building is self-contained if it consists of a vertical division of a building and the structure is such that it could be redeveloped independently from the rest of the building in which it is situated.
(c) The total number of flats held by qualifying tenants is not less than two-thirds of the total number of flats in the premises.

The tenants must have leases exceeding twenty-one years, including interests subject to forfeiture, perpetually renewable leases or long leases acquired under the public sector right to buy provisions (s.7). Joint tenants are considered as one in order to preserve the principle that there can be only one qualifying tenant per flat (s.5(3)). The freehold of all the flats need not be owned by the same person (s.3(1) as amended by the Housing Act 1996 s.107) so an application can still be made after some of the flats have been disposed of.

Exclusions

The following are excluded from the right to collective enfranchisement

(a) Any premises to which the resident landlord exemption applies and which contains no more than four units. Any premises are premises with a resident landlord at any time if (i) they are not, and do not form part of, a purpose built block (i.e. they have been converted into flats – or a mixture of flats and other units used as dwellings such as bedsits) (ii) the same person has owned the freehold of the premises since before the conversion of the premises into two or more flats or other units, and (iii) the freeholder or an adult member of his/her family has occupied a flat or other unit in the premises as a principal home for at least twelve months prior to the tenants' claim for enfranchisement (s.10(1)). Alternatively, where the freehold is held on trust, there must have been such an interest under the trust since before the conversion. In *Slamon* v. *Planchon* (2005) the issue was whether the freeholder (whose mother was the occupier of one of the three flats in the building) had an adequate interest. She relied on her mother's occupation together with her own interest in the freehold of the house which stretched back to before the time of its conversion into flats. However, although she was both legal and beneficial owner at the beginning and end of the period between conversion and the bid for enfranchisement, there had been a period in the middle in which she had had only an equitable interest under a trust. The Court of Appeal held that the interests could not be mixed with each other to result in a continuous whole. The defendant would not only lose the freehold therefore but would also have no right to participate in the future management of the freehold with the other qualifying tenants who were acquiring it.

(b) Properties in mixed residential and non-residential use where the internal floor area of the non-residentail parts exceeds 25 per cent of the total internal floor area of the property, disregarding the common parts (s.4).

(c) Business tenancies, sub-tenancies whose interests were granted in breach of covenant without any subsequent waiver and tenancies of charitable housing trusts (s.5). In *Richmond Housing Partnership Ltd.* v. *Brick Farm Management Ltd.* (2005), a charitable housing trust owned two blocks of flats in which at least half of the flats were held on long leases. The remainder, which were allocated by the trust in pursuit of its charitable purposes, were the subject of assured tenancies. The fact that the trust let some flats in the blocks in the pursuit of its charitable objects was held not to disqualify the participating tenants from the right to collective enfranchisement. It was clear that 'housing accommodation' provided by a housing trust was the social housing it provided; in this case the flats let on assured tenancies, but not those on long leases. To conclude otherwise would mean that when a charitable trust acquired the freehold of a block of flats, the majority of which were let on long leases and the minority on assured tenancies, the tenants with long leases would lose both their right to collective enfranchisement and their individual right to acquire a new lease under Part I of the 1993 Act. At the expiration of their long leases they would have no capital asset and would become assured tenants. If Parliament had intended to exclude such cases from the right to collective enfranchisement, s.5 would have expressly excluded 'relevant premises that include accommodation provided by a charitable trust in the pursuit of its charitable purposes'.

17.7.3 Enfranchisement (ss.11–38)

If the conditions above are all met *and* two-thirds of all the qualifying tenants agree to do so they may proceed collectively to enfranchise, provided they occupy at least half of the total number of flats in the premises. Section 11 allows them to obtain identifying information about the freeholder, and s.26 gives the courts powers to make vesting orders if the freeholder cannot be traced.

The first step in the acquisition procedure is the service on the landlord of a s.13 initial notice by a Right To Enfranchise (RTE) company which has among its participating members a number of qualifying tenants which is not less than half the total number of flats in the premises. Where there are only two qualifying tenants, both must be participating members of the RTE Company. An RTE Company is a private company limited by guarantee whose memorandum of association states that its object – or one of its objects – is the exercise of the right of collective enfranchisement with respect to the premises. (One of its other objects may be to acquire and exercise the Right to Manage the premises as a Right to Manage Company.) Once the initial notice is issued all subsequent proceedings are carried out by the RTE company. The RTE Company cannot make its claim until a notice of invitation is given to all qualifying tenants. By s.12A(2) it must

(a) state that the RTE Company intends to exercise the right to collective enfranchisement with respect to the premises;
(b) state the names of the participating members of the RET Company;
(c) explain the rights and obligations of the members of the RTE Company with respect to the exrcise of the rights;
(d) include an estimate of the price payable for the freehold and the associated costs;
(e) invite the recipients of the notice to become participating members of the RTE Company.

The initial s.13 notice must contain specified information including: premises involved, interests to be acquire of flats contained in the premises on the relevant date names of those applying, price proposed and a date for reply not more than two months after this initial notice. The price is assessed by an identified qualifying surveyor according to valuation rules set out in s.32 and Schedule 6. These rules allow for the landlord to receive market price, and half of the 'marriage value' which is the difference between the market value of the property and its value once it becomes a freehold or following an extension. Market value means what the property would fetch on the open market assuming a willing seller; it is not sale in a market limited to the landlord and tenant. The claim is invalid if the initial notice does not propose a realistic price (*Cadogan* v. *Morris* (1999)).

After the initial notice is received the landlord (or person acting on his behalf, known as the reversioner) has a right of access (s.17) so as to have a chance of confirming or not the proposed valuation. The landlord may not dispose of the premises while the notice subsists and must formally respond to the applicants through a counter-notice. In *9 Cornwall Crescent London Ltd.* v. *Kensington and Chelsea RLBC* (2005) the tenants' initial notice proposed a purchase price of £210 but the landlords' counter-notice proposed a price of £130,000. Instead of referring the premium to a Leasehold Valuation Tribunal (as they could have done, had they been unable to negotiate another price with the landlords), the tenants challenged the validity of the landlords' notice in the county court. Relying on *Cadogan* v. *Morris*, they argued that because it imposed an unrealistically high price, the landlords' counter-notice was invalid. Dismissing their appeal, the Court of Appeal held unanimously that the rule in *Cadogan* v. *Morris* does not apply to the landlord's counter-notice, largely because of the consequences should such a rule be applied. (Here the leaseholders would have acquired the freehold for £210 and the landlords would have lost the chance to challenge the leaseholders' valuation.) However, the judges differed on the issue of whether the landlord's counter-proposal must be genuine or made in good faith. Arden L.J. accepted the landlords' submission that the landlord could 'take any figure out of the air' while Auld L.J. thought that the landlord's proposal should be made in good faith.

If the landlord fails to respond to the initial notice, the tenants can apply to the county court for a declaration of their entitlement. If the court accepts that the tenants have met the necessary conditions, it must grant the declaration and also direct the terms upon which the acquisition is to proceed. The contract must be completed within two further months. If the the landlord issues a counter-notice accepting the tenants' right to enfranchise, terms are agreed and the applicants acquire the freehold. Any disputes as to terms are resolved in this instance by the Leasehold Valuation Tribunal once two months have lapsed since the landlord's or Court's notice. Finally, the landlord may contest the right to enfranchise either on the basis that the qualifying conditions as set out above are not met or / and because of an intention to develop the site (s.23). To succeed in this latter claim he must be able to show that the leases in question are due to terminate within five years of the date from which the new interest is to start. He must also be able to show an intention to demolish or reconstruct, or carry out substantial works of construction which could not reasonably be achieved without obtaining possession.

The result of a successful application to enfranchise will be the acquisition by the qualifying tenants of all interests superior to their own (s.2), the freehold of the property, and 'any garage, outhouse, garden, yard and appurtenances belonging to, or usually enjoyed with, the flat' (s.1(7)). On completion the tenants must pay all the reasonable costs of their now former landlord, including legal and valuation fees.

The landlord may set up a management scheme following enfranchisement in order to regulate redevelopment, use or appearance, ensure maintenance or to empower work (ss.69–75). If proposed, such a scheme would have to be approved by the Leasehold Valuation Tribunal. This option is not dissimilar to powers contained in the 1954 Act.

17.7.4 Extended Lease (ss.39–61)

Where ss.5–8 apply and the tenants are qualifying, but enfranchisement is not possible, perhaps because the limit on non-residential use is infringed, or there are insufficient qualifying tenants, the tenants – this time only individually – may use the notice and counter-notice procedure set out above to obtain ninety-year extended leases (ss.39 and 56) provided additionally that the applicants have been qualifying tenants for the last two years before the exercise of the right. The extension will be on the same terms, subject to modifications necessary to take account of physical or other alterations since the original lease (s.57). On completion of this process the tenants will pay a peppercorn rent and a premium calculated in accordance with Schedule 12 (s.56) that is broadly similar to Schedule 6 described above, subject to an allowance for the landlord retaining the freehold. The landlord may again refuse an application to extend (s.47) and indeed may terminate an already extended lease (s.61) if he or she can show an intention to redevelop, as mentioned above.

Summary

- A long lease is one which exceeds twenty-one years. In addition, it will usually have a low rent – that being defined in different ways depending on when the lease began.

- In long leases of any residential property, service charges must not be unreasonable and restrictions are placed on the ability of the landlord to forfeit the lease for non-payment of service charges.

- In the event of dispute between landlord and tenant during the currency of the lease, an application may be made to the court for variation of the terms, appointment of a manager, or acquisition of the property.

- When a long lease expires, it will continue on the same terms until one of the parties takes steps to change the situation.

- Under the Landlord and Tenant Act 1954, the landlord may either propose that a long lease which has expired be converted to a statutory tenancy, or may attempt to regain possession.

- The Leasehold Reform Act 1967 gives those who have been tenants of houses for the requisite period and who can meet other conditions rights either to a new lease or to enfranchise. The 1967 Act applies only to premises which are vertically divided.

- The Leasehold Reform Housing and Urban Development Act 1993 gives similar rights to occupiers of flats.

- Enfranchisement means the right to purchase the freehold at a price calculated according to a statutory formula. It may be exercised before the end of the lease.

- The right to an extension may be exercised only at the end of the lease, and leads to a grant of a new lease of fifty years under the 1967 Act or ninety years under the 1993 Act.

Exercises

17.1 What is a qualifying tenant? How does the definition change for the various pieces of legislation in this chapter?

17.2 What protection do tenants have from excessive service charges?

17.3 If the landlord has the remedy of forfeiture for breach of covenant by the lessee, what remedy does the tenant have if the landlord is in default?

17.4 Why is s.3 of the Landlord & Tenant Act 1954 to the tenant's advantage?

17.5 How can a landlord prevent a long lease being converted to a statutory tenancy?

17.6 What are the preconditions for exercise of powers under the Leasehold Reform Act 1967?

17.7 What benefits can a tenant obtain under the 1967 Act? What are their relative advantages and disadvantages?

17.8 Why might a landlord be reluctant for the tenant to use the 1967 or 1993 Acts?

17.9 In what ways does the 1993 Act extend the 1967 Act?

17.10 Can all long lessees enfranchise following the 1993 Act?

17.11 Can all long lessees claim extensions following the 1993 Act?

Workshop

1 In 1982, Noddy granted Tariq a twenty-one-year lease of a corner shop with a flat above, situated at the end of a residential terrace. In 1990 Tariq assigned the lease to Aisha, who immediately sublet the shop to Sally. Aisha lived in the flat and has continued to do so except for three months every winter when she goes to stay in Barbados. In 2003 Noddy granted Aisha a further ten-year lease and soon afterwards sold the reversion to Robbo.

(a) Advise Aisha
   (i) as to whether she can require Robbo to sell her the freehold of the property; and
   (ii) if she does have a right to enfranchise, the procedure which she should follow.

(b) How, if at all, would your answer to (a)(i) differ if Aisha and Sally had vacated the property in 2002, and in 2003 Noddy had granted a ten-year lease of the property to Timto Properties Ltd. which had immediately sub-let the flat and shop to Sharon and Sol respectively?

2 The freehold of Celestial Towers – an eleven storey tower block, consisting of 20 flats – is owned by Acme Enterprises Ltd. The ground floor consists of a caretaker's flat, together with a gym and other social amenities. Most of the tenants hold ninety-nine-year leases, although a few of the flats are let to companies on yearly leases.

Advise Olga, the secretary to the residents' association, as to whether, and if so how, the residents could

(a) together buy the freehold of the block; or

(b) exercise the right to manage.

Chapter 18

Public sector residential accommodation

18.1 Introduction and Scope

Rented property in the public sector, like other types of rented property, has been subjected to considerable pressures over the decades. Its significance grew after the First World War when Lloyd George, the then Prime Minister, realised that one way of meeting his election pledge of 'homes fit for heroes' was to increase the stock of local authority accommodation. Between the First and Second World Wars housing was a political football kicked to and fro between the opposing parties. The Conservatives supported private enterprise and regarded state intervention merely as a temporary measure while Labour envisaged a permanent role for public housing but was hampered by a lack of political power and economic resources. Even so, there was a high output of new houses in both the private and public sectors and by 1938 local authorities owned 11 per cent of housing stock. Millions of residential properties in Great Britain were destroyed or damaged during the Second World War and, not surprisingly, new building had been at a virtual standstill. After 1945 both Labour and Conservative governments promoted the building of local authority housing (albeit with varying degrees of enthusiasm) and the sector grew every year until, by 1979, it accounted for 29 per cent of housing. By 2003 it had dropped to 11 per cent. The decline can be attributed to a number of factors. Local authority tenants have exercised their 'right to buy' (introduced by the Housing Act 1980), fewer local authority homes have built, and many authorities have transferred the whole or part of their housing stock to new owners – usually Registered Social Landlords (i.e. housing associations registered with the Housing Corporation).

In its 1987 White Paper the Conservative Government acknowledged the contribution made by council housing to increasing the total housing stock and clearing slums. However, it criticised the 'distant and bureaucratic' housing operations of local authorities in many big cities, and the insensitive design and bad management of some housing. It contended that some housing had been badly maintained, tenants alienated, and a wide range of social problems had emerged: an increase in crime and violence; the departure of many people for better opportunities elsewhere; the disappearance of local enterprise and employment; and the welfare dependancy of whole communities. A 'more pluralist and more market oriented system' was advocated which would ensure that housing supply could respond more flexibly to demand, provide tenants with more choice and allow 'greater scope for private investment and more effective use of public sector money.' A 1987 White Paper proposed that responsibility for providing social housing should pass from local authorities to housing associations (Department of the Environment, *Housing: The Government's Proposals* Cm. 214, 1987). The idea was (and is) that local authorities should act as facilitators or enablers, rather than providers, of housing. This shift of responsibility continues under current government policies (Department of the Environment, Transport and the Regions, *Quality and Choice: A Decent Home for All: The Housing Green Paper*, 2000).

There are over 2,000 housing associations in Great Britain and, between them, they own or manage about 1.8 million homes. About two-thirds of them are registered with the Housing Corporation. Registration with the Housing Corporation or Housing for Wales is an essential prerequisite of eligibility for public grants but private finance has become the main source of funding for housing association projects. When the Housing Act 1980 created statutory security of tenure for local authority tenants, the same provisions were also applied to the tenants of housing associations with the additional protection of rent regulation under the Rent Act 1977. However, the Housing Act 1988 gave effect to the recommendation contained in the 1987 White Paper that, henceforth, all housing associations should grant assured and assured shorthold tenancies in the same way as the private rented sector. The reason given for this change in status was to give housing associations 'the essential freedom and flexibility in setting their rents to enable then to meet the requirements of private sector finance instead of relying on funding from public sources' (Department of the Environment, *Housing: The Government's Proposals*, Cm 214, HMSO, 1987). Reference should be made, therefore, to Chapter 16 when considering the security of tenure of housing association tenants whose tenancies have been granted since 15 January 1989.

18.1.1 The Scope of the Legislation

Local authorities have wide powers in relation to housing. They can control development through implementation of planning policies; they can take action (under the Housing Act 1985, as amended, and the Environmental Protection Act 1990) where property is in disrepair, either by forcing the owner to act or by acting themselves and then recovering the cost; they can make grants for work to private houses under the Housing Grants, Construction and Regeneration Act 1996; they can build or convert housing individually or on a large scale; and they can provide accommodation.

The Housing Act 1996 Part VI, ss.159–74, as amended by the Homelessness Act 2002, contains the scheme which governs the allocation of public sector accommodation. A local authority allocates accommodation when

(a) it selects someone to be a secure or introductory tenant of one of its dwellings, or
(b) it nominates someone to be a secure or introductory tenant of another landlord (e.g. a housing action trust), or
(c) it nominates someone to be an assured tenant of housing held by a registered social landlord.

The provisions of Part VI do not apply when an introductory tenancy (see below) becomes a secure tenancy, nor to tenancies which were in existence at 1 April 1997 when Part VI was implemented. Further exceptions come into play when succession rights are acquired or following an assignment or an exchange, or following an assignment under the Matrimonial Causes Act 1973 or under the Children Act 1989.

Section 160A provides that allocations may be made only to 'eligible persons', a category which does not include people subject to immigration control under the Asylum and Immigration Act 1996. Further, a housing authority may treat as ineligible for an allocation an applicant (or a member of the applicant's household) whom it is satisfied is guilty of unacceptable behaviour serious enough to make him unsuitable to be a tenant (s. 160A(7)). The only behaviour which can be regarded as unacceptable for these purposes is behaviour which would have entitled the housing authority to a possession order under s.84 of the Housing Act 1985 on any of the grounds in Part I of Schedule 2 (other than Ground 8) had the applicant already been a secure tenant (s.160A(8)).

Authorities are required to have a scheme of allocation which explains how priorities between applicants are determined and applied. They must, however, give 'reasonable preference' to those who are homeless (within the meaning of Part VII of the 1996 Act) or are owed a duty under the homelessness legislation, or occupy insanitary or overcrowded housing or are otherwise living in unsatisfactory housing conditions, or need to move on medical or welfare grounds or to a particular locality in the authority's district if failure to meet that need would cause hardship.

18.2 Secure Tenancies under the Housing Act 1985

Before 1980 the rights of local authority tenants were governed by the common law and the terms of their tenancy agreements. It had not been thought necessary to give them the same kind of rights afforded to tenants in the private sector because, even though local authority landlords had 'a complete discretion with regard to the eviction of public sector tenants', it was felt that they could be relied on 'to exercise such discretion fairly and wisely' (Brandon LJ in *Harrison* v. *Hammersmith & Fulham London Borough Council* (1981)). The Housing Act 1980 changed this, introducing a system that was similar to, but simpler than, that operating in the private sector (then governed by the Rent Act 1977). The 1980 Act has since been amended and consolidated, and the law is now contained in Part IV of the Housing Act 1985 ss.79–117 and Schedules 1–3. These provisions deal with security of tenure and confer a number of rights (often referred to as the Tenants' Charter) which include rights of succession. The 1985 Act appears to go further than the Rent Act and the Housing Act 1988 in that security of tenure and the benefits of the 'tenants' charter' are extended to licensees (s.79(3)). It should be noted, however, that s.79(3) does not apply where (a) the licence is granted as a temporary expedient to a person who entered the dwelling-house as a trespasser (s.79(4)), or (b) the occupier does not have exclusive possession of the premises (*Westminster City Council* v. *Clarke* (1992)).

Part IV of the 1985 affords protection to 'secure' tenants. A secure tenancy is 'a tenancy under which a dwelling-house is let as a separate dwelling . . . at any time when the conditions described in sections 80 and 81 as the landlord condition and the tenant condition are satisfied' (s.79, Housing Act 1985). The 1985 Act applies equally to fixed and periodic lettings, although the latter are the norm.

18.2.1 Security of Tenure

To be a secure tenant, and entitled therefore to security of tenure, three conditions must be met:

(a) To satisfy the 'tenant condition' of s.81, the occupier must:
   (i) Be an individual or one of up to four joint tenants who are individuals. A company cannot be a secure tenant. Simply moving in with an existing tenant, for example as his or her spouse, will not automatically give rise to a joint tenancy.
   (ii) Occupy a dwellinghouse let as a separate dwelling (s.79). The interpretation of this provision is the same as with the Rent Act 1977 and the Housing Act 1988 (see 16.2). Any lingering doubts on marginal cases are removed by the absence, in the 1985 Act, of anything equivalent to s.22 or s.3 of the 1977 and 1988 Acts, respectively, which extend protection to tenants sharing living accommodation with other tenants (confirmed in *Westminster City Council* v. *Clarke* (1992)). Section 79 does, of course, ensure that lodgers within s.93 cannot get security.

(iii)   Occupy the dwelling as his or her only or principal home (s.81). In *Crawley BC* v. *Sawyer* (1988) a weekly tenant left his local authority flat to live with his girlfriend in a property he was helping her to buy. The gas and electricity supplies to the flat were cut off but the tenant carried on paying the rent and rates. He visited the flat about once a month, and once spent a week there. The relationship between the tenant and his girlfriend ended and he returned to the flat soon after the expiry of the notice to quit with which he had been served by his landlord. The local authority brought possession proceedings. The tenant asserted throughout that he had every intention of returning to the flat and did not intend to give it up. The Court of Appeal upheld the decision of the county court judge that the flat had always remained the tenant's principal home, even while he was living with his girlfriend. It took the view that there is no material difference between occupying premises as a home and occupying them as a residence and that two houses can be occupied at the same time as a home so that actual physical occupation is not necessary. The fact a secure tenancy is conferred *at any time* 'the tenancy condition' is satisfied means that the tenant can move in and out of protection. In *Hussey* v. *Camden LBC* (1995) the tenant ceased to occupy the flat in question as his only or principal home but was again living there at the date the notice to quit expired and was held therefore to have regained security. In *Ujima Housing Association* v. *Ansah* (1998) the tenant lived in the flat before subletting it on an assured shorthold tenancy. The Court of Appeal held that he was not in physical occupation nor entitled to occupation on the expiry of the notice to quit, and he had left no personal possessions in the property. Viewed objectively, therefore, he did not have the necessary intent to maintain occupation of the flat as his principal residence.

(b) The landlord, according to s.80 of the 1985 Act and s.35 of the 1988 Act, must be one of the following:
 (i)   a local authority;
 (ii)   a new town corporation;
 (iii) an urban development corporation;
 (iv)   a housing action trust;
 (v)   a housing co-operative.
     The property must have been formally allocated to the occupier. Obvious though that may sound, moving into vacant property of one of the listed landlords will not mean acquisition of security in the absence of payment for occupation which is acknowledged by the

landlord. A joint landlord arrangement is permitted, but both must be on the above list to claim the benefit of the 1985 Act.

(c) The tenancy must not be one of those set out in Schedule 1 of the 1985 Act, that is:

(i)   long tenancies, as discussed in Chapter 17;

(ii)   where the landlord (as defined in (b) above or a police or fire authority) employs the tenant and the contract of employment requires occupation of the dwelling-house for the better performance of his duties. In *Hughes* v. *London Borough of Greenwich* (1994) a headmaster of a boarding school was employed under a contract providing free board and lodgings. The education authority later built a house for him nearby, outside the school grounds. In 1988, upon his imminent retirement, the headmaster served a notice on the authority claiming a right to buy as a secure tenant. The House of Lords held that because his occupation of the house was not essential for the performance of his duties, he was not a service occupier but a secure tenant and could indeed exercise the right to buy;

(iii) the dwelling is on land acquired for development, where the dwelling is being used for temporary purposes only (see further *Hyde Housing Association* v. *Harrison* (1990));

(iv)   it is granted in pursuance of a local authority's obligations to house the homeless;

(v)   it was granted for up to one year to provide temporary accommodation for those seeking employment in a new district, *provided* there was an offer of work in the area at the start;

(vi)   it was leased to the landlord for temporary housing;

(vii) it was granted to the occupier while works were carried out on his or her home, for example because the works were so substantial that the established residence had to be cleared;

(viii) an agricultural letting, as discussed in Chapter 20;

(ix)   a business letting, as discussed in Chapter 19;

(x)   a student letting;

(xi)   a licence to occupy an almshouse where the licence was granted by a charity which has no power under its trusts to grant a tenancy of the almshouse.

18.2.2   Introductory Tenancies

Introductory tenancies were created by the Housing Act 1996 Part V, ss.124–43, having been described in the 1995 White Paper as 'tenancies on a probationary basis' which, if they belong to 'the minority of tenants who do not behave responsibly', may be terminated at any time during the probationary period (Department of the Environment, *Our Future Homes: Opportunity, Choice, Responsibility*, Cmnd 2901, HMSO, 1995). Local authorities and housing action trusts trusts *may* choose to operate an introductory tenancy regime under which all their new periodic tenants and licensees are granted introductory tenancies rather than secure tenancies (s.124, Housing Act 1996). Such a tenancy lasts for one year beginning with the date the tenancy is entered into or, if later, the date when the tenant is first entitled to possession (s.125(2)).

A landlord who wishes to bring an introductory tenancy to an end during the probationary period must obtain a court order (s.127(1)). There is no need to prove that a ground for possession exists but the court cannot entertain proceedings for possession unless the landlord has served a notice which

- sets out the landlord's reasons for seeking possession (s.128(3));
- specifies a date for the beginning of proceedings, which must be no earlier than that of a common law notice to quit (s.128(4)); and
- informs the tenant or licensee of the right given by s.129 to seek a review and thereby challenge the reasons given by a landlord for its decision (Introductory Tenants (Review) Regulations 1997, SI 1997/22).

The court *must* make a possession order once it has ascertained that the requirements regarding notice of proceedings have been satisfied but it *may* grant an adjournment to allow the tenant to apply for judicial review of the landlord authority's conduct of the review (*Manchester City Council* v. *Cochrane* (1999)). In *R (on the application of McLellan)* v. *Bracknell Forest BC* (2002) the Court of Appeal held that the introductory tenancy regime is not incompatible with the Human Rights Act 1998 and that the applicants' rights under Articles 6 (right to a fair trial) and 8 (right to respect for a person's private and family life and home) of the European Convention on Human Rights had not been violated by the local authority's decision to end the introductory tenancy. Waller LJ pointed out Convention jurisprudence affords a wide 'margin of appreciation' to domestic legislatures to identify areas of public concern (such as housing) and the measures needed to deal with them. Parliament had decided that the introductory tenancy regime was necessary in the interests of social housing tenants and landlords generally. While the scheme does not require the local authority to be satisfied that any breaches of the tenancy agreement have taken place, a review procedure is in place and the scheme contains a number of important safeguards. Although the review panel did not exhibit the degree of independence required by Article 6 there was no reason why the review process as a whole could not do so. Furthermore, the remedy of judicial review provided an adequate safeguard for those tenants who wished to challenge a decision on the grounds of unfairness or contravention of Convention rights.

Introductory tenancies automatically become secure at the end of the probationary period. A tenancy will cease to be introductory if the tenancy could never become secure, if the local authority or housing action trust ceases to be the landlord, if the tenant dies without a successor or if the landlord's election to operate an introductory tenancy scheme is revoked. Introductory tenants do have certain rights: of succession, to have urgent repairs carried out under the Housing Act 1985 s.96 (see below) and under the Landlord and Tenant Act 1985 s.11 (see section 5.3), and to be informed of the terms of their occupation – all within the twelve months' period only.

18.2.3   Demoted Tenancies

Since 30 June 2004, as an alternative to obtaining suspended or outright possession orders, local housing authorities, housing actions trusts (HATs) and registered social landlords (RSLs) have been able to apply to the county court for a demotion order in circumstances related to anti-social behaviour (s.82A, Housing Act 1985; s.6A, Housing Act 1988). Secure tenancies of local authorities and HATs become demoted tenancies (s.143A(5) Housing Act 1996) while assured or secure tenancies of RSLs become demoted assured shorthold tenancies (s.20B, Housing Act 1988). Demoted tenancies last for a year during which – as with an introductory tenancy – the tenant may be evicted without the landlord needing to prove any grounds for possession. If there is no notice seeking possession or the tenancy has not been terminated, the demoted tenancy reverts to its former status after 12 months.

Landlords seeking demotion must first serve the secure tenant with a notice in the prescribed form under s.83 of the Housing Act 1985 unless the court considers it just and equitable to dispense with service of such notice. It must specify the date after which proceedings may be begun and state that no proceedings will be begun after the end of 12 months from the date when proceedings first began. The court will not make a demotion order unless the tenant or a person residing in or visiting the property has engaged or threatened to engage in conduct which is either (a) capable of causing nuisance and annoyance to any person and directly or indirectly relates to or affects the landlord's housing management functions; or (b) involves using or threatening to use, for an unlawful purpose, housing accommodation owned or managed by the landlord. In either case the ciurt must be satisfied that it is reasonable to make the order.

18.2.4 The Terms of a Secure Letting

Secure tenants will have certain covenants included in their leases. These terms, some of which have been explained elsewhere, will be included by virtue of either common law or statute:

(a) a right to, almost invariably, qualified quiet enjoyment;
(b) a restriction to residential user;
(c) an obligation to pay rent;
(d) liability for forfeiture if there has been breach of covenant during a fixed-term lease;
(e) a right to receive a rent book (Landlord and Tenant Act 1985 ss.4 and 5);
(f) the benefit of the Landlord and Tenant Act 1985 s.11;
(g) varying restrictions on taking in lodgers, subletting, assigning and exchanging with other secure tenants. These complex controls are contained in Housing Act 1985 ss.89–94 and are designed to provide a legitimate framework for activities which public sector tenants had carried out for many years before the 1980 Act came into effect.

   (i) Taking in lodgers (s.93): despite the difficulty encountered in the private sector in defining the word 'lodger' (see Chapter 1 on licensees), s.93 specifically uses the word and states that any secure tenant has the right to take in lodgers without the consent of the landlord.

   (ii) Subletting (s.94): this is permitted provided the landlord consents, consent not being unreasonably withheld. Should there be a dispute as to reasonableness or not, the onus will be on the landlord who should be able to discharge this by showing that written reasons were given (s.94(5)) within a reasonable time and that refusal turned on the risk of overcrowding and/or long-term plans for the premises. Should the landlord not reply to a request from the tenant, this is presumed to be an unreasonable refusal. Whether the occupier is a lodger or a subtenant was considered in *Monmouth B.C. v. Marlog* (1994). The premises were a three-bedroomed council house one bedroom of which was occupied by the tenant, the other two by the defendant and his two children. The rest of the property was shared. The Court of Appeal held that the arrangement was an informal one permitting no conclusion other than that the defendant was a lodger.

   Should the tenant attempt to surrender the lease, a lodger can only take it over if surrender has been agreed and rent then accepted from the lodger by the landlord authority. Should the occupier be a subtenant, possession against the mesne tenant will not be possession against the subtenant, whose interests will be unaffected. In any event the landlord will have to show that the tenant has another principal or main home if parting of all possession is alleged: without that the allegations will not succeed (*Hussey* v. *Camden LBC* (1995)).

(iii) Exchange (s.92): this is possible where both parties agree and where both are secure tenants or where one is a secure tenant and the other an assured housing association tenant – not necessarily of the same landlord. The landlord(s) do, however, have to consent although the grounds for refusal are limited, being set out in Schedule 3 of the 1985 Act:

– the assignee is already obliged by court order to give up possession; or

– a notice of seeking possession under s.83 has been served or possession proceedings have been started on any of Grounds 1–6 (see below);

– the accommodation is substantially greater than the proposed assignee needs;

– the extent of the accommodation is not reasonably suitable for the needs of the tenant and his/her family;

– the accommodation has been let to the tenant in consequence of employment, related to non-housing purposes;

– the premises, or the landlord, provides accommodation for people with specific needs (for example, the disabled, those with special needs, or those with special circumstances), and the exchange would bring in occupiers outside these categories; this exception also covers charitable landlords who provide accommodation for particular groups.

Within 42 days of the tenant's application for consent, the landlord must serve on the tenant a notice specifying and giving particulars of the ground on which consent is withheld (s.92(4)). If it is withheld for any reason other than one of the grounds set out in Schedule 3, the tenant may treat it as having been given (s.92(3)). Consent can be made conditional upon the tenant paying any outstanding rent or remedying any breach of obligation (s.92(5) and (6)).

(iv) Assignment (s.91): assignment of all or part of the premises, and for that matter subletting all the premises, are prohibited. A tenant who does any of these things will *prima facie* be in breach of Ground 1 (see below). Assignment is permitted in the following limited circumstances:

- to a potential successor in title provided it is in the form of a deed;
- when the tenancy has been transferred under the Matrimonial Causes Act 1973 following a decree of divorce, nullity or judicial separation;
- when there has been an exchange.

Transmission on death under s.89 (see below) is also classified as a permissible assignment.

(h) improvements (ss.97–101): although the general rule is that secure tenants cannot carry out any improvements (defined widely to include alterations, decorations and additions), they are permitted to do so if consent has been obtained from the landlord. The rules as to consent are the same as for partial subletting (above). If improvements are permitted, the landlord may agree that the tenant can be compensated at the end of the lease.

(i) repairs (s.96 as repealed and re-enacted by the Leasehold Reform Housing and Urban Development Act 1993): tenants may claim compensation if they have given notice of repairs due under their lease which the landlord has failed to arrange. The Secure Tenants of Local Housing Authorities (Right to Repair) Regulations 1994 detail and define 'qualifying repairs' as being those to a dwellinghouse not exceeding £250 in cost which the landlord has covenanted to do, expressly or impliedly, and which remedy defects listed in the same regulations.

(j) variation (ss.102–3): apart from statutory covenants, other terms can be varied by both sides agreeing. The landlord alone can vary rent, Council Tax, or service charges provided proper notice is given.

(k) ss.104–6: introduced in 1980 as the core of the 'tenants' charter'. These sections require lessors of secure tenancies to publish allocation rules, to consult on changes in housing management and to provide all their tenants with up-to-date copies of their tenancy agreement. The inherent difficulties of implementing these obligations, in the context of the sections on variation, is illustrated by the case of *Palmer* v. *Sandwell Metropolitan Council* (1987). The plaintiff was a council tenant whose property suffered from condensation which is, of course, usually outside s.11 of the Landlord and Tenant Act 1985, and for which the Council was therefore not liable. Following introduction of ss.104–6 the Council distributed a *draft* agreement which suggested that the authority would be liable for a wide range of defects that would include condensation damage. The plaintiff assumed the new clauses had become part of her lease even though she had not been fully consulted. It was held that, despite the fact that the booklet was muddled and sometimes misleading, it was not a new lease; nor was it a variation of any existing agreement and the authority had not become liable; distribution amounted merely to an opening of discussions.

(l) right to buy (Part V ss.118–88): secure tenants who satisfy the 'qualifying period' (i.e., have held a public sector tenancy which fulfils the 'landlord condition' and the 'tenant condition' for at least five years (two years for tenancies granted before 18 January 2005) (s.119)) have the right to purchase the freehold of their house or a lease of 125 years of their flat, as the case may be, subject to discounts depending on the length of their residence and the part of the country in which the property is siutated. Purchasers exercising the right to buy following succession may claim a discount to include the years of their predecessor in title's residence (*McIntyre* v. *Merthyr Tydfil District Council* (1989). Purchasers who resell within five years of buying their properties must repay some or all of the discount which they received. Certain groups cannot claim the right to buy, either because their landlords are exempt (for example charitable housing associations, housing trusts or housing co-operatives), or because of the accommodation they occupy (that is it is for the disabled, elderly or mentally ill, and has been let to a member of that group – so classified by the local authority). Tenancies excluded from security under Schedule 1 of the 1985 Act are also excluded from the right to buy provisions. Tenants who acquire leases are obliged to pay service charges thereon (*Coventry City Council* v. *Cole* (1994)), although the Housing Act 1996, ss.219–20, allows the Secretary of State to direct that the charges be reduced or waived.

18.2.5 Succession (ss.87–90 and 113)

On the death of a periodic or fixed-term secure tenant a surviving spouse, civil partner or member of that tenant's family may be able to require the tenancy to be assigned to him or her. On succession, the new tenant is in the same position as the previous one for all purposes, for example able to exercise the right to buy, and liable for debts. Succession is possible when:

(a) There has been no previous succession of the tenancy. Thus, for example, transmission from parent to parent is permitted, but not from parent to parent and then to surviving child. Furthermore, on death of one joint tenant the survivor acquires a sole tenancy by succession; no further succession, for example to children or new partners, is possible – although a new tenancy may be granted.

(b) The survivor is a spouse or civil partner of the tenant who occupied the dwelling-house as his or her only or principal home at the time of the tenant's death.

(c) Alternatively, the claimant is a member of the deceased's family who resided with the deceased for the twelve months prior to death. The period of joint residence does not all need to have been at the premises in dispute provided there is a clear intention of sufficient quality to return (*Camden LBC* v. *Goldenberg* (1996)). 'Member of the tenant's family is defined by s.113 Housing Act 1985 to include those who live together as husband and wife or as if they were civil partners, and those who are the parents, grandparents, children, grandchildren, brothers, sisters, uncles, aunts, nephews and nieces of the deceased. Relationships by marriage are treated as relationships by blood, the half-blood as the whole, step-children and children and illegitimate children as legitimate children of their mothers and reputed fathers.

(d) The claimant had a right of occupation. Thus, the survivor of two people living in a flat intended to be occupied by one person will not be able to claim in the absence of prior consent by the landlord to shared residence (*South Northamptonshire DC* v. *Power* (1987)).

It should be noted that a person under 18 who comes within one of the categories listed in s.113 may succeed to a secure tenancy so long as he or she is the tenant's spouse or civil partner or is a member of the tenant's family who satisfies the twelve month residence requirement. In *Kingston-upon-Thames BC* v. *Prince* (1999) the secure tenant's daughter and granddaughter were living with him at the time of his death in July 1996. His daughter had only been living there for about six months and was not, therefore, qualified to succeed. His grand-daughter, however, who was thirteen years old, had been living with him for about three years. The Court of Appeal held that although, by virtue of s.1(6) Law of Property Act 1925, a minor cannot hold a *legal* estate, there was nothing to stop the grand-daughter from succeeding to an *equitable* secure tenancy. A similar conclusion was reached in *Newham LBC* v. *R (A Child)* (2004).

In the event of a dispute between survivors, spouses always have priority over other members. The landlord has power to adjudicate in disputes between other members, unless the parties can reach agreement for themselves. Although ultimately the court would have to decide, it will take notice of stipulations or written agreements entered into by claimants: *Newham LBC* v. *Phillips* (1997).

18.2.6 Rent

Pre-Housing Act 1988 housing association tenants will continue to pay fair rents assessed by the Rent Officer. Rents for housing association tenancies created since the Housing Act 1988 came into force are determined in the same way as other private sector tenancies. Local authority tenants, on the other hand, have their rent fixed according to annual government-controlled funding levels, as well as 24 of the Housing Act 1985 which empowers a local housing authority to make 'such reasonable charges as they may determine for the tenancy or occupation of their houses.' By s.24(2), 'the authority shall from time to time review rents and make such changes, either of rents generally or of particular rents, as circumstances may require.' Unlike the Rent Act 1977, the Housing Act 1985 contains no formal machinery for challenging the rent payable. Theoretically, the tenant can seek judicial review of the local authority's exercise of its discretion but, in practice, such a course of action is unlikely to be successful. The discretion given to a local authority is such that the court can interfere only if the tenant can prove that it has been exercised in a manner which no reasonable person could consider justifiable (*Backhouse* v. *Lambeth BC* (1972) 116 SJ 802).

In its Green Paper (DETR, *Quality and Choice: A Decent Home for All*, 2000) the Government expressed its commitment 'to keeping social rents at an affordable level, well below private sector rents'. Noting that rents for properties rented from registered social landlords were around 20 per cent higher than rents for local authority housing, it took the view that 'there should not be arbitrary differences between the rents of similar properties in a locality, just because some are local authority owned and others are registered social landlord properties'. The Government has now set in motion a process of 'rent restructuring' (to be carried out over a ten-year period ending in 2012) which is intended to reduce the gap between rents in the two sectors.

18.2.7 Termination of a Secure Tenancy

– By the tenant
A secure tenancy remains secure so long as the tenant occupies the dwelling as his or her only or principal home, although in the case of a joint tenancy only one of them need so occupy. A sole tenant can bring his or her tenancy to an end by giving the necessary notice (usually four weeks but less is possible by agreement) to the landlord. Notice by one joint tenant brings the tenancy of them all to an end (*London Borough of Hammersmith & Fulham* v. *Monk* (1990)).

– By the landlord
Fixed-term lettings can be brought to an end during their term only by forfeiture proceedings. Periodic tenancies and fixed-term tenancies whose term has expired must be determined, apart from surrender, by a 'notice of possession' (s.83) that has been given to the tenant in the prescribed form specifying the Ground alleged (see below) and particularising the allegations

therein. The court may dispense with the notice requirement if it thinks it just and equitable to do so. If a notice is served its content must meet the requirements of the Protection from Eviction Act 1977 s.5. The notice of possession must state the earliest date on which proceedings may begin and will last only one year, so must still be in force when proceedings do begin.

Local authorities are clearly 'public authorities' within the meaning of s. 6 of the Human Rights Act 1998 which means that it is unlawful for them to act in a way which is incompatible with a Convention right. Not surprisingly, a number of human rights challenges have been made to substantive housing provisions in the English courts but the vast majority has been unsuccessful. As regards recovery of possession, Sedley LJ in *Lambeth LBC* v. *Howard* (2001) assumed that Article 8(1) was engaged by 'any attempt to evict a person, whether directly or by process of law, from his or her home' but interference will usually be justified under Article 8(2) because it is 'in accordance with the law and . . . necessary in a democratic society in the interests of national security, public safety or the economic well-being of the country, for the prevention of disorder or crime, for the protection of health or morals, or for the protection of the rights and freedoms of others'. Thus, in *Sheffield City Council* v. *Smart* (2002) it was held that although the commencement of possession proceedings had interfered with the tenants' right to respect for their home, the interference was justified given the existence of housing legislation which balanced tenants' individual rights and housing policy as a whole.

There are seventeen Grounds (set out in Schedule 2) and they can be divided into three groups:

A   Where possession will be granted only if the order is reasonable, Reasonableness could include, for example, account being taken of the order resulting in intentional homelessness which could in turn lead to the local authority no longer being obliged to provide accommodation under the homelessness legislation. However, in *Bristol City Council* v. *Mousah* (1998) there had been serious breaches of the tenancy conditions and the Court of Appeal held that only rarely would it not be reasonable to make a possession order in such cases. The judge had been wrong to speculate as to how the the local authority would respond to any application for housing by the tenant after the order was made and there was no evidence that he would become a danger to the public if made homeless.

The first four categories in this group are similar to some of those applying in the private sector. They were dealt with in some detail in Chapter 16.

   1   Arrears of rent *or* breach of obligation. Rent arrears is by far the most commonly used ground for possession. Numerous authorities confirm that

tenants who make realistic offers to pay the current rent and also to begin to clear accumulated arrears should have judicial discretion exercised in their favour by the imposition of a possession order suspended on terms. Other authorities indicate that tenants whose physical or mental health problems caused the arrears will be similarly treated, although less specific personal difficulties will probably need substantiation before the courts will be sympathetic. It should be noted, however, that where the tenant breaks the terms of a suspended possession order, the order becomes effective and the tenancy is terminated from that moment. The landlord is not obliged to take any further steps to notify the tenant of its intention to seek a warrant for possession (*Thompson* v. *Elmbridge BC* (1987).

This ground also covers breach of obligation – by the tenant and with his knowledge. The scope of this limb is illustrated by *Green* v. *Sheffield City Council* (1994) in which the defendant had been a tenant since January 1978 in a small local authority property under a lease which included a prohibition on keeping pets. He acquired a dog, apparently to protect his wife from possible assaults by the Yorkshire Ripper. This reason might have been grounds to refuse possession but it was not because he did not meet the local authority to explain his reasons: his marriage had broken down, and the Ripper had in any case been caught and incarcerated.

2   Originally, Ground 2 was worded in the same way as Case 2 of the Rent Act 1977 but it was extended by the Housing Act 1988 and is now identical to Ground 14 of the 1988 Act (see Chapter 16.5) except that the notice of possession may provide for immediate inception of proceedings rather than inception after expiry of the notice period (s.83(3)). Recent years have witnessed an ever-expanding catalogue of measures attempting to deal with anti-social behaviour by one neighbour against another. Traditionally Ground 1 (see above) was perceived as sufficient because local authority tenancy agreements commonly contain a covenant by the tenant not to commit a nuisance or annoyance etc. In such circumstances, courts may grant possession where, for example, tenants are using their rented premises for the distribution of drugs, or they or their children have become out of control to the extent of frightening or racially abusing those living nearby. In *Kensington & Chelsea Royal London Borough Council* v. *Simmonds* (1996) a single parent living in a council maisonette appealed against a decision to grant the local authority a suspended possession order in respect of her flat after her thirteen-year-old son was found to have caused annoyance and offence to neighbours amounting to a breach of the tenancy agreement. The tenant argued that because she was not personally at fault, the possession order should not have been made. Dismissing the appeal, the Court of Appeal held that Ground 2, which specifically refers to the behaviour of the tenant or other persons living in the property, was in any

event satisfied. Moreover, it would go against common sense and the interests of justice for neighbours to be left without a remedy just because 'some ineffectual tenant next door' was unable to control her children.

Where the court is considering whether it is reasonableness within the context of ground 2, it must consider, in particular:

(a) the effect that the nuisance or annoyance has had on persons other than the person against whom the order is sought;
(b) any continuing effect the nuisance or annoyance is likely to have on such persons; and
(c) the effect that the nuisance or annoyance would be likely to have on such persons if the conduct is repeated.

In *Manchester City Council* v. *Romano and Samari* (2005), the Court of Appeal was called upon to consider the interface between housing legislation and the Disability Discrimination Act 1995. Section 22(3) of the 1995 Act makes it unlawful to discriminate 'by evicting the disabled person [or] subjecting him to any detriment'. By s.24(3), a person discriminates against a disabled person if 'for a reason which relates to the disabled person's disability, he treats him less favourably than he treats or would treat others to whom that reason does not or would not apply' and he cannot show that the treatment in question is justified. In *Romano* the local authority landlord had obtained orders for possession against two secure tenants under Ground 2. The tenants – each of whom was suffering from a recognised mental illness – contended that they were discriminated against under s.22(3). The Court held that, in order to interpret s.24(3) in a way which was compatible with the ECHR, a court had to ask (i) whether the landlord held the opinion that it was necessary to seek possession in order that the health of a person or persons would not be endangered and (ii) whether that opinion was objectively justified. Brooke L.J. delivering the judgment of the Court, pointed out that there were evident difficulties in ss.22 and 24 which – unless Parliament took remedial action – could result in the courts being confronted with 'a deluge of cases in which disabled tenants are resisting possession proceedings'. As he explained:

> One difficulty lies in the fact that these sections are not confined to residential tenancies, so that a business tenant might invoke the 1995 Act if he asserts that the reason he has broken the conditions of his lease relates to his mental disability. A further difficulty arises from the fact that a tenant could assert that his landlord could not recover possession for non-payment of rent because the reason why he could not manage his financial affairs efficiently relates to his mental disability. Another difficulty lies in the fact that a private landlord who does not have to establish a 'reasonableness' ground for possession may nevertheless be confronted by an assertion that he has caused detriment to a disabled tenant by selecting him for eviction.

Local authority powers have been reinforced by the introduction of Ground 2A (see below) and the Housing Act 1996, s.153 which allows local authority landlords, housing action trusts and RSLs to apply for an injunction where, e.g. there is conduct which is capable of causing nuisance or annoyance to any person, and directly or indirectly relates to or affects the housing management functions of a relevant landlord' or which consists of or involves using or threatening to use housing accommodation owned or managed by a relevant landlord for an unlawful purpose (such as drug dealing or as a brothel). Alternatively or additionally the injunction may exclude the person in respect of whom it is granted from any specified premises or any specified area.

On a separate but related point, s.1 Crime and Disorder Act 1998, as amended by the Anti-Social Behaviour Act 2003, empowers a local authority, a registered social landlord, a housing action trust or the police to apply for an anti-social behaviour order (ASBO). An ASBO can be made in respect of any person aged 10 or over who has acted in a manner that caused or was likely to cause harassment, alarm or distress to one or more persons not of the same household as the perpetrator. An order contains conditions prohibiting the offender from carrying out specific anti-social acts or from entering defined areas and is effective for a minimum of two years. Breach of an order is a criminal offence. Finally, the Protection from Harassment Act 1997, considered in Chapter 16.8, gives remedies to occupiers themselves.

2A This ground, which was introduced by the Housing Act 1996, is identical to Ground 14A of the Housing Act 1988 (which is set out in Chapter 16) except that, in the case of Ground 2A, the court shall not entertain possession proceedings unless it is satisifed that the landlord has served a copy of the notice of seeking possession on the partner who has left or has taken all reasonable steps serve a copy of the ntoice on that partner (s.83A).

3 Committing an act of waste in the leased premises or in any of the common parts.

4 Committing an act of waste to a piece of furniture.

5 The landlord was induced to grant the tenancy by virtue of a false statement made knowingly and recklessly by the tenant, or (by virtue of the Housing Act 1996 s.101) by someone else acting at the instigation of the tenant. Since the statement would have had to be made prior to entry, it is submitted that it would have to be serious for possession to be granted, and becoming ever more serious as time passes.

6 The tenancy was assigned to the tenant or her or his predecessor and a premium was paid in connection with the assignment.

7 The tenant is a service tenant and has been guilty of conduct such that, having regard to the purpose for which the buidling is used, it would not be right for him to continue in occupation.

8   The dwelling at present occupied by the tenant or his or her predecessor was provided as a temporary measure while work now completed was carried out on his or her previous dwelling, of which he or she was a secure tenant.

B   Where the court is bound to order possession once the Ground is proved but must be satisfied that suitable accommodation will be available once the order comes into effect.

9   The premises are overcrowded according to criteria specified in the Housing Act 1985 Part X, relating to number of occupants per room and room space per occupant.

10   The landlord intends to demolish or reconstruct the premises or carry out work on the building or land surrounding it and cannot reasonably do so without obtaining possession. To succeed on this Ground the authority must provide clear evidence of intention to carry out the works. Thus in *Wansbeck District Council* v. *Marley* (1988) the appellants occupied a cottage adjacent to a swimming pool. The respondent wished to incorporate both into a country park development but failed to obtain possession because of failure to adduce at the trial any documentation in support (in spite of its being in existence).

10A   The local authority wishes to dispose of the whole estate on which the tenant lives and needs vacant possession in order to do so.

11   The landlord is a charity and the tenant's continued occupation would conflict with the objects of the charity.

C   Where the court has a discretion whether to grant possession but if it does so must be satisfied that suitable accommodation will be available for the tenant when the order takes effect.

12   The letting is a service letting to someone who has ceased to be an employee of the lessor who has not acquired security by virtue of paying rent after leaving the tied employment, and the premises are required for a new employee.

13   The premises were adapted for use by a handicapped person, and let to such a person who no longer lives there and the landlord requires possession in order to relet to a handicapped person.

14   The landlord is a housing association or housing trust which lets to persons in special need, no such person lives there and the landlord requires possession in order to relet to a person with special needs.

15   The premises are one of a group of such premises let to persons with special needs, no such person lives there and the landlord requires possession in order to relet to a person with special needs. It seems that to be classified as a 'group' there needs to be, for example a common call

system, a warden system, or physical proximity of buildings with each other.

16 The accommodation afforded by the dwelling-house is more extensive than is reasonably required by the tenant who, as a member of the previous tenant's family, succeeded to a *periodic* tenancy by virtue of s 89. Proceedings under this ground must be initiated between six and twelve months after succession and In determining whether it is reasonable to make an order the court must take into account the present occupier's age, period of occupation, and any financial or other support given to the previous tenant.

Suitable alternative accommodation is defined in Schedule 2, Part IV of the Housing Act 1985. The Schedule sets out a set of criteria broadly similar to those in Schedule 2, Part III of the Housing Act 1988 (see Chapter 16) with the notable difference that 'character' is not included in the Housing Act 1985 list. The impact of this was considered in *Enfield Borough Council* v. *French* (1985). Mr French, the tenant, had spent much time working on the garden attached to the two-bedroom flat that he and his mother occupied. He had turned a wilderness into what was obviously a pleasant garden, installing a pond stocked with fish and an aviary, as well as building a shed in which he did some arc-welding. On his mother's death he was offered a one-bedroom flat with no garden which he said was not suitable for his needs. The court held that Mr French's needs had to be balanced against the needs of others on the waiting list, that absence of 'character' from the list made it harder to take account of the garden, and that presence of the criterion unique to the Housing Act 1985, namely the nature of the accommodation to which it was the practice of the authority to allocate persons with similar needs, meant that the plaintiff must take the accommodation on offer if he wished to remain a tenant of the authority.

18.2.2 Tolerated Trespassers

Once a possession order has been made, s.85 of the 1985 Act gives the court the same powers to postpone and suspend as exist in relation to private sector tenancies (see Chapter 16). Thus, for example, as noted in the discussion of Ground 1, where the landlord seeks to recover possession on the basis of rent arrears but the tenant makes reasonable proposals for clearing the debt, the court is likely to suspend the possession order on terms that the tenant pays the arrears at a stated amount each week together with the current rent. When a possession order takes effect, i.e., on the date specified in the absolute order or when the terms of a suspended order are breached, the secure tenancy comes to an end. However, local authority landlords will often allow the former tenant to remain in occupation so long as they maintain a satisfactory rent account and, indeed, there are probably many thousands of people occupying public sector housing in such circumstances. They are known as 'tolerated trespassers', a term coined by Lord Browne-Wilkinson in *Burrows* v. *Brent LBC* (1996). Here, Ms Burrows made an arrangement to pay off rent arrears seven days before the court awarded possession to her local authority landlord. She failed to keep up payments and two years later the authority issued a possession warrant which was executed. Ms Burrows then applied for a declaration that she was a secure tenant because the agreement to pay arrears had had the effect of reinstating her secure tenancy. The House of Lords held that prior to the execution date the parties could indeed have created a new tenancy or licence or could have reached an alternative arrangement, depending on their intention. In this case, however, the only intention was to defer execution of the possession order as long as Ms Burrows carried out her part of the agreement; while she did a limbo existed, the former tenant paying the arrears and the landlord forbearing to execute the order. Had she met the conditions in full and paid off all the arrears, she could have applied under s.85(4) to have the possession order discharged , with the effect that her tenancy would have been retrospectively revived. In the absence of such application, the occupier's secure status will be revived only if the intention of both parties was to create a new tenancy. This will require more than the acceptance of rent by the landlord or, indeed, the service of notice of rent increases upon the tenant (*Lambeth LBC* v. *O'Kane* (2006)) but was held to have occurred in *Swindon BC* v. *Aston* (2003) in which the local authority had not only received the rent but had also provided the occupier with a new tenancy agreement.

Tolerated trespassers have no security of tenure or other statutory rights and are unable to enforce any covenants in the former tenancy against their landlords. There can be no succession if the former tenant dies while a tolerated trespasser and the potential successor will have no defence to possession proceedings. However, because these causes of action arise from the law of tort rather than from the tenancy agreement, a tolerated trespasser can still claim damages from the landlord for nuisance, negligence and trespass to property.

Summary

- Most secure tenancies are granted by local authorities. Tenancies granted by housing associations before 15 January 1989 will generally be secure; those granted after 15 January 1989 are assured tenancies subject to the Housing Act 1988.

Summary cont'd

- ◗ The law relating to secure tenancies is primarily contained in the Housing Act 1985.

- ◗ To be regarded as secure tenants, occupiers must meet conditions relating to themselves, their landlord and the tenancy.

- ◗ The lease of a secure tenant will have implied into it common law covenants relating to quiet enjoyment, forfeiture, use and an obligation to pay rent.

- ◗ The lease of a secure tenant will also have implied into it statutory covenants relating to repairs, improvements, taking lodgers, subletting, assigning, exchanging, information, right to buy, provision of a rent book and procedures for variation.

- ◗ Spouses and members of the family residing with a secure tenant can, on death of that tenant, claim transmission of the tenancy to themselves.

- ◗ Possession against secure tenants can only be on proof of one of seventeen Grounds of Possession. Unlike the Rent Act 1977 and the Housing Act 1988 there are no mandatory grounds for possession.

Exercises

18.1 Are all occupiers of local authority residential property secure tenants?

18.2 When will occupiers of local authority property be licensees?

18.3 When is a local authority landlord's consent needed to dispose of all or part of a tenant's interest?

18.4 What are the differences between security in the private sector and security in the public sector?

18.5 What will be the effect of refusal of an offer of suitable alternative accommodation?

18.6 What is the significance of transmission for secured tenancies compared with similar provisions for assured tenancies?

18.7 Large estates often generate tensions between the tenants. Will a complaint from one tenant to the authority landlord about another tenant automatically lead to a possession order?

18.8 Both local authorities and housing associations are the prime providers of accommodation for the disabled and elderly. How far are these properties protected from acquisition by the able-bodied?

Workshop

No. 6 Acacia Avenue is a council house which for some years has been let to Leeroy and his wife. Last week Leeroy died and Anita, a woman claiming to be Leeroy's cohabitant of some time, has just visited the local housing office. How would you advise given the following facts?

- Leeroy's wife is still alive but no longer living on the premises.
- Leeroy's brother lives on the top floor which he and Leeroy have made virtually self-contained.
- Anita's brother has one room on the ground floor, sharing meals and sitting room with Anita.
- Leeroy's grown up child, Kyle, lives at No. 6.
- Anita would like a smaller home, and has found two nearby. One is occupied by a single elderly man whose accommodation has been converted for him as he is handicapped. The other is occupied by a family, who are intentionally in rent arrears because the council has not carried out essential repairs to their home.
- Next door to Anita is a family who are always having noisy parties. Leeroy and Anita complained frequently but the authority refused to intervene.
- The authority offers anybody who wants to move alternative accommodation several miles away on a new estate. Moving there would mean Anita losing contact with her friends, and Kyle having to give up his job because of the travelling problems. The accommodation itself is smaller but with much better facilities.

Chapter 19

Business tenancies

19.1 Introduction

Until the coming into force of the Landlord and Tenant Act 1954, Part II, business tenants mostly had no security of tenure. If the tenant had a periodic tenancy, it could be terminated by the landlord by notice to quit at common law, and the tenant would have to vacate when the notice expired. If the tenant had a fixed-term lease with no option to renew, the tenant could only hope that the landlord might agree to grant a new lease at the expiration of the contractual term. A business tenant obliged to leave might have to incur substantial expense in relocation, and it could suffer loss of both goodwill and the value of any improvements that it had made.

The absence of security of tenure and the disturbance to business activity had undesirable economic consequences, not merely for the tenants, but for the nation as a whole, and there was therefore a public interest in providing business tenants with security of tenure. In the first half of the twentieth century there were a few half-hearted, short-term, stop-gap measures.[1] The most important of these was the very limited and complex scheme for security of tenure introduced by the Landlord and Tenant Act 1927, which proved unsatisfactory, and which has long since been repealed. That Act also introduced a scheme whereby tenants, on quitting the holding, can in some circumstances obtain compensation for improvements. This scheme, contained in Part I, remains in force (subject to modifications). It will not be considered further, however, since it is in practice moribund: its requirements and procedures are impractical and cumbersome, and many tenants are unaware of the need to take the requisite steps. Furthermore, although the parties cannot contract out of the compensation provisions, a landlord can easily circumvent them by imposing an obligation on a tenant either to carry out the improvements or to reinstate at the expiration or earlier determination of the lease.[2]

It was not until the economic revival after the Second World War that a general regime for security of tenure was introduced in Part II of the Landlord and Tenant Act 1954. Part II has generally been considered to work well, and, although it was amended in 1969 and in 2004, it remains in essence the same as when it was enacted over fifty years ago. If a business tenancy is within Part II, the tenant has a basic right to remain in possession at the end of the contractual term, which is statutorily extended for an indefinite period. This will be the position unless the landlord or the tenant serves a statutory notice on the other to start a procedure which could either result in the grant of a new lease, or the tenant's having to quit. In certain circumstances, a landlord who successfully opposes a renewal may have to pay the tenant compensation. Unless the landlord successfully opposes a renewal, the court will itself determine the terms of the new tenancy, so far as the parties cannot agree them.

The most recent amendments to Part II are the result of an extensive government review of this area that began in 2001. The review indicated that, whilst the basic structure of the regime was sound and should be retained, it was in need of important modifications in detail.[3] As a result, changes to Part II were introduced, as from 1 June 2004, by the Regulatory Reform (Business Tenancies) (England and Wales) Order 2003.[4]

The changes involve largely a simplification, rationalisation, and streamlining of the procedure for termination and renewal in Part II. Landlords and tenants are now treated more even-handedly than before. For instance, until the recent changes, a landlord who was prepared to grant a new lease could not initiate the renewal process by serving a notice setting out its own proposals for a new tenancy. Now the landlord can do so, thereby expediting the negotiations (see 19.5.3 below). Another example is that, whereas previously only landlords could apply for an interim rent, now tenants can apply as well (see 19.7 below). The changes also reflect the prevailing attitude to the involvement of the court in civil proceedings underlying the Woolf reforms to the civil justice system contained in the Civil Procedure Rules 1998. The overriding objective of the Rules is that each case is dealt with justly (CPR Para. 1.1), which includes (*inter alia*) ensuring that the resources of the court are allocated appropriately. This approach is carried into the reform of Part II, notably in the new procedure for contracting out (see 19.3 below), and in the extended deadline for making applications to the court (see 19.6 below).

The traditional institutional lease of twenty-five years is largely a thing of the past, and most business leases are now granted for far shorter periods (often for a term of just seven years, although the length tends to vary according to the nature of the business concerned). With much shorter leases being the trend, renewals under the Act are occurring much more frequently than in the recent past. There are several reasons for the prevalence of shorter terms:

(a) Economic conditions have changed since the late 1980s, and are now generally more favourable to tenants, who often prefer shorter leases with either an option to renew or the protection of Part II. A shorter lease restricts the length of time that the tenant might be potentially liable after assignment (i.e. by virtue of continuing contractual liability under a pre-1996 lease, and under an authorised guarantee agreement in a post-1995 lease). A tenant under a long lease that provides for upwards-only rent review might eventually find itself having to pay a higher rent than the market rent. If the tenant had had a shorter lease, the rent that would be determined on a renewal under Part II would be only the market rent.

(b) A lease granted for a term not exceeding seven years is not registrable substantively at the Land Registry, and so is free from the risk that any commercially sensitive information that it contains may be publicly accessible.[5]

(c) As stamp duty land tax (introduced on 1 December 2003 by the Finance Act 2003) is essentially calculated on the aggregate of the rents payable for the whole term, shorter leases are likely to bear less tax.[6]

19.2 Tenancies within Part II

Part II applies to any tenancy where the property comprised in the tenancy is or includes premises which are occupied by the tenant, and are so occupied for the purposes of a business carried on by him or for those and other purposes: LTA 1954, s.23(1). As the statute refers to present occupation and use, Part II protection is lost if any of these requirements ceases to be met. The ingredients will be considered in turn.

19.2.1 Tenancy

A tenancy includes an agreement for a tenancy and a sublease (s.69(1)), even if the latter was granted in breach of a covenant against sub-letting without the landlord's consent: *D'Silva* v. *Lister House Developments Ltd.* (1971). A tenancy by estoppel has also been held to be a tenancy within Part II: *Bell* v. *General Accident Fire & Life Assurance Corp. Ltd.* (1998).

The following fall outside the protection of Part II of the 1954 Act:

(a) Licences

Chapter 1 on licences explores their limitations, and the comments made there apply equally to business lettings – exclusivity, terms and conditions, and the amount of rent. It became clear soon after the decision of the House of Lords in *Street* v. *Mountford* (1985) that the principles that their Lordships had there laid down applied not only to residential but also to business premises. In *London & Associated Investment Trust plc* v. *Calow* (1986), the issue was whether an arrangement by a firm of solicitors to use office space had created a lease. Applying *Street* v. *Mountford*, the judge held that it had: there was exclusivity of occupation, the payment of rent, and the parties' clear intention to enter into legal relations, as evidenced by a draft under-lease and assignment that were drawn up but not executed.

In *Essex Plan Ltd.* v. *Broadminster* (1988), occupation under a licence for one year with an option to take a thirty-year lease from the start of the licence did not create a business tenancy, since the occupier had not exercised the option. The occupier therefore had no rights under Part II. Even if (contrary to the judge's conclusion) exclusive possession had been conferred, the circumstances were analogous to one of the exceptions to the creation of a tenancy mentioned in *Street* v. *Mountford*, namely the occupation of a purchaser before completion.

In *Clear Channel UK Ltd.* v. *Manchester City Council* (2006), various agreements for the use of advertising sites did not specify the precise areas of land concerned, but merely identified the sites by a general address. The Court of Appeal affirmed the decision of the trial judge, who had held that this was a factor from which he could conclude that the agreements created licences only. The result was that the occupier had no security of tenure under Part II. Parker L.J. (with whom the other members of the court agreed) also noted, without wishing to cast any doubt on *Street* v. *Mountford*, that as this was 'a contract negotiated between two substantial parties of equal bargaining power and with the benefit of full legal advice', and the agreements had clauses that unequivocally declared themselves to be licences, he would 'have taken some persuading' that their legal effect was otherwise. (For further discussion of this case, see Chapter 1.6).

(b)   *Express or implied tenancies at will*

A tenancy at will is outside Part II, whether it arises by operation of law (*Wheeler* v. *Mercer* (1957)), or by express agreement (*Hagee (London) Ltd.* v. *AB Erikson & Larson* (1976)). The express creation of a tenancy at will provides an easy escape from Part II, but only if it is a genuine tenancy at will. As Scarman L.J. pointed out in the *Hagee* case, parties 'cannot impose upon an agreement, by a choice of label, a nature or character which upon its proper construction it does not possess'. In accordance with *Street* v. *Mountford*, mere labelling will not turn what is in substance a lease into something else. Nevertheless, if the parties are of equal bargaining strength and have legal advice, and there is an unequivocal clause in the agreement stating that it creates a tenancy at will, the courts might adopt the same approach as they did in the *Clear Channel* case. Contracting out, however, is now easy, and it is a more certain way of avoiding Part II (see 19.3 below).

(c)   *Service lettings (s.43(2))*

(d)   *Tenancies within s.43(3)*

This sub-section excludes from protection tenancies not exceeding six months where there is no provision for extension or renewal, unless the tenant has been in occupation for a period which, together with any period of occupation of his predecessor carrying on the same business, exceeds 12 months. In *Cricket Ltd.* v. *Shaftesbury plc* (1999), the plaintiff had been in occupation for some ten months under two successive tenancies of about five months each, but had remained in occupation thereafter as a tenant at will. The total period of occupation therefore exceeded 12 months. It was nevertheless held that occupation within s.43(3) refers to occupation as a tenant, so that the period of occupation under the tenancy at will (not being a tenancy for the purposes of Part II) had to be excluded. The plaintiff could not therefore claim security of tenure under Part II.

(e)   Extended leases created under the Leasehold Reform Act 1967 (s.16(1)(c)(d) of the 1967 Act)

(f)   Tenancies within s.57(3)(b)
These are leases granted subject to a notice that by a particular date the use of the premises will have changed. The only leases for which such notices can be issued are those where the landlord is a government department, a local authority, a statutory undertaking, or a development corporation.

(g)   Agricultural lettings
Agricultural lettings are considered in Chapter 20. Such lettings are specifically excluded from Part II by sections 43(1)(a) (agricultural holding) and 43(1)(aa) (farm business tenancy).

(h)   Mining leases
These are excluded from Part II: s.43(1)(b). The rationale is that the tenant's business necessarily involves depleting the land's resources.

Leases of on-licensed premises used to be outside the protection of Part II unless a substantial proportion of the business involved the sale of food or other non-intoxicating items. They were brought within the scope of Part II, however, by the Landlord and Tenant (Licensed Premises) Act 1990, s.1(1).

19.2.2   Premises

In *Bracey* v. *Read* (1963), Cross J decided that the word 'premises' in s.23(1) was synonymous with the word 'property' in that sub-section, and so could include land with no buildings on it. He therefore held that a lease of down-land as gallops to train and exercise racehorses fell within the sub-section. Whilst an incorporeal hereditament, such as an easement, can comprise 'premises' as part of a comprehensive demise including a corporeal hereditament as well, Shaw L.J. expressed the view in *Land Reclamation Co. Ltd.* v. *Basildon DC* (1979) that an easement standing by itself cannot be 'premises' within Part II.

19.2.3 Occupation

It has been held that the grant of a right of way, not being part of a grant of land, cannot fall within Part II because the grantee of such a right cannot be said to be in occupation of it: *Land Reclamation Co. Ltd.* v. *Basildon DC* (above). This leaves open the possibility that the grant of an easement which involves some degree of occupation, such as an easement of parking or storage, might fall within Part II. Dicta in *Pointon York Group plc* v. *Poulton* (2006) suggest that an easement of parking can be occupied for business purposes even though the demise of land to which it is ancillary is not. It is, however, difficult to see how there can be a renewal under Part II of the easement alone: the subject matter of the grant not being a legal estate, there would be no 'tenancy' within s.23(1), and the benefit of the easement would no longer be appurtenant to a dominant tenement.

The tenant can be in occupation under Part II even before he has started trading, as when he is having the premises made suitable for his business. This was held in the *Poulton* case, where the tenant was having carpets laid; the court applied the same broad meaning to occupation in s.23 as had been applied to s.37 in the *Bacchiocchi* case (1998) (see 19.9.3 below). Even if the tenant has to be away for a short period, its occupation can be maintained through the storage of its goods on the premises: *I & H Caplan Ltd.* v. *Caplan (No 2)* (1963). In *Flairline Properties Ltd.* v. *Hassan* (1999), the premises had been damaged by fire and the tenant, through no fault of his own, had to re-locate his restaurant business to other premises. The tenant retained the key, and left some fire-damaged items of some commercial value in the premises. It was held that the tenant remained in occupation for the purposes of Part II.

It does not matter that the tenant's occupation is likely to be temporary. In *Narcissi* v. *Woolf* (1960), the tenant, Celeste Narcissi, who had a lease of a building with several storeys and a basement, ran a restaurant on the ground floor. Having been warned by the public health authority not to store food in the basement, she stored it instead in the first-floor flat, which she had previously let, but which had just become vacant. This was evidently intended as a short-term measure until the basement had been repaired and made suitable for food storage. Roxburgh J emphasised that the occupation must be genuine; and, having found that it was, he held her to be in occupation of the first floor for the purposes of Part II, with the result that the first floor was included in the grant to her of a new lease.

The issue of occupation has often arisen where the landlord allows somebody else into the premises. In *Bagettes* v. *GP Estates Ltd.* (1956), one of the early cases decided under the 1954 Act, the tenant had used the premises (which were divided into residential flats) for the purpose of sub-letting. However, although it was accepted that the tenant *used* the flats for the purpose of its business of letting, it could not show that it was in *occupation* of the let flats for the purpose of its business, and so was held to be outside the protection of the Act. This decision seemed to indicate that a tenant who had sub-let could never have protection under Part II.

A qualification to the principle in *Bagettes* was, however, introduced in the difficult case of *Lee-Verhulst* v. *Harwood Trust* (1973). There the tenant company had sub-let a number of self-contained furnished rooms, but it retained keys to the rooms (which it could enter without notice), it could control the use of the cooking facilities, and its employees had access in order to provide services. This degree of control, which was much more extensive than would usually be found in a residential letting, was sufficient to establish that the tenant company was in occupation of the rooms and so protected by Part II. The Court of Appeal considered that the occupation of the rooms for residential purposes by the sub-tenants (who might have had security of tenure under the Rent Acts) did not preclude their also being occupied by the tenant company for the purpose of its business.

It is now clear that a tenant and a sub-tenant cannot both be in occupation of the same premises for the purposes of the 1954 Act. This was laid down by the House of Lords in the leading case of *Graysim Holdings Ltd.* v. *P&O Property Holdings Ltd.* (1996). The rationale is that, under Part II, a tenant who fails to obtain a renewal of the lease and who is obliged to quit the holding may in certain circumstances obtain compensation; if both the sub-tenant and intermediate landlord could have the protection of Part II, the head-landlord might have to pay compensation twice.

The facts of the case were that the tenant, Graysim, had been granted a twenty-one-year lease of an enclosed market hall, which it fitted out with thirty-five secure stalls. Stall-holders paid a weekly charge and a service charge in return for which they received services, facilities and a superintendent on site during opening hours. Graysim did not retain any keys to the stalls, it had no right to enter them, and it had conceded that the stall-holders had leases within Part II. The House of Lords held that, although Graysim did occupy the retained area (the common parts), it did not occupy the stalls, so there was no holding in respect of which it could claim that it had a tenancy, or in respect of which it could claim compensation. Lord Nicholls, who gave the main speech in the House of Lords, said that occupation for the purposes of Part II connotes physical occupation.

Whilst *Graysim*, therefore, excludes the possibility of both the landlord and the tenant being in simultaneous occupation *for the purposes of Part II*, it does not preclude the possibility of occupation of both the landlord and the tenant (as in *Lee-Verhulst*) under *different* Acts. Nevertheless, later authorities suggest that *Lee-Verhulst* is an exceptional case that turns on its own facts.

In *Bassairi Ltd.* v. *Campden LBC* (1999), there was a sub-letting of rooms for residential purposes, where some services were, allegedly, provided. The judge at first instance thought that there was a certain amount of 'window-dressing', in that the services might not actually have been supplied. More generally, however, he commented that, as the occupiers of the rooms were tenants, it was proper to infer that they had exclusive occupation of their rooms. His decision was upheld by the Court of Appeal.

In *Smith* v. *Titanate Ltd.* (2005), the tenant company held a lease of a building that it used for the letting of self-contained flats on either assured shorthold tenancies or very short lettings of a few weeks (all of which were held to be tenancies). The landlord provided various services, including the provision of tea and coffee, a twice-weekly change of linen, and a daily change of towels. Lettings and the co-ordination of services were dealt with by an on-site manager. The county court judge said that even this high level of management was insufficient to indicate occupation within Part II, as (applying *Graysim*) it did not involve the tenant company's physical occupation. The crucial differences from *Lee-Verhulst* were the self-contained nature of the flats and the landlord's right of entry being exercisable only on reasonable notice.

19.2.4   Occupation for the Purposes of a Business

The occupation must be for the purposes of a business: LTA 1954, s.23(1). If the premises are used for purposes ancillary to a business carried on elsewhere, they will be within Part II only if the occupation is necessary for the business. In *Chapman* v. *Freeman* (1978), the respondent, who owned and ran a hotel, rented a small cottage nearby to accommodate the hotel's head barman and his wife. The cottage was held to be 'occupied' by the respondent through his employees. It was held not to be occupied for the purpose of a business, however, as the housing of staff, whilst convenient, was not necessary for the running of the hotel. The lease of the cottage therefore fell outside Part II.

If the tenant is not in occupation of the premises at the date upon which the contractual term expires, the tenancy is not protected by Part II: s.27(1A).

Various provisions (considered below) allow trusts (s.41) and companies (s.42) to be deemed to be in occupation even though actual occupation is (as the case may be) by the beneficiaries, the members, subsidiaries or other companies in the same group.

19.2.5   Business

Section 23(2) states that 'the expression "business" includes a trade, profession or employment and includes any activity carried on by a body of persons, whether corporate or unincorporate'.

The wording of s.23(2) seems to suggest that an activity carried on by an individual (i.e. under the first limb of the sub-section) will qualify as a 'business' for this purpose only if it is a 'trade, profession or employment'; whereas an activity carried on by more than one person or by a company (i.e. under the second limb) will comprise a 'business' whatever its nature. The relationship between the two limbs is, however, by no means clear.

The courts have mostly interpreted s.23(2) broadly, so as to treat the second limb as free-standing, and not restricted by the first. Thus in *Addiscombe Garden Estates Ltd.* v. *Crabbe* (1958), the tenants, who were the trustees of a members' lawn-tennis club, took a lease of a club-house and tennis courts. It was held that their activities fell within the second limb of s.23(2) because they were carried on by a body of persons. The Court of Appeal was unconcerned that the activities might not be in the nature of a 'trade, profession or employment' under the first limb. Indeed, Parker L.J. considered it to be 'quite impossible to argue that there is any real limitation on the words "any activity."' He said that those words must be read as enlarging the scope of what goes before.

In *Hillil Property and Investment Co. Ltd.* v. *Naraine Pharmacy Ltd.* (1979), however, the Court of Appeal made it clear that, under the second limb, the activity that a body of persons is carrying on must be correlative to a trade, profession or employment. In that case, the tenant (a body of persons corporate) was developing nearby freehold premises which it owned and from which it carried on trade as a pharmacy; it hired builders who, instead of putting waste from the pharmacy premises into a skip, left them in the demised premises further down the street. It was held that the temporary dumping of spoil as part of these building operations was not on the facts an 'activity' within s.23(2), as it was not in the nature of a business that the tenant was carrying on. Megaw L.J. said that the word 'activity' connotes some general use by the persons occupying, and not some particular or casual operation such as was being carried out by the contractors in that case.

A similar approach to that in the *Hillil* case is evident in the recent case of *Hawkesbrook Leisure Ltd.* v. *Reece-Jones Partnership* (2004). There it was held that a body can be treated as carrying on a 'trade' within s.23(2) even though it is forbidden to distribute profits amongst its members (as where it is a charity or a company limited by guarantee); it was held sufficient that its activities are carried on with a view to making a profit or surplus. The court dealt only with the first limb, presumably because it was accepted that an 'activity' must be in the nature of a trade, profession or employment.[7]

A case where the tenant fell between two stools is *Abernethie* v. *AM & J Kleinman* (1970). There the tenant, Mr Abernethie, used the premises for just one hour a week as a Sunday-school, and without receiving any payment. It was held that he was not carrying on a business within s.23(2), so the lease was outside Part II. The activity could not fall under the second limb, as it was carried on by the tenant alone and not by a body of persons; and the Court of Appeal held that it was not a business under the first limb either, as it was only as a spare-time activity without any commercial involvement.

Mixed business and residential use

Whilst leases that are solely for business use, or solely for residential use, are protected by the appropriate legislation, many thousands of premises have mixed use, e.g. where there is a letting of a shop together with a flat above, or of a house with consulting rooms. Section 23(2) of the 1954 Act permits lettings for mixed use to fall within Part II, as it applies not only where the premises are occupied by the tenant for the purposes of a business but also 'for those and other purposes'.

Not all mixed use tenancies, however, fall within Part II. Where there is mixed use, the applicable legislative regime is determined by the controlling use, which is decided on a finding of fact by the court of first instance. In one of the appeals in *Cheryl Investments Ltd.* v. *Saldhana* (1978), there was a lease of a maisonette to a doctor who resided there, but who also (with the landlord's consent) used one room as a consulting room to see patients, although this occurred only once or twice a year in an emergency. Here the Court of Appeal, upholding the trial judge, decided that the only significant purpose of the occupation was residential, and that the occasional business use was merely incidental. The doctor therefore had a regulated tenancy. Similarly, in *Gurton* v. *Parrott* (1991), the Court of Appeal affirmed the decision of the trial judge that the tenant's running a business of kennelling and breeding dogs on the premises was merely incidental to her occupation for residential purposes; it was more akin to a hobby.

The regime which applies is significant because it determines whether the tenant has security of tenure and rent control. Residential leases governed by the Rent Act 1977, section 1, (i.e. those granted before 15 January 1989), enjoy security of tenure and significant rent control. On the other hand, residential tenants holding under assured shorthold tenancies (granted on or after 15 January 1989) have no right to renew the lease at the end of the term, and enjoy little significant rent control. If no statutory notice is served, an assured shorthold tenancy becomes an assured periodic tenancy at the end of the term, but the tenant has no security of tenure after the landlord has terminated such tenancy by notice to quit. Nowadays, therefore, a business tenant enjoying the protection of Part II of the 1954 Act essentially has greater security of tenure than a residential tenant holding under an assured shorthold tenancy or an assured periodic tenancy.

The regime which applies is also important if there is a change from business to residential use, or vice versa.

If the tenancy is initially a business tenancy within Part II, it cannot fall into the residential tenancy regime at a later date if the business activity stops. This was the position in *Pulleng* v. *Curran* (1980), where, at its grant, a lease of a shop with residential accommodation above came within Part II. Subsequently the tenant ceased his business activities, and claimed that, as he continued to reside upstairs, he had a regulated tenancy within the Rent Acts. The Court of Appeal rejected this argument, holding that a tenancy could be a regulated tenancy only if it was so at the start of the lease.[8] Such a tenant may therefore effectively lose the protection of either regime, since the lease will cease to be protected by Part II when the business use ends, and the landlord may then terminate it by notice: s.24(3). The position might be otherwise if the landlord consented to the tenant's user for residential purposes of premises that had been leased for business user only. If a residential tenant resumes residential use after a period of unauthorised business use, he may risk forfeiture, unless the landlord waives the breach.

Subject to the rather narrow exception in s.23(4) (unauthorised business user) discussed below, a tenant who changes from residential to business use acquires the protection of Part II, since s.23 looks to current use. The fact that the change of use occurs without the landlord's knowledge, or without his consent, is to this extent immaterial. This is seen in the other appeal in *Cheryl Investments Ltd.* v. *Saldhana* (above), where the landlord had let a flat to a tenant for residential purposes. However, although the tenant lived in the flat, he concealed from the landlord the fact that he also carried on a significant amount of trade (importing sea foods) from the premises, having installed a telephone for business calls and using the hall as his office. The Court of Appeal, reversing the trial judge, held that, although the tenant's business user was surreptitious, it was a significant purpose of his occupation, with the consequence that he had clandestinely acquired a tenancy within Part II. Lord Denning MR commented that some might call this a strange result, but he saw no escape from the wording of the Act. In such circumstances the landlord's remedy might be to forfeit the lease for breach of the user covenant, assuming that he has not waived his right to do so.

More complex is the status of a residential sub-tenant whose immediate landlord has a lease of premises used for mixed business and residential purposes. An example is the lease of a house which comprises a ground-floor shop and a residential flat on the first floor; if the tenant lawfully sub-lets the flat to a residential occupier, is the sub-tenant to be treated as a residential tenant as against the head-landlord on the termination of the intermediate tenancy? The question is particularly important if the sublease was granted before 15 January 1989, since if the answer is yes, the (former) sub-tenant will have security of tenure under the Rent Act 1977 against the head-landlord. The issue was considered in *Church Commissioners* v. *Baines*

(1998), which involved consolidated appeals in three cases from the county court. In each appeal, the headlease had been a business lease within Part II of the 1954 Act, but had come to an end. The Court of Appeal held that in such circumstances the residential sub-tenant could be treated as occupying a dwelling-house for the purposes of the Rent Act 1977, s.137(3). The court approved the test set out by Romer L.J. in *Whiteley* v. *Wilson* (1953), namely, whether 'the building should in a broad sense be regarded on the one hand as a dwelling-house which is partly or even substantially used as a shop, or on the other hand as a shop which is used in part for residential purposes'. In each case, the Court of Appeal held that, on the facts, the premises constituted a dwelling-house. Each sub-tenant therefore had security of tenure under the Rent Act 1977, s.137(3), against the head-landlord, even after the termination of the intermediate lease.

Even if the tenant of mixed-user premises is protected under Part II of the 1954 Act, the Protection from Eviction Act 1977 still applies, so the landlord cannot re-enter without a court order: *Pirabakaran* v. *Patel* (2006) (where the court observed that there might otherwise be a breach of Article 8 of the European Convention on Human Rights).

Unauthorised business user

Under s.23(4), a tenant who uses the premises for business purposes in breach of a prohibition on business user does not acquire the protection of Part II unless the immediate landlord or his predecessor in title has consented to the breach, or the immediate landlord has acquiesced in it. In considering this sub-section in *Bell* v. *Alfred Franks & Bartlett Co. Ltd.* (1980), Shaw L.J. commented that acquiescence refers to 'something passive in the face of knowledge', whereas consent 'must involve a positive demonstrative act', whether by words or conduct.

The exclusion from security of tenure in s.23(4) is, however, of limited scope, since:

- It applies only to a prohibition that relates to the whole of the premises, and only to certain types of prohibition. A lease of a ground-floor shop and a residential flat above will often contain a prohibition on the use of the flat for business purposes; but, as the restriction does not apply to the whole of the premises demised, the tenancy will remain within Part II even though the tenant extends the business in breach of covenant into the flat.
- It applies only to a general prohibition on business use, or to a prohibition on one or more of the classes of business set out in s.23(2): namely to a trade, profession or employment. It does not apply to a prohibition on use for (or other than for) a specified business. Therefore

a lease which permits use as a confectioner's only, or which permits any trade except that of newsagent's, will remain within Part II even though the tenant begins using the premises as a newsagent's.

Since s.23(4) provides that acquiescence in the breach affects only the immediate landlord and not his predecessor. In *Bell* v. *Alfred Franks & Bartlett Co. Ltd.* (1980), the tenant could not rely on the sub-section because the current landlord had not acquiesced in the breach, and the previous landlord, although acquiescing in it, had not consented to it. A landlord who has acquiesced in a breach of a user covenant can therefore effectively ensure that the lease loses Part II protection by assigning the reversion to his nominee or associate.[9]

Changes from residential to business use in breach of covenant, and then back to residential use, will reinstate any residential security of tenure only if there has been a waiver of the breach.

Whether the breach of the user covenant causes the lease to lose Part II protection or not, the landlord still has the remedy (assuming there is a proviso for re-entry) of forfeiting the lease. Even if the breach of the user covenant does not cause Part II protection to be lost under s.23(4), the lease will come to an end on forfeiture: s.24(2).

19.2.6 Carried On By Him

Trusts

Under s.41, where the tenancy is held on trust (so that the tenant is trustees), the occupation and carrying on the business by all or any of the beneficiaries is treated as the occupation and carrying on a business by the tenant (i.e. the trustees).

Companies

Under the doctrine of corporate personality, a company is a separate person from the person or persons who control it. Before the changes to Part II on 1 June 2004, the effect of this doctrine was that if the tenant was an individual, but the business was carried on by the tenant's company, or if it was the tenant's company (not the tenant) that was in occupation, the lease fell outside Part II: *Christina* v. *Seear* (1985). This created a loophole whereby, for instance, a landlord could prevent the lease from falling within Part II by requiring a trader to form a separate company so that the premises would be leased to the company, even though the business being carried on was that of the trader. Similarly, a trader with a lease in his own name who later decided to incorporate, and to transfer his business (but not his lease) to a company, would thereby lose the protection of Part II.

The position has now been changed. Under the new s.23(1A), the occupation or carrying on of a business by a company in which the tenant has a controlling interest, or (where the tenant is a company) by a person with a controlling interest in the company, is treated as the occupation or carrying on of a business by the tenant: s.23(1A)(1B). A person has a controlling interest if, had he been a company, the other company would have been its subsidiary: s.46(2). 'Subsidiary' has the meaning given in Companies Act 1985, s.736.

Previously, whilst companies in a group were treated as one, they were treated as in a group only if one was a subsidiary of the other, or if both were subsidiaries of a third. In consequence, companies fell outside the provision if they were merely controlled by the same person. Under the amended s.42(1), the meaning of group has been extended to include two companies controlled by the same person: see s.42(1), (2). The effect of the amendment is that where two companies, A and B, are both controlled by the same person, a lease to company A is now within s.23 even though it is company B which occupies and carries on the business.

Partnerships

There is also special provision for partnerships in s.41A (which dates back to 1969). This section deals with the problem that can arise where there is a letting to several partners (which will necessarily be to them as joint tenants), and one or more of them subsequently leave the partnership. The section applies only where there remain two or more joint tenants: if only one remains, then the section does not apply. The section uses the expression 'the business tenants' to refer to the joint tenants who are for the time being carrying on the business. The section deals with several matters:

- *Service of statutory notices.* In order to avoid the problem of notices under Part II having to be served by or on all the joint tenants, including those who have since left the partnership, it is provided that it is sufficient if such notices are served by or on the business tenants. The statutory notices to which the section applies are a tenant's s.26 request, a tenant's notice to quit under s.27, and a landlord's s.25 notice.
- *Liability during continuation tenancy.* If the business tenants alone make an application for a new tenancy, only the business tenants are liable in respect of any rental period after the termination date specified in the s.25 notice or the equivalent in the tenant's s.26 request.
- *New tenancy.* The court may make an order for a new tenancy (under s.29) to the business tenants, or to them jointly with the persons carrying on the business in partnership with them. Such grant may be made subject to such conditions as to guarantors, sureties or otherwise as appears to the court to be equitable, having regard to the omission of the other joint tenants from the new tenancy.

▶ *Compensation.* It is the business tenants who are entitled to any statutory compensation on quitting the holding under s.37 or (in special cases) s.59.

19.3 Contracting Out

Before 1 June 2004, a lease could be contracted out of Part II only with the approval of the court. However, in the vast majority of cases under the old law, where the tenant was legally represented or had at least received legal advice, the courts did not consider the application on its merits, but merely 'rubber-stamped' it.

Since 1 June 2004, it has no longer been possible to obtain the court's approval to contract out of the security of tenure of Part II. Instead, there is a new procedure for contracting out.[10]

Under the new law, if the lease is to be contracted out, the landlord must serve what might be called a '*health warning*' on the tenant before the tenant enters into, or becomes legally bound to enter into, the tenancy, and the tenant must make a declaration in the prescribed form, which states that it has read the health warning and accepts the consequences of contracting out of the protection of Part II. If the health warning notice is served on the tenant at least fourteen days before the lease (or contract for a lease) is entered into, the tenant need only make an *ordinary* declaration; if it is served less than fourteen days before, the tenant must make a *statutory* declaration before a solicitor. If these statutory requirements are not complied with, the agreement to contract out is void.

Although the new contracting-out regime sounds simple, it is fraught with potential dangers for the landlord:

(a) A change in the identity of the tenant between the service of the health warning and the grant of the lease would invalidate the contracting out. (Contrast the position under the old law, where there was a change in the identity of the tenant after the court had approved the contracting out: *Brighton and Hove City Council* v. *Collinson* (2004)).

(b) It is unclear whether it is sufficient if the health warning notice is served in respect of an agreement (necessarily subject to contract) of 'heads of terms' (i.e. material terms) only, or whether the exact terms of the lease need to have been agreed (subject to contract). (Contrast *Receiver for the Metropolitan Police District* v. *Palacegate Properties Ltd.* (2001), which deals with the position under the old regime).

(c) The health warning requirements seem to have overlooked the fact that, where (as is common practice) a guarantor (which could be an assignor under an authorised guarantee agreement) agrees to take a new lease in its own name in the event of disclaimer by the tenant's liquidator or trustee in bankruptcy, a health warning will need to be served on the guarantor. It is uncertain when the guarantor's obligation to enter into a new lease arises: if, for instance, the tenant agrees to enter into an authorised guarantee agreement on assigning the lease, it is unclear whether the obligation arises from the moment the original lease is entered into (with the problem of the landlord's having to serve potentially a multiplicity of health-warning notices in respect of leases that will probably never be granted) or only later if and when the landlord calls upon the guarantor to take up a new lease.[11]

These difficulties aside, the ease with which business leases can now be contracted out may lead to increased numbers of such leases being granted with no security of tenure. However, the market rent for a contracted-out business lease (unless it contains an option to renew) is likely to be less than that for a lease within Part II.

19.4 The Continuation Tenancy

If neither the landlord nor the tenant takes any steps to terminate a business tenancy protected by Part II, on the expiration of the contractual term it is statutorily continued for an indefinite period: s.24(1). The continuation tenancy does not confer a new form of interest on the tenant; the effect of the statute is to prolong the estate, subject to a statutory variation as to the mode of determination: *Bolton (HL) Engineering Co. Ltd.* v. *TJ Graham & Sons Ltd.* (1957). As the tenant retains an estate in the land, it can assign the continuation tenancy. The section does not extend merely contractual rights and liabilities (such as those of a guarantor) unless the contract expressly includes the period of holding over: see the conjoined appeals in the House of Lords in *City of London Corporation* v. *Fell* (1994) and *Herbert Duncan Ltd.* v. *Cluttons* (1994).

19.5 The Statutory Notice Procedures

Either party may initiate the procedure under Part II by serving a statutory notice upon the other. A tenant may serve on the landlord a statutory request for a new tenancy under s.26. Alternatively, the landlord may serve on the tenant a notice under s.25 to terminate the tenancy; and such notice must state whether it is opposed to the grant of a new tenancy, and (as the case may be) either set out its grounds of opposition, or its proposals for a new tenancy. Only one such statutory notice can be served, i.e. if the tenant has served a s.26 request, it is too late for the landlord to serve a s.25 notice, and vice versa. After service of one of these statutory notices, the other party may respond to it in the appropriate way. All statutory notices must be in the prescribed form set out in regulations.[12]

A s.25 notice or a s.26 request must be served not more than twelve months nor less than six months before the date of termination specified in the notice: ss.25(2), 26(2). In each case, the termination date cannot be earlier than the date on which the tenancy would come to an end by effluxion of time or could be brought to an end by a notice to quit given by the party serving the notice: s.25(3)(a), s.26(2). If the contractual term of the lease expires before the termination date specified in the s.25 notice or the equivalent date in the s.26 request, the tenancy is statutorily continued under s.24.

The landlord and tenant each needs to consider carefully its strategy in deciding whether to serve a notice or request, when to serve it, and what period of notice to give. The process might be likened to a game of chess or (because the party which initiates the procedure can choose whether to serve a long or a short notice) it might also be likened to a very slow game of tennis.

19.5.1 Methods of Service

All statutory notices under Part II are deemed served if served personally, or if left at the intended recipient's last place of abode (which includes a place of business: *Price* v. *West London Investment Building Society* (1964)), or if send to him there by post in a registered (or recorded delivery) letter, and a notice to a landlord can be served on its authorised agent.[13]

There are two reasons why, from the server's point of view, such a notice is best served by recorded delivery: first, it is deemed served from the date it is handed to the Post Office or other postal operator (not when it is actually received, or might be expected to be delivered); secondly, it is deemed served at that date even if it is returned undelivered or goes astray in the post: *Beanby Estates Ltd.* v. *Egg Stores (Stanford Hill) Ltd.* (2003), applied in *CA Webber (Transport) Ltd.* v. *Railtrack plc* (2004), each also holding that this interpretation did not infringe either Article 6 (the right to a fair trial) or Article 1 to the First Protocol (the right to the protection of property) of the European Convention on Human Rights enshrined in the Human Rights Act 1998.[14]

19.5.2 Tenant's Request (s.26)

A tenant may initiate renewal only if it has a tenancy for a term of years certain exceeding one year, or a tenancy for a term of years certain and thereafter from year to year: s.26(1). There is no similar provision restricting a tenant's replying to a landlord's notice under s.25. A tenant cannot initiate renewal if the landlord has already served a s.25 notice (s.26(4)), or if the tenant has already given notice to quit or a notice to terminate the tenancy under s.27: s.26(4).

If it is entitled to do so, a tenant may initiate renewal by serving a statutory request for a new tenancy (a s.26 request) in the prescribed form:

s.26(3). The request must specify the date such new tenancy is to begin: s.26(2). The request must also set out the tenant's proposals as to the property, the length of the term, the rent, and the other terms to be contained in the new tenancy: s.26(3). In one case, the tenant's request omitted the length of the term of the proposed new lease, but stated that the other terms should be the same as those of its existing tenancy. It was held that the request was valid, as it implied a request for a new tenancy for the same term as that of the existing tenancy (seven years): *Sidney Bolsom Investment Trust Ltd. v. E Karmios & Co. (London) Ltd.* (1956).

The time-limit imposed on the tenant by s.26 (see 19.5 above) may be waived by the landlord's conduct. This occurred in *Bristol Cars Ltd. v. RKH Hotels Ltd.* (1979), where the tenant's s.26 request was defective because it specified too early a date; it was held that the landlord had waived the defect because it had initially indicated that it would not oppose a new tenancy, had failed to serve a counter-notice under s.26(6), and had applied for an interim rent on the basis that the tenancy was continuing. It did not matter that the landlord had not appreciated that the tenant's request had been bad.

It might appear surprising that a tenant should sometimes prefer to ask for a new tenancy by serving a s.26 request rather than waiting for the landlord to initiate the statutory procedure, since the result might be the grant of a new lease on more onerous terms or the tenant's having to leave. Many tenants do indeed choose to sit tight, and to wait for the landlord to take the first step, failing which, on the expiration of the contractual term, the tenants would simply hold over under Part II. There are, however, several reasons why a particular tenant might favour initiating the Part II procedure itself:

(a) *Certainty.* A tenant whose lease is nearing the end of its term might prefer to have the uncertainty of its position resolved as soon as possible, particularly if it is planning to expand its business.

(b) *Goodwill.* Although an intangible asset and often difficult to put a price on, goodwill can be very valuable. An assignee is not going to pay so much for the goodwill of a business where the lease has only a few months to run or is a continuation tenancy under Part II. A tenant who is intending to retire and to assign the lease with the goodwill might therefore prefer to have the lease renewed, so that it can turn the goodwill to account on a sale of the renewed lease, rather than effectively allowing the landlord to profit from it (as might happen if the tenant simply quits the holding when the lease expires).

(c) *Time.* By serving a s.26 request before the landlord serves a s.25 notice, the tenant might effectively extend the term of its existing lease by a period of up to six months. If, for instance, the contractual term has six

months to run, there is still time for the landlord to serve a s.25 notice
to terminate the lease at the contractual term by serving a short notice
(six months). If, however, the tenant were at that time to serve a s.26
request first, it could, by serving a long notice (twelve months), ensure
that its tenancy would (at the least) continue for six months after the
expiration of the contractual term.

In *Garston v. Scottish Widows' Fund* (1998), the tenant tried to obtain a novel
advantage from the service of a s.26 request. The tenant, who had a fixed term
lease with a right to break, attempted to serve a s.26 request for a new lease
from the break date. It did this because it wished to remain in the premises
on the more favourable terms that it believed it would secure under a new
lease settled by the court under Part II. Had the tenant also served a notice to
break under the lease, it would have lost the protection of Part II (s.24(2)). A
break notice ranks as a notice to quit for this purpose (s.69(1)), so a tenant who
serves a break notice under the lease cannot then serve a s.26 request for a
new tenancy. In this case, however, the tenant served a s.26 request without
having served a break notice under the lease. The tenant pointed out that a
s.26 request could specify a termination date no earlier than the date the
tenancy '*could be* brought to an end by a notice to quit given by the tenant':
s.26(2) (italics supplied). This looks like a case of the tenant's trying to have
its cake and eat it, so it is not surprising that this argument lost both at first
instance and in the Court of Appeal. In this context the words italicised above
would seem to refer to notice to quit a periodic tenancy, rather than to the
exercise of a break clause in a fixed-term lease; nevertheless, the Act is
unhappily worded, as the definition section (s.69) does not make provision
for a different meaning where the context otherwise requires.

19.5.3 Landlord's Notice (s.25)

A landlord cannot initiate the Part II procedure if the tenant has already
served a s.26 request (s.26(4)), but in practice it is usually the landlord who
initiates the procedure. The landlord must serve on the tenant a s.25 notice
in the prescribed form: s.25(1). The notice must specify the date at which the
tenancy is to come to an end ('the date of termination') (s.25(1)), and it must
state whether the landlord is opposed to the grant of a new tenancy to the
tenant (s.25(6)). The notice must be served within the time limits set out
above (para. 19.5).

(a) If the landlord is opposed, the notice must specify one or more of the
    grounds of opposition in s.30(1): s.25(7).
(b) If the landlord is not opposed, the notice must set out the landlord's
    proposals for the terms of the new tenancy (i.e. the property, the rent,

and the other terms) (s.25(8)). It is not clear precisely how detailed the landlord's proposals need to be: it seems that 'heads of terms' suffice, but whether the landlord must, for instance, specify the actual amount of rent proposed, or whether it is enough to propose 'a market rent' is as yet uncertain. The requirement for a non-opposing landlord to set out its proposals for a new tenancy was introduced by the 2003 Order. It mirrors the tenant's obligation under a s.26 request, and is designed to help speed up negotiations and the renewal process. The landlord's proposals must be accompanied by a warning informing the tenant that it is not obliged to accept the terms.

Where the notice is invalid and has to be re-issued, the landlord may, of course, amend or change entirely the grounds for opposing renewal of the lease. The ways in which invalidity can arise are as numerous as the opportunities for human error. In *Herongrove Ltd.* v. *Wates City of London Properties plc* (1988), there was a lease of office premises on the ninth floor of a building, together with storage accommodation on two other floors and free car-parking spaces. The landlord served a s.25 notice that referred only to the ninth floor. The notice was ambiguous (and so held void) because a reasonable tenant might assume that the notice meant that the landlord was opposing a new lease only of the ninth floor, and so was going to offer the tenant a lease of another floor in the building together with the existing storage and car-parking spaces. This being so, even the principle in the *Mannai* case (mentioned below), developed since the *Herongrove* case, would not have assisted the landlord.

In *Barclays Bank plc* v. *Bee* (2001), the landlord's solicitors mistakenly served on the tenant two conflicting notices (on standard printed forms) on the same day. One (notice A) stated that the landlord would be opposed to a renewal, but did not specify the particular grounds; the other (notice B) stated that an application for a new tenancy would not be opposed. The tenant's solicitors pointed out the conflict to the landlord's solicitors, who thereupon served a third notice (notice C) stating that a renewal would be opposed, and specifying the ground. The Court of Appeal, applying the *Mannai* principle[15] (discussed more fully at Chapter 13.2), held that, although notice B by itself would have been a valid notice (whereas notice A was not), a reasonable recipient receiving two inconsistent notices simultaneously would not have been clearly informed of the landlord's intention. Notices A and B were therefore void, and it was notice C that was held valid.

If the lease can be terminated at common law by a landlord's notice to quit (which will be the case if it is a periodic tenancy, or a fixed-term lease with a landlord's break clause) such common law notice merely terminates the contractual term, whereupon the tenant's continuation tenancy arises under

Part II. If the landlord wishes also to terminate the continuation tenancy under the Act, it will need to serve both a common law notice to quit, and a s.25 notice. If the lease enables the landlord to terminate by notice to break, a single notice will suffice if it is capable of complying (and does in fact comply) with the break clause and with s.25: *Keith Bayley Rogers & Co. v. Cubes Ltd.* (1975).

19.5.4 Landlord's Counter-notice to Tenant's s.26 Request

If the tenant has served a s.26 request, the landlord, if it opposes a renewal, must serve a counter-notice within two months of the s.26 request, indicating the statutory grounds of opposition: s.26(6). If the landlord does not do this, he must grant a new lease to the tenant in accordance with the proposals set out in the tenant's s.26 request.

By contrast, a tenant does not have to serve a counter-notice following a landlord's s.25 notice. There used to be such a requirement, but it was abolished by the 2003 Order. In the past, omitting to serve statutory notices under the 1954 Act within the requisite time limits proved a fruitful source of negligence actions against solicitors; the abolition of the tenant's counter-notice should help to save solicitors' claims on their professional indemnity insurance.

19.5.5 Competent Landlord

The foregoing statutory notices can be given only by or to the 'competent landlord', as defined in s.44(1). The competent landlord is not necessarily the tenant's immediate landlord. It will be the immediate landlord if the landlord is the freehold owner, or has a lease which has at least 14 months to run. If the immediate landlord does not satisfy these criteria, then they are applied to his immediate landlord, and so on until the competent landlord is identified.

The effect of these provisions is that if a freehold owner (L), grants a fixed-term lease to a tenant (T), and T grants a Part II protected sublease to a sub tenant (S) for a term which expires more than 14 months before the expiration of T's head lease, there will be a period during which S's competent landlord will be T, not L. The risk for L in such circumstances is that the person negotiating a renewal of S's sublease will be T, who will have no interest in the terms of the sublease after its own headlease expires, and who is therefore unlikely to be concerned to protect the interests of L. To guard against this, L could ensure that T's headlease prohibits the grant of any sublease for a term which ends 14 months or more before the contractual expiration of T's headlease, unless the sublease is contracted out of the protection of Part II.

19.5.6   Duty to Give Information

In order to operate the statutory termination and renewal procedure, a landlord may need to obtain relevant information from the tenant, and *vice versa*. Either party, for instance, may need to determine the identity of the competent landlord for the purposes of s.44. The extent of the duty to give information when requested has been extended by the 2003 Order. The request for specified information must be made in each case in the prescribed form, and must be provided by the addressee in writing. No such notice can be served more than two years before the tenancy would (apart from Part II) come to an end by effluxion of time or could be brought to an end by notice to quit given by the landlord: s.40(6).

A reversioner (whether or not the immediate reversioner) may serve on the tenant of business premises a notice requiring the latter to state whether he occupies the premises for the purposes of a business carried on by him, whether there is any sub-tenancy (and to supply relevant details about it); and (to the best of his knowledge and belief) to give the name and address of any other person who owns an interest in reversion: s.40(1). A tenant's notice requires a reversioner or his mortgagee in possession to state whether he is the owner of the fee simple or the mortgagee in possession, and (where appropriate) to give specified information about the immediate landlord, any other person with an interest in the reversion, and any mortgagee in possession: s.40(3).

The person served must give the information within one month of service of the notice. The 2003 Order has imposed the further duty to tell the inquirer about any subsequent changes that occur within six months from that date: s.40(5). It might be difficult to comply with this further duty if the person served disposes of his interest within six months. This is recognised by s.40A, which relieves him of such further duty after transfer, provided that he gives written notice to the appropriate person (tenant or reversioner as the case may be) of the transfer and the name and address of the transferee: s.40A(1). If the person who served the notice transfers his own interest within six months, he or his assignee can notify the person served of this, and the duty to keep informed of subsequent changes is then owed to the assignee: s.40A(2). The 2003 Order has given teeth to the duty to give information: non-compliance with any duty imposed by s.40 is now a breach of statutory duty for which the remedy is an order to comply or an award of damages, or both: s.40B.

19.5.7   Tenant's Notice to Terminate: s.27

A tenant can terminate a tenancy for a term of years certain by giving to its *immediate* landlord, not less than three months before the end of the contractual term, a notice in writing that it does not desire the tenancy to be continued; but such notice cannot be given unless the tenant has been in occupation under the tenancy for one month: s.27(1). This exception is designed to prevent a landlord from extracting a notice to terminate from the tenant at the time the lease is granted, when the tenant may wrongly believe it has no choice.

Part II does not apply, however, if the tenant is not in occupation of the property at the end of the contractual term: s.27(1A). This sub-section (which was inserted by the 2003 Order) puts into statutory form what had previously been held to be the position by the decision of the Court of Appeal in *Esselte AB* v. *Pearl Assurance* (1997). A tenant who has left it too late to quit at the end of the contractual term can therefore avoid the statutory obligation (applicable to tenancies within Part II) to give three months' notice of termination simply by ceasing to occupy before the term date. The landlord's position is weakened, as the tenant's vacating at the eleventh hour may leave the landlord with a void (i.e. a period during which the property is untenanted and so not earning rent) before the premises can be re-let. A landlord might be able to guard against this by serving a s.25 notice on the tenant well in advance, in the hope that if his tenant does not intend to remain it is unlikely to wish to incur the expense of renewal proceedings, and so might prefer to make its intentions clear.

The enactment of s.27(1A) does not clarify the precise time at which a tenant ceases to occupy. Occupation could cease the moment the tenant vacates, in which case a tenant who moves out before midnight on the last day of the contractual term ceases to occupy immediately and is not liable for rent for the period after midnight. Analogies can be drawn with the meaning of 'occupation' under other provisions of Part II (see 19.9.3 below). A tenant which closes down its business and vacates only few days before the contractual term expires might be treated as still in occupation at the term date if its chosen date of vacating is effectively geared to the term date.

The principle in the *Esselte* case does not apply once the contractual term has ended, so that a tenant under a continuation tenancy cannot end its rights and liabilities under the lease simply by ceasing to occupy. It must give three months' notice in writing to its immediate landlord: s.27(2). This can be any period of three months: since the 2003 Order was enacted, it does not have to be notice to terminate on any particular day. Such notice cannot be given unless the tenant has been in occupation under the tenancy for one month.

19.5.8 Landlord's Termination Notice Where Tenancy Ceases to be Subject to Part II: s.24(3)

If a tenancy is subject to Part II, it does not come to an end merely because it ceases to be subject to Part II, but if it was granted for a term of years certain and is now extended into a continuation tenancy, it can be terminated by the landlord by between three and six months' notice in writing given to the tenant: s.24(3). If therefore a tenant under a continuation tenancy ceases to carry on a business, this does not itself terminate the tenancy, but the landlord can then give notice to bring it to an end.

19.5.9 Tenant's Notice to Quit: s.24(2)

Part II protection is lost if the tenant serves a notice to quit. This includes both a notice to quit a periodic tenancy, and a tenant's notice to terminate under a break clause in a fixed-term lease (s.69(1)). A notice to quit is not, however, effective to end the tenancy unless the tenant has been in occupation under the tenancy for one month. This exception has the same underlying rationale as the equivalent exception in relation to a tenant's notice to terminate under s.27(1) (see 19.5.7 above).

19.5.10 Surrender: s.24(2)

If the tenancy is surrendered, Part II protection is lost. There is an exception where the surrender was executed before, or in pursuance of an agreement made before, the tenant had been in occupation under the tenancy for one month. The rationale for this is the same as in the other situations already mentioned.

19.5.11 Forfeiture: s.24(2)

The tenant loses the protection of Part II if the tenancy, or a superior tenancy, is forfeited; but, if the landlord has an order for possession the statutory protection remains so long as there is a pending application for relief: *Meadows* v. *Clerical, Medical and General Life Assurance Society* (1981).

19.5.12 Frustration or Repudiatory Breach

As they had not been admitted as methods by which a lease could determine in 1954, it is hardly surprising that Part II does not specify frustration or repudiatory breach as methods of termination. It seems likely, however, that frustration or a tenant's acceptance of a repudiatory breach by the landlord would have an overriding effect to terminate the lease: cf. *Chartered Trust plc* v. *Davies* (1997). Were the position otherwise, a tenant accepting a landlord's repudiatory breach during a continuation tenancy would not be able to bring the lease to an end except by giving notice under s.27(2), which would result in its having to pay any rent due under the lease for at least a further three months.

19.6 Applications to the Court

If the landlord has served a s.25 notice or the tenant has served a s.26 request, either party may apply to the court for the grant of a new tenancy: s.24(1). Alternatively, if it has served a s.25 notice or a counter-notice to the tenant's s.26 request, the landlord may apply to the court for an order for the termination of the tenancy without the grant of a new tenancy: s.29(2). As soon as one party has served an application, neither party can make another (ss.24(2A),(2B), 29(3)), and the landlord may not withdraw its application (whether for a new tenancy or for termination of the existing tenancy without the grant of a new tenancy) without the tenant's consent: ss.24(2C), 29(6).

The deadline for court applications is the date stated in the landlord's s.25 notice or the day before the date specified in the tenant's s.26 request: ss.29A, 29B. (In each case, this is the date the existing tenancy is to determine, which, in the case of the tenant's s.26 request, will be the day before the requested new lease is to begin). The parties can agree to extend the deadline for such applications (to enable further negotiations to take place) without having to go to court. This relatively long deadline (which was introduced by the 2003 Order) is intended to facilitate negotiations, and to minimise the involvement of the court. Previously, court applications had to be made within only a few months of the notices being served, with the result that applications often had to be made even in circumstances where negotiations were making good progress. The change is also likely to reduce the number of negligence claims against solicitors for missing the deadline for applications.

19.7 Interim Rent

The contractual term may expire either because the renewal procedure is still in progress, or simply through the inaction of either party. The terms of the statutory continuation tenancy will be the same (save as to length of term) as that of the expired contractual tenancy, including the rent; but in many circumstances (notably where the general level of rents has risen or fallen since the last rent review) it may be unfair to one of the parties that the same rent should continue to be payable during the period of the continuation tenancy.

As originally enacted, the 1954 Act made no provision for an interim rent, so that tenants had every incentive to delay proceedings. The position was changed in 1969, when, with the insertion of s.24A into the 1954 Act, it became possible for a landlord to apply for an interim rent during the period of the continuation tenancy. This provision was, however, defective in a number of ways.[16] First, only the landlord could apply, so that in a falling market (such as occurred generally in the recession of the early 1990s) the tenant would have no means of seeking a lower interim rent. Secondly, the method of calculating an interim rent was not only uncertain, but involved an element of discounting: the interim rent would usually be lower than the rent ultimately settled under any new tenancy that might be granted. There therefore remained an incentive for tenants to use delaying tactics to prolong the continuation tenancy for as long as possible. Thirdly, although a landlord could *apply* for an interim rent as soon as it had served a s.25 notice or received a s.26 request, the earliest date from which an interim rent could actually *take effect* was the termination date set out in the landlord's s.25 notice, or the equivalent date evident from the tenant's s.26 request. If the contractual term of the lease had six months to run, then by serving a s.26 request for a new tenancy 12 months ahead, the tenant could effectively use the renewal machinery to delay the earliest date on which an interim rent could take effect to six months into its period of holding over. Fourthly, in any event, an interim rent could take effect only from the date on which the landlord applied for it; an application could not be retrospective. Thus, no application for an interim rent could be made after the continuation tenancy had come to an end.

These defects in the interim rent machinery were addressed by the reforms introduced by the 2003 Order. Now, either party can apply for an interim rent, so landlords and tenants are for the first time on an even footing. As before the changes, a landlord can avoid the need to apply to the court for an interim rent by ensuring that the lease contains provision for rent review at the end of the term. Now, however, this device does not guarantee a higher rent after the expiration of the contractual term, as the tenant might apply for an interim rent if it considers that this will probably be less than the rent calculated under an end-of-term review.

The earliest date of application for an interim rent remains the service of a s.25 notice or a s.26 request: s.24(A)(1)). However, an interim rent can now begin much sooner than under the previous law. It now starts from the *earliest* date that *could have been* specified in whichever statutory notice was served (i.e. the landlord's s.25 notice or the tenant's s.26 request): s.24B. Since the earliest date that could have been specified in either notice is six months, the interim rent cannot start earlier than that. The change now precludes the tenant's serving a long s.26 request in order to delay an interim rent. In a rising market, the landlord should be aware that, unless a s.25 notice or a s.26 request has been served at least six months before the expiration of the contractual term, it will begin to lose the benefit of a (higher) interim rent from the commencement of the period of holding over. If, for instance, it were to serve a s.25 notice only two months before the expiration of the contractual term and to apply immediately for an interim rent, the date from which it would be payable would be four months into the continuation tenancy. There is an ultimate deadline: no application for an interim rent can be made more than six months after the determination of the continuation tenancy: s.24A(3).

It will be appreciated that an interim rent can now be awarded retrospectively, and so can become payable even before the date on which application for it was made. If (as will usually be the case) the interim rent is higher than that payable under the old lease, the tenant will have to pay, at the date of the award, a lump sum equal to the difference between the rent that it has been paying and the (higher) interim rent from the date the interim rent became payable. The tenant should be aware of the potential financial consequences of this, particularly if it has been holding over for a long period.

19.7.1   Method of Calculating the Interim Rent

Under the new law, where a new tenancy is granted, the interim rent will usually be the *same* as the rent under the new tenancy if the landlord's s.25 notice or the tenant's s.26 request applies to the whole of the property let, the tenant occupies the whole of the property, and the landlord does not oppose the grant of a new tenancy: s.24C(1)(2). As these circumstances will pertain in many cases of renewal, many tenants will be paying a higher interim rent than they would have been paying under the former regime.

The new provision could, however, work hardship to one of the parties if the terms of the new lease are different. In these circumstances, the method of calculation is modified: s.24C(3)–(7). If the *rental market conditions* have changed significantly (e.g. if rents have risen substantially at the time the court hears the interim rent application, so that the effect would otherwise be to compel the tenant to pay an interim rent for an earlier period that would have been much higher than a market rent at the time), the court will base the interim rent on the occupational terms of the new lease, but adjust it according to open market conditions. If the *occupational terms* of the new tenancy are significantly different (e.g. if the repairing obligations are changed), the court may fix an interim rent that it considers reasonable to both parties.

In other cases, (as where no new tenancy is ultimately granted), the interim rent will be the rent that it is *reasonable* for the tenant to pay during the continuation tenancy: s.24D(1). In determining what is reasonable, the court must have regard to the rent payable under the existing tenancy and under any sub-tenancy, but otherwise s.34(1) and (2) apply to the determination of the interim rent as they would apply under that section if a new tenancy *from year to year* of the whole property were granted to the tenant by order of the court: s.24D(2). This method of calculation continues the old fiction of a yearly tenancy, with the similar result that an interim rent calculated on this basis is likely to be less than is eventually settled for the new lease. Furthermore, in *English Exporters (London) Ltd.* v. *Eldonwall Ltd.* (1973) and in *Fawke* v. *Viscount Chelsea* (1980), the court said that, in having regard to the rent payable under the existing tenancy, it was from the rent calculated on the basis of an annual tenancy that the discount should be made. In *Ratners (Jewellers) Ltd.* v. *Lemnoll Ltd.* (1980), this approach led the court to discount the rent of the yearly periodic tenancy by 20 per cent. This approach, which was unfavourable to the landlord, was not applied in *Regis Property Co. Ltd.* v. *Lewis & Peat Ltd.* (1970), where the judge treated the rent under the old lease as relevant only as providing some evidence of the market value of the notional yearly tenancy.

19.8 The Landlord's Grounds of Opposition

The landlord may state that it is opposed to the grant of a new tenancy either in its s.25 notice or in its counter-notice to the tenant's s.26 request. There are seven grounds of opposition, which are set out in paragraphs (a) to (g) of s.30, as elaborated in sections 31 and 31A. Paragraphs (a) to (c) and (e) set out grounds in view of which the tenant 'ought not' to be granted a new tenancy, so that under these four grounds, the court has a discretion, which enables it to take all circumstances into account. Paragraphs (d), (f) and (g) set out mandatory grounds, so that provided the landlord can prove its case, the court must refuse the application for a new tenancy.

The first three grounds, (a) to (c), all involve an element of fault on the tenant's part. As these are discretionary grounds, the court is entitled to consider all the circumstances relating to the breaches and the conduct of the tenant as a whole. Such circumstances may include evidence of other breaches that are not themselves relied on as separate grounds of opposition. In *Eichner* v. *Midland Bank Executor & Trustee Co. Ltd.* (1970), the landlord had relied on grounds (a) and (c). It was held that, in determining whether a new tenancy ought not to be granted under these grounds, the court was entitled to take account of a long unhappy relationship between the parties, including a history of litigation and non-payment of rent, even though the landlord had not set out his opposition under ground (b) (persistent delay in paying rent).

The fault-based grounds are:

19.8.1   Para. (a): Tenant's Breach of a Repairing Obligation

The first ground is where the premises are in disrepair as a result of the tenant's breach of its repairing obligation. As this is a discretionary ground, the court will take into account the extent of the disrepair, a history of previous breaches, and any undertaking to repair that the tenant is willing to give: *Lyons* v. *Central Commercial Properties London Ltd.* (1958).

19.8.2   Para. (b): Tenant's Persistent Delay in Paying Rent

The reference to persistent delay enables the court to take into account the number of occasions on which the payment of rent has been delayed, and the length of the delays. As this is a discretionary ground, the court can also take account of the reasons for the delays, and whether there are rent arrears at the date of the hearing: *Gill* v. *Moore* (1989). It can also consider ways in which the landlord might be safeguarded in the future, such as by requiring the tenant to pay a security deposit, as was mentioned by Sachs L.J. in *Hopcutt* v. *Carver* (1969).

19.8.3   Para. (c): Other Substantial Breaches by the Tenant of its Obligations under the Tenancy, or any Other Reason Connected with the Tenant's Use and Management of the Holding

Under the first leg, the court can look at the nature and seriousness of the breach, whether it is remediable, and whether the right to forfeit for the breach has been waived by the landlord. The second leg does not involve any existing breach of covenant on the tenant's part; but it could take account of future conduct, or breaches of obligations to public authorities (e.g. contravention of a planning enforcement order, as in *Turner and Bell* v. *Searles (Stanford-le-Hope) Ltd.* (1977)).

In *Beard* v. *Williams* (1986), the landlord opposed a renewal under the second leg of this ground where the tenant, who ran a greyhound-training business from the demised premises, lived in a van which he parked (possibly illegally) on the grass verge of the highway nearby. The Court of Appeal accepted that, whilst a tenant's living arrangements would not normally be connected with the tenant's use and management of the holding, they were in this case because the tenant's business would be at risk if he had to leave his place of abode. Even so, this was a discretionary ground, and as the court considered that it did not have sufficient evidence to determine whether the tenant 'ought not' to be granted a new tenancy, it remitted the case to the county court.

The last four grounds, (d) to (g), do not involve any fault on the part of the tenant. These non-fault based grounds are:

19.8.4 Para. (d): Landlord's Offer of Alternative Accommodation

This ground is that the landlord has offered and is willing to provide or secure the provision of alternative accommodation for the tenant. The terms of such accommodation must be reasonable having regard to the current tenancy and all other relevant circumstances. The time at which such accommodation will be available must also be suitable for the tenant's requirements (including the preservation of goodwill) having regard to the nature and class of his business and to the situation and extent of the holding, and the facilities that it affords.

It is uncertain whether the suitability of the alternative accommodation is to be determined solely on the basis of any original offer that the landlord has made, or whether the court can take account of any improved offer that the landlord might make during the trial. The point was left open by the Court of Appeal: *Mark Stone Car Sales Ltd.* v. *Howard de Walden Estates Ltd.* (1997). It would be more consistent with the policy of the Act of encouraging negotiations (particularly in its amended form after the 2003 Order), for the court to be able to take account of later offers, and county court authority tends to support that view: *M Chaplin Ltd.* v. *Regent Capital Holdings Ltd.* (1994).

If the court finds the landlord's offer to have been reasonable, so that the landlord establishes ground (d), the court must refuse the application for a new tenancy. The tenant is not precluded from then accepting the offer, so long as it remains open. The risk for the tenant is that the landlord may withdraw the offer before the tenant has time to accept, so that the tenant will have to quit the premises without being provided with suitable alternative accommodation (and without statutory compensation, which is not available under this ground).[17]

19.8.5 Para. (e): Where the Tenancy is an Uneconomic Subletting of Part

This ground can apply only where the tenancy is a sub-tenancy comprising only part of the premises demised by a superior tenancy, in circumstances where the competent landlord is the holder of the reversion. These circumstances pertain if L leases premises to T, who in turn sub-lets part only of those premises to S, and where, there being less than 14 months before the termination of T's headlease, L is S's competent landlord. L can successfully oppose S's application for a new tenancy if it can establish:

▶ that the aggregate of the rents reasonably obtainable on separate lettings of the holding and the remainder of that property would be substantially less than the rent reasonably obtainable on a letting of that property as a whole; and

▶ that on termination of the current tenancy the landlord requires possession of the holding for letting or otherwise disposing of it as a whole; and

▶ that in view thereof the tenant ought not to be granted a new tenancy.

This ground is rarely relied upon because it is both narrow in scope and obscure in meaning: *Betty's Cafés Ltd. v. Phillips Furnishing Stores Ltd.* (1959) (HL).

19.8.6   Para. (f): Landlord Intends to Demolish, Reconstruct, etc

This ground is that, on termination of the current tenancy, the landlord intends to demolish or reconstruct the whole or a substantial part of the premises or to carry out substantial work of construction on the holding or part of it, and that he could not reasonably do so without obtaining possession of the holding.

To succeed under this ground, the landlord must establish three things:

(i)   Intention

He must satisfy the court that he has the requisite intention. This has two aspects: a settled intention and a reasonable prospect of fulfilment.

The first aspect, a settled intention, means that there must be definite proposals: it is not enough if the landlord is merely feeling his way: *Reohorn v. Barry Corporation* (1956). The landlord must have 'moved out of the zone of contemplation – the sphere of the tentative, the provisional and the exploratory – into the valley of decision': per Asquith L.J. in *Cunliffe v. Goodman* (1950). On the other hand, there need be no detailed scheme of development, and the intention may be established even if contracts with the developers have not been entered into: *PF Ahern & Sons Ltd. v. Hunt* (1988). The landlord needs to show only that general arrangements have been made regarding finance, building and planning permission: *Capocci v. Goble* (1987). The requisite intention can be shown even if the landlord hires contractors to do the work and grants a building lease: *Spook Erection Ltd. v. British Railways Board* (1988). Motive, such as a plan to sell at the end of a short building lease, is irrelevant: *Turner v. Wandsworth LBC* (1994).

The second aspect of intention, that the landlord's scheme has a reasonable prospect of being fulfilled, is closely connected to the first, since it has been said that a person cannot intend what he has no reasonable possibility of bringing about: *Cunliffe v. Goodman* (1950). There was held to be no reasonable prospect of fulfilment in *Wessex Reserve Forces & Cadets Association v. White* (2006). The tenant in that case was occupying various structures, the most substantial being two huts, but also other lesser fabrications, all of which (apart from a small stone shed) the tenant had itself introduced. The landlord's opposition under ground (f) failed because the structures were held to be mostly tenant's fixtures, which the tenant planned to remove at the end of the lease: the landlord therefore had no reasonable prospect of demolishing them.

The date the intention must be shown is the date of application to the court: *Betty's Cafés Ltd.* v. *Phillips Furnishing Stores Ltd.* (1959) (HL). If the landlord changes his mind afterwards, the tenant can do nothing, unless it can show misrepresentation or concealment of material facts, and so claim compensation for damage or loss: s.37A.

As a tenant refused a new lease is given three months (after the expiry of time for an appeal) to vacate, the landlord must show that he can begin work by that date. If he cannot show this, but he can satisfy the court that he could begin within the period specified in s.31(2), then he might still be able to prevent the grant of a new tenancy: see 19.9.1 below.

(ii) Demolition, reconstruction, or construction

The landlord must show that his intended acts are those of demolition, reconstruction, or construction. Whilst, as already discussed, bare land can be premises for the purposes of s.23(1), it seems that only structures on the land can be demolished for the purposes of paragraph (f) of s.30(1): *Housleys* v. *Bloomer-Holt Ltd.* (1966). Similarly, in *Coppen* v. *Bruce-Smith* (1998), intended works of breaking up of tennis courts (both hard and grass) and leaving them as shallow pits were held not to be acts within ground (f). On the other hand, acts within the paragraph can include works affecting an 'eggshell tenancy', i.e. a lease of the space within part of a building, including only the internal skin: *Pumperninks of Piccadilly Ltd.* v. *Land Securities plc* (2002).

Demolition or reconstruction must involve at least a substantial part of the premises, but the premises themselves do not have to be substantial. In *Houlsleys* v. *Bloomer-Holt Ltd.* (1966), the tenant, motor engineers, had a lease of a site on one third of which stood a wooden garage, and the rest of which, apart from a wall, was covered in cinders. The landlord wanted to demolish the wall and the garage and to turn the whole site into concrete hard-standing for its lorries. It succeeded under ground (f). Sellars L.J. said that what was to be demolished was all that there was to demolish on the site, 'and that seems to be demolishing the whole of the premises so far as any structure was to be demolished.'

There must be a substantial interference with the existing premises. In *Botterill* v. *Beds CC* (1985), merely removing the topsoil of a field without buildings, depositing waste and landscaping the site, did not amount to reconstruction. To qualify as construction, the works must affect the structure of a building; so mere refurbishment or improvement (such as re-roofing, re-siting a staircase or the insertion of wooden partitions) is insufficient: *Barth* v. *Pritchard* (1990).

(iii)   *Need for possession*

The landlord must establish the need for possession in order to carry out the work. However, by s.31A(1), the landlord will not be able to establish this if the tenant can satisfy either paragraph (a) or (b) of that sub-section. The first is where:

(a) the tenant agrees to the inclusion in the new tenancy of a term giving the landlord access and other facilities for carrying out the work, and, as a result, the landlord could reasonably carry out the work without obtaining possession and without interfering to a substantial extent or for a substantial time with the tenant's business user.

Whether the interference with the tenant's business is substantial, both in extent and in time, is a matter of fact. In *Blackburn* v. *Hussain* (1988), the landlord's intended works involved demolition of walls and of shop-fronts, and removal of lavatories and of the stairway leading to the tenant's café; it would be impossible for the tenant to run his café in anything like a reasonable way for twelve weeks, and the Court of Appeal held that the interference was substantial. In *Cerex Jewels Ltd.* v. *Peachey Property Corp plc* (1986), where the works would necessitate the closure of the tenant's business for only two weeks, the interference was held not to be substantial. The tenant cannot waive the requirement that there be no substantial interference with its business: *Redfern* v. *Reeves* (1978).

The obtaining of possession means the putting to an end of the tenant's rights to possession under the present tenancy, so the landlord cannot establish a need for possession if the tenant's lease reserves to the landlord the right to enter to carry out the works. This was held by a majority of the House of Lords in *Heath* v. *Drown* (1973), where the tenant had a lease of two floors of a building, the front wall of which was in a dangerous state. The landlord was responsible for the repairs, which would involve substantial works; but the lease entitled the landlord to enter to carry out any necessary repairs, and it was conceded that the landlord's proposed works fell within this description. As the landlord was able to carry out the works under the existing lease, his opposition under ground (f) failed. Section 31A did not apply, so it was irrelevant that the works would make it impossible for the tenant to carry on her business for between four and nine months.

The alternative basis on which the tenant can prevent the landlord's establishing a need for possession is where:

(b) the tenant is willing to accept a tenancy of an economically separable part of the holding, and either paragraph (a) is satisfied with respect to that part or possession of the remainder would be reasonably sufficient to enable the landlord to carry out the intended work.

The tenancy is of an economically separable part only if, after the works have been completed, the aggregate of the rents reasonably obtainable on the separate lettings would not be substantially less than the rents that would then be reasonably obtainable on a letting of the premises as a whole: s.31A(2).

19.8.7 Para. (g): The Landlord Intends to Occupy the Premises Himself for Business Purposes or as his Residence

To succeed under this ground, the landlord must show that, on the termination of the current tenancy, he intends to occupy the holding for the purposes, or partly for the purposes, of a business to be carried on by him therein, or as his residence.

By virtue of what is often called 'the five-year rule', a landlord cannot rely on paragraph (g) if his interest was purchased or (where he has a leasehold interest) created within five years of the termination of the tenancy, and at all times since the holding has been comprised in a business tenancy within Part II: s.30(2). This is intended to prevent speculators from buying up business leases near the end of their terms with a view to gaining possession by relying on ground (g): *Artemiou* v. *Procopiou* (1965).

References in ground (g) to landlord include a company controlled by the landlord: s.30(1A). They also include, where the landlord is a company, the person who controls the company: s.30(1B), unless the landlord's controlling interest in the company was acquired within five years of the termination of the current tenancy: s.30(2A). The five-year rule is thereby extended to the latter circumstance. A landlord may therefore oppose under this ground if it is his company that is intended to occupy for business purposes, or if (subject to the five-year rule) the landlord being a company, it is the person who controls the company who is intended to occupy for such purposes.

The requisite intention for this ground is similar to that needed to be shown for ground (f). For ground (g), the landlord must have a firm and genuine intention to occupy the demised premises for the purposes of a business or as his residence within a reasonable time after the termination of the tenancy: *Gregson* v. *Cyril Lord Ltd.* (1963). The landlord must also satisfy the court that he has a reasonable prospect of achieving such intention. To use the words of Laws L.J. in *Gatwick Parking Services Ltd.* v.

Sargant (2000), the landlord has to show that, in the carrying out of his proposals, he has a real, not merely a fanciful, chance. The landlord does not have to establish the probability of achieving the start of such business, nor its likely success once established: *Dolgellau Golf Club* v. *Hett* (1998). The court will not therefore examine the financial wisdom of the landlord's plans: *Cox* v. *Binfield* (1989). The landlord may intend to occupy the premises through an agent: *Skeet* v. *Powell-Sheddon* (1988). If the landlord intends to demolish the premises, he cannot have an intention to occupy them under ground (g): *Nursey* v. *P Currie (Dartford) Ltd.* (1959). As in ground (f), the date the intention must be shown is the date of the hearing.

19.9 Landlord Establishes Ground of Opposition

19.9.1 Termination of the Existing Lease

If the landlord successfully opposes a renewal under any ground, no new tenancy will be ordered: s.31(1). The existing tenancy will continue, but it will generally come to an end on whichever is the later of the following dates:

- the termination date specified in the landlord's s.25 notice or the equivalent date evident from the tenant's s.26 request (as the case may be);
- three months after the application is finally disposed of: s.64(1). As an application is not finally disposed of until the time for any appeal (four weeks) has expired, the effect is that (unless an appeal is lodged) the tenancy determines four months after judgment.

By lodging even a hopeless appeal, the tenant may be able to defer the date on which it has to relinquish possession. Whilst this makes sense where the appeal relates to a ground of opposition, it seems inappropriate where it relates solely to compensation: *Mark Stones Car Sales Ltd.* v. *Howard De Walden Estates Ltd.* (1997).

In special circumstances, where refusal is based on grounds (d), (e), or (f), the tenancy may come to an end at a later date. This is by virtue of s.31(2), which deals with the position where the landlord cannot satisfy the court under ground (d), (e), or (f), but the court would have been satisfied of that ground within one year of the termination date stated in the landlord's s.25 notice or of the date for a new tenancy stated in the tenant's s.26 request. The court must make a declaration to that effect, specifying the date it has so determined. No new lease is then granted, and the existing lease will then terminate at the date specified in such notice unless the tenant applies to the court within 14 days to have the date of termination of the existing lease extended to that so determined by the court.

19.9.2   Misrepresentation or Concealment

If the court makes an order for the termination of the current tenancy but does not make an order for the grant of a new tenancy, or refuses an order for the grant of a new tenancy, but it later comes to light that the court's refusal was induced by misrepresentation or concealment of material facts, the court may order the landlord to pay compensation to the tenant for its damage or loss thereby sustained: s.37A(1). The tenant may similarly be awarded compensation where it has quit the holding after making (or making but withdrawing) an application under Part II, where it later comes to light that he did so by reason of the landlord's misrepresentation or concealment of material facts: s.37A(2). A misrepresentation does not include a change of mind by the landlord after judgment, e.g. where he successfully opposed a renewal on ground (f) with a genuine intention to demolish or reconstruct, but later decided not to do so.

19.9.3   Compensation

No compensation is payable by the landlord if he successfully opposes under grounds (a) to (d). It is self-evident why this should be so for the fault-based grounds, (a) to (c). The absence of compensation under ground (d) means that a tenant declines the offer of reasonable alternative accommodation at his peril.

Under s.37(1), the landlord is obliged to pay the tenant compensation on quitting the holding if:

- upon an application to the court (brought by either party) the landlord successfully opposes a renewal under grounds (e), (f) or (g) only; or
- if the landlord relies solely on grounds (e), (f) or (g) in his notice or counter-notice, and the tenant does not make (or makes but later withdraws) an application for a new tenancy. Compensation can therefore be awarded without the tenant's having to apply to the court and have its application dismissed.

Compensation is calculated as the product of the appropriate multiplier, and either the rateable value, or twice the rateable value, of the holding: s.37(2). The appropriate multiplier is laid down by statutory instrument (s.37(8)), currently the Landlord and Tenant Act 1954 (Appropriate Multiplier) Order 1990.[18] Twice the rateable value is used in the calculation if, during the whole of the fourteen years immediately preceding the termination of the current tenancy, the premises have been occupied for the purposes of a business carried on by the occupier (or for those and other purposes): s.37(3)(a). If during that period there was a change of occupier, twice the rateable is still used, provided the occupier immediately after the change was the successor to the business carried on by the immediately preceding occupier: s.37(3)(b). The termination of the current tenancy in this section refers to the date of termination specified in the landlord's s.25 notice or the date specified in the tenant's s.26 request for a new tenancy: s.37(7). A tenant who has been in occupation for the purpose of a business for fourteen years therefore obtains twice the compensation of a tenant who has occupied for such purposes for only thirteen years and eleven months.

The parties can by agreement exclude or modify the landlord's obligation to provide compensation: s.38(3). Such agreement is, however, void if the tenant has, or the tenant and his immediately preceding occupier in the same business have, been in occupation of the premises for the purposes of a business for the whole of the five years immediately preceding the date the tenant is to quit the holding: s.38(2). In *Bacchiocchi* v. *Academic Agency Ltd.* (1998) it was held that if a tenant vacates the premises before the date he is to quit, he can still be regarded as having been in occupation for the five years 'immediately preceding' that date, provided that his leaving the premises is reasonably incidental to the running down of his business. It was said that the same principle would apply to the starting of a business, and to periods of inactivity (as where business premises are occupied for a business that is seasonal in nature) provided that such periods of non-attendance are business-related. The tenant in *Bacchiocchi* made a mistake as to the date he was to quit and left two weeks early; but he was treated as having been in occupation until that date, and so the term in the lease excluding his right to compensation was held void.

It was assumed in *Bacchiocchi* that the date the tenant is to quit for the purposes of the restriction on contracting out in s.38(2) is the date by which the tenant must leave the premises under s.64. However, in *Sight & Sound Education Ltd.* v. *Books etc Ltd.* (1999), the High Court took the view that for the purposes of calculating the period of fourteen years (for double compensation) in s.37(2), the relevant date is the termination date specified in the landlord's s.25 notice or the equivalent date in the tenant's s.26 request. The tenant in *Sight & Sound* had moved out five months before that date with no intention to return, and it could not be said that he was still in occupation during that period. He was therefore held not entitled to double compensation.

19.10 Court Orders Grant of New Tenancy

If either party has applied to the court for a new tenancy, the court will grant a new tenancy unless the landlord makes out a ground of opposition, or the special circumstances set out in s.31(2) apply (see s.19.9.1 above): s.29(1). The court will settle the terms of the new tenancy to the extent that the parties themselves cannot agree.

19.10.1 Property: s.32

The court will order a grant of a new tenancy of the holding, and in the absence of any agreement between the parties as to what that property is, it will be designated by the court by reference to the circumstances existing at the date of the order: s.32(1). 'The holding' means the property comprised in the tenancy excluding any part which is occupied neither by the tenant nor by his employee for the purpose of a business: s.23(3). If, for instance, a tenant has sub-let a part of the premises so that it cannot satisfy this requirement, the court can grant it a new tenancy only of the part that it is itself occupying for the purpose of a business. The landlord may however require that the new tenancy be of the whole of the property comprised in the current tenancy: s.32(2). This provision ensures that the landlord is not unwillingly made the landlord of two or more tenants each holding a tenancy of part of the premises comprised in the current lease.

If the landlord opposes a renewal under ground (f) (demolition, reconstruction, etc), but the tenant is willing to accept a tenancy of an economically separable part (see 19.8.6 above), the order will be for the grant of a new tenancy of that part only: s.32(1A).

Any rights enjoyed with the tenancy in connection with the holding are included in the new tenancy except as otherwise agreed by the parties or (in default of such agreement) as the court determines: s.32(3). Easements, such as rights of light, rights of way, and drainage, which benefit the current tenancy, will therefore normally be included in the new tenancy.

19.10.2 Duration: s.33

The parties themselves can agree a term of any length; in the absence of agreement, the court will determine such term as is reasonable in all the circumstances, but for a term not exceeding fifteen years, to begin on the ending of the current tenancy: s.33(1). Before the 2003 Order came into force, the maximum term that the court could order was fourteen years; the Order increased this to fifteen, as the latter period suits the inclusion of both three-yearly and five-yearly rent reviews, these being more common nowadays than when the Act was passed in 1954.

In determining the length of the term, the circumstances that the court takes into account include the length of the current tenancy. The court will rarely order the grant of a longer term, and in practice the new lease will often be for the same term as the current tenancy. The court is not restricted by the tenant's wishes, and may determine a term longer or shorter than the tenant desires. In *Betty's Cafés Ltd.* v. *Phillips Furnishing Stores Ltd.* (1957), the tenant had been in possession of the premises for over forty years, but under a succession of short leases, none of which had exceeded eight years. In view of this, the Court of Appeal substituted a term of five years for the fourteen years that the tenant had sought and successfully obtained at first instance.

Other factors that the court may take into account include the nature of the business (the existence of substantial goodwill tending to the grant of a longer lease), the length of time the tenant has been in business, the premises' age and state of repair, and the comparative hardship between the parties (as where a very short lease might reduce the value of the landlord's reversion, which he intends to dispose of: *Ganton House Investments* v. *Crossman Investments* (1995)).

The landlord's intended plans for the premises are also relevant. If the landlord intends to do work which would fall within ground (f), or to occupy as required by ground (g), but cannot establish an intention to do so within one year of the termination of the current tenancy (so falling outside s.31(2), see 19.9.1 above), the court can take this into account in determining both the length of the new lease and whether (as another term, under s.35) it should contain a break clause. The court endeavours to balance the principle that the tenant should have a measure of security of tenure with the genuine wishes of the landlord to carry out its demolition or reconstruction works or to occupy. To this extent, it is a question of balancing the hardship between the parties.

Sometimes the courts have balanced these factors by ordering a shorter term, as in *London and Provincial Millinery Stores Ltd.* v. *Barclays Bank Ltd.* (1962), where the premises were ripe for development. In this case the landlord intended to demolish and reconstruct a row of buildings, the ground floor of one being occupied by the tenant, who had a millinery shop. The landlord had, however, omitted to serve a counter-notice to a s.26 request, and so was reduced to contesting the terms of the new lease (settled by the judge at first instance as a term of nine years). The Court of Appeal reduced this to a term of one year because of the landlord's urgent need to demolish and reconstruct, the upper floor and the adjoining buildings being in a very dilapidated state and capable of falling down at any time. In deciding upon the term of the new lease, the court also took account of the tenant's having been in occupation under a continuation tenancy for more than four years. In the circumstances, a one-year term was appropriate to give the tenant a reasonable period to find alternative premises.

On other occasions, the courts have granted a longer lease with a break clause, sometimes operable by either party. This often takes the form of a rolling break clause that requires a relatively long period of notice. A landlord's break clause might be made exercisable only on the landlord's intention to develop (a development break clause).

The court might prefer to grant a longer lease with a break clause rather than a shorter lease, where the landlord's plans for development or occupation are prospective rather than immediate. Thus in *Adams* v. *Green* (1978), the landlord owned a row of small shop premises that were a hundred years old. The landlord intended to redevelop the whole row in the near future, probably by selling to a developer, and had therefore re-let all the other shops in the row on leases containing a landlord's development break clause operable on two years' notice. The judge at first instance had ordered a seven-year lease with no break clause. The Court of Appeal instead ordered a fourteen-year lease with a landlord's rolling two-year development break clause. It considered that the break clause was appropriate so as not to thwart the landlord's intention to redevelop the whole row; and it pointed out that, even if the landlord served such break notice, the tenant would still have the protection of Part II.

If a rolling break clause is inserted, the court will often prefer to defer the date on which notice can first be served so as to give the tenant a useful period of occupation under the new lease free from the risk of disturbance. In *Davy's of London (Wine Merchants) Ltd.* v. *City of London Corp.* (2004), where the landlord intended to develop, the parties had agreed on a fourteen-year term, but could not agree on a break clause. As the landlord's fall-back strategy was to sell to a developer within two to four years, the Court of Appeal specified that there should be a rolling development break clause exercisable on eleven months' notice, but not before the tenant had effectively had the benefit of three-and-a-half years' occupation.

Different circumstances pertained in *National Car Parks Ltd.* v. *Paternoster Consortium Ltd.* (1990), where the tenant claimed a 10-year lease. Browne-Wilkinson V-C granted the landlord, who had a genuine intention to develop within that period, a rolling development break clause exercisable on six months' notice from the beginning of the new lease. An important factor here was that, as the premises were a car park, the disturbance to the tenant's business in having to give up possession at short notice was small compared with the majority of cases.

On the other hand, in *Becker* v. *Hill Street Properties Ltd.* (1990), the judge had determined that the new lease should be for four and a half years. The Court of Appeal rejected the landlord's appeal for the insertion of a break clause. The new lease was already for a short term, the end of which coincided with the time that the tenant, a dentist, was planning to retire. If the landlord were able to determine the lease earlier, it would be difficult for the tenant to relocate his practice and equipment for the short period

324 Leases: the statutory codes

remaining before his retirement. Such comparative hardship to the tenant was the decisive factor.

19.10.3   Rent: s.34

In default of an agreement between the landlord and tenant, the rent to be determined by the court as payable under the new tenancy is that at which, having regard to the terms of the tenancy (other than those relating to rent) the holding might be expected to be let in the open market by a willing lessor, but with specified factors being disregarded: s.34(1). As the court must have regard to the other terms of the tenancy, these must be settled before the court can determine the rent: *O'May* v. *City of London Real Property Co. Ltd.* (1983). The presence of a ransom element, such as there being no other premises to which the tenant could move without incurring great expense, does not justify a higher rent: *Northern Electric plc* v. *Addison* (1997). An open market can exist even where most of the occupiers belong to a particular profession or trade*: Baptist* v. *Trustees of the Honourable Society of Gray's Inn* (1993).

The statutory disregards in s.34(1) are:

(a) any effect on rent of the occupation of the holding by the tenant or his predecessors in title,
(b) any goodwill attached to the holding by reason of the carrying on there of the tenant's business (whether by him or his predecessor),
(c) any effect on rent of certain types of improvement, and
(d) any addition to the value of licensed premises attributable to the tenant's licence ('tenant' here including a company in which the tenant has a controlling interest, or a person with a controlling interest in the tenant company: s.34(2A)).

For an improvement to be disregarded under paragraph (c), there are two requirements. First, it must have been carried out by the person who was tenant at the time it was carried out, otherwise than in pursuance of an obligation to his immediate landlord. An improvement is treated as carried out by the tenant even if it is performed by a third party, provided the tenant finances or supervises the work or is otherwise involved: *Durley House Ltd.* v. *Earl Cadogan* (1999). Secondly, it must have been carried out either during the current tenancy or completed not more than twenty-one years before the application to the court was made, and (in the latter case) the holding affected by the improvement must at all times since completion have been comprised in tenancies within Part II, and no tenant since such time must have given notice to quit: s.34(2). The effect of this provision is that an improvement made more than twenty-one years earlier is disregarded if it was carried out during the term of the lease being renewed, but not if it had been made under an earlier lease.

Each party will usually present evidence of the rental values of comparable properties, where these are available. Failing this, relevant evidence to determine open-market value may be the general level of rent increases (or decreases) in the area concerned: *National Car Parks* v. *Colebrook Estates Ltd.* (1983). Where the business is exceptional, such as a hotel or a theatre, the profitability of the tenant's business may be relevant, as indicating the premises' earning potential: *Harewood Hotels Ltd.* v. *Harris* (1958). The open-market rent must be assessed on the basis of the most profitable use which the tenant could make of the property in compliance with the user covenant, rather than the tenant's actual use: *WJ Barton Ltd.* v. *Long Acre Securities Ltd.* (1982). A serious breach of the repairing covenant may also affect the open-market rent; so that, where the breach is the landlord's, the open-market rent may be reduced: *Fawke* v. *Viscount Chelsea* (1980).

Where the court is determining the rent, it may make provision for rent review: s.34(3). Under this sub-section (unlike when it is settling other terms under s.35) the court does not have to have regard to the terms of the current tenancy. Nevertheless, in *Charles Follett Ltd.* v. *Cabtell Investment Co. Ltd.* (1986), the judge at first instance thought that he should not tinker around with the upwards-only rent-review clause in the existing lease; and, there being no evidence that rents in the area might go down, he ordered an upwards-only clause in the new lease.

Leases granted before the 1960s (a period when inflation took hold) are less likely to contain any machinery for rent review. There have been several cases in which the existing lease has not contained a rent-review clause, but the parties have agreed that the new lease should. In these cases the court has merely been called upon to determine whether the review clause should be upwards only, or up-and-down. In *Janes (Gowns) Ltd.* v. *Harlow Development Corporation* (1980), the court ordered up-and-down review, there being evidence that a nearby development would have an unpredictable effect on the general level of rents in the area. There was no such specific evidence in *Boots the Chemist* v. *Pinkland Ltd.* (1992) (applied in *Forbouys plc* v. *Newport BC* (1994)), but the judge made an order for a two-way review, commenting that, whilst he had no crystal ball, a long-term decline in rental values would wreak injustice on a tenant tied into an upwards-only review.

If the rent is too small (or the term too short) to justify a rent-review clause, the rent will be set at an appropriately higher level to take this into account: *Northern Electric plc* v. *Addison* (1997) (where the rent under the existing lease of an electricity sub-station was only £10 per annum).

19.10.4   Other Terms: s.35

In default of agreement between the landlord and the tenant, the other terms of the tenancy (i.e. those not relating to duration and rent) may be determined by the court, which is to have regard to the terms of the current tenancy and to all relevant circumstances: s.35(1). Usually, the other terms of the current lease will be imported into the new one, and any variation or new term will need to be justified as fair and reasonable by the party proposing it, and should take account of the comparatively weak bargaining position of a sitting tenant requiring renewal: *O'May* v. *City of London Real Property Co.* (1983). Thus it has been held that a landlord could not insist on a relaxation of the user covenant of no value to the particular tenant solely in order to obtain a rent increase: *Charles Clement (London) Ltd.* v. *Rank City Wall Ltd.* (1978). Conversely, a tenant could not attempt to narrow the permitted user in order to secure a rent reduction: *Aldwych Club Ltd.* v. *Copthall Property Co. Ltd.* (1962).

If a variation is made or a new term introduced to the benefit of one party, it is unlikely to be treated as fair and reasonable unless there is a compensatory change elsewhere for the benefit of the other party. Even if actuarial evidence shows that the *quid pro quo* is likely to maintain a financial balance, the variation may still not be fair and reasonable. In *O'May* v. *City of London Real Property Co.* (1983), the landlord wished the new lease to contain a service charge (not contained in the current lease) in return for a reduction in rent. The House of Lords dismissed the landlord's claim. Even assuming that the rent reduction was adequate compensation, it was not fair and reasonable that, instead of a fixed rent, the tenant should be subject to a fluctuating and unpredictable liability under the service charge.

A variation which essentially preserved the *status quo* (and so required no compensating changes) was approved in *Cairnplace Ltd.* v. *CBL (Property Investment) Co. Ltd.* (1984). There, the current lease did not require the original tenant to provide guarantors, but it did require guarantors if there was an assignment to a company. The lease had been assigned to a company, and guarantors obtained. In settling the terms of the new lease to be granted to that company, the judge at first instance had ordered that the new lease should require the tenant company to provide guarantors, and his decision was upheld by the Court of Appeal.

It was also held in the *Cairnplace* case that the new lease should not contain an agreement under which the tenant was to pay the landlord's solicitor's costs of preparing the lease, even though such an agreement was contained in the current lease. The Court of Appeal, reversing the judge at first instance on this point, referred to the Costs of Leases Act 1958, which, in the absence of written agreement between the parties, relieves either party from being required to pay the other's legal costs of the lease. The Court of Appeal considered that, as that statute had been designed to relieve tenants of a specific obligation, it would not be a correct exercise of judicial discretion to use the wide power under s.35 of the 1954 Act to deprive the tenant of the protection of the relieving statute. It was apparently of no significance that the existing lease had been granted in 1972, after the 1958 Act had been passed.

The relevant circumstances to which the court is to have regard under s.35(1) expressly include the operation of the Landlord and Tenant (Covenants) Act 1995: LTA 1954, s.35(2). A pre-1996 lease is likely to impose continuing tenant liability after assignment, whereas tenant liability under a post-1995 lease must end on a lawful assignment. Where post-1995 leases are granted without the involvement of the court, it is standard practice that the lease contains a clause under which the landlord is entitled to demand an authorised guarantee agreement (AGA) when the tenant assigns. In *Wallis Fashion Group Ltd.* v. *CGU Life Assurance Ltd.* (2000), however, it was held that, when the terms of renewal of a pre-1996 lease are being determined by the court under Part II, the new lease should not give the landlord an entitlement to an AGA on assignment; rather he should be able to require an AGA on an assignment only if it is reasonable to do so, in accordance with the fall-back provision in the 1995 Act. What remains to be decided is whether the court will take the same approach under s.35 when settling the renewal terms of a post-1995 lease under which the landlord is entitled to an AGA. By analogy with *Cairnplace*, the court might well decline to give the landlord an automatic right to an AGA in the new lease. In each case, it might be considered fair that the terms of the existing lease be modified to take account of the statutory protection that Parliament intended to confer on tenants.[19]

<h3>19.10.5　Carrying out the Court Order</h3>

If the court has made an order for the grant of a new tenancy, the landlord must execute a lease or agreement for a lease in the terms agreed or determined by the court, and the landlord can require the tenant to execute a counterpart or duplicate: s.36(1).

The court must revoke the order for the grant of a new tenancy if the tenant applies for a revocation within fourteen days of the order's being made. If the order is revoked, the current tenancy ceases to be protected by Part II, and continues for such period as the parties may agree or the court determines is necessary to afford the landlord a reasonable opportunity for re-letting or otherwise disposing of the premises: s.36(2).

Notes

1 For the historical background, see Haley, *The Statutory Regulation of Business Tenancies*, Oxford University Press, 2000, Chapter 1.

2 See *Landlord and Tenant Law: Compensation for Tenant's Improvements*, Law Com No 178 (1989), paras 3.5–3.14.

3 Department of the Environment, Transport and the Regions, *Business Tenancies Legislation in England and Wales: The Government's Proposals for Reform* (March 2001); Department for Transport, Local Government and the Regions (DTLGR), *Outcome of Consultation on Business Tenancy Reforms*, (February 2002); see also Haley, 'Reforming Business Tenancies: a Critique of the Current Proposals', [2003] JBL 252.

4 SI 2003/3096.

5 See Freedom of Information Act 2000, ss.1, 3, 43; Land Registration Act 2002, s.66; and Land Registration Rules 2003, rules 131 (definition of 'prejudicial information') and 136–138 (exempt information documents).

6 The details of SDLT are outside the scope of this book, but essentially the tenant pays it on the grant of the lease if the annual rents over the whole period of the term granted (after a small percentage discounting) exceed, in the case of a business lease, £150,000. No refund of SDLT is made if the lease is terminated before its term date by the exercise of a break clause. This regime therefore encourages the grant of shorter leases with options to renew. (The tax is less if the option is not exercised; if it is, the new lease is treated as associated with the old, and additional SDLT may be payable). If a tenant holds over under the LTA 1954, Part II, after the expiry of the contractual term, even for a day, the tenant may need to pay (or to pay additional) SDLT on the basis that the lease has been extended for a further year (a growing lease). See Slessenger [2005] Conv 7–13.

7 For criticism, see Morgan, [2005] JBL 235.

8 See also *Webb* v. *Barnet LBC* (1989).

9 See Law Commission, *Part II of the Landlord and Tenant Act 1954*, Working Paper No. 111 (1988), paras. 3.1.26–32.

10 See LTA 1954, ss.38 and 38A, and Regulatory Reform (Business Tenancies) (England and Wales) Order 2003, SI 2003/3096, Schs 1 and 2.

11 For further discussion, see Colby, Wallis and Fenn, [2004] Estates Gazette 29 May, 133–134; Fenn, 'Mind the traps' [2004] Estates Gazette 5 June, 116–117; Fenn, Colby and Highmore, 'A procedure guaranteed to confuse' [2004] Estates Gazette 19 June, 166–167; Murdoch, 'A potential trap' [2004] Estates Gazette, 26 June, 191 (note on *Brighton & Hove CC* v. *Collinson* [2004] 21 EG 150 (CS)).

12 Landlord and Tenant Act 1954, Part II, (Notices) Regulations 2004, SI 2004/1005.

13 LTA 1927, s.23, applied by LTA 1954, s.66(4); and see Recorded Delivery Service Act 1962, s.1(1) & Sch. 1, para. 1, and Postal Services Act 2000, s.127(4) & Sch. 8, para. 3.

▶ **14** See Luxton, 'The service of notices in business tenancies by recorded delivery' [2004] JBL 564.

▶ **15** *Mannai Investment Co. Ltd.* v. *Eagle Star Life Assurance Co. Ltd.* (1997)

▶ **16** For a discussion of the defects in the interim rent procedure under the old law, see Haley, *The Statutory Regulation of*

Business Tenancies, Oxford University Press, 2000, Chapter 6.

▶ **17** For practical suggestions on the use of ground (d), see Bonye, [2006] 8 Estates Gazette 170.

▶ **18** SI 1990/363.

▶ **19** For comment, see Luxton [2001] JBL 84.

Summary

▷ Business leases are protected by the Landlord and Tenant Act 1954, Part II unless the parties have contracted out of the statutory protection. Before the 2003 Order (which came into force on 1 June 2004), contracting out needed the approval of the court. Since that date, contracting out does not involve the court, but is valid only if the landlord has served a prior 'health warning' and the tenant has made an appropriate declaration.

▷ Section 23 defines 'business', and also sets out the conditions for the tenancy to fall within Part II, viz. a tenancy, occupation, and business purpose.

▷ At the expiration of the contractual term of a business lease within Part II, it is statutorily continued indefinitely unless and until it is either forfeited, surrendered, terminated by a tenant's notice, or brought to an end in accordance with the statutory notice procedure contained in Part II (whether or not a new lease is granted).

▷ Either the landlord (by serving a s.25 notice) or the tenant (by serving a s.26 request) can initiate the procedure under Part II. These are formal notices that must contain specified information. If the procedure is initiated by a tenant's s.26 request, the landlord must respond with a counter-notice within a specific time or the tenant will acquire a right to a new tenancy in accordance with the proposals contained in its request.

▷ Either party may apply to the court for a new tenancy as soon as the landlord has served a s.25 notice or the tenant has served a s.26 request.

▷ The landlord can apply to court for an order to terminate the tenancy as soon as it has served a s.25 notice or a counter-notice to a tenant's s.26 request.

▷ Either party may apply for an interim rent. Such rent may be applied retrospectively, but cannot begin earlier than six months from the service of the landlord's s.25 notice or the tenant's s.26 request (as the case may be).

Summary cont'd

▶ Although the court can order a new lease and settle its terms, the parties are encouraged by the Part II procedures to negotiate their own settlement. The 2003 Order furthered this policy by extending the deadline for applications to the court.

▶ If the court orders a new tenancy, it can determine the property to be contained in the tenancy, the duration of the lease, the rent, and any other terms. However, although Part II apparently gives the court very wide powers, the courts are in practice reluctant to depart from the terms of the original lease.

▶ A landlord who opposes a renewal must satisfy the court on one of seven specified grounds. Four of the grounds are discretionary, the others mandatory.

▶ Depending on which of the grounds of opposition the landlord relies, the tenant may be able to claim compensation on quitting the holding.

Exercises

19.1 Do all business leases fall within the 1954 Act, Part II?

19.2 Are lettings that were within Part II when granted always entitled to its protection towards the end of their terms?

19.3 What are the advantages to justify the complex renewal process contained in ss.24–29 of the 1954 Act?

19.4 Why was Part II of the 1954 Act amended by the 2003 Order?

19.5 How might a landlord who wishes to grant a lease contracted out of Part II seek to minimise the uncertainties in the contracting-out procedure?

19.6 What are the differences between s.25 notices and s.26 requests?

19.7 Why should a tenant sometimes prefer to serve a s.26 request rather than waiting for the landlord to serve a s.25 notice?

19.8 Which is the best method of serving a statutory notice under Part II?

19.9 Do you consider that the changes to interim rents made by the 2003 Order mostly benefit landlords at the expense of tenants?

19.10 Sections 32–35 of the 1954 Act apparently give the courts enormous discretion; but how wide is this in reality?

19.11 How would you advise a landlord who appears unlikely to succeed in an attempt to obtain possession of business premises relying on ground (f)?

19.12 How would you advise a tenant whose landlord appears likely to succeed in an attempt to obtain possession of business premises relying on ground (f)?

Workshop

1 Look again at Question 2 in the Workshop at the end of Chapter 16.

2 Turnover Cars owns a row of three shops with living accommodation above. The company is expanding and needs more showroom space. It therefore wants to turn all the shops into one display area for new cars, and use the space above one of them for storage and offices. The shops are occupied at present as follows:

No. 1　The ground floor is let to and occupied by a charity, whose second six-month lease is about to end. The upstairs is vacant.

No. 2　This is leased to an old-established family grocery business. The lease has eight months more to run. The family use the ground floor as the shop. The family live upstairs; their residential entrance, however, is separate from the shop entrance.

No. 3　This was leased to Tony ten years ago. Tony still holds the lease, but two years ago he moved his business operations to larger premises, and now uses only the ground floor of No. 3, and this only for storage. Shortly after moving out, Tony sublet the upstairs (with Turnover Cars' consent) to a hi-fi dealer, Harry. The contractual term granted under Tony's lease ends in 15 months' time; Harry's sublease has one year to run.

Advise Turnover Cars:

(a) how they might best obtain possession; and

(b) if they obtain possession, whether they will have to pay compensation to the occupiers for having to leave.

3 Outline the steps to be taken by a landlord of business premises who wishes to obtain possession at the end of a ten-year lease due to expire in nine months' time.

4 Greenfingers Ltd. runs a shop selling gardening supplies. The contractual term of its lease ended four months ago. Both sides want to renew the lease, but discussions have broken down because of disagreement over the amount of rent to be payable under the new lease. Consider the steps each party should take to safeguard its position.

5 Stephen is the landlord of business premises leased to Yvonne under a fixed-term lease due to expire in three months' time. The premises have become dilapidated because Yvonne, who admits she is at fault, has not carried out her repairing obligations under the lease. The parties are negotiating for the grant of a new lease, but Yvonne will not agree to Stephen's proposal that the new lease should impose more stringent repairing obligations on the tenant, and (unlike the existing lease) should require the tenant to provide a guarantor for the performance of her obligations under the lease. Advise Stephen.

Chapter 20
Agricultural holdings

20.1 Introduction

The general law of landlord and tenant as set out in Part 1 of this book applies as much to agricultural tenancies as it does to the tenancies discussed in the previous four chapters. However, the nature of agricultural activities means that there has had to be some response to the particular problems arising from animal husbandry and crop rotation. Crops planted by one tenant may not ripen until after he has moved on, and might not ripen at all if there has been bad weather. Either way, the incoming tenant will have no choice but to put up with the crops which are in the ground, since it will almost certainly be too late to change them. Again, the configuration and productivity of a particular piece of land will be the result of many years of work including planning, planting, draining and fertilising. For centuries a mass of customary practices which varied from county to county (and sometimes varied within counties) governed the relationship between landowners and tenants of agricultural land. Custom and common law had their limitations, however: they did not compensate the outgoing tenant for any improvements, nor did they allow for removal of any fixtures that might have been installed. Further, given that most agricultural tenancies were yearly tenancies, terminable at common law by six months' notice to quit, the tenant's occupation of the land was far from secure. From 1875, therefore, legislation intervened, initially to provide for the payment of compensation to the outgoing tenant, then to extend length of notice, and finally (in 1947) to confer security of tenure.

The mass of nineteenth- and early twentieth-century legislation was almost entirely consolidated into the Agricultural Holdings Act 1948, but subsequent developments were incorporated in further statutes. These, and the 1948 Act, were consolidated into the Agricultural Holdings Act 1986 which, together with the Rent (Agriculture) Act 1976 as amended, provided a comprehensive code governing the contents and variation of agreements, security of tenure, compensation, and fixtures.

However, the security enjoyed by tenants under the 1986 Act and its predecessors was blamed for the decline in tenanted agricultural land from 90 per cent in 1910 to 36 per cent in 1991 (MAFF, *Consultation Paper on the Reform of Agricultural Tenancy Law*, 1991). Landlowners grew increasingly reluctant to let under the 1986 Act and, in order to avoid giving security to their tenants, turned to short-term grazing agreements, or lettings of more than one year but less than two (see *Gladstone* v. *Bower* below) thereby exploiting gaps or loopholes in the legislation. These strategies caused legal problems and ran counter to the enduring cycle of agricultural activity described above.

The deregulation of the landlord and tenant relationship, leaving the parties to negotiate their own letting arrangements, was seen as the way forward. The Agricultural Tenancies Act 1995 therefore represents an attempt to stimulate the market and to create an environment in which landowners will be more disposed to let to tenant farmers. It allows landowners to determine the length of the tenancy and gives the tenant no security beyond the contractual term. In return, tenants (who may diversify into non-agricultural activities provided that their tenancy agreement permits it) must be given a minimum of twelve months' notice (provided the letting is for two years or more), and are entitled to compensation for agreed improvements. Research carried out in 2001 concluded that the 1995 Act had succeeded in its first objective in encouraging more letting of land (33 per cent of agricultural land in England and Wales is now let), but had not been successful in increasing opportunities for new entrants, and had had only limited success in promoting greater economic efficiency in agricultural land use. In particular it noted the short term nature of many farm business tenancies which inhibits longer term planning and investment by tenants ((I. Whitehead *et al.*, *An Economic Evaluation of the Agricultural Tenancies Act 1995*, DEFRA).

The 1995 Act applies only to lettings beginning on or after 1 September 1995 (s.2) which means that the previous legislation will be important for many years to come and must still be considered in some detail. The 'old' law continues to apply in certain clearly specified cases, such as under the statutory succession provisions of the 1986 Act or where the parties have agreed in a written contract made before 1 September 1995 that it is to apply to tenancy which will begin thereafter (s.4).

20.2 The 1986 Legislation

An 'agricultural holding' is the land comprised in a contract of tenancy provided the activity carried out on the land is agricultural, and the land is used for a trade or business (s.1(4)). 'Agriculture' is defined as including horticulture, fruit growing, seed growing, dairy farming, livestock breeding and keeping; use of the land for grazing, meadow, osiers, market gardens and nurseries; and use for woodland provided this is ancillary to the agricultural activity (s.96). These provisions have been judicially interpreted to mean that the 1986 Act applies provided the substance of the property is used for agricultural purposes; the fact that some part is used for the tenant's residence and that some other area is not being cultivated need not matter (*Blackmore* v. *Butler* (1954)). If the use is not agricultural, the activity may still fall within the business lettings legislation discussed in Chapter 19. In *Bracey* v. *Read* (1963) a tenancy of downland used as gallops for the training of racehorses was held to be subject to the Landlord and Tenant Act 1954, Part II. In *Rutherford* v. *Maurer* (1961), five acres were let for grazing horses which were employed in a riding school; it was held that, while the riding stable was a business letting, the grazing fell within what is now the 1986 Act. Alternatively, provided there is no breach of user covenant, the residential lettings legislation considered in Chapter 16 could apply, subject to planning controls which could also severely restrict transfer of use into the agricultural sector.

A 'contract of tenancy' is a letting of land or an agreement for letting of land for a term of years or from year to year (s.1(5)). Section 2(2) extends the scope of the 1986 Act by deeming lettings for less than from year to year (thus weekly, monthly and quarterly tenancies as well as fixed term tenancies for part of a year only) to be yearly, while s.3 allows fixed term leases of two years or more to continue as yearly tenancies after their expiry. Section 2(2) also allows a licence to be defined as a tenancy from year to year within the scope of the Act. In order to do so however it must confer an exclusive right under which the licensee can prevent the licensor, or anyone claiming through him, from making use of the land during the period of the licence (*Bahamas International Trust Co. Ltd.* v. *Threadgold* (1974)). As to whether there is sufficient consideration, the courts have been more interested in finding a commercial element than a high rent or even a monetary rent. Thus in *Padbury* v. *York* (1990) an arrangement for cultivation and cropping in return for exclusive occupation was held to be a licence which attracted the protection of the 1986 Act. In *Evans* v. *Tompkins* (1993), however, a written agreement for a year's use of grass and of a barn did not fall within s.2 because there was no exclusivity of possession. The defendant occupier had failed to discharge the burden upon him to show he had a tenancy. All he had demonstrated was that he had use of the land and barn for twelve months, not that use was exclusive to him alone – indeed others had the right to graze at the same time. In *Davies* v. *Davies* (2003) a landowner granted his brother a right to graze cattle on a large field in return for the payment of an annual sum. This arrangement continued for some years until the landowner gave his brother permission to plant a crop of winter barley. This effectively meant that the brother acquired sole use of the land from ploughing in the autumn until harvesting in the following summer. It was agreed that, after the crop had been harvested, the brother would reseed the land to grass but, instead, he planted another crop of winter barley. He claimed that the land was held under an agricultural tenancy and, as a result of the variation which allowed him exclusive possession, he was entitled to continue using the land for growing winter barley. The Court of Appeal held that the agreement to plant winter barley had been a variation of the existing annual agreement for summer grazing and the undertaking to reseed the area to grass had been sufficient consideration to support the agreement as a contract in law. It was however a one-off variation which did not lead to the conversion under s.2 of the 1986 Act of the tenancy to a secure agricultural tenancy.

The rights of subtenants under the 1986 Act are relatively limited. They have the usual rights against their immediate landlord and can claim relief against the landlord in forfeiture proceedings. However, unlike long lessees or business tenants, statute has granted them no legal relationship with their head landlord (and no consequential protection therefore) should the latter give the mesne tenant a notice to quit which results in possession being granted.

Certain interests are outside the range of the 1986 Act, notably

– grazing or mowing leases for 'some specified period of the year' (s.2(3)). This includes a letting or licence for 364 days (*Reid* v. *Dawson* (1955));
– leases excluded with permission from the Department of the Environment, Food and Rural Affairs either because the landlord wants to be able to recover possession (s.2(1)), or because the parties to a lease of between two and five years have agreed to exclude the Act under s.5;
– leases to employees of the landlord (s.1(1));
– fixed term leases of more than one year but less than two years – *Gladstone* v. *Bower* (1960).

20.2.1   The Terms of an Agricultural Lease

Common law rules requiring a tenant to behave in a tenant-like manner – that is, not to commit waste – and the landlord not to derogate from the grant will apply to agricultural leases in the same way as to other types of lease, although they have largely been usurped by statute. Sections 10 and 11 of the Agriculture Act 1947 contain general rules of good estate management and good husbandry requiring the owner to allow 'an occupier of the land reasonably skilled in husbandry to maintain efficient production', while the occupier is obliged to maintain a reasonable standard of efficient production. These objective criteria are supported by s.22 of the 1986 Act which allows either party to require the compilation of a record of the condition of fixed equipment on the holding and of the general condition of the holding itself, or the tenant to require a list to be made recording any fixtures or buildings which he is entitled to remove and improvements. These requests can be made at any time, and are obviously important should there be a dispute at the end of the lease as to how far conditions have or have not deteriorated.

The 1986 Act, Schedule 1, sets out provisions which either party may, through s.6, insist are included in a written agreement within its scope: items such as the parties' names, the term, the holding, amount of rent, liability for rates, insurance obligations, and provisions on assigning and subletting. If the parties cannot reach agreement on these matters there is provision for referral to an arbitrator who can specify the terms as varied by agreement, and can supplement the terms through inserting the provisions of Schedule 1.

In addition to the above, there are specific and detailed provisions relating to particular terms.

Repair

Subject to any agreement the parties may reach on repairing obligations, the Agriculture (Maintenance, Repair and Insurance of Fixed Equipment) Regulations 1973 and the 1986 Act include provisions as to repairs and replacements which are the responsibility of the landlord. If the tenant serves an appropriate notice on the landlord (or, in some specified cases, on an agent) requiring repairs or replacements to be done then, if such notice is not contested as the Regulations provide and if the work is not done, the tenant may himself carry out work and then recover the cost from the landlord. In order to trigger any such liability, the landlord has to have received the notice or it has to have been given or served upon another for him in one or more of the ways described by the Act. Disputes may be referred to arbitration.

Rent

Schedule 1 of the 1986 Act includes the rent as one item to be specified in the agreement. Schedule 2 allows for review at no less than three-yearly intervals, subject to twelve months' notice being given by the party applying for the review and subject to there being a review clause in the agreement. Together, s.12 and Schedule 2 set out the items to be disregarded and also give some guidance as to the criteria for the calculation of rent. To be disregarded are the tenant's presence, tenant's improvements, tenant's dilapidations or deteriorations, and landlord's grant-aided improvements. Included in the calculations are the terms of the tenancy, the character, situation and locality of the holding, the productive and earning capacity of the property, comparables and its profitability. Applying these rules, the arbitrator will assess 'the rent at which the holding might reasonably be expected to be let by a prudent and willing landlord to a prudent and willing tenant' (Schedule 2, para. 1).

Disposal of produce

Under s.15 of the 1986 Act the tenant is free to dispose of all produce of the holding and organise any cropping system in all but the final year of the tenancy.

20.2.2   Security of Tenure

Statutory protection

Provided the requirements of 20.2.1 are met, the 1986 Act provides some security for agricultural tenants, although this is not as extensive as that provided for residential or business tenants. The provisions set out below on protection do not apply if the parties agree to surrender, nor will they apply if the tenant gives a unilateral notice to quit. In this last event, the tenant's notice must be twelve months in advance of the intended departure unless it follows a rent review in which case it need be only six months.

The first step in the possession process is for the the landlord to give the tenant at least twelve months' notice to quit (s.25). The notice must make it clear whether the reason for requring possession is one to which the Agricultural Lands Tribunal must consent, or whether one of the Cases set out below is being alleged; ambiguity as to which of these two options applies makes the notice invalid. On receipt of the notice the tenant has the choice of leaving voluntarily, possibly serving a counter-notice under s.26, or disputing the Case in the county court. In *National Trust* v. *Knipe* (1999) the tenant failed to challenge the landlord's notice to quit by arbitration under the 1986 Act, and later contended that the landlord's notice was defective as it failed to carry the information prescribed by s.5 of the Protection from Eviction Act 1977 (see 16.8.3). The Court of Appeal held that premises let as an agricultural holding were not 'premises let as a dwelling' for the purpose of s.5 of the 1977 Act and that the landlord had accordingly served a valid notice to quit. The information statutorily required by s.5 did not assist an agricultural tenant since the 1986 Act required not legal advice but a counter notice within a restricted time scale, and the relevant period of notice was 12 months not four weeks.

Unless the landlord alleges one of the Cases contained in Schedule 3, Part I the tenant has the right to serve a counter-notice. The effect of the counter-notice is to prevent the notice to quit from taking effect unless the Agricultural Lands Tribunal consents. Provided the tenant's counter-notice is served within a month of receipt of the landlord's notice the Tribunal will consider whether the latter's application should be allowed to proceed further. To do so it must be satisfied that at least one of the following five Grounds contained in s.27 exists (there is no restriction as to how many the landlord may allege):

- the landlord's proposals are desirable in the interests of good husbandry;
- the landlord's proposals are desirable in the interests of good estate management;
- possession is desirable for the purpose of agricultural research education, experimentation or demonstration, or will allow development of allotments or smallholdings;
- there will be greater hardship if possession is not granted than if it is, requiring the balancing of interests of both the landlord and the tenant;
- the landlord proposes to use the land for non-agricultural purposes not included in Case B below.

The landlord who does satisfy the Tribunal under one of the five Grounds may still be refused possession because 'a fair and reasonable landlord would not insist on [it]' (s.27). Even if the Tribunal does allow him to proceed, it may either postpone termination for up to twelve months or impose conditions to ensure that the landlord actually does what he says he is going to do (s.27(4)).

A covenant in the lease of an agricultural holding purporting to prevent a tenant from serving a counter-notice will be invalid as being contrary to public policy (*Johnson* v. *Moreton* (1980)). However, there is nothing which obliges the tenant to serve a counter-notice. In *Barrett* v. *Morgan* (2000) the defendant had been the sub-tenant of an agricultural holding since 1980. In 1992 the freeholder, who wished to sell the land with vacant possession, agreed with the head tenant (who was a member of the freeholder's family and also in favour of the sale) that a notice to quit would be served and that the head tenant would not serve a counter-notice. Overruling the Court of Appeal (which had held that a notice to quit given in such circumstances amounted to a surrender), the House of Lords held that a notice to quit served by a landlord on the common understanding or agreement that the head tenant would not serve a counter-notice, was an effective notice at common law which determined both the head tenancy and any sub-tenancy held under it.

If in the notice to quit the landlord specifies one of the Cases set out in Schedule 3, Part 1 of the 1986 Act, the tenant will not be able to serve a counter-notice (s.26(2)). In this case, all the tenant can do is to refer the matter to arbitration within one month of service of the notice to quit (or possibly allege that the notice was invalid due to fraudulent statements (*Rous* v. *Mitchell* (1991)) The Cases are contained in Schedule 3 and are:

Case A   The letting is a smallholding entered into after 12 September 1984, the tenant has reached the age of 65, the Case has been referred to in the lease, and the tenant has been offered suitable alternative accommodation.

Case B   The land (and probably the whole of the land) referred to in the notice to quit is required for a non-agricultural purpose for which planning permission has either been obtained or is not required under the relevant legislation. 'Required' involves both a genuine intention and a reasonable prospect of carrying it out (*Paddock Investments Ltd.* v. *Lory* (1975)).

Case C   Not more than six months before the notice to quit is given, the Agricultural Land Tribunal granted a certificate that the tenant was not fulfilling his duties to farm in accordance with the rules of good husbandry. It is up to the landlord to apply for such a certificate.

Case D   At the date of the notice to quit, the tenant has failed to comply with a written notice from the landlord requiring him:

(a) within two months of service of the notice, to pay any rent due, or
(b) within a reasonable period as specified in the notice, to remedy any breach of the terms and conditions of the tenancy capable of being remedied by him.

A notice to remedy may itself be one of two types: a notice to do work (of maintenance or repair); or a notice to remedy a breach of any other kind. The two types notices are treated quite differently. The tenant who receives a notice to do work has the opportunity, before he receives a notice to quit, to contest his liability to do the work and may ask the arbitrator to delete any unnecessary or unjustified items in the notice or substitute different materials or methods of work for those specified. The arbitrator may also extend time for compliance. If the tenant does not comply with the notice to do work and is served with a notice to quit, he may serve a counter-notice with the effect that the notice to quit will not take effect unless the Agricultural Lands Tribunal consents to its operation. The Tribunal must not give consent if it appears to them that a fair and reasonable landlord would not insist on possession, having regard to (s.28(5)):

(a) the extent of the tenant's failure to comply with the notice;
(b) the consequences of his failure to comply, and
(c) the circumstances surrounding the failure.

   By contrast, the tenant who is served with a non-work notice to remedy cannot refer any dispute to statutory arbitration until he has been served with a notice to quit. Furthermore, he has no right to serve a counter-ntoice. In *Lancashire CC* v. *Taylor* (2005), the tenancy required the tenant to use the holding for agricultural purposes only but his local authority landlord discovered that he was processing, bottling and distributing milk and fruit juices which had not been produced on the holding. The tenant failed to remedy the alleged breaches and was served with notice to quit citing Case D. The arbitrator determined that the notice to quit was valid and effective. The tenant complained that the notice to quit scheme under the 1986 Act was incompatible with the European Convention on Human Rights because it discriminated – contrary to Article 14 – between an agricultural tenant facing eviction for failure to maintain a holding and one facing eviction for failure to improve it, since (as indicated above) the former could apply for arbitration before a notice to quit had been served whereas the latter had to wait until he had been served with notice to quit. He argued that this discrimination made the entire scheme incompatible with the Convention. It did not matter therefore that Mr Taylor's breach was a breach of a user clause and not of a covenant to do works of improvement. Article 14 provides that 'the enjoyment of the rights and freedoms set forth in this Convention shall be secured without discrimination on any grounds such as sex, race, colour, religion, political or other opinion, national or social origin, association with a national minority, property, birth or other status'. The Court of Appeal held that the differential treatment of tenants under the 1986 Act did not depend on their property or status within Article 14 but solely on the content of the covenant alleged to have been breached. There was in any event a rational objective justification for the different routes available to agricultural tenants facing allegations of breach of covenant because the covenant to maintain could easily become an 'engine of oppression'. As Lord Woolf explained, it was 'entirely intelligible that Parliament chose to draw a line, on one side of which were to be farmers who were at risk of inflated notices to repair, maintain or replace, and for whom an early arbitration to sift the proper from the improper was desirable, and on the other side of which there remained tenant farmers facing other alleged breaches of covenant'.

Case E   The tenant has committed an irremediable breach of the tenancy agreement, which have materially prejudiced the landlord's interest. The authorities on remediability within the context of forfeiture (see 15.5) may be relevant here too.

Case F   The tenant has become insolvent.

Case G   The tenant has died and the Case is being alleged within three months of formal notice of death to the landlord by the personal representatives or by someone acting on their behalf. It must be clear to the landlord that the object of the communication was to serve formal notice so informing the landlord of the tenant's death, or paying the next rent instalment with a cheque signed by an executor, has been held insufficient (*Lees* v. *Tatchell* (1990)).

Case H   The landlord is the Department of the Environment, Food and Rural Affairs and notice was given to the tenant when the tenancy was granted that possession might be wanted in order to amalgamate or reshape the unit.

An agricultural landlord who wants to recover part of the property may do so through Case B, or if he had sufficient foresight and wishes to avoid unnecessary aggravation he may do so under an express power reserved in the lease. Alternatively, s.31 of the 1986 Act allows recovery of part of the demise for erection of farm cottages, for allotments or smallholdings, or for mining or quarrying.

Succession

In 1976 legislation was introduced to allow limited transmission of agricultural tenancies on death and thus reduce the rigours of Case G. Such was the complexity of the provisions, however, that they were modified in 1984 by the introduction of limited opportunities for relatives to apply to succeed on the tenant's retirement. Both schemes apply only to leases granted before 12 July 1984.

In order to claim transmission on death the applicant must:

– be a 'close relative' of the deceased tenant. This includes the deceased's wife or husband;
– have earned a living, either wholly or principally, for five of the previous seven years through working on the holding. In *Welby* v. *Casswell* (1994) the tenant and his son ran the farm as a partnership, both having drawing rights on the accounts as partners: income to the accounts came from the farm and from outside sources. It was held by the Court of Appeal that the son could succeed on his father's death since he was economically dependent on the land and could draw on the accounts only because he was engaged in agricultural work;
– not occupy some other holding which could provide the applicant with a living;
– be suitable to run an agricultural holding on the basis of experience, health and financial viability;
– apply to the landlord within three months of being given notice of opportunity by the personal representatives; and
– not be excluded from applying because there have been more than two transmissions.

If the application is successful, the new occupier acquires a yearly lease which cannot be assigned or sublet, but which is governed by the provisions discussed above as to terms.

Apart from the above provisions, tenants of pre 12 July 1984 leases may nominate successors, related and eligible as defined above, one or two years in advance of their intended retirement. This provision is intended to cater for tenants who would otherwise remain indefinitely so there are restrictions on its operation, notably that the tenant must be over 65, must be unable to work, and must not be the subject of proceedings under Cases B, D or E.

20.2.3   Compensation

Once again the nature of agricultural lettings has given rise to rules designed to cope with tenants moving out who have invested a great deal of time and effort in improving an asset which they cannot take with them. There are several heads of compensation:

- for tenant-right – that is, payments made on the termination of the tenancy through effluxion or some other cause (not abandonment or forfeiture);
- for long-term or short-term improvements as listed in Schedules 7 and 8 of the 1986 Act;
- for disturbance, which can be claimed by tenants who have had to leave in consequence of a notice to quit under either the Tribunal or County Court jurisdiction provided the notice was not for Cases C, D, E, F, or G.

The amount of compensation will vary depending on the category involved. Thus under the head of tenant-right the tenant can recover crop value and reasonable husbandry costs. Improvements will *prima facie* carry compensation related to their value but will be subject to depreciation as well as being subject to the landlord initially giving consent to the works (s.67). Disturbance will qualify for at least one year's rent, but may last for up to five years if conditions set out in s.60 of the 1986 Act are met. The landlord can claim compensation for dilapidations either during the tenancy or at the end of the lease. In the former case, the landlord can enter and do the work or claim damages for breach of covenant. In the latter case, the claim will cover making good and damages for loss of value.

Market gardens are subject to special provisions relating to compensation in response to their capital-intensive activities. The rules are contained in s.79 and will apply if the parties or the Tribunal (s.80) have agreed that the leased property is a market garden. Once this status is settled, the tenant can either take all his fixtures with him at the end of the term or leave them all and claim compensation. He may also claim compensation for specific crops and buildings, installed with or without the landlord's consent.

20.3 The Agricultural Tenancies Act 1995

20.3.1 The Agriculture, Notice and Business Conditions

Landowners and tenants entering into agreements on or after 1 September 1995 will fall within the 1995 Act, provided they meet all three of the agriculture, notice and business conditions. If they do they will become parties to a 'farm business tenancy' (s.1).

So far as the agriculture condition is concerned, the tenancy must be 'primarily or wholly' agricultural (s.1(3)) having regard to its terms, the use of the land comprised in the tenancy, the nature of any commercial activities on the land, and any other relevant circumstances. The 'primary' provision allows only limited diversity: too much and the tenancy will drift into the altogether different and more secure regime of the 1954 Act discussed in Chapter 19. All the circumstances will have to be considered to see how far, if at all, the use has departed from agriculture as defined in s.38 (1), a provision that is identical to the 'old' s.96 (see 20.2 above).

Parties who want to diversify outside the limits of s.1(3) and still remain within the 1995 Act regime must exchange notices (s.1(4)) at the start of the tenancy, identifying the land to be comprised in the tenancy or proposed tenancy, containing a statement to the effect that the person giving the notice intends that the tenancy or proposed tenancy is to be, and remain, a farm business tenancy, (to which therefore the 1995 Act is to apply) and confirming that at the start of the lease the tenancy was primarily or wholly agricultural. Compliance with this notice condition allows the tenant to diversify and ensures that the landlord can always recover possession without difficulty.

Finally, the business condition (s.1(2)) requires that all or at least part of the land is farmed for the purpose of a trade or business (that is not a hobby) from when the tenant goes into possession (s.38(4)) – which need not necessarily be the start of the lease. The requirement in this condition is for the activity of 'farmed' and not the narrower 'agricultural' found elsewhere in s.1.

Unlike the 1986 Act, only tenancies, including subtenancies, fall within the 1995 Act (s.38) tenancies at will being excluded. Equally important, there is no provision allowing conversion of licences into tenancies; licences might be granted for grass keep and will confer no benefits unless exclusion of possession is conferred. Even then, the absence of security makes the farm business tenancy a less appealing concept.

20.3.2 Rent

Once granted, Part II (ss.9–14) creates a statutory framework for rent reviews unless the parties at the start of the agreement either opt out or expressly create their own scheme, which might be by fixing a rent for the whole tenancy or by determining a specified formula (s.9).

Assuming no opting out, either the landlord or the tenant can instigate a rent review twelve to twenty-four months in advance of when it will fall due by issuing a statutory review notice. The parties can, of course, proceed to agree any or all of the time when the review is to start, the period between reviews and the review date but, if they cannot, s.10(6) provides a default of an earliest review three years after the start of the lease and at three year intervals thereafter. Failure to agree means resolution by an arbitrator (s.10 and s.12) whose task will be to determine the rent properly payable on the open market by a willing landlord under the terms of the tenancy (s.13). The arbitrator must disregard the following: the tenant's occupation, dilapidation caused by the tenant, and tenant's improvements prior to the current lease, or for which the tenant has been compensated in cash or in kind (s.13 (3), (4)).

20.3.3   Security of Tenure

Instead of terminating on the term date, a farm business tenancy for a term of more than two years continues from that date as a tenancy from year to year, but otherwise on the same terms as the original tenancy. The tenancy can be terminated by either party giving to the other at least twelve months but less than twenty-four months' written notice of his intention to terminate the tenancy (s.5(1)). No grounds need be given in support of the notice. No notice is required to terminate a tenancy for a term of two years exactly or for a term of less than two years; such tenancies expire by effluxion of time in accordance with the common law.

By s.6, in the case of a farm business tenancy from year to year, a notice to quit the holding or part of the holding is invalid (notwithstanding any provision to the contrary in the tenancy) unless:

(a) it is in writing;
(b) it is to take effect at the end of a year of the tenancy; and
(c) it is given at least 12 months but less than 24 months before the date on which it is to take effect

These requirements apply to notices given by tenants as well as landlords. Again, no grounds need to be given in support of the notice to quit.

20.3.4   Removal of Fixtures and Compensation for Improvements

The end of a farm business tenancy may lead to disputes as to removal of fixtures or payment of compensation for improvements by the tenants.

Fixtures and buildings installed by the tenant for agricultural or other purposes can be removed at any time provided damage is made good (s.8). This right exists irrespective of the tenant's compliance with the terms of the lease and without need to give notice to the landlord: both preconditions of the 1986 Act. The only restrictions are that the tenant must not have been required to install, and leave, the fixtures, nor must he have obtained compensation (s.8(2)).

Part III (ss.15–27) creates a new and complex regime to compensate the tenant for improvements whose benefits would otherwise be lost on termination (s.16). Section 15 defines improvements broadly, as physical improvements carried out by the tenant's own efforts or expense or as intangible advantages resulting from his own efforts or expense and attached to the holding intended to reward effort, always provided the landlord has agreed to the improvements being carried out (s.17). The parties will in many instances resolve disputes as to the amount of compensation among themselves. If they cannot, s.22 provides for resolution by arbitration. In either event the amount of compensation is, according to s.20, a restitution figure, that is 'an amount equal to the increase attributable to the improvement in the value of the holding at the termination of the tenancy as land comprised in a tenancy' (s.20(1)) less a proportionate reduction for grants received or allowances already made (s.20(3),(2)). Since compensation is only payable when the tenant leaves, rights can be 'rolled over' on renewal (s.23). There may, of course, be some overlap between the fixtures provisions described above and those relating to compensation.

20.4 Allotments and Smallholdings

The Allotments Acts 1922–1950 require local authorities to provide allotments for residents in their area. There are detailed rules on size, and limited provisions for compensation. Every County Council is constituted a smallholding authority in order that it can let small areas of land to those wishing to farm it. The rules as to size and selection of tenants are contained in the Agriculture Act 1970.

20.5 Agricultural Tied Homes

The Rent (Agriculture) Act 1976 – which is largely modelled on the provisions of the Rent Acts – gives security of tenure and a considerable degree of rent protection to 'protected occupiers' with regard to their tied accommodation. Many agricultural workers were excluded from Rent Act protection, either because they were not tenants at all or because their tenancies were at a low rent or fell within the agricultural holdings exemption. The Housing Act 1988 – which regulates tenancies and licences granted to agricultural workers after 15 January 1989 – seeks to bring agricultural workers within the assured tenancies regime by creating the specific category of 'assured agricultural occupancy'.

By s.2(1) of the Rent (Agriculture) Act 1976 'where a person has, in relation to a dwelling-house, a relevant licence or tenancy and the dwelling-house is in qualifying ownership at any time during the subsistence of the licence or tenancy . . . he shall be a protected occupier if

(a) he is a qualifying worker;
(b) he has been a qualifying worker at any time during the subsistence of the licence or tenancy . . .'

In order to be a qualifying worker, the applicant must have worked full-time (currently 35 hours per week) in agriculture for at least 91 out of the previous 104 weeks. Agriculture is defined widely by s.1 to include, for example, dairy farming, livestock breeding and keeping, the production of consumable produce for sale or consumption and using land for grazing. Livestock includes any animal kept for the production of food, skin or fur or other agricultural activity. Although 'animal' includes birds, the Act expressly excludes fish. In *Mcphail* v. *Greenwich* (1993) a mechanic based on the farm and employed to repair and maintain farm tractors and machinery was held to fall within the provisions but in *Earl of Normanton* v. *Giles* (1980), a gamekeeper employed to rear phesants was held not to be protected. This was because his primary role was to provide birds for sportsmen to shoot. The fact that the birds were later sold as food was incidental.

A relevant licence or tenancy is one which would be a protected tenancy under the Rent Act 1977 but for the provisions in the 1977 Acts which exclude tenancies at low rents, tenancies of dwelling-houses comprised in agricultural holdings and those where the rent includes payment for board or attendance. The premises must be of a dwellinghouse let as a separate dwelling (see Chapter 16.2). However, for present purposes the interest need only be of a right to occupy. It should be remembered that tenants sharing with their landlords will have only very limited security under the Protection from Eviction Act 1977, as amended by the Housing Act 1988. The requirement that the dwelling-house is in qualifying ownership at some time during the relevant period means that either the employer is the owner of the dwelling-house or he has made arrangements with the owner of the dwelling-house for it to be used as housing accommodation for persons which he employs in agriculture.

Section 4(1) of the 1976 Act provides that where a person ceases to be a protected occupier of a dwelling-house he shall, on the termination of his licence or tenancy, be the statutory tenant of it, if and so long as he occupies the dwelling-house as his residence. By s.3(2) where the original occupier was a man who died leaving a widow who was residing in the dwelling-house immediately before his death then, after his death, if the widow has a relevant licence or tenancy in relation to the dwelling-house, she shall be a protected occupier (or statutory tenant, as the case may be). To recover possession against a statutory tenant, the landlord must prove one or more of the thirteen grounds for possession set out in Schedule 4 to the Act. These are similar to the grounds for possession in the Rent Act 1977, except that there is no equivalent to case 8 (dwelling required for the landlord's employee). If the landlord has other property available, and can meet the criteria of Case 1 (which are the same as in Chapter 16) he may be able to insist on the tenant moving. If the landlord has nowhere else to offer, the 1976 Act allows the landlord to require the Local Authority to rehouse the former employee 'in the interests of good agriculture' – or at least to show good reason why not. Possession in each of these cases is discretionary.

So far as assured agricultural tenancies are concerned, the requirements for protection are very similar to those of the 1976 Act. Once it has been established that an assured agricultural occupancy exists, it is treated exactly in the same way as an assured tenancy even if it is simply a licence. The court will order possession only on grounds 1–15 of the 1988 Act. The landlord cannot, however, recover possession under Ground 16 (i.e. where the landlord can show that the dwelling-house was let to the tenant in the consequence of his employment and that employment has now come to an end).

Summary

▶ The law on agricultural lettings is now contained in the consolidating Agricultural Holdings Act 1986 for tenancies granted up to 31 August 1995, and in the Agricultural Tenancies Act 1995 for tenancies granted after that date. There are transitional, protecting, provisions.

▶ The 1986 Act provides for the creation of agricultural tenancies, the 1995 Act for the creation of farm business tenancies.

▶ To fall within the 1986 Act a lease must comply with ss.1, 2, and 96 of that Act, which require a yearly tenancy of a trade or business to be carried out on land that is being used for agricultural purposes.

▶ Farm business tenancies under the 1995 Act are created if all of the agriculture, business and notice conditions are satisfied.

▶ The parties to an agricultural tenancy may negotiate their own terms or may use those contained in the 1986 Act.

Summary cont'd

▷ Security of tenure for agricultural tenants involves the landlord giving notice to quit and the tenant giving a counter-notice so that the landlord has to satisfy the Agricultural Lands Tribunal that the matter should proceed. Alternatively, the landlord can prove one of the Cases contained in the 1986 Act.

▷ The rent of a farm business tenancy can be regularly reviewed by virtue of the statutory framework unless the parties opt out of it. The 1995 Act allows the landlord to recover possession automatically following service of a written notice that contains specified details.

▷ Lessees who have to leave their agricultural tenancies or their farm business tenancies may claim compensation, although its scope varies depending on the statutory regime that applies.

▷ The Rent (Agriculture) Act 1976 provides security to occupiers of tied agricultural accommodation. The Housing Act 1988 governs licences and tenancies of tied agricultural accommodation granted after 15 January 1989.

Exercises

20.1 What is meant by an 'agricultural holding'?

20.2 What period of notice is usually required to terminate the tenancy of an agricultural holding?

20.3 Outline the two types of notice which may be served by a landlord who wishes to recover possession of an agricultural holding to which the Agricultural Holdings Act 1986 applies.

20.4 What is a 'farm business tenancy' for the purpose of the Agricultural Tenancies Act 1995?

20.5 What will happen to a five-year lease of an agricultural holding which expires at common law by effluxion of time?

20.6 Which of the following will fall within the (a) Agricultural Holdings Act 1986; (b) the Agricultural Tenancies Act 1995?

   (i) a field let to a local riding school for the grazing of its horses;
   (ii) a fishery;
   (iii) a market garden.

20.7 In the context of the Rent (Agriculture) Act 1976, explain the what is meant by a qualifying worker.

20.8 What are the similarities between the Rent (Agriculture) Act 1976 and the Rent Act 1977?

Workshop

1 Walter is sixty-six. His employer has told him that in a few weeks' time he must retire, and leave the home that he has occupied throughout the time he has worked on the farm in order that it can be used by a new employee. Advise Walter's employer.

2 George has a fifteen-year lease of some land he uses for a mix of grazing cattle and horses, for horse training, letting to campers in the summer months, and the remainder as a market garden. He has spent a lot of money on the market garden, building greenhouses and installing irrigation systems, although he has never obtained consent for the works. The lease expired a few months ago. Craig, the landlord who acquired the freehold last year, has given George notice because he wants to combine George's property with his own in order to form a more viable economic unit.

(a) Does George have any security of tenure?
(b) If he does have to leave can he claim any compensation?

3 Martin took possession of a three-year farm business tenancy on 3 September 1995. Being energetic, he has improved and drained the land, installed outbuildings (with consent) and is well on the way to turning a rundown smallholding into a profitable enterprise that is further enhanced by income from a caravan site he has set up on the river running across the land. His landlord died recently and his interest has passed to his son, who has shown some interest in recovering possession in order to sell on at a profit. Advise Martin.

Index

Pearson New International Edition

Personality
Classic Theories and Modern
Howard S. Friedman   Miriam W. Schustack
Fifth Edition

PEARSON®

Pearson Education Limited
Edinburgh Gate
Harlow
Essex CM20 2JE
England and Associated Companies throughout the world

Visit us on the World Wide Web at: www.pearsoned.co.uk

© Pearson Education Limited 2014

ISBN 10: 1-292-02225-6
ISBN 13: 978-1-292-02225-3

British Library Cataloguing-in-Publication Data
A catalogue record for this book is available from the British Library

Printed in the United States of America